# Reviews of the Horse Travel Handbook

**The *Horse Travel Handbook* is destined to become the Long Rider's Bible.**
It has been an honour and a privilege, a pleasure and a surprise, to be among the first
to read this wonderful work. Only CuChullaine O'Reilly could accomplish this task. I
know of no other person with such energy, dedication and the knowledge needed to
put together such an incredible effort.
*Argentine Long Rider Benjamin Reynal rode in South America and is the author of*
Cuando La Distancia Revela.

**I can't say enough about this magnificent book.**
*The Horse Travel Handbook* by CuChullaine O'Reilly is without doubt one of the
finest equestrian books of any kind ever written. I can't say enough about this
magnificent book. Between these covers is an astonishingly comprehensive and vital
wealth of information about travel with horses under any circumstance the rider
would ever encounter on planet earth. This is a book for the ages.
*American Long Rider Doug Preston is a Fellow of the Royal Geographical Society,
who rode across the Despoblado Desert and is the author of* Cities of Gold.

**This Handbook is the Holy Grail for Long Riders.**
This is an amazing book, and it covers EVERYTHING. CuChullaine O'Reilly should
be proud of his contribution to not only the equine world, and the world of Long
Riding, but of his contribution to history, literature, and the preservation of the age
old practice of slow travel on horseback in this modern day of technology and such
fast paced movement.
*Australian Long Rider Kimberley Delavere rode solo along the Bicentennial National
Trail.*

**CuChullaine O'Reilly's tireless work in creating the *Horse Travel Handbook* is an
invaluable gift to all those wanting to pursue the magic of equestrian travel.**
In an era of jet travel, smart-phones and satellite technology, it is often claimed that
the world is becoming smaller, more homogenous, less diverse, and generally
travelled out. And yet step into the saddle, point your horse to the horizon, leave
roads, fences, and Monday-to-Friday life behind, and it becomes obvious that the
world is still as large, enchanting, and forever surprising as perhaps it has ever been.
*Australian Long Rider Tim Cope is a Fellow of the Royal Geographical Society who
rode from Mongolia to Hungary and is the author of 'On the Trail of Genghis Khan.'*

**A New Classic.**
CuChullaine O'Reilly, founder of the international Long Riders' Guild, has distilled
hundreds of Long Riders' accounts and tips into a manual dense with information on
every conceivable aspect of planning, preparing for, and surviving a long-distance
ride.. O'Reilly speaks eloquently of the spiritual changes many Long Riders undergo,
the necessity of leaving competitiveness and timetables behind, and the perils of
chasing fame and fortune. Again and again, the *Horse Travel Handbook* emphasizes
the ethics of equine travel: conducting oneself honourably and always, always putting
the welfare of one's equine companion(s) first.
*American Long Rider Katie Cooper rode from Mississippi to Arizona.*

**The *Horse Travel Handbook* is a MUST READ for anyone even considering a long ride.**
It is the only primer available that details the unique experiences of those who set out on long distance equestrian journey. I wish it had been available when I was planning my first ride years ago -- it would have saved me the frustration of sifting through bad and inadequate information.
*American Long Rider Samantha Szesciorka made equestrian journeys through the deserts of Nevada.*

**The Horse Travel Handbook is written for all modern Long Riders worldwide.**
It is quite extraordinary in the global range and depth of its practical content and advice, and in its sense of ethic, its vision and its passion. It is written for those planning their first journey and those already highly experienced.
*William Reddaway and his horse Strider completed the first modern equestrian journey to thirty of Great Britain's historic cathedrals and abbeys.*

**Essential for the horseman!**
The importance and value of the Handbook cannot be underestimated, as well as being a practical 'how to?' Guide for anyone planning a long ride, it also preserves a treasure of equestrian knowledge gathered through the ages in an easy to read and entertaining form.
*New Zealand Long Rider Ian Robinson made solo journeys across Mongolia, Tibet and Afghanistan. Author of the award-winning "Tea with the Taliban".*

**Providing all Equestrians with a Moral Compass.**
The *Horse Travel Handbook* is receiving well deserved accolades from a growing number of Long Riders, who have been there and done that. To those who are becoming inspired to become legends, themselves, this book details the "how to." However, for the millions of us, who ride a bit less, this book is of historic importance, because the Handbook, itself, honours the animals by providing all equestrians with a moral compass by which anyone can understand our sacred responsibility to protect and defend our fellow travelers, upon whose backs we ride.
*Robert Ferrand, USA*

**The Horse Travel Handbook explains how the trip serves as a gateway to self-discovery.**
*The Horse Travel Handbook is an informative, accurate and valuable travel guide that is of scientific value. Yet the book serves another purpose too. It encourages the traveller to view the horseback journey from a philosophical perspective. It explains how the trip serves as a gateway to self-discovery.*
*Turkmen Long Rider Geldy Kyarizov is a Fellow of the Royal Geographical Society who rode across Central Asia and Russia.*

# The Horse Travel Handbook

## CuChullaine O'Reilly F.R.G.S.
## Founder of The Long Riders' Guild

# Copyright

Cover Design was conceived and created by Brian Rooney of R7 Media.

Cover Image – The cover image of Jamie Maddison appears courtesy of Matt Traver. In 2013 these exemplary British Long Riders prematurely concluded their journey across northern Kazakhstan rather than imperil the welfare of their horses.

Images – Image of securing horse shoe appears courtesy of American Long Rider Tracy Paine. Image of Guatemalan pack saddle appears courtesy of American Long Rider Orion Kraus. Image of adjustable pack saddle appears courtesy of Custom Pack Rigging. Image of river crossing appears courtesy of Israeli Long Rider Koreen Kahn. Image of quicksand rescue courtesy of Mary Anne Leighton. Image of Siberian horseman appears courtesy of Swedish Long Rider Mikael Strandberg. Image of African traffic courtesy of English Long Rider Christine Henchie. Image of documents and border crossing courtesy of Brazilian Long Rider Filipe Leite. Image of traffic courtesy of American Long Rider Doc Mishler. Image of river crossing courtesy of Irish Long Rider Hugh MacDermott. Image of ferry courtesy of English Long Rider Lisa Adshead. Image of quicksand courtesy of West Midlands Fire Service. Image of Central Asian nomad knot appears courtesy of Australian Long Rider Tim Cope. Image of lead rope knot appears courtesy of Belgian Long Rider Robert Wauters.

Dedicated to Count Pompeii,
the flying logo of The Long Riders' Guild,
and to the beloved Road Horses who faithfully
carried us to the ends of the Earth and enriched our
lives throughout history.

# Table of Contents

# Section Four – The Challenges

# Section Five – The Journey

# Section Six – The Aftermath

# Section Seven – The Equestionary

# Foreword

For those who long for the independence and contentment of days in the saddle, away from the rat race of civilization and the crush of overpopulated lands, here is a real "bible". For the novice Long Riders it is a comprehensive guide and for the experienced hands it will be a source of much interest and perhaps even some useful tips.

CuChullaine deserves congratulations for producing such a full, fascinating and comprehensive handbook, loaded with the experience and wisdom of numerous international equestrian explorers over many years.

Whether one is seeking advice on horses' health and feeding, handling bureaucratic obstacles at borders or even fleeing for one's life, this is the ideal book to have in one's saddle bag.

John Blashford-Snell
Honorary President
The Scientific Exploration Society

*Colonel John Blashford-Snell OBE is a former British Army officer, explorer and author. Blashford-Snell was educated at the Royal Military Academy Sandhurst and then commissioned into the Royal Engineers. He would serve for 37 years in the Army and see active services in many areas. In 1969, he founded the Scientific Exploration Society. Amongst his expeditions were the first descent of the Blue Nile during which he invented white water rafting (in 1968); crossing of the Darién Gap (1971 to 1972) and overseeing the first north–south vehicular journey from Alaska to Cape Horn; and a complete navigation of the Congo River (in 1974 to 1975). He was awarded the Segrave Trophy in 1974 and the Livingstone Medal by the Royal Scottish Geographical Society in recognition of his leadership of the expeditions. In 1993 he was awarded the Patron's Gold Medal of the Royal Geographical Society.*

# Introduction

During the course of the last six thousand years countless generations of bold men and women evolved a special type of equestrian knowledge. They preserved skills, lore and traditions that enabled them to ride to the far corners of the globe. But the onset of the motorized age brought about a case of collective equestrian amnesia. The result was that the majority of mankind had no memory of the traditions and wisdom of their mounted ancestors.

Other types of knowledge had not suffered from such neglect.

For example, Abu Bakr ibn Badr ad-Din al-Bitar was a Mamaluke veterinarian, author and horse expert who died in 1340; but not before creating an extensive study which listed all the known equestrian sources and manuscripts from India to Andalusia.

And Ahmad ibn Majid of Oman was the premier Arabic sailing master. His book, *Kitab al-Faw'id fi Usul 'Ilm al-Bahr wa l-Qawa'id* (Book of Useful Information on the Principles and Rules of Navigation), which was published in 1490, contains an encyclopedia of nautical wisdom, including the history and basic principles of navigation, an explanation of lunar monsoons, the difference between coastal and open-sea sailing, the locations of ports from Africa to Indonesia, a treatise on star positions, a warning about typhoons and other topics of immense interest to professional sailors. All this wisdom was drawn not only from the author's own experience, but the lore of generations of other sailors as well.

Yet though six hundred years have passed since Ahmad ibn Majid last dropped anchor and wrote his book, no such global study had ever been penned for equestrian explorers. The result was that unlike mariners, modern equestrian travellers could not profit from the achievements and experiences of previous generations of Long Riders; forcing them to learn all the basic skills again and again.

The *Encyclopaedia of Equestrian Exploration* which I wrote was designed to not only preserve mankind's collective knowledge from extinction but to provide posterity with the first in-depth study of its kind. That book contains the largest collection of horse travel information in history, including the wisdom and warnings of 393 Long Riders, the knowledge gathered from more than 200 books, and the visual evidence of nearly a thousand images. Such a book, while of tremendous importance, was never designed to be taken on a journey. It is hoped that any would-be equestrian traveller will have taken the time to carefully study the *Encyclopaedia of Equestrian Exploration* at home prior to departure.

The *Horse Travel Handbook* differs fundamentally from its larger literary brother. Whereas the *Encyclopaedia* takes care to identify each Long Rider who shared a story or insight, the *Handbook* does not identify the source of the knowledge on offer. That is because unlike the *Encyclopaedia*, the *Handbook* has been designed to accompany the Long Rider on an equestrian expedition. For this reason only the most critically important information is presented in as concise a manner as possible.

The goal of the *Horse Travel Handbook* is to provide the Long Rider with a small, light-weight volume that can be carried in a saddle bag and referred to when necessity forces the traveller to solve a problem, deal with an emergency or recall vital advice.

You will inherit a different world from the one we knew. It will be up to you to summon the courage needed to ride through and help shape future events. Thus this is a new type of horse book designed specifically to help guide and guard you during your journey. Within these pages is everything all the generations of Long Riders have collectively learned, discovered or endured. This knowledge is our gift to you. It is designed to enable you and the rest of mankind to continue to explore the globe with our noble friend the horse and to keep our endangered equestrian travel heritage alive for generations to come.

*Author's note:* For the sake of simplicity, I have referred to all Long Riders and horses as "he".

# Introduction

# Section One – The Preparation

## Chapter 1 - Reality versus Romance

The idea of equestrian travel is always romantic because one never realizes what lies ahead. There is instead a hazy notion of you and your horse riding peacefully across a nature-filled landscape. In such an equestrian reverie you never think about where you're going to sleep at night, because the sun is always shining. Nor do you give any thought to what you and your mount are going to eat, because in your day dream you're too busy being happy.

No one would be naïve enough to announce they were going to fly around the world if they didn't possess the basic skills needed to operate an airplane. Yet time and time again people think they can purchase a horse and then ride towards the sunset on what they mistakenly believe will be an extended pony picnic. Nothing could be further from the truth!

Saying you are going to ride from Point A to Point B is one thing. Actually reaching that distant goal is something altogether different. Equestrian travel requires the acquisition of specialized skills. Do not let your enthusiasm overrule your common sense. Without planning, practice, and a bit of luck, your chances of success are minimal.

## Chapter 2 - Overcoming Resistance

You might be tempted to think that no one would object to someone else setting off on an equestrian journey. Yet regardless of the date on the calendar, whatever pedestrian culture is in power at the time will attempt to coerce the population into believing that it is better for them to remain where they are.

There are many reasons for this discouragement, all of which are a variation on the same theme. It's dangerous or deserted, cold or hot, infested with beasts or crawling with bandits. When a young woman said she wished to ride across England, her outraged critics reminded her that she couldn't possibly make such a journey "in this modern age." They uttered that objection in 1939!

Regardless of the reason, the first thing you must learn is that there are many people who are going to present you with what they believe are perfectly logical, legal, emotional and spiritual reasons why you should not make your ride. If it isn't the unsuitability of your horse, it will be some vague danger just waiting around the corner to get you, or the unstable political climate, or some other ghost. It all boils down to one thing. They're afraid of doing what you're planning to attempt. Therefore, feeling inadequate, they try to undermine your dream of setting off on an equestrian journey.

So before you go any further with your planning, before you buy a map, dust off your saddle, look at horses and think about the onset of warm weather, you have an emotional test to overcome. Every person who became a Long Rider first had to make an initial lonely decision before they could swing into the saddle and began their journey. They have to overcome the often vocal and vehement opposition aimed at them by the current generation of well-meaning nay-sayers. Thus the decision to protect your personal resolve represents an act of individual bravery in a person's life and marks the beginning of the journey.

## Chapter 3 - Understanding the Journey

All Long Riders have asked themselves, "Why set off on a difficult and perhaps dangerous equestrian journey?" Likewise, it is a question that intrigues the pedestrians who meet us. "Why are you doing this," they've asked us in a multitude of tongues in countries scattered around the globe. The answer to this ancient question is as complex as the wide variety of equestrian explorers represented by The Long Riders' Guild. Equestrian travel is not merely about covering vast amounts of mileage. Such a journey is about change as much as discovery.

3

History provides examples of the primary reasons people have set off, across the ages, in search of answers.

**The Personal Pilgrimage.** There are many accounts depicting the plight of a "normal" person, like you, who left the safety of "home" and, having overcome numerous trials and temptations, underwent a personal transformation. Such tales bring into play the eternal themes of self-reliance, loyalty, resolve and valour. Plus, Long Riders have the added power of the semi-magical horse to carry them on their journey of self-discovery.

**Life is short.** If Reason One is dominated by youth, Reason Two is the realm of maturity. There comes a time when we realize with a shock that our life isn't about time passing, it's about what little time remains. Linked to that discovery is the realisation that life is about time, not things.

**The Horse.** Despite having spent their lives with horses, many Long Riders discover that the journey gave them a new perspective on the horse-human relationship. At some indefinable point the human and horse ceased to be two separate entities. They learn to trust each other for safety and comfort. It is a seamless melding of the two spirits so complete, they can no longer be defined as individuals. They have become a Centaur.

**Curiosity.** As long as humans have ridden horses, people have been intrigued enough by a sense of geographic, cultural, spiritual or political curiosity to ride off in a sense of discovery. It may be no more than what is over the next mountain. It might entail undertaking a ride like the one made by Erich von Salzmann who rode 6,000 kilometres (3,700 miles) from Tientsin, China, across the Gobi Desert, to Tashkent, Uzbekistan in 1903.

**Charities, Campaigns and Crusades.** Long Riders have made journeys for a wide variety of reasons, including raising money for various types of medical research, educational efforts, etc. While every one of these efforts was in itself worthwhile, you do not need to justify the journey. Riding for a cause complicates the trip. It detracts from the daily events. It intrudes upon your time. It forces you to be a book-keeper, when your number one duty is to your horse. And the longer you travel, the further away will seem the cause which you once held dear. By all means ride. And ride for a cause, if you hold it dear. Just don't think that you need to have a crusade in order to justify the journey. The journey is the cause!

No matter what reason motivates you, the world still belongs to those brave enough to venture out into its unknown dangers, and horses still stand eager and willing to take us there. The map of your life is yours alone to draw.

## Chapter 4 - Age and Ability

Just as there are no such things as national, religious, cultural, political or sexual restrictions against becoming a Long Rider, you will likewise find that there are no age limitations either.

Jessica Chitty was only three years old when she completed a 4,800 kilometre (3,000 mile) journey from Spain to Greece. The child had ridden while the parents walked beside. Being sixty-seven years old didn't stop Bill Holt from riding his aged cart horse, Trigger, 9,500 kilometres (6,000 miles) across Europe.

Nor is equestrian travel reserved for physically fit athletes. Despite being born with only tiny stumps, instead of fully formed arms and legs, it was his love of riding that unlocked the world to Arthur Kavanagh. The adventurous young man rode from Circassia, across Persia and on to India in 1849, where he became a government dispatch rider and hunted tigers.

## Chapter 5 - Seeking Advice

Historically there has been no equestrian literary point of reference for men and women such as you.

The earliest mounted Argonauts of the past scoffed at book learning. Yet even after the majority of mankind had learned to read and write, equestrian travellers in later ages still failed to write down how they made equestrian decisions.

For example, one 19$^{th}$ century equestrian explorer set off with 94 horses in his expedition. Six months later only seven of these equines had survived. That meant that during the course of 182 days the explorer had lost an average of one horse every two days. Yet the explorer didn't bother to explain or justify his actions. He didn't devote any part of his book to discussing how he fed the horses, whether he shod them, what type of saddle he rode, etc. Why? Because these early equestrian travellers did not see any reason to retain easily accessible communal wisdom for unforeseen generations. They took such knowledge for granted.

This isn't to say that you are not going to meet a host of horseback people who are eager to offer you their opinions on everything from your route, your horse and gear. Don't let their costume fool you. The vast majority of people who are dressed like Cowboys, Cossacks, Gauchos, Mounties and Mongols, are little more than well-meaning opinionated descendants of once-great equestrian cultures. Whereas their forefathers might have been able to guide you, chances are that the man wearing the big cowboy hat knows more about Chevrolets than he does about Criollos. Burdening mules, chasing cows, performing dressage, jumping over painted sticks or riding a trail on Sunday isn't the same thing as leaving behind everything you know to become an equestrian explorer.

Despite the passage of thousands of years, equestrian travel has changed very little. There have been improvements to the equipment but the basic laws still apply. Travelling for great distances demands special skills - and even though there are millions of horse owners in the world - only a handful of them have ever ridden far from home. That is why you must be careful of accepting well-meaning advice. This obviously doesn't apply to people who are teaching you how to groom, tack and ride horses. Those sort of basic equestrian skills are essential. By "advice" I mean when it comes to horse travel.

It takes another Long Rider to tell you about the reality of equestrian travel. Never accept equestrian travel advice from anyone who hasn't ridden at least five hundred miles in a straight line.

## Chapter 6 - No Preparation, No Success

History has demonstrated that those who fail to plan more often than not never reach their goal. Even worse, the journey ends up being made at the horse's expense. If one is preparing to set off on an equestrian exploration, then you must realise in advance that penalties occur from inexperience, that nature is unforgiving, that the rider's lack of planning may have direct results on the horses' health and even life.

The best defence against the problem of equestrian disaster is EEE - Equestrian Exploration Education. The more background information you can soak up before your departure the better are your chances to succeed in a journey near home or a life-threatening ride across the wilds. More importantly, such education not only translates into a greater chance of expedition success, it greatly increases the very survival of the animals you cherish so highly to begin with.

The first thing you need to do therefore is match your dreams against your skills. Equestrian travel has no room for false heroism. It is about preparation. To face the unknown perils of the road without knowledge or skill brings only hardship, suffering, injury and possible death to you and your horses.

Before you leave you should be asking yourself a lot of basic questions.

Do you have the required equestrian skill needed to make a journey? Will anyone ride with you? What sort of horses should you acquire? Do you have the proper riding and pack saddles? How do you handle the pack horse? How many miles should you travel every day? Do you walk, trot or canter? How do you go uphill, downhill, through tunnels, across bridges, through rivers and past traffic? When do you water and feed? When do you start to think about stopping for the day? What kind of place should you look for? What do you feed the horse if you don't recognize any of the native food on offer? Do you picket, hobble, highline or stable the horse? How do you handle horse thieves? What measures have you taken regarding governmental interference?

Advance preparation will prove your salvation later on and help you realize that the more trouble one takes beforehand, the more successful a journey is likely to be. Don't attempt to follow your dream unless you are prepared to learn what is first needed first; and that does not mean merely taking riding lessons. It means acquiring a far wider range of skills, including the time to find out your horses' physical and psychological needs. It means being prepared to change your route and timetable as necessary to work within the horses' best interest. And it means putting your horses first at all time, however tired, wet and footsore you may be.

These basic laws of equestrian travel always hold true. Adventures occur due to inexperience. Recklessness will jeopardize your journey. Determination is not enough. Luck will not get you through. The goal must be clearly defined. Preparation is all important. Planning must be meticulous. Time spent learning is never wasted.

# Chapter 7 - Finances

Regardless of how excited you are, in spite of all your noble intentions, you can't overlook this ancient law of travel. Even Columbus needed money. Finances are a critically important part of equestrian travel. You are no exception to that non-negotiable rule. Plus, unlike a bicyclist, you have the added responsibility of providing daily feed and care for your mount. So the ride proceeds only as and when you have the funding necessary to ensure the financial safety of you and your horse.

Before you proceed to purchase a horse, saddle, etc, you will need to determine two things: What kind of equestrian traveller are you and how much money do you need? There are three types of equestrian travellers: a) independently wealthy b) corporate sponsored c) any combination of traveller/pilgrim/explorer. Which one are you? Regardless, all three are valid because the problems encountered on the road are the great leveller of both Long Riders and Road Horses.

In order to help you arrive at some idea of the amount of funds needed, construct an approximate route for your proposed trip. Divide the total number of proposed miles by twenty miles per day to arrive at the minimum length of your trip. Figure on $15 a day for rider and one horse. Add an additional $5 per day for a pack horse. What's the total amount? Now factor in the cost of purchasing your Road Horse, Pack Horse, riding and pack saddles. Do you have the basic funds needed to even proceed on a horse trip? Can you raise it?

Here is a list of potential expenses. Road horse and riding saddle. Pack horse and pack saddle. Bridle, halters, lead ropes, and saddle pads. Rider's personal equipment such as clothes. Horse's equipment such as brushes, hoof picks, etc. Tent, camping and cooking gear. Food and lodging for Long Rider and horses. Diplomatic charges for visas, human and equine passports, and medical evaluations at border crossings. Insurance for health of horse and rider. Transportation costs, ranging from local ferry across a river to air fare across oceans. Local labour, be it a guide, veterinarian or farrier.

Before you can swing into the saddle, you must carefully consider all of these potential financial handicaps, because lacking the funds for any portion of your overall expedition will diminish your chances of successfully reaching your distant geographic goal.

Regardless of where you're riding, the cost of the journey will always turn out to be higher than budgeted, so handle your financial preparations with extreme care. Plan to spend twice as much as you expect both in time and money.

Carry your paper money in small denominations, with enough money close at hand so as to handle expected daily expenses. Maintain the rest of your cash in a deeply secure wallet, hidden vest pocket or in a secret bag kept under your shirt. Keep a reserve of traveller's cheques in case of an emergency, especially as border guards and immigration officials may demand that you verify you have enough funds to transit through their country. Use an ATM card with caution, regardless of what country you're riding in. If you must carry a large sum of cash, for example to buy several horses, disguise it, hide it and don't discuss it. Don't expect foreign banks to adhere to the same rules observed by your local banking institution. Money transfers can almost certainly take longer than expected and charges will often be exorbitant. Like many aspects of riding in foreign lands, you will need a tremendous amount of patience, tolerance and good humour.

Finally, ask yourself this question. Is money a deciding factor in deciding whether you leave on an equestrian adventure? If so then you're not ready to depart.

## Chapter 8 - Sponsors

Perhaps you are considering enlisting the aid of a financial sponsor. Is this a reasonable idea?

No one would realistically expect to contact one of the major American automobile companies, announce they wanted to see the United States, and then ask a Detroit car maker to be so kind as to donate a new car and a tank of gas so they can make the trip. Yet all too often would-be equestrian travellers don't hesitate to ask for an assortment of free items including saddles, clothing and feed.

What many amateur travellers don't appreciate is how small the majority of equine connected companies are. So making payroll and keeping the doors open is already tough, before you show up asking them to sponsor your dream.

Also, don't forget that you're signing away a share of your independence in exchange for an assortment of "freebies," such as sleeping bags, tents and clothing. That's because you make a Faustian deal when you tie your expedition to a sponsor, as they expect media, demand reports and thrive on exposure. Anything you get comes with invisible strings attached. So if you can maintain your financial independence, by all means do so.

One financial aspect of equestrian travel which has never been adequately explained is how the general rules of expedition planning can, and should, also be applied to equestrian travel. It's going to take more than an impressive letterhead to sway cynical corporate accountants. What's needed is an easy-to-read synopsis of your proposed journey. This document should include facts, images and maps which explain the significance of your journey. Your proposal should provide information regarding your equestrian qualifications and how those talents will help you overcome any difficulties you might encounter while travelling. The proposal should include intended departure dates and list the costs of the various aspects of the journey. It should also detail how the journey will benefit the corporate sponsor or individual donor.

As the leaders of other major types of expeditions know, most corporations set their budgets and allocate donations at least a year in advance. Any donation proposal should be professional, and presented long before your actual departure, as a last-minute prospectus will not inspire either confidence or financial input.

## Chapter 9 - Work

Don't plan on mixing working and riding. It may happen but you can't count on it. No matter how hard it is to find a job at the best of times back home, your problems are going to be multiplied a thousand fold when you have the additional emotional burden of worrying about your horses in a strange place. So take this lesson to heart. Don't depart until you have enough money to guarantee the safety of you and your animals.

## Chapter 10 - Donations

Even if you ask for the moon a year in advance, what are your chances of getting it? Not very encouraging, I'm afraid.

In the early 1980s, when French Long Rider Jean Claude Cazade rode from France to Arabia, a company dispatched equine medicine to some of the cities along the route. When the Russian Long Rider Vladimir Fissenko, rode 30,500 kilometres (19,000 miles) from Patagonia to Alaska, the Easy Boot Company agreed to provide his mount with protective hoof boots. These two Long Riders were lucky. The North American Long Rider John Egenes spent two fruitless years trying to entice corporate sponsorship for his 1972 ocean to ocean ride.

One final point about donations; if you receive them, use them, otherwise, return them! There are several notorious examples of unethical horse travellers who exploited the generosity and trust of equine companies. What these sorts of people do is poison the well of generosity for legitimate equestrian travellers. If you receive a financial donation, acknowledge it. If you're given valuable equipment or services, repay the companies generosity by publicly endorsing their product on your website and to the equestrian press. If you don't depart, then have the ethical courage and courtesy to return the equipment.

# Chapter 11 - Choosing your Destination

Where we travel to is just as important as how we get there. That is why you need to spend time determining where you're going, personally and geographically.

The destination for some may be easily defined in geographic terms, such as those equestrian travellers who relish the challenge of riding three thousand miles "ocean to ocean" across the United States. Yet equestrian travel isn't restricted to geographical goals, nor must it be overtly influenced by either current political or geographical events.

If it is true that the age of national exploration is now past, the Long Riders' Guild believes we are witnessing the dawning of the age of the citizen-explorer, an enlightened era wherein individuals set out not to exploit the natural resources of their neighbours, nor to plant the flag of their country atop a mighty peak in another land, but rather to explore the frontiers of this planet and our own souls.

Obviously no matter what they have to offer, places are just places. What makes them special or not is the complex combination of you, the place and the moment. What you should fear, in terms of determining your destination, is the danger of making a predictable ride to a stagnant location. You should approach equestrian travel as an adventure, not an advertisement. When you consider "where" you're going, you must recall that you are making two journeys, an inner and outer one. Your journey's destination should serve to unlock the complexity of your soul, instead of trying to control it. Your time in the saddle should be spent learning from the obstacles which you will undoubtedly encounter, not pretending that life is trouble free, as the colourful tourist brochures preach to the unwitting.

Organized travel is designed to turn you into a moveable conformist. Guidebooks tell you where to eat and what places to avoid. In contrast, when you explore the world on horseback you are stimulated physically, geographically, intellectually, linguistically, emotionally and spiritually. When you become a Long Rider you saddle up and then slow down. Your choice of destination should reflect your desire to embrace personal change, as well as geographic achievement.

What you must do is base your destination decision on modern equestrian reality, not mythology. Don't set off thinking you are going to re-discover the Old West, the Old East, or any other 19th century legends. Roads now criss-cross continents. Barbed wire halts progress along historic pathways. Caravanserais are a dim memory in Central Asia. More Long Riders are injured in the United States by road-raged motorists than by wild animals.

One final thought you should bear in mind about your travel plans. After you've invented them, don't enshrine them: you're travelling by horse, not bus. Your schedule is largely dependant on his stomach and the weather. If something or someone exciting comes along, don't be afraid to linger or explore.

## Chapter 12 - Equestrian Brotherhood

One of the primary principles of safe horse travel is to always try and ride within the boundaries of an established equestrian culture.

When someone is encased in a speeding car they don't travel slowly enough to meet and speak to other people. There are no encounters at seventy miles per hour, only the isolation of man. Nor are mechanized societies prone to understand or tolerate you and your mount.

Equestrian traditions still run strong in numerous parts of the world and it is those horse-friendly cultures which you should always seek. What they lack in numbers they make up for in hospitality. Such traditional equestrian cultures are always more intrigued, and hospitable, than completely mechanized countries.

You will find that there is a sympathetic impression in the souls of other horse people, regardless of the obvious visual differences which separate you. Even if they're not equestrian travellers, horse riders relish how their mounts make them feel like they are part of the wider world you are riding through. Thus, regardless of who first rode him, the horse has helped create a mounted celebration of mankind's diversity. Planning your trip through a horse-friendly environment is a positive first step.

But you must leave any naive feelings of native cultural superiority at home. You should instead set out on this trip to seek knowledge, not to push your own cultural opinions on people who have the right to disagree with the personal views you hold based on your own limited understanding of a vast and culturally diverse planet.

## Chapter 13 - Planning Your Route

Once you've decided on a physical location, you must ask yourself what is the safest way you can go about arriving at your destination. Your immediate task is to construct a route that will take you and your horse along a line of travel designed to eliminate as many busy roads and topographical challenges as is possible.

In order to accomplish this seemingly-easy task, you should make a giant mental leap away from your current existence as a motorized citizen. Geography is no longer to be ignored. It must be studied carefully. Equestrian travellers are not motorists. A mile-long bridge across the vast Mississippi river causes a driver to glance idly at the muddy water swirling below, while a Long Rider takes his life in his hands to make the same crossing. When planning your route never think in terms of motorized distances, as the geographic challenges routinely ignored by drivers will imperil the lives of you and your horses.

One of the most common failings of would-be equestrian travellers is to over estimate their daily mileage. With their map spread out before them, novices cheerfully decide in advance that they're going to ride from Point A to Point B in so many months, weeks, days and hours. These people are making the fundamental error of mistaking mathematical progress for equestrian reality. Equestrian travel is never about a preconceived set of miles. If you haven't already ridden the road, you don't have any idea what challenges and delays are waiting around the corner.

Distance by horse is measured by time! It is measured in miles only in hindsight.

Do not be too optimistic about your proposed mileage. Do not think you're going to ride an average of thirty miles a day. Such dreams are meant to be broken by the waves of reality on the rocks of disappointment. Plan instead on averaging between fifteen and twenty miles a day for five days, allowing two days for rest and repair.

You may not think you need the rest, but your horse does. While you use the first day to do chores, repair equipment and send mail etc., your horse will be busy eating. The second day he will eat as well. But it is the rest gained during the second day that will allow him to restore his energy. Using this technique you can have an accurate idea before departure of how long your journey will actually take.

# Chapter 14 - The Paperwork

There is a great deal more paperwork involved in equestrian travel than most Long Riders realize. It is critical that you document the legal, diplomatic and medical progress of your trip. Your documentation needs to be started early because every one of these steps is time-consuming and takes longer than you might think,. We shall be discussing equine paperwork in a later section. What needs to be realized first is that unless your own papers are in order, there's no point in worrying about those of your horses.

When you are on your horse, away from home, you are in danger from more subtle hazards than robbers. Chances are your journey won't be stopped by obvious dangers. You run a greater risk from petty officials who are apt to delay or antagonize you. This arises wherever you ride because officials around the world are eager to enforce laws. Therefore no equestrian traveller can hope to escape from this bureaucratic threat because a stranger riding a horse is a nuisance to busy officials.

This antagonism to travellers is an ancient evil, one which earlier equestrian explorers foresaw and took precautions to protect against. They did so by use of the firman.

**The Firman.** The firman is a letter issued by a high-ranking government minister. The firman instructs local officials to treat the traveller with respect, not to obstruct his journey and to afford him every possible assistance. This idea has been used by various cultures. Its most celebrated example was the pass issued by the powerful Genghis Khan to his ambassadors, friends and couriers. The mere sight of this potent travel icon instantly procured polite behaviour from obstructionist officials, inspired efficiency instead of arrogance, provided support in government guest houses and even opened jail cells. You should make every effort to obtain some sort of firman from the authorities prior to your departure. If your journey is to be a domestic one which keeps you within the borders of your own country, have your governor, state senator, local congressman, mayor or even police chief, issue you a document urging other officials to respect and expedite your journey through their areas of influence. If your journey will take you through foreign countries, then arrange a courtesy call to the embassies of each of the lands you wish to ride in. If possible, ask for a brief meeting with the ambassador. During that meeting ask the ambassador if he would be kind enough to sign a letter you have prepared in advance which describes your intentions, route and the fact that you have discussed your journey with this high-ranking government official. If possible, have the letter stamped with an official seal. And in this age of instant digital photography, ask if someone can take your photo as the ambassador hands you the firman. Such diplomatic precautions may save you countless delays, or rescue you and your horses from unforeseen bureaucratic entanglements.

**Letters of Introduction.** A letter of introduction from a person of authority to other officials will smooth away many small difficulties and give you a recognized position during your travels. If possible obtain letters of recommendation to ambassadors, bankers, merchants, doctors, lawyers, booksellers and respectable tradesmen. In addition to being helpful, such people are able to give you a great deal of interesting information

**Passport.** Keep your passport with you at all times. But be sure to also make a photocopy of it and keep it somewhere separate. Never keep your passport and other vital papers in your saddlebag. One unlucky Long Rider's horse ran away on the steppes of Mongolia. She watched in horror as her passport and money disappeared in the distance. Always carry your passport, documents and money on your person.

**Health Certificates.** Regardless of where you're planning on riding, it is imperative that you confirm what medical tests, inoculations and health certificates you and your horse will require before setting out.

**Explanatory Flyers.** There is one other powerful piece of paper you should arm yourself with; the Explanatory Flyer.

Regardless of where you ride, day after day curious people will ask you the same questions. Where are you coming from? Where are going? What kind of horse are you riding? How much did you pay for him? Why are you making this ride? Aren't you afraid you're going to be a)

killed, b) kidnapped c) robbed d) all of the above? Are you married? Do you want to be? How much money do you make? What religion are you? And on and on and on, every day.

To offset these endless questions, compose a one-page piece of paper that provides all the details about you and your trip. If possible include a photo of you and your horse on the flyer. Carry copies of this document in your saddlebag. The Explanatory Flyer works anywhere and saves you the trouble of having to deal with an annoying daily barrage of repetitive questions. Plus it will provide reporters with an accurate description of your journey.

**Friendship Book.** Long Riders have recognized the need to document the accuracy of their journeys. These travellers carried a special book which contained the names of the people they met, along with that person's signature, date and a personal comment.

Friendship Books not only provide vital evidence which proves the accuracy of your journey, they can also ease your way through local difficulties. Smart Long Riders make a point of collecting the autographs and stamped entries of all the policemen they meet. If you get one policeman to sign your book and stamp it, then the next policeman you find will also want to sign, to be part of your trip, to have his picture taken with you. Also, the growing collection of police signatures helps create a clear path when trouble arises.

Argentine Long Rider Benjamin Reynal documented how this important literary tool serves other functions as well. The book quickly proves the legitimacy of your journey to a potential host.

"The book is a great ice breaker," Benjamin explained. "With its growing collection of pictures, letters, stamps etc it is a very fast, easy and truthful way of explaining your travels. I learned that after seeing the book 99% of the people wanted to help and become part of the trip. And because you travel short distances one day at a time, people may recognize the place you stayed at the night before or recognize the name of the last person who wrote in the book."

The book also provides a strong strategic purpose.

Benjamin discovered that by collecting the signatures of all the policemen he met, the Friendship Book helped ease his way through local difficulties and created a clear path when trouble arose. "The reason for this is very important and I would recommend it to future travellers. If you get one policeman to sign your book and stamp it, as I did fifty times, then the next policeman you find will also want to sign, to be part of your trip, to have his picture taken with you."

Finally, besides being a useful tool during the ride, the Friendship Book will eventually become a beautiful reminder of the journey. Benjamin collected personal letters, poems and pictures from the people he met.

"Years go by and I read people's notes and everything comes back again. Without a doubt, from all the things I brought back from my ride, this book is the only item that makes me drop a tear," Benjamin said.

Thus, though it began life as a strategic tool, the Friendship Book becomes an emotional treasure.

**Hints.** Other suggestions made by Long Riders include making copies of your driving license and birth certificate. And because many countries require a traveller to provide several photos per visa application, always carry extra passport photos so as to stave off problems en route. If possible obtain your visas in advance and always be aware of their expiration date. South African Long Rider Billy Brenchley wrote, "When it comes to paperwork and documents, be practical not paranoid. I carry several colour copies of my original documents. This way, if a corrupt official threatens to confiscate it unless you pay a bribe, say go ahead, keep it."

# Chapter 15 - Your Choice of Companions

The choice of a comrade is a preliminary test filled with unseen perils, many of which are not recognized by Long Riders prior to their departure. Equestrian travel is complex and difficult in its challenges. That is why you must determine if you will ride alone or with a companion.

**The Requirements.** Only a few people can become Long Riders. That is why it is difficult to find anyone to accompany you. There are few people capable of summoning the courage to set off on such a journey. The chances of finding such person to accompany you are therefore slim. What you need in a companion on the ride is a guide at the crossroads, strength when you are weak, defence against danger, solace in moments of discouragement and firmness of purpose, for an equestrian expedition is only as strong as its weakest link. If your journey is to succeed, everyone must come together to form a powerful team that shares the same vision.

**Emotional Disaster.** Nine times out of ten this is your dream and a potential companion often serves as a convenient emotional security blanket which you think you need at this early stage of the trip's development. What you will discover is that as your mounted skills increase on the trail, your previous emotional need will diminish as your confidence grows. Plus the further you ride into your new world the more interactions you will enjoy with an exciting assortment of newly-met friends. As your own courage and resolve increase, your original companion's value will often diminish.

As history has demonstrated, the immense physical and emotional hardships of an equestrian journey place a tremendous strain on friendships, families and marriages, many of which will not survive unless everyone involved is equally passionate about completing the trip. The majority of companions, though initially intrigued with the idea, soon discover that they either suffer through or end up hating the experience. When that occurs, the Long Rider is facing hell in the saddle.

Your equestrian dream will turn into a nightmare if you set off with the wrong companion! When this occurs you are facing a critical social disaster, one which has scuttled many an otherwise carefully planned equestrian journey.

**Riding Alone.** Having discovered what happens when you set off with the wrong person, it's no wonder that the majority of would-be Long Riders decide to travel alone. Solo travelling certainly has its compensations. You have no one to consider but yourself. You can go where and when you like, stop when you want to, eat what and when you fancy, without reference to the curious and unpredictable tastes of a comrade. But don't be afraid, you already have the ideal companion.

**Your Best Friend.** Though it may seem obvious, most humans overlook this fundamental truth. A great portion of the journey is about the involved relationship which develops between two species, namely you and your mount. Your horse is your primary companion! Part of your mission is to explore, expand and understand the journey alongside this majestic animal. It is the horse who will spark more interest, talk, friendliness and hospitality than any human companion.

**Recipe for Success.** You can't wish for a perfect Long Rider but here's a recipe for emotional and tactical success. When looking for a companion, remember personal qualities mean more than money. Find a person who is inclined to your own view and sympathetic to the things you enjoy. Always choose enthusiasm before academic knowledge. Courtesy is priceless. A sense of humour is a must. Tolerance, resilience and adaptability in the face of emergencies are always required. Endurance and keen motivation are foundations for success. The ability to thrive in isolation is necessary. Courage can never be underestimated. A proficiency in equestrian skills is a delight, as are linguistic and cooking skills. Above all else, prize loyalty, as this gift will help overcome the stresses and strains found on any rigorous journey.

When considering a companion, you will be tempted to compromise. Listen to your instincts. Ask yourself if you would be willing to spend long periods of time with this person, trapped in a small room, facing unexpected troubles, should plans gone awry? Forsake any type of inflexible expert. Shun anyone whose political or religious convictions cannot be constrained. Leave drunkards and party animals behind, as their lack of discipline will translate into future trouble for your horses. Above all, avoid anyone who is selfish, immature, immoral and lazy. Equestrian travel will test the toughest and break the weak. Don't burden yourself with the wrong companion.

# Chapter 16 - Travelling with Dogs

Long Riders are often tempted to take a dog as a travelling companion. There have been rare exceptions but this usually proves to be a fatal decision for the trusting canine.

Their presence provokes fights with other dogs. They attract predators. They are often seriously injured by kicks from irritated horses. Dogs have died of snake bite. They are often wounded by porcupines and skunks. They suffer from sore paws and are susceptible to heat stroke. They have been kidnapped and nearly eaten by hungry natives. The leading cause of death occurs when dogs wander in front of traffic.

There are other reasons not to take a dog. Some national parks will not permit them. Locating their food is an additional challenge. If the dog becomes injured or ill the pack horse is employed to carry the canine's additional weight. They represent an extra emotional and logistical burden at a time when your priority should be your horses.

# Chapter 17 - Before You Saddle Up

As this information demonstrates, equestrian travel is uncompromising. It must be viewed through the disenchanting view of reality. Yet there are two things certain to be awaiting you – excitement and freedom. The shackles of civilization are left behind. There are no planes to be caught, no crowded hotels to stop at. Camp after camp is pitched and then struck, inducing an eagerness to press on. And yet there is no hurry about it. The journey stops at the pleasure of the Long Rider.

**Getting Ready for the Road.** Your horse needs no favours. He only looks for a square deal. If you already have a suitable Road Horse, then now is the time to start training rides. Get your horse used to traffic without delay. It's a different universe once you leave the safety net of the stable. Learn to slow down, while you're learning to ride ahead.

If you're going to make your journey overseas, then speak to the airline about the cost of transporting your tack and equipment. Saddles and Long Rider gear are heavy, bulky and valuable.

Start work on your paperwork immediately. Investigate your medical, legal and travel document needs. Create your firman by asking your lawyer, mayor, congressman, senator, Member of Parliament, and vet to provide you with this critically important paper protection.

**Rewards.** What you must realize before you leave is that regardless of the dangers and disappointments you will be awarded an immense emotional reward that you would never have found while participating in traditional equestrian activities. What you will discover instead is what other Long Riders have found before you - the deepest possible emotional bond with your horse and an intense love of life that can't be adequately described to anyone who is not a fellow equestrian explorer.

Thus, there is no "failure" if you are a Long Rider. Every journey presents a brilliant opportunity for you to enshrine a lesson for years to come; namely, that the richness of life isn't dependent on the miles, but on the value of where you rode emotionally and what you learned spiritually along the way. If you come away with that lesson then you will make this journey a success that isn't dependent upon reaching a distant geographic goal. If you learn that going is more important than arriving, then you'll have accomplished something of immense value before you ever leave.

# Section Two – The Horses

## Chapter 18 - A New Herd Ethic

Long distance travelling alters a horse. He becomes more alert and accepting. On the move he will eat food that he would not have accepted back home. Most importantly, he becomes tightly fused to his companions; (to the other horses and his Long Rider). He calls for his rider if he walks away. He recognizes him from afar.

Long Riders have made a number of consistent emotional discoveries regarding their horses. After a certain number of days travelling, the road horse develops a new herd ethic. As ancient genetic impressions are aroused, the horse's memory of 'home' is replaced by a new cosmic order which centres on his rider and the sun.

Because his geographic world is now constantly changing, the road horse develops an intense emotional bond with his rider. The sun comes up – the road horse sets off and observes the world around him changing – again and again. Despite that day's emotional surprises, the Long Rider is there to reassure the horse. The sun starts to set – and the horse learns that his rider will provide food and security throughout the night.

This constant geographic alteration prompts an intense sentimental need among many road horses who long for a sense of stability. As the journey starts to take hold, the horse learns that food and safety can be found close by the Long Rider's camp. The emotional connection and sense of trust that exist between horse and Long Rider is a hundred times deeper than that of a ring-ridden horse and his weekend rider.

Like man, horses take up deep friendships and form intense emotional bonds. In a world that changes every day, where every night brings a new roof or no roof, where one day brings feast and the next famine, you will represent emotional consistency to your horse. No bond in your life will ever be stronger than the one you develop with the horse you sleep, travel and share the road with.

## Chapter 19 – One Horse or Two?

One of the first decisions you have to make is - one horse or two? The answer depends upon a number of factors.

Where will you ride; in a country rich with easily obtained resources or across a terrain filled with geographic and climatic challenges?

Will you be travelling across a lonely landscape devoid of traffic or riding alongside busy roads inhabited with motorized threats?

Shall the countryside aid or hinder you: can you count on encountering a regular series of hospitable hosts or will friendly faces be few and far between?

Can you depend upon routinely obtaining food and grazing; or will a lack of supplies require the employment of a pack animal?

How much is needed to ensure your safety and comfort; are you one those who can sleep comfortably in a roadside ditch or do you require amenities such as a hot meal every night?

Are you strong enough; can you carry supplies in a backpack and walk for miles alongside your horse?

If the decision is made to only use one horse, will you be able to locate an animal with the suitable strength and emotional loyalty?

**A Fundamental Problem.** Let us say for the sake of argument that you are thinking about making an equestrian journey and are debating the idea of employing a pack horse.

In his book, *Horses Saddles and Bridles*, cavalry General William Harding Carter wrote, "All soldiers of experience know well the value of carefully preserving the strength of the horse. While the weight of the pack saddle does not appear to diminish the rate of speed upon the march, it necessarily increases the fatigue of the horse and ultimately tends to reduce his length of service."

Carter went on to explain that the more weight the horse carries, the higher the chance he will suffer a sore back. That is why, he wrote, "It is customary to reduce the weight of the pack saddle to its lowest limit."

Cavalrymen like Carter knew the hazards of placing a heavy weight on a horse. Thus deciding not to employ a pack horse means the road horse will be required to carry more weight, which increases the rate of risk.

This provokes an important strategic and ethical question before departure. Can you travel safely with one horse?

As some Long Riders have proved, given the right set of circumstances the answer can be 'yes.'

**Size Matters.** First a Long Rider needs to ideally employ a big horse, one with plenty of power. Louise, DC Vision's Shire mare, was the ultimate example of this one-horse philosophy. Having been previously employed pulling logs out of the Maine forest, Louise loved the idea of making a journey. The lovable mare happily carried DC and all his possessions for 22,500 kilometres (14,000 miles).

Lucy Leaf's horse Igor was 16.1, weighed about 1300 pounds, was big of bone and had size 3 hooves. His thick skin, mane and tail provided him with protection from bugs in summer and cold in winter. Like Louise, Igor had a tremendous appetite and his strong stomach enabled him to eat nearly anything.

**Mounted Experience.** Let's say that the idea of using one horse is appealing but you still harbour doubts. Then let us begin this investigation by seeking the opinion of a Long Rider who is uniquely qualified to comment on the differences between using a pack horse as opposed to travelling with one equine.

In 1982 Lisa Stewart made a 4,900 kilometre (3,000 mile) equestrian journey across the USA in the company of Len Brown and five horses. More recently the experienced Long Rider completed another journey; only this time she chose to only use her horse, Chief.

"I loved feeling so free with just one horse. I loved knowing I could control my horse. And I liked the idea of asking to stay on someone's property, knowing it was only one horse, not five like with Len's and my trip. This meant I didn't have to call ahead or plan in advance. I could just ride up to a house that felt right and knock."

Lisa felt so strongly about the subject of how many horses to employ, that she wrote, "As far as whether to take one horse or two, I would never again make a ride in which I had to lead a pack horse. I want both hands on my road horse at all times."

In her opinion, "The only reason to take a second horse is if you are riding through country that is so remote you literally cannot restock once a week."

**Careful Planning.** Unlike Lisa, who had equestrian travel experience, William Reddaway described himself as "an inexperienced 65 year old."

Yet that didn't stop him from riding his horse Strider to the four corners of England.

William recognized the need to take precautions regarding the largely urbanized environment in which he would be travelling.

"I chose to make my ride in England because I am neither much of a rider nor of a horseman and I wanted to be in an environment with easy access to advice and professional support."

He had reason to be concerned. England is a densely populated country and eighty per cent of William's route lay along roads that took him through busy cities. The idea of leading a pack horse in traffic was unappealing. Plus there were other reasons why William decided to only use one horse.

"I planned the ride to be done with one horse because a) I could not afford to buy and keep more than one horse and b) I had little enough experience for managing one horse and none in working with two."

William realized additional benefits included, "lower ongoing costs (feed, farrier, vet, insurance etc); easier passage through the many gates off-road; a narrower and more agile profile on-road; easier to find people who could accommodate one horse."

Having made the decision to travel with one horse, William spent a great deal of time carefully planning his route. He then contacted people in advance so as to arrange for him and Strider to be fed and sheltered.

"I reckoned that the travelling would be tough enough for me as an inexperienced 65 year old and that a bed, shower and food each night would be a better bet than camping. I had 85% of our accommodation arranged before I started. For 99% of our nights either both of us, or Strider, was spent staying with people who had horses."

In addition, William organized to have feed for Strider delivered along the way. He also scheduled appointments with the farrier in advance.

"These factors were important in reducing what we needed to carry."

**Drawbacks.** There are disadvantages to using one horse.

Travelling with one horse requires you to reduce what you can carry, including cooking gear and food.

Packing and unpacking takes a shorter amount of time; but balancing the weight being carried is of vital importance.

Long Riders routinely walk. Using one horse requires them to walk more often.

There may be an emotional disadvantage in that most horses are gregarious by nature. A lonely horse may seek company during the night, leaving the Long Rider stranded.

# Chapter 20 - The Road Horse

The term "Road Horse" was once commonly used to describe an equine capable of successfully completing extended journeys under a variety of conditions, across any type of country, in any type of weather. In 1847 equine travel expert Rollo Springfield defined what qualities were needed for such an animal. "The Road Horse is a strong, vigorous, active kind, capable of enduring great hardship; its stature rather low, seldom exceeding fifteen hands; the body round and compact; its limbs strong," Springfield wrote, then went on to say, "sadly this breed has of late been neglected by those preferring fashion instead of utility." Regardless of the year and place, your chances of geographic success are directly linked to your choice of mount. This will be the most important decision you make in planning your journey. Not only will it greatly determine if you reach your goal, it will affect every step of your trip. But finding a road horse in the early 21$^{st}$ century is difficult. You should begin your search by realizing that not any horse will do.

**A Challenging Proposal.** Every road horse must be capable of carrying heavy loads, consisting of the saddle, the Long Rider and their mutual essentials. He must be able to work even in difficult terrain. But the rise of the automobile has seen the decline of the horse, in terms of overall strength, perseverance and travel performance. When it comes to deciding what you will ride on a journey, understand that a horse which has spent its life living in a luxurious stall will be sensitive to the weather, less apt to endure hunger and prone to fatigue. Such a horse will require a lengthy time to transition to the rigours of a life on the road, with the chances of that success being dependent upon a great many unforeseen factors.

**Your Own Horse.** Perhaps you already own a horse. That doesn't automatically mean that this animal is capable of making a long and challenging journey. While it is correct to assume that it helps to be mounted on a horse you already trust and ride, you must not allow love to overrule logic. What is needed is a merciless evaluation of the animal's strengths and weaknesses. Does the horse have the physical strength required? Does he have the temperament needed to face a vast array of emotional obstacles? Can he adapt to spending the night in a variety of strange places? Can he travel through traffic calmly? Is he a hearty eater? If you already own such a horse, fine. However, if you have any doubts about the horse's suitability, look for another mount. Any journey requires a horse to tap into its deepest reserves of emotional courage and physical fortitude. Therefore do not be blinkered by misplaced loyalty into placing an animal you care for into a situation which he cannot withstand, overcome or even survive.

**Breeds.** You must never allow a romantic vision to cloud your better judgement. When we look for a road horse we must be careful not to fall into the trap of setting our hearts in advance on riding a specific breed, rather than locating a suitable animal. Blood lines are not the ultimate deciding factor. It is individual ability that counts. Long Riders want horses that are strong, brave and faithful. They're searching for courage not fairy-tale origins. They are pragmatists not preservationists. That is why there is no "chosen" breed for equestrian travel. One line of horses doesn't warrant greater praise than another. Long Riders give every breed and every individual horse a chance, and when the breed or individual horse fails to live up to the rigours of the road, he must give up his place to others. You steer the course but it is the strength and courage of the road horse that gets you both through. Do not allow an illusion to set your heart in advance on a particular breed! The most important criterion is to pick the horse from a breed that has the correct model and a body weight in accordance with the Long Rider and his equipment. Such an ideal road horse is one who enjoys travelling, can eat and drink anything, has strong feet and is happy being in a new place every day. This is a state of mind, not a breed.

**Climate and Terrain.** Think climate, not papers. It is imperative that the horse chosen for any journey must be suited to the local conditions as far as possible. For example, don't take a tropical horse into the mountains as horses do not adjust well to radical changes in climate and terrain. Fear terrain, not a lack of social standing. Consider if you will be riding through rugged country or alongside more sedate roadways. Where you are going will affect what you ride, so a local horse should always be considered a priority as acclimatised native animals are found to be more effective than imported mounts.

**Strength & Conformation.** Because the road horse must perform hard physical duty and carry continuous loads, he can't have any weaknesses in his general conformation, as any faults in build or balance must be compensated for by the use of extra energy. That is why in terms of the road horse small physical defects that may not make big differences in jumping, dressage or the show ring can create larger problems for a road horse. Beauty should be a secondary consideration. In choosing a road horse you should look for a sturdy type with sound limbs. A road horse needs to have heavier bone than the casual weekend riding mount. One then looks for a good teeth, a strong back, a wide deep chest, a free-moving shoulder, supple knees, flexible tendons, very hard hooves and high endurance. The withers are the most important aspect of the back. A round-backed horse will not hold the saddle well. This causes the saddle to roll from side to side, increasing the chance of sores and creating a horse that may require constant attention to re-pack a slipped load. For these reasons the withers should be well defined.

**Gender.** Depending on where you go, the gender of the road horse has a tremendous influence on daily events and will affect your long-term chances of success. The first thing to realize is that all horses, regardless of their gender, have the potential to become good road horses. What you have to consider are the cultural implications of where you ride, before you decide what you mount.

There is a strong prejudice currently afoot in North America and parts of Western Europe against stallions. Also, whereas it is difficult to cross any border with a medically certified mare or gelding, it is ten times more complex to attempt this with a stallion. The worst problem of travelling with a mare is that she runs the risk of becoming pregnant during the journey. This occurred to mares belonging to several equestrian travellers. History demonstrates that the gelding is nearly always the ideal travelling horse, as the medical procedure generally renders him pleasant, but spirited, brave, but not uncontrollable, tractable, but confident. According to his individual personality, if the horse is operated on at an older age, he often retains the characteristics of the stallion but without its wildness. Overall, a strong, reliable, well-trained gelding will be found to maintain the majority of those characteristics needed by a Long Rider.

**Colour.** When it comes to the perfect colour for a road horse, there isn't one. What you need to consider is that a lack of pigment makes a horse more prone to sunburn. This is especially true about horses with pink noses and pale skins. The other drawback of having a light-coloured horse is that as and when they roll in dung, you find your pretty pony is now adorned with a garish green coat. Always choose a darker rather than a lighter shade.

**Age.** The road horse should be at least six years old to ensure that the skeleton is solid. Plus, the majority of horses conclude their physical growth before they reach a state of emotional maturity. Because of these various reasons, you should avoid choosing a young horse. As long as the horse is in good health, there is no reason an older animal cannot travel with confidence.

**Height and Weight.** Just as you wouldn't purchase a pair of boots that were too big you should not obtain a horse too large for your purposes. When considering a possible road horse, the first thing to note is its height and weight-carrying power. Does it match your logistical and physical needs? Larger riders require heavier horses. Smaller riders can make do with lighter-limbed animals. When considering the height of your possible mount, what you must bear in mind is that the taller he is the higher you must reach to put on the saddle. Saddles are heavy, and become even more so as they are taken on and off day after day. So avoid adding to your work by purchasing a extremely tall horse. What you are seeking is a sturdy combination of strength and a capacity to endure.

**Emotional Stability.** One of the major problems we face is the need to form a reliable estimate of the horse's temperament, by no means an easy task in the fleeting time we have at our disposal. An emotionally-sound horse is one that creates no trouble and does not have a dominant personality that is difficult to control. Nor are stubborn trouble-makers suitable. What is needed is a calm temperament that can bear up under all challenges. This sort of quiet disposition results in a horse that is able to maintain a constant pace all day, then eat what's on offer, before bedding down in a strange stable. You may get where you are going on a horse that isn't right for you but it won't be much fun.

**Confidence.** A road horse should be fearless. His sense of independence is of far more importance than his good looks. A pretty horse is useless if he can't make the miles.

**Gait.** One of the most essential requirements in a potential mount is that he has a long, forward and ground-covering walk. This should be a fast, pleasant pace, so as to ensure that your daily miles become a pleasure instead of a constant struggle.

**Training.** A lack of fundamental training will not only place the successful outcome of your journey in question, it may well place your life at risk, as no amount of post-sale tenderness can overcome a horse's flaws in basic courtesy and education. You are looking for a horse that not only has a certain level of training but takes his work seriously. A road horse should stand still when being brushed, saddled and mounted. He should not pull back when tied. In addition to being quick to walk, trot and canter, he must move forward with a minimum of urging, turn easily and stop quickly. It helps if he neck reins, but it is essential that he respond to the bit and reins, regardless of what local system you decide to use. He must not evade being caught, as a runaway horse is a time-waster who will eventually leave you stranded and afoot. Depending on where you travel, he must quietly agree to be hobbled, picketed or placed in a barn other than his own. While it is essential to encourage him to exercise his own personality and judgment when encountering obstacles on the trail, etc., because the final decision is the rider's, the horse must be obedient and trusting. This is why a solid equestrian education is a fundamental requirement for a road horse and the further you stray from these principles of mutual respect, common courtesy and basic training the more likely you are to encounter trouble or be injured. Be sure that any horse you consider shows signs of being able to adapt to the emotional uncertainties encountered during a journey. You are searching for bravery, absolute trust and eagle-eyed attention. What you are seeking is a physically strong, emotionally rock solid, dependable horse.

**Hooves.** Regardless of what system you decide to use, barefoot, boots or shoes, a horse who acts badly around the farrier will be a constant source of trouble. A road horse should stand quietly when he is trimmed or shod.

**Feeding.** Because the road horse has been removed from his original home, he must be able to adopt an attitude of nutritional independence. He can't just be a good feeder. He should be a glutton that will eat absolutely anything. This type of horse is a survivor. They're always looking for food, which shouldn't be discouraged, as this is a valuable characteristic in a travelling horse.

**Hints.** Things will not "work themselves out" when you are on the road. Nor will a physically or emotionally unsuitable horse mysteriously transform itself into a wise road horse after you have set off. While your efforts to locate a suitable road horse may be fraught with difficulties and inevitable disappointments, there are several points which you should always keep in mind while undertaking your search. Sore backs, youth and pregnancy are the chief things to avoid. Don't begin your ride with an exhausted or underweight horse. Don't accept any dangerous stable vices, such as rearing or biting. Don't underestimate the importance of a rapid, ground-covering walk. Don't place beauty before wisdom and a large appetite. Don't allow a romantic pedigree to take precedence over strength and emotional confidence. Don't buy a horse which is too tall, seek instead for intelligence, bravery, maturity, hearty appetite, strong bones and rock-hard hooves. Don't overlook the need for the horse to stand when mounted, lift his feet for the farrier and act sensibly in traffic.

# Chapter 21 - Before You Buy Horses

Purchasing the proper road and pack horses is critically important because when the horse is bad the road is long. Be on your guard against making any mistakes as it is more difficult to judge horses than men. You must know what definition of horse suits your needs, matches your personality and fits your budget.

**Hire or Buy?** You don't have to own horses to make an equestrian journey. It is possible to lease them. Given the current global financial recession, many horse owners are facing economic hardships, which might entice them to provide you with a riding or pack horse in exchange for guaranteed long-term care of their animal. Breeders who are anxious to promote the strength and durability of their favourite horse might be another option. While leasing, borrowing or having a horse donated is possible, the vast majority of Long Riders, especially those preparing to travel in Asia, Africa and Latin America, must be prepared to begin bargaining.

**Cautious Shopping.** Before we think about "where," let's not forget "when." Many horse owners will be anxious to sell an animal before the onslaught of winter to offset the high cost of feeding during the cold weather months. Likewise with the resumption of warmer riding weather, buyers are more frequent. When you buy determines what you pay.

**Buyer Beware.** With the onslaught of the internet, it is possible to shop on line for horses in any part of the world, as this free service will allow you to inspect thousands of horses from your home. Yet if it's true that a piece of paper will lie down and let you write anything on it, the same holds true for a deceptive internet horse advertisement. When shopping for a horse on line, you should be extremely cautious as the factors of distance and anonymity create a peculiar mixture of vulnerability and trust between buyer and seller. This is especially true if you see a horse being sold on extraordinarily good terms. Throughout history cheapness has been the surest bait in the world for catching the majority of customers.

**Other Options.** Another option is to purchase a horse at a livestock auction. However be warned. Unless you are extremely knowledgeable about horses, this is a method fraught with menace as there is little time to adequately inspect a horse prior to sale. Many times auctioneers turn a profit on your lack of experience.

**Cultural Traps.** While buying horses is always fraught with economic peril, if you attempt to purchase them in many foreign countries you must be prepared to encounter additional cultural challenges during an already-complicated psychological procedure. Long Riders visiting Kyrgyzstan encountered such a trap. When potential horses were presented, the Kyrgyz asked the naïve English travellers if the horses looked good. Fearing to offend the sellers, the travellers said the horses looked fine. The Kyrgyz took this to mean the travellers had agreed to the asking price. The travellers learned they could not ask for a lower price after they said they approved of the horses. You must not remain a prisoner to your upbringing but should instead take the practices and beliefs of the local equestrian culture into account. Also, there are some cultures where lying is considered a fine art and there is no shame in being found out. While they expect you, the rich foreigner, to be honest, they believe they are justified in lying through their teeth.

**Trial and Error.** It takes time to find horses and strike a bargain. That is why when you set out to purchase horses you must prepare yourself for a challenging quest. Unless you are carefully prepared, you are facing a long, frustrating, expensive and fruitless search.

**A Word of Caution.** Regardless of where you look for a horse, everyone is an expert, even if they've never ridden down the road. When you are buying a horse it is the faults you want to know about, not the virtues. Yet many buyers will seldom find what they have expected. In their disappointment some will call the horse-trader a fraud, though the responsibility is really with the buyer himself. This is because all too often the buyer was hasty, ignorant, greedy, naïve or ill prepared. Great vigilance and thorough knowledge is needed. The latter can only be obtained by practising, never from theory or a book.

**The Seller.** There is no object of trade that is harder to buy than the horse. Tradition demonstrates that trickery, fraud, and deception are inherent in this situation. This is because the buyer and seller base their estimates of value on very different grounds. Who is the seller? He is any person who tries to present his horse in the best possible condition in order to reap the greatest profit from the sale. The difference between one seller and another will be merely a difference in degree, the result being that the most honest man in the world, whose word would pass in the bank for any amount, cannot help lying when it comes to selling a horse. History proves that the buyer has all too often been on the losing end of this arrangement. Even the most scrupulous seller will acknowledge only certain defects in their horses; the discovery of others they will leave to the knowledge of the purchaser. Thus a man's own mother cannot be trusted in a transaction of this kind without looking into the horse's mouth and examining its feet. As to those who are less honest, they conceal everything except the qualities which they exaggerate. To denounce these practices is a waste of time. Your only defence is to be able to judge the quality of the horse you are about to buy.

**Tricks of the Horse Trade.** Purchasing an animal from a professional horse dealer has always been fraught with hazard. It is a notorious truth that honesty and horse-selling seldom dwell together and no dealer keeps a horse unless he hopes to gain some financial advantage by doing so. Thus the time honoured warning, "Caveat Emptor: let the buyer beware," still rules as there are scoundrels about who keep alive the ancient practice of deluding and plundering travellers and horsemen. Modern crooks have been known to use a bait and switch method, where they advertise one horse on the internet, then replace it with a similarly marked animal. The good news is that most modern horse dealers have a reputation to maintain, therefore they are dutiful, have access to valuable knowledge and can show you a great many horses in a short period of time. The best advice that can be offered is to deal with a horse dealer to whom you have been recommended, one who is of fair character and established circumstances, as such a person has every reason not to forfeit his credibility.

# Chapter 22 - Inspecting Horses

**Early Selection Process.** Many Long Riders have found themselves in the same position as the inexperienced traveller who wrote, "Other than some advice about buying a horse with a leg on each corner, I didn't have a lot to go on." Logic dictates that the buyer only purchases a healthy horse. The buyer should have determined exactly what type of animal he is attempting to purchase; this includes knowing the size, sex, age and approximate price. Once you have made these basic decisions, you need to rule out unsuitable animals prior to physical inspection. To do this you must present sellers with as many preliminary questions as possible so as to confirm the horse's strengths and weaknesses.

**Basic Questions.** Either by phone, or before you ever walk to the barn or the pasture, you can save yourself a lot of time by asking these sort of questions.

Why is the seller disposing of the horse? If it is because the horse is old, infirm or dangerous, terminate the interview.

Is the horse fitted by training and disposition to the task at hand? If it is too young or unbroken, terminate the interview.

Is its confirmation sound? If it is partially sighted, sway backed or suffering from any type of open wound, terminate the interview.

Is its temperament good? If it bites, bucks, strikes, kicks, rears or runs away, terminate the interview.

Can it be easily caught, groomed, saddled and bridled? If it doesn't stand quietly when mounted, terminate the interview.

Will the horse be able to use your saddle and bridle? If it requires special expensive gear, terminate the interview.

When was the last time the horse was ridden and how far did it go? If there is any hint that the animal is disobedient or dangerous, terminate the interview.

Has the horse ever travelled and was it road worthy? If the horse runs away from dogs or spooks in front of traffic, terminate the interview.

Has the horse been ridden on trails and if so does it cross water and load into a trailer? If it bucks while being ridden on a trail ride, terminate the interview.

Is it a hearty eater? If it is severely underweight, requires a special diet or suffers from colic, terminate the interview.

Does the horse behave quietly while being shod? If it has bad feet or can't be shod, terminate the interview.

Can it be hobbled, tied to a picket pin or a high line? If it fights with or runs away from strange horses, terminate the interview.

Has it been wormed and vaccinated? If it has any sign of disease, terminate the interview.

Are the horse's medical papers up to date and is its Coggins test negative? If the owner can't provide medical certificates and a bill of sale proving he is the legal owner, terminate the interview.

There is nothing more frustrating than buying the wrong horse. That is why these types of basic questions will help you determine the horse's ability, performance, dispositions, habits, training and health. When you phone the seller, listen to the answers carefully so as to get a sense of whether the person is telling the truth or withholding vital information. If you believe the seller is being evasive, deceitful, or if there are negative or dangerous aspects associated with the horse, then be prepared to conclude the discussion before you've ever seen the horse.

**Misleading Emotions.** What you are seeking is a horse that is fit and guaranteed free from disease or defects. What you don't want is the "love at first sight horse." Bad horses have as good an appetite as the best. You're in the market for a road horse, not an emotional commodity. You must be brutally candid with yourself. When we first look at a horse we must keep our emotions in check. Sadly, buyers rarely seek for latent good qualities, preferring to focus on a dramatic exterior instead. True equine judgement is displayed when you select a horse possessing great powers, though they might be hidden under the cover of an ill-favoured outward appearance.

**Public and Private Examinations.** The examination of the horse cannot always be made at one's leisure, although enough time should always be taken so as to make the inspection a detailed one. The location of the inspection is of tremendous importance. If you plan to buy a horse in a foreign country, despite your desire for privacy you may well be surrounded by an audience of curious locals who are equally interested in observing you. Such circumstances tend to make an already-complicated investigation all the more cumbersome, as the locals may feel free to offer advice, tease the horse or attempt to assist the seller in cheating you. Add in the element of a foreign language and you can foresee the problems. In contrast, the initial benefit of examining a potential horse at the stable of a private owner is that the purchaser can proceed in privacy. Regardless of where the inspection takes place, the best time to initially inspect the horse is when you are not expected, as in this manner you will find out more defects than any other way.

**Age.** Regardless of where you shop for the horse, his age plays a critical role in your potential geographic success. Various factors demonstrate that young horses are unsuitable for extended equestrian journeys. To begin with, it is a mistake to suppose that young horses will last longer than old ones. A mature horse does not tire so soon. After a night's rest, he will come out of his stable settled and sober, then proceed to work a younger horse off his legs. Another consideration is that as your road horse travels cross country, he will be constantly exposed to various equine ailments. Here again, a well-seasoned older horse is less liable to disease than a younger one.

For these reasons a road horse should be at least six years old, especially if he is to be ridden near traffic. Horses that have not been taught how to behave in such situations are extremely awkward, unmanageable and often cause accidents. A horse of six, if sound in wind, limb and sight, should last you eight or nine years.

**Colour and Pedigree.** Don't be surprised if the seller attempts to entice you to pay more because the animal in question is an excellent representative of a special breed. Horses are like angels. They have no nationality. This is an equestrian journey, not a beauty contest. A good horse is never a bad colour.

**Vices.** Bear in mind that a vicious horse may also be a sound one. While there are a number of offences, the discovery of any dangerous vice should automatically rule out purchasing the animal.

You should never ride a horse addicted to any vice or one having a fault likely to endanger your safety. It is not only disagreeable but dangerous to ride an animal that is ready upon the least excitement to buck, shy violently, endeavour to run away or attempt to harm you.

Of all the defences which a horse makes, that of rearing is the most dangerous. Some horses will rear so high as to fall backward on top of the rider. When a horse rears, the rider must immediately cease bearing on the reins, and incline his body well forward, so as to throw his weight upon the horse's shoulders and oblige him to come down. Under no circumstance purchase such a horse.

Running away is a serious vice and horses addicted to bolting are very dangerous, both for the rider and those they encounter. It is necessary to turn the horse's head strongly around to the left or to the right in such a way as to slacken his gait, hamper his movements, and produce a sharp pain upon the bars of his mouth. Even if such an animal is offered as a gift, the wisest thing to do is not to accept it, nor ever attempt to use it on a journey.

Never purchase a horse which threatens or frightens you, for such an animal keeps the rider in fear and anxiety. Some horses have a trick of suddenly stopping when going at a fast pace. A horse of this kind is dangerous because of the likelihood of throwing the rider over his head. Your road horse should be free from the slightest suspicion of stumbling, which leads to falls. Avoid buying a fearful horse. Never purchase a horse that sets his ears back or stamps his feet when you approach or try to groom him. A horse which is difficult to saddle or mount has no place on a journey. Horses which are difficult to shoe should also be avoided, as the neglect of this basic requirement will result in very serious consequences once the journey has begun. Kicking at other horses, or at people, denotes an ill nature. Likewise a biter should always be avoided. A horse who has acquired the habit of backing up, so as to avoid the bit, is not only a danger to the rider but may injure anyone in close proximity. Any horse which is indolent, timid, bad mouthed, balky, stubborn, cowardly, skittish or spiteful is to be rejected however perfect he may otherwise be.

Beware, as sellers use tricks so cunning that the best judges of horse flesh may be deceived into believing the horse has none of these defects. When determining the price, any negative element works in your favour. The journey requires you to obtain a horse which is free from any life-threatening, harmful or disturbing vice. As prevention is better than cure, an animal

22

addicted to a dangerous vice should never be selected. Thus the discovery of such defects does not lower the price, it kills the deal. If you don't want trouble, don't mount it and never buy it.

**Defects.** Lameness is the language of pain and its presence automatically rules the horse out. It tells the plain and honest truth, with the greatest simplicity. When horses are more tender in one foot than the other, they droop their head when they step upon the unsound hoof, then raise it again when stepping on the sound one. Visually impaired horses shy frequently, stumble easily and should never be considered.

**First Impressions in a Public Market.** In order to buy the right horse, you must follow the proper steps. Yet many people get the first impression wrong. When a horse which seems to answer the requirements has been found at a public horse market he should be brought away from the other horses and led to a quiet place, where he can be easily observed.

Upon first seeing the animal, ask yourself if this horse is equipped by nature to handle your route. For example, if the horse has been bought in a warm land, chances are that when ridden up into a colder climate the animal will suffer. Therefore are you looking at a lowlands horse, before you set off over the Himalayan Mountains or perhaps a grassland horse who won't survive in the desert?

Only a general inspection of the whole animal need be made at this point so as to determine if he pleases or he displeases. As you first approach cast your eye over the animal to determine if by his size, weight and general development he fulfils the required purpose. Does he appear to be in a healthy condition? Is he standing quietly on firm feet and does he seem well mannered? As you near, how does he react? Manners make the horse and never more so than in an equine travelling companion. After you've had time to study the horse, ask the seller to provide the horse's age and breed. Finally, his price should be asked. If these first impressions are not favourable, or if the price is too high, it is useless to proceed further with the examination.

**First Impressions in a Private Stable.** Your initial inspection begins the moment you near the horse in his stall, as valuable information is on offer even though you're still several feet away.

Before you even glance at the horse, look around the stall for any evidence that the horse cribs or chews. This is a self-destructive habit that is often taught to other horses. If the animal cribs, conclude the inspection, as travelling horses are required to lodge in a different place every night. The last thing you need is for your road horse to spend the night eating part of your host's barn or stripping the bark off his trees.

As you near the stall, you should note the manner in which the animal is tied to the manger, how he stands in the stall, the way in which he holds his head, the expression of his countenance, the movements of his ears. As you draw near; this is the time also to observe the conformation. When the stall door is opened, does the horse stand easy or does he pace about the stall nervously? Does he move towards his visitors or back away?

While there are a variety of things to observe at this stage, the first is temperament. There is as much difference in the tempers, dispositions and intelligence of horses as in human beings.

When the animal is being groomed, observe his general manners, study his disposition and watch his eye. The eye of a horse is a good index of a horse's temper. A horse never plays a vicious trick without showing his intention to do so by his eye. Therefore, if much of the white is seen, and that restless and cast backwards, it may be suspected that he is dangerous and is an indication of the kick which he is about to aim. If you are near, it would be advisable either to go boldly up to his head and seize it, with the right hand on the halter close to his muzzle, or else keep out of the range of his heels; for you may rest assured that the horse is slyly watching for an opportunity to do you a mischief.

The other indicators of temper are the ears. The hearing of the horse is much more acute than that of a human being and the ears are the interpreters of his passion, particularly of fear, anger or malice. They are always in motion; quivering, and darting their sharp points towards every object that presents itself. This holds true for groups and individuals. Where four or five horses travel in a line, the first always points his forward, and the last points his backwards. An experienced observer can often tell by the motion of the ears most of what the horse means to do. This is especially important when the horse lays his ears back flat upon his neck and keeps them so, as he most assuredly means to harm the bystander with either heels or teeth.

**A Closer Look.** Upon taking the horse out into the yard, a closer examination must be made of the animal.

On the horse being led out of the stable, first walk up to the horse's withers to ascertain if he is of the required height. Too often buyers look at horses as butchers do at cattle, and value them in proportion to the amount of fat they carry. This is an error.

The horse having been led out, have the owner stand in front of him, placing the animal a step forward or backward until his fore-feet and hind feet are respectively on a line with each other; after which the horse's head is kept in a fixed position.

Then visually examine the animal in sections (feet, pasterns, fetlocks, canons, knees and hocks; forearms and legs, arms and thighs, shoulder and croup, neck and withers, back, chest, abdomen and flank). As to the head, it is to be reserved for the last, because the eyes, nostrils, mouth and ears should be particularly examined.

Take your time studying the horse in profile, on both sides, in front, behind, and obliquely from in front and from behind. This survey should be made at a distance of four or five steps, while walking around the animal slowly, stopping for an instant at each of the points we have just enumerated.

In judging on the whole, we should take into account the general harmony of the lines, the height, length, size, equilibrium and expression of the horse's face.

Perhaps this is as good a place as any other to remark upon the absurdity of buying an animal that had once in his life preformed a particular feat well, instead of seeking to possess horses of capacity for general usefulness. Choose a horse based upon his current ability and willingness, never upon a former sporting victory.

This part of the examination should be made as much as possible without touching the horse. The purchaser should have sufficient experience to recognize at a glance if serious blemishes exist. If there be any doubt in his mind, he should remove it by examining the parts with the hand.

**The Intensive Inspection.** Having carefully studied the horse, you should move toward the animal and commence a careful hands-on evaluation. To begin with, never consent to inspect an animal that is either saddled or wearing any type of blanket. One of the oldest tricks in the book is to distract an unwary seller with a lot of fast talk, all the while presenting the horse fully saddled and ready for a test ride. The purpose of this deception is to conceal saddle sores under the saddle or blanket. No horse can be properly evaluated if its defects have been hidden in this manner.

Pay no attention to the seller's misleading chatter. Ensure instead that the animal's physical condition is not camouflaged in any way and then order the horse to be held quietly for your further inspection.

To begin with study the animal's overall weight. Because of the inherent rigours of equestrian travel, never purchase an animal which is underweight. Unlike pampered animals kept in stalls, road and pack horses work in an environment where feeding is an open-ended daily challenge. While it is possible to keep your travelling horses in excellent shape during their journey, hard exercise and sporadic diet will almost certainly ensure that they never grow fat. Thus you need to purchase animals that are not fussy feeders or initially undernourished.

Regardless of how calmly the animal has acted around its owner, don't forget that when a horse is startled or suspicious, he can kick or bite with great speed. Thus, always use extreme caution when first approaching a strange horse, making sure his head is being held up and that the animal is paying attention to your approach. Because horses have good and bad days, they experience strong emotions which can cause them to become impatient or turn angry. Furthermore, since the horse is remarkably perceptive, he will respond to any impatience or fear he may sense from you.

Move toward him in a confident, unhurried manner, initially approaching in the direction of his left shoulder. This is known as the safe zone and by standing slightly ahead of the shoulder and to the left; you reduce your risk of injury. Always maintain a point of contact with the horse. This permits the horse to know where you are at all times, while also allowing you to feel if the animal is about to shy away abruptly.

**The Back and Withers.** Begin by gently stroking his shoulder and withers, as these are his least threatened areas. Next, gently rub your hand along the horse's back. Then run your hands up his neck, across his chest and finally along the length of his stomach. An animal that has been properly groomed should experience no displeasure at this attention.

Because equestrian journeys can be halted due to saddle sores, you must next pay close attention to the horse's withers and back. The withers for a road horse should be of a moderate height, so as to provide a surface for the saddle. Low, thick withers are undesirable as they allow the saddle to slip. When it comes to bearing a load on a long journey, a long back is a weak one.

Neither the withers nor the back can sustain undue pressure without injury. It is not uncommon for such previous injuries to leave white hair, where the saddle has pinched, galled or injured the animal. Though a previous injury might not influence a horse's current performance, begin this critical part of the inspection by asking the owner to provide an explanation for every visible discoloured mark or scar on the animal's back, as each and every one represents a potential weakness in the animal's future travel performance. While these parts of the body might be slightly weaker, they do not necessarily mean the horse is actually injured at the time of the inspection.

Next, carefully run the palm of your hand along the withers, top of the shoulder blades, along the spine, and the top of the rib cage, all the while looking for any signs of swelling or heat, as these are strong indicators of saddle-related injuries. As you carefully move your hand along this portion of the horse's body feel for lumps under the skin. Meanwhile, use your eyes to look for evidence of hard skin and search for any signs that the hair is coming off. These clues indicate the horse is carrying invisible injuries caused by a saddle.

Subsequently, use the tip of two fingers to apply an even amount of pressure along the horse's withers, his back and anywhere the saddle comes in contact with his body. Do not let your fingernails hurt the animal. What you are attempting to locate is any area which may be tender. As you press on his withers and spine, watch the horse's ears and eyes, as they are strong indicators of pain. Also, note any tension in the animal's skin. If, during this part of your investigation, you discover a place which appears to be tender, stop pressing, inspect the area visually for any confirmation of a saddle sore, then carry on your investigation.

Be sure that you carry out this portion of the examination with equal care on both sides of the horse's body. If the animal becomes distressed, attempts to shy away from the pressure of your fingers, or tries to bite or kick you, then regardless of the lack of any strongly overt visual evidence, you may be inspecting a horse which is carrying undisclosed saddle sores. These wounds can, in a very short time, become open sores, which in turn will immediately conclude your journey.

If you find any hint of damage to the horse's back, quiz the seller ruthlessly about the nature and date of the injury. If he protests that the animal is in fine condition, then reapply finger tip pressure to the affected area. If the horse reacts painfully, pulls away, or attempts to move his back so as to escape the pressure, ask the owner to explain the circumstances. If you have any hint that the seller is being evasive, terminate the investigation, as the physical evidence suggests that you are being lied to.

**The Head and Mouth.** During the time that you are inspecting the animal, don't forget that most people are injured by so-called "gentle" horses, so always keep a wary eye on the horse that is strange to you. There should be a general look of leanness about the head, with the nostrils standing well open, so as to provide a capacity for easy breathing during exertion. The neck should be strong but light. The ears should be carried upright and forward. Lop ears, which flop down sideways, usually denote a lack of energy. The lips should be thin, but firm and regularly closed. Flabby, pendulous lips indicate weakness or old age, dullness and sluggishness.

It is imperative that a road or pack horse have good teeth. Ask the seller when the horse's teeth were cared for. If you lack experience, make this part of the subsequent veterinarian examination. Should the teeth need attention, have the vet carry out this quick and painless procedure prior to your departure.

The eyes of a road horse require a very careful examination. The eyes should be set well out at the side of the head so as to command a wide range of vision. Examine each eye carefully. They should be clear and dry. Any disease which results in rheumy eyes stamps the horse as unsound.

Likewise pass up any horse that has saliva dripping from its mouth, a discharge running from its nose and any evidence of a cough or chest infection.

**The Bones and Muscles.** Having inspected the upper portion of the horse, you should now inspect the bones, muscles, hooves and lower part of his body.

The hind-quarters, providing as they do the propelling force for the horse's body, must be muscular and proportionate to the rest of the frame, with enough bulk being essential so as to provide strength.

The ribs should be well sprung and deep so as to give plenty of room for heart, lungs, stomach and bowels. Shallow bodies wanting depth are to be avoided as they are not shaped to withstand hardship or long travel.

On the inner side of leg may be noted a horny prominence known as the chestnut or castor. This growth does not denote weakness or illness.

Check the horse's legs by slowly running both hands down the length of each leg. Each limb should be cool and the horse should show no sign of pain while his legs are being handled.

**The Feet and Shoes.** The integrity and conformation of the hoof are of the utmost importance, for a horse with bad feet is like a house with a weak foundation. Therefore you must carry out a careful examination of each hoof.

In appearance, the feet should be smooth and tough, with dark coloured hooves preferred to lighter ones. Avoid feet which are brittle, spongy or rotten. The heels should be firm, the frogs horny and dry. The sole, which is somewhat hollow, should resemble the inside of a bowl. In terms of size, large hooves are more difficult to shoe, especially if your journey takes you into countries which have no history of horse shoeing. Hard, dark, medium-sized hooves will be less likely to disappoint.

It is critically important that a road horse will allow you to work with his feet.

Before you begin this part of the inspection, ask the seller when the horse was last shod, and how the animal reacts to his feet being worked on or inspected? Once you have obtained that information, begin by comparing it to the evidence available for your inspection.

Starting with the left front leg, run your hands down to the fetlock, then see if the horse allows you to lift his hoof. Any well-trained horse will permit you to pick up any of his hooves, and while it is being inspected, be able to stand quietly on his other three legs. Tap on the bottom of the hoof, or shoe, to see if the horse objects or tries to drop his foot. If the animal refuses to allow you to work on his feet, then neither you, nor a farrier, will be able to keep him shod without difficulty during your trip. Such an animal is not ready for a journey.

After you've picked up the horse's foot, inspect the hoof to determine its overall condition. If the horse is shod, is the shoe nailed firmly in place? Has the frog been overly trimmed? Are the heels cracked? Is the foot cool to the touch? Is there any sign, or smell, of the hoof disease known as thrush?

If the horse stands calmly, lower the hoof, then work your way towards his haunch. Once again, brush him gently, this time attempting to lift his rear hoof. During this part of the inspection, your left shoulder should be in close contact with the animal's flank. If the horse shies, or attempts to kick while you are checking his hooves, then move away.

If any of the hooves are found to be injured, or the horse refuses to allow you to lift his feet, then terminate the inspection.

**The Tail.** Finally, check the animal's tail. Making sure that you are still standing next to the animal, not behind him, gently move the tail in various directions. If the animal has been used as a pack animal, inspect under the root of his tail to make sure a crupper has not blistered him.

If at any time during the close inspection a horse attempts to bite or kick, then terminate the inspection. If the animal can't be handled by the seller during a quiet routine inspection, in its own stable and under the best of conditions, then you will be risking life and limb later on the road.

Any potential road horse must be sound in eyes, wind and limb, before you proceed to the next stage of the inspection.

**Examining the horse in action.** If the horse has passed the physical inspection, it is important, after this, to witness the animal being tested at the walk and trot. If possible, this trial should take place on a paved surface, as this assists in detecting any lameness.

In the first of these exercises the horse will be led by the halter. The buyer must ensure that the seller's hand does not furnish a point of support for the horse's head. With this in mind, the seller is to be instructed to allow considerable freedom to the horse's head while the animal is moving at the walk and trot. Moreover, the seller should be requested to abstain from any means of excitement, such as cracking a whip, shouting, gestures, etc.

Have the seller walk and trot the horse in a straight line as you stand behind. Observe well if the horse demonstrates any inequality in his motions, favours one leg or bobs his head in pain. Take notice to see if he steps firmly on the ground. Have him stopped often. Then order him to start again. Observe whether in setting off he has a partiality for either leg.

It is vital that a road horse have easy gaits, be firm on his feet, and, above all, possess a fast walk. During this exercise, the horse should be examined in profile, from the left and right, in front and from behind, either by running him successively from one side of the yard to the other or making him turn around in a circle. This will give an opportunity of noticing how he turns and how he backs.

**The Cold Ride.** As a final test, there must be the trial under saddle, what is known as the cold ride. To begin this mounted trial, it is sensible to see a horse ridden by the owner before trying him oneself, as this gives the opportunity of judging whether the animal is quiet to mount and quiet to ride.

Does the animal stand calmly while he is being groomed and his feet picked out? Does he object to have the girth tightened or does the horse allow himself to be bridled and saddled peacefully? Does he stand still while being mounted? Does he perform the walk, trot and canter calmly, or does he buck, halt, resist and run away? By putting the horse through its paces in such a way, the observant buyer can judge the horse's action, wind, strength and training, with no risk to himself.

This portion of the test begins when the horse is saddled and bridled, so as to notice if he bears both calmly. While the seller rides, the horse should be seen in profile, right and left, in front and from behind during this test, all the while the buyer observes how the animal starts off, trots, turns, backs and canters. Also, have the seller walk and trot the horse in a straight line as you stand behind, as this affords you a better opportunity to detect any subtle signs of lameness. Have the horse stopped often, then ask for him to move on again, all the while you watch carefully for any signs of lameness.

By observing every detail the buyer can determine how the animal allows himself to be ridden and if he enjoys the experience. If the animal acts disagreeably with his current rider, in this familiar environment, then chances are that the horse is unsuitable for travel. You should ascertain also that the horse is gentle, that he steps firmly on the ground and that he does not become frightened at unfamiliar objects or noises.

At the conclusion of this test you should have a good idea if the horse suits you and matches your riding ability.

**The Test Ride.** If all has gone well during this preliminary mounted examination, the last test is the mounted trial by the buyer. Begin by taking the reins and walking beside the animal for some distance by yourself. Does the horse follow quietly, stop when required, and walk on when asked? Does he invade your space and act pushy or is he respectful and calm? Aggressive behaviour is a characteristic which will add to your worries while travelling.

What you must concern yourself with is having a horse which is comfortable to mount and whose weight corresponds in proportion to your own.

A Long Rider's horse should be safe on its legs. Nothing destroys nerve more than a stumbling, falling animal. Likewise, a horse that shies badly is very trying to a rider with a weak seat. Thus, you are seeking an equine whose level of composure will reassure you about the task at hand.

Begin your test by noting how quietly the horse stands when you mount. And let me interject a note of caution about mounting – some cultures mount on the right.

Once you are in the saddle, take up the reins and begin to judge how sensitive the animal's mouth is. The road horse should be a fast walker, as this is the quality most desirable. though not often sufficiently considered, so begin by determining if he has a brisk walk.

As you proceed to trot, notice if his gait is smooth and if the horse carries his head up. Can you ask him to give you a collected canter without risk of a runaway? Is he observant and tranquil under saddle or does he shy and fret? Does he feel deliberate, calm, relaxed and fun to ride?

If at any time you detect a limp, then ask the horse to trot on a hard surface. If he is in pain, his head will bob up and down with each step.

After a sufficient amount of exercise, listen attentively to the sound of the horse's respiration and observe the movements of his flanks, to be sure he is not short-winded.

If a safe opportunity presents itself, ride the horse near traffic to see how it reacts.

A final test is whether the horse will allow you to quietly ride it away from the stable and/or his equine companions. If the animal is psychologically herd bound, he may become belligerent and fight if asked to depart from his home. Such an animal is obviously unsuitable for a journey. It is better to discover this damaging fact prior to purchase, than discover it after the horse has been loaded onto a trailer and the obstinate animal is then deposited, upset, angry and fearful, at your home.

You are searching for a road horse that is ready to assist you with your journey. Travel is already filled with enough unforeseen hardships and dangers without taking on the additional burden of purchasing someone's training project. If at any time during your test ride the horse acts nervous, becomes fearful, attempts to buck, or tries to run away, you should terminate the ride and the inspection immediately.

**After the Ride.** There are several things you should look for at the conclusion of the test ride.

To begin with, once the saddle has been removed, inspect the horse's back and withers again for any signs of swelling or soreness. Does the horse pull away from your two finger when you test his muscles for soreness?

If there is a pasture or pen nearby, ask the seller to turn out the horse. Watch how the animal reacts once he is released. Does he appear calm and relaxed? If there are other horses nearby, carefully observe how this horse reacts and is treated in turn. If he becomes aggressive with other horses, he may in turn present an emotional challenge once you are on the road. After he has had a few minutes of freedom, try and catch the horse yourself to see how he reacts.

Should the animal seem sound, and if it rides well, then it is time to ask the veterinarian for a final inspection.

**Vet Check.** Let us assume that the seller is an honest person who believes the horse is sound. Nevertheless, a little knowledge is a dangerous thing and even horsemen of great experience stipulate a veterinary examination, on the principle that two heads are better than one.

Regardless of what country you plan to ride in, if the option is available, you should not hesitate to call in the aid of a medical expert. Whatever the expense of consulting a professsional, it is not to be compared with the loss which would result from a wrong selection. Veterinarians in every country will be found to be the safest guides in such matters. Their special studies and knowledge enable them to give the best advice and to judge the qualities, defects and blemishes of the animal presented and of his state of health or of disease.

28

Explain the nature of your journey to the veterinarian, making sure the medico understands that while the horse will not be involved in hard galloping or jumping, you need to be ensured that the horse's stamina is sound, that his feet are good, that his eyes and teeth are in working order and that he has no previously undetected ailment.

If a horse has good vision, turns normally in either direction, has a brisk walk, trots out gaily on hard ground, makes no unusual noises when cantered, has clean healthy feet, shows no heat or swelling about his legs and comes out sound when cooled down after work the traveller may buy him, knowing that he has done all that can be expected of him to secure himself from fraud.

Having now checked the animal thoroughly, let us attempt to purchase him.

# Chapter 23 - Purchasing Horses

Telling a person how to buy a horse is akin to advising another on how to carry on a romance. Because we are discussing two human beings, buyer and seller, the alternative endings are incalculable. If you factor in the possibility of attempting to make the purchase in a country other than your own, then sprinkle that experiment with a smattering of a foreign language, you are contemplating becoming a participant in one of mankind's most difficult business transactions. The trick is how do you ride away on a good horse, without having your pocket's turned out by the seller?

**The Dealer's Excuses.** In order to protect yourself from deception, you need to use your logic against the seller's emotional, misleading, and often fraudulent, appeals. You are under no legal obligation to purchase the horse, so if at any time you feel threatened or you sense the seller is deceiving you then terminate the transaction. This is especially important if you are in a foreign country where you may have little or no recourse to legal action if, after the purchase, you discover you have been swindled.

After having carefully examined the horse, your job is to keep your hand on your pocketbook, all the while you proceed cautiously through this minefield of a marketplace manoeuvring. To begin with, you should count on the seller having plenty of excuses at hand to explain anything suspicious or discouraging that may have been discovered during the various parts of the physical examination.

If the horse tried to bite you when you first approached, it was because he is so affectionate and will be such a close friend during your trip.

If the horse is underweight, all the good grass encountered during the journey will soon rectify that.

If the horse bucked, snorted, and reared when the seller first mounted, it was the first time the animal had ever behaved this way and is evidence of the strength he will have to bear you and your luggage.

No matter what went wrong, the seller will do everything possible to appeal to your vanity, all the while he works to convince you that black is white and that what you witnessed with your own eyes was not what you saw.

Don't let his honeyed words distract you. What you must assume is that the horse has been produced for the trial in the best condition possible. Thus, do not argue, as the facts speak for themselves. Nor should you allow yourself to be cajoled or bullied. You must begin this stage of the procedure by carefully considering the accumulated evidence.

**Three Options.** Having ended the inspection portion of the experiment, there are now three courses open to you. First, you may refuse the horse outright. Second, you may make an offer on the horse, subject to a veterinary examination. Third, you may stipulate a further trial. If you refuse the horse the decision should be conveyed to the owner firmly, ignoring any pleas about how his children will starve because of your stinginess and cruelty, etc.

**Asking Price is no Guarantee of Value.** Should you decide that you wish to buy the horse, then straight away you should realize that the asking price does not reflect the animal's true value. A seller can ask a million pounds, yet the horse will remain a wreck. Likewise, a fabulous animal might be found disguised under a low price.

**Determining the Price.** The purchase of a horse is a difficult and delicate matter and arriving at a proper price is one of the largest obstacles you must overcome.

Too many people set off to find a horse equipped with large dreams and a small bank account.

To begin with, you must be inspecting a horse which fits within your budget. Not only do you place your journey in financial risk, you place yourself at a tremendous emotional disadvantage if you attempt to purchase a horse you cannot afford. There must be an absolute financial high point beyond which you will not yield, as to do so imperils your mission. Your task is to obtain a suitable horse for as low an amount as circumstances, and your sense of personal honour, allow. In order to determine what you offer you should consider these aspects of the horse in question.

Is the horse the proper size and weight for your journey? You need a weight-carrying animal which is easy to mount.

Is the horse sound and free from any visible defect that affects its ability to travel? You need a horse with sharp eyes, a strong back, feet like iron and legs of steel.

Is the horse emotionally dependable, obedient, courteous, kind and eager to befriend you? Your life depends on riding an animal you can trust.

Is the horse the right gender for your journey and your equestrian experience? Geldings generally make the best road horses, while stallions and mares both have drawbacks.

Is the horse responsive when ridden and does it have a fast walk? A slow horse makes for a long journey.

Is the horse's price comparable to similar animals in that market or locality? This last point can be of vital economic importance, because if you are purchasing a horse in a foreign country you must try not to allow your national origin to be used against you so as to inflate the asking price beyond what locals would be expected to pay. Prior to bargaining, you should have made a dedicated attempt to establish what locals normally pay for the type of horse you are attempting to purchase.

One way to uncover this vital information is by using the "hair cut and bananas" rule. While obtaining a hair cut, ask the barber what bananas cost? While buying a bunch of bananas, ask the seller how much a hair cut costs? By appealing to various members of the local economy, none of whom have a vested interest in horses, you may be able to establish a rough idea of local horse prices prior to trying to buy the animal.

Another option is to enlist a sympathetic local to help you establish what local prices are. Such a person may not only help locate horses but bargain for them, so as to ensure that the foreign Long Rider isn't overcharged.

**Making an Offer.** One thing which can be relied upon throughout the march of history is the fact that it is not possible to close a transaction for a horse without bargaining. Thus regardless of what age, or country, in which the transaction takes place, you can count on the seller asking as much as he dares.

Buying a horse is akin to a magic trick. You know the magician is deceiving you, yet regardless of being forearmed with this knowledge you can't uncover his secret. Like the magician, the seller is working in the open, all the while trying to mislead you by asking more than the two of you know will ultimately be accepted. He in turn expects you to proceed on the principle that you will attempt to start low enough in the hope that the two of you can meet somewhere in the middle.

By allowing the seller to set the asking price, you instantly surrender part of your power.

Horses are not saddles. A saddle can be kept for years and then sold for a profit. Yet every day the seller retains possession of the horse, the animal eats a portion of his potential revenue. This psychological fact plays in your favour, especially if the seller is anxious to dispose of the animal. Plus, the seller knows that the world is full of potentially suitable horses, any one of which might better fit your needs than his horse. Thus, the most powerful tool at your disposal is your firm, and obvious, determination to walk away at a moment's notice, as your emotions are under control and your pocketbook shall remain resolutely closed unless there is movement from the other party.

For the sake of this experiment, ignore the asking price of $500.

Offer 25% or $125.

The seller will probably counter with $450.

Up your offer to 30%, or $150.

If the seller says no and offers his last price again, refuse his offer, thank him and walk away.

He if calls you back, re-offer $150.

Often, if you've done your homework, established the local price, and made an offer close to this amount, the seller will accept your lower offer.

If he insists on continuing the bargaining, you are now working upwards from $150, and not from his inflated asking price of $500.

Never pay more than your previously-determined limit.

Another thing to anticipate is that the seller might accept your original offer without any hesitation. This is disconcerting as it indicates that your original offer was too high. On the other hand, while you can always offer more, you cannot reduce your bid; hence your need to cautiously begin at the low end of the possible sales price.

All the while you are attempting to protect your economic interests; you must not lose sight of the fact that you should not offend the seller. Driving a hard bargain is one thing, but haggling over a few dollars will only cause hard feelings and may lose you the horse. Make sure the seller knows you appreciate his horse; however you have restrictions which do not allow you to compromise beyond a certain financial point.

**Conditions of Sale.** Even if all goes well, and the price is agreed upon to your satisfaction, your work is still far from done.

In common with any type of business arrangement, the details are as important as the price and it is critically important that seller and buyer agree on all points concerning payment, transfer of ownership, medical condition at the time of sale, and transport after the sale.

For example, how and where will the funds be paid? Will you be presented with papers proving that the seller is the recorded owner of the horse? Is the seller willing to guarantee the overall health of the animal for 48 hours after the sale? If the sale occurs in North America, did the seller provide you with medical evidence demonstrating that the horse has a negative Coggins test at the time of the sale? Will the seller provide you with all of the horse's registration papers and any relevant medical documentation at the close of sale? If the horse has to be moved, is it clear how much time you have to transport the animal? Does any equipment come with the horse?

The best way to protect yourself is by clearly defining all aspects of the sale. It isn't necessary to have a solicitor to draw up such a document, as both parties can compose a letter describing the responsibilities of both parties. After the seller and buyer have both signed and dated this paper, you will possess a legal document detailing everyone's intentions. This in turn works to protect you, especially if a disagreement occurs later. It strengthens the document if it is also signed and dated by a witness. While it is imperative to record the details of the sale, the document proving you are the new owner is even more critically important.

**Bill of Sale.** This book provides you with a sample of the *Long Rider International Equine Bill of Sale*. This is a simple piece of paper that makes men honest and keeps them so. Thus, if you have no wish to be disappointed, summon to your assistance the aid of those powerful refreshers of memory, your allies, the pen, this document and a witness. An honest man will have no objections to signing a written contract. Therefore, when concluding the agreement, never accept a verbal agreement on the sale of a horse. Don't shake hands and give anyone your money. Make the seller provide evidence that he is the legal owner, is entitled to sell the horse and can offer every bit of necessary paperwork at the time of sale, and never accept a promise to receive the papers at a later date.

Take care to note the horse's brands and distinguishing markings. When the document is signed, witnessed and dated, have it notarised if this service is available.

31

Depending on what country you are in, you may need to register the sale with the government office for agriculture. For example, in Argentina you must register the sale of your horses with the SENASA office. This requires you to obtain an official "certificado" from the local justice of the peace registering the sale and documenting you as the new owner.

Also, be sure that you keep separate copies of these papers, so that you can prove ownership if you lose the originals.

**Buyer's Remorse.** Finding a great road horse isn't simply a matter of saving or spending money.

There should be an intangible element to the animal which makes you eager to set off with him on your exciting mutual journey. Even if you've received a good deal financially, to offset any trace of buyer's remorse, you should ask yourself two questions before sealing the deal.

Do you believe you have chosen the best horse you can afford? Are you willing to trust your life to this animal?

The ease with which a person can lose his loyalty for a horse is notorious. That is why the old saying goes, "The horse has only two faults, one that it takes a long time to catch him in the field, the other that he's not worth a damn when caught."

Trust is more important than money. If you don't trust the horse, don't close the deal.

# Long Rider International Equine Bill of Sale

This sales agreement, dated the      day of _____,2_____
between

_____ of _____
(Name of Seller)                    (Seller's City, Province and Country)


and _____ of _____
(Name of Buyer)                   (Buyer's City, Province and Country)

is for the sale of one _____
               (List sex of animal – gelding, mare or stallion)

Parties agree as follows on the following description of the equine including name, age, date of birth, colour, markings, breed and registry number.


Seller warrants that the equine is in good health with no known defects or injuries and will furnish Buyer with health records on the equine. Seller also guarantees that he is the lawful owner of the equine and has the right to sell the animal.

The total sales price for this equine is _____
               (List Dollars, Pounds, Euros, Pesos, Yen, etc.)
(Paid in cash or travellers' cheques.)

the receipt of which is hereby acknowledged.

             Signed and dated this      day of _____, 2_____.


_____
Seller

_____
Buyer

_____
Witness/Notary

33

# Chapter 25 - Long Rider Horsemanship

It is only common mythology which states that equestrian travel doesn't produce excellent horsemen.

A dramatic example was D.C. Vision, a Founding Member of the Guild, who rode 22,500 kilometres (14,000 miles) on a four-year journey through the United States. While the mileage is impressive, what is astonishing is that D.C. had never even been near a horse before he swung into the saddle.

Likewise, Gordon Naysmith rode 20,000 kilometres (12.000 miles) from South Africa to Austria, Vladimir Fissenko rode 30.500 kilometres (19,000 miles) from Tierra del Fuego to Alaska and Otto Schwarz rode 48,000 kilometres (30,000 miles) on five continents. What these extraordinary Long Riders demonstrate is that true horsemanship isn't about style. The Long Rider views riding not as an art but as an indispensable accomplishment. The road horse invites you to feel, to respond, to reawaken your soul. He is concerned with riding, not rituals. He doesn't care how you ride but where you go. Long Rider horsemanship satisfies the human soul, respects the horse and reflects a mutual initiative. It's about connection, not collection.

**Riding and Horsemanship.** It is not to be expected that Long Riders be perfect riding masters, nor that their road horses should perform complicated dressage movements. What is required is that every Long Rider should have his horse under thorough control at all times and be able to ride him with confidence and pleasure.

**Our First Goal - Safe Riding.** The primary goal of Long Rider horsemanship is accident-free riding. A major distinction between accident-prone sporting events and equestrian travel is that the latter is largely calamity free, regardless of the enormous mileage involved. This is because Long Rider horsemanship minimizes the risk of the horse shying and is aimed instead at preventing horse and rider from falling.

**Riding the Road Horse.** Nearly everyone can become a competent rider. The skilful Long Rider can sit skin-tight at all gaits, through dense forests, down hills, across streams, in rough country. A person who can thus control the horse will feel confident enough to cross tricky bridges, make their way through heavy traffic, swim a river or avoid dangers. When you ride, you should always be looking for ways to conserve your horse's strength. It is the duty of every Long Rider to continually correct your position in the saddle. You always remain sitting straight up in the saddle and never lean your weight back against the cantle. Such an action places enormous pressure on the horse's kidneys and causes severe saddle sores.

**The Gaits.** The Long Rider must maintain control during three gaits, the walk, trot and canter. These paces enable the traveller to advance, turn in both directions and, in an emergency, move backwards.

**Discipline.** It is critically important that the road horse be well-mannered and disciplined, as these are the bedrocks of respect and safety. The horse must not be defiant. He should recognize that during the journey the Long Rider is the herd leader. This requires the traveller to maintain discipline, especially when his road horse is confronted with fearful challenges. You can be kind, but confident, considerate, but strong. The result is that when a horse adapts to the authority of the Long Rider a sense of mutual confidence is born.

**A Test of Basic Skills.** In terms of creating confident riders, one month's training along trails in the open is equal in value to five months in an indoor riding school. But regardless of how you arrive at it, you must be a competent horseman capable of achieving the following list of equestrian goals before you depart.

You must be able to confidently catch, handle, halter, lead and tie the horse; groom, brush and clean his hooves correctly; be able to saddle and bridle and know when the saddle and tack are properly adjusted; be able to judge stirrup length correctly; be able to mount from both sides; able to maintain quiet hands, soft reins, a strong sense of balance and the correct position in the saddle; be able to control the horse at the walk, trot and canter; be able to halt, back up and travel up and downhill; be able to recognize if the horseshoes are in order and able to remove one if required. You must be able to off-saddle correctly and recognize the signs of saddle sores; know how to feed, water and bed down the horse; know how to clean your tack.

The ultimate goal of Long Rider horsemanship is to achieve a state wherein two separate biological entities merge into a single harmonious Centaur, one representing the horse's strength and the human's intelligence.

# Chapter 25 - Getting Your Horse Fit

**At Home or Abroad:** If you travel to a foreign country, you may not have the luxury of getting your horse fit. If that is the case, start slowly. If you are in your home country, follow this advice.

Horses that have not been rigorously exercised prior to departure must not be asked to suddenly perform hard labour. An animal which has been treated tenderly, and has been warmly bedded in a hot stable, cannot be turned out onto the cold road without negative consequences. Such horses are not only weaker; they are susceptible to a vast number of infirmities. For example, a horse in soft condition is always liable to get a sore back just as a man who has not ridden for some time is apt to chafe on the saddle.

Unfortunately, not only do most horses lack conditioning, their riders mistakenly believe they can build up the strength of the animal during the course of the journey. This is a flawed philosophy! Regardless of how stout and healthy the horse appears at the commencement of a journey, if he is ridden hard when first setting out, he soon becomes exhausted and every additional mile adds to his physical discomfort.

This is all the more important if the horse has been regularly stabled and has previously worn an outdoor coat to protect him against harsh weather. If this is the case, then he should be prepared by diminishing his clothing and gradually accustoming him to all weathers. Such a soft horse should be brought into work slowly. Nor should he be asked to carry a great weight for long periods until his muscles and back have hardened.

War horses in England were given four or five weeks tough training prior to a campaign to ensure they were in good condition. That is why it is critically important that your road horse be healthy and strong before you depart. A training regime launched prior to leaving on the journey will not only reduce the chance of causing possible pain to your road horse during the first few days, it may also offset serious injuries and delays.

**Training the Road Warrior.** The majority of horses will be fat, not fit. You should begin by riding the horse for a minimum of two hours a day, with one day a week off. This time in the saddle should gradually be extended over the course of the training period until the horse can easily do four hours of rapid road work without showing signs of distress.

As most of your travelling will be done at the walk, this is the pace which you should concentrate on. When training, encourage your horse to maintain a brisk, steady, mile-eating walk. Never allow him to stroll or stumble, as he's working, not picnicking in the country.

A moderate amount of trotting should be included in your training routine, the proportion being three parts walking to one part trotting. Don't be afraid to combine trots, and a strong walk, over as wide a variety of terrain as is possible. A collected canter will help develop his wind. But bear in mind that the walk and trot are the essential gaits for any journey.

Your training program should never be so severe as to exhaust the animal, as his muscles will suffer and he will lose weight. Never work a tired horse. He will be prone to falls and injuries. Create instead a training programme that increases the horse's condition, all the while being careful to never overburden him.

Because of the vagaries of travel, you may find yourself forced to dismount on a steep trail or onto a hillside. That's why it is important to teach your horse to permit you to mount from either side.

During the training period, when you dismount to walk alongside your horse, make sure he is trained to maintain a safe distance. His trust in your judgment should be so profound that if you

35

are in the lead, he will follow you through, across, over, under or around a challenging obstacle.

Make sure the road horse is trained not to take fright if you open a map, pull on your rain coat, adjust your hat, reach for your canteen, etc. He should stand rock solid when you stop him.

Once the horse has reached his peak condition, calculate his rate of travel at both the walk and trot. This will allow you to estimate how long it will take you reach each day's destination.

Never shoe your horse just before you start. You must be certain that the nails have not lamed him and that the shoes are firmly in place. Therefore, have your horse accurately shod some days before you set out on a journey.

**Vary the Exercise.** In addition to hardening his muscles, the exercise regime should stimulate your horse's intelligence and steady his nerves as well. While being careful not to attempt anything too hazardous, you and the new road horse should attempt to explore narrow trails, go up and down hills, cross shallow streams, traverse bridges and travel along traffic-laden roads. If your journey will require you to cross urban areas, then it is imperative that your training rides include places where your horse will encounter cars, crowds and noise, as you need a horse that is comfortable in traffic.

The four cornerstones for this physical training must be patience, consistency, kindness and forgiveness.

# Chapter 27 - The Pack Horse

**Why a Pack Horse?** If you are planning an equestrian journey of any distance, you need to consider the weight you will be asking your road horse to carry. If you find that geographic and climatic challenges force you to bring extra food for you and your mount, as well as cooking gear, a tent and additional clothing, then you should not overburden your mount. The answer lies in using a pack horse to carry every extra ounce of weight that you can relieve the road horse from carrying.

Not only is it kinder on the road horse, additionally a pack horse also grants you a tremendous sense of independence. You can take more equipment along if you have a pack animal; you can travel further without resupplying; and horses, being very gregarious, enjoy themselves much more when in company. Thus the basic law of equestrian travel still applies, whether you are using a pack horse or not. The more you know the less you need. However, if you need it, then put it on your pack horse. Don't overburden your road horse!

**An Ally not a Machine.** It would be a mistake to think that the pack horse is a lowly beast of burden. He is strong, clever, patient, and above all, loyal. Yet most first-time travellers are tempted to overload their pack horse. Such people forget that this is not a four-legged rental truck designed to be over burdened then cruelly used. This is a highly intelligent animal whose ability to assist you must never be exploited. The pack horse is more prone to injury because his burden is greater than the road horse's. This is why the pack horse should be treated with great respect, as his need for protection is all the more acute.

**The Perfect Pack Horse.** How do we physically define a pack horse? Though it is a bit like trying to identify the perfect mate, here are some reliable guidelines.

**Breeds.** A Long Rider focuses on deeds not breeds. What you need is physical strength, mental agility and deep emotional devotion, not papers proving an illustrious pedigree. An inexpensive mustang, a sturdy farm mule or perhaps a former logging horse are the type of blue collar worker you require for a journey.

**Sex.** Geldings make the best pack horses, as mares in heat and stallions both become distracted by sexual issues.

**Age.** Don't choose a young horse to be your pack animal. The body and bone structure of equines less than six years old will be damaged by the intense rigours of equestrian travel. Plus older horses possess a sense of maturity as well as a strong work ethic which serve a Long Rider well. A calm gelding between the ages of eight and sixteen will match the task at hand.

**Body type.** Unlike the flexible weight carried by the road horse, the pack horse is burdened by a relentless dead weight which always bears straight down onto his body. This is why the pack horse should have a short back, well-defined withers, well-sprung ribs, strong chest and good loins. A short back and pronounced withers are especially important as they work together to keep the pack saddle in place.

**Size and Strength.** Because you are required to lift the pack saddle and panniers on and off his back, you should avoid purchasing a tall pack horse. A large horse is not only more difficult to pack; he may have trouble negotiating his way through trees and over obstacles. A shorter animal is easier to saddle. Fifteen hands (150 cm) is adequate; anything over sixteen hands (160 cm) increases your work. Your pack horse works twice as hard as your road horse; another reason to avoid excessively large pack horses, as the availability of food in the countryside you will be travelling through will have a direct impact on the pack horse's performance. A horse that isn't a good feeder doesn't belong on the road, as a skinny horse will never put on weight during a journey.

**Hooves.** His hooves should be rock-hard, so as to endure the sharp stones and harsh roads encountered on a journey. Most equestrian cultures believe that a dark hoof is tougher than a lighter coloured one. But do not disregard an otherwise suitable pack animal over the colour of his hooves. Concentrate instead on making sure that none of the hooves are chipped or cracked.

**Emotions.** A pack horse must be quiet, gentle, and manageable. He must have two reliable characteristics, trust and obedience. He should exhibit his trust by allowing you to load him quietly. He must demonstrate his obedience by calmly following you through every type of obstacle, including steep trails, alongside busy roads and away from danger. He must learn to trust the road horse to warn him of any hazards ahead. His emotional mission is to ensure that your supplies are safely on hand when the sun sets.

**Intelligence.** Most people overlook the fact that road horses receive directions from the reins or are guided by the rider's voice, while pack horses are required to make independent decisions. While a pack horse spends much of his time hooked to a lead rope, occasions will arise when the animal may be asked to make his own way over, around or through obstacles along the trail. The pack horse must not only overcome these challenges without assistance, he must do so while maintaining and balancing the load on his back.

**Agility.** Pack horses are often confronted with downed trees, sizeable rocks, intimidating mud holes, narrow trails and watery obstructions, any one of which will force the horse to weave his way around danger. This ability is all the more important when you remember that the road horse will see the problems rising to confront the Long Rider. Yet the same obstacle will often take the pack horse by surprise because his view is partially blocked by the road horse. When this occurs, your pack animal should have the skill to side step peril.

**Endurance.** A pack horse should be a hardened animal that is able to ignore the elements, overcome slight thirst, bed down anywhere and eat everything. What you don't need is a soft, sensitive, stable-bred animal that requires special food and inordinate amounts of emotional attention. A pack horse should thrive on living out of doors, delight in spending his night in a strange field and eagerly devour a dinner of fresh grass. Such an animal is a recipe for success.

**Specific Skills.** A pack horse must be easy to catch, enjoy being groomed, allow his feet to be handled, stand still while being loaded and serene on the trail. He should never lay back his ears, show the whites of his eyes, and threaten to bite or kick you. Replace such an animal prior to your departure.

**Training.** A well-trained pack horse should be able to follow your road horse like a faithful shadow, keeping close to you, all the while he neither crowds the road horse nor crashes the pack saddle painfully into your leg. He must be able to manage difficult terrain. This includes watching where he puts his feet and being so surefooted that he never trips over obstacles. He must also be able to avoid crashing his load into trees or other obstructions.

**Gait.** Pack and road horses cannot work equally if they are not similar in size, enjoy a complimentary temperament, posses the same basic strength and have an equal pace. Like your road horse, the pack horse should have a long, smooth, mile-eating gait. The pack horse must be

37

eager to travel alongside the road horse otherwise every day's travel becomes a plague wherein your right arm is tugged out of joint, the lead rope burns your hands when it is yanked backwards or you are pulled out of the saddle when the pack horse balks.

**Unacceptable Behaviour.** Unlike the average riding saddle, a pack saddle and panniers can frighten an untrained horse or mule. Therefore before purchasing a potential pack animal, it is imperative that you test his physical skills and emotional capabilities. Will he follow you easily when you lead him on foot? Will he stand quietly when you load him? Will he move alongside another horse quietly, without nipping or pulling back on the lead rope? If he doesn't follow you and your road horse like a quiet shadow, your life on the road will be a constant heartache. Horses who have become overly attached to either their home or companions are prone to fight the Long Rider in an effort to return. Such horses seize every opportunity to begin pulling, bucking and even rearing, prior to running back home. Above all, stay away from horses that pull back while being led. Horses that resist the lead rope fall behind, and then rush forward, often banging the panniers into the rider's leg. This is not only painful; it can throw the Long Rider off balance, which is dangerous.

# Chapter 28 - Mules

For the sake of brevity, I have intentionally confined the wording in this book to use the words "pack horse." This is not meant to overlook the suitability of mules. The history of equine travel is filled with stories of Long Riders who either rode or packed mules with great success. The arguments, both pro and con, for mules are many, long standing, and are often based on subjective personal experience or opinion. As Long Riders our focus should be on the journey, not the species. What works is what counts. While the choice is yours, there are a few things to keep in mind.

To begin with, there's the biology. A mule is produced by breeding as mare horse to a stallion donkey. The result is a mule. If you reverse the order, by breeding a stallion horse to a mare donkey, you obtain a hinny. The latter tends to look more like a horse than a mule. While mules are commonly found world wide, hinnys are less common. Both animals carry many of the emotional characteristics of their donkey forebears.

The size of the mule depends upon the breed of the dam. For example, if a Belgian mare is bred, the resultant mule is exceptionally large. Thus mules, like horses, vary in size based upon their parentage. Once again, the same basic requirements of size, speed and strength which you look for in a pack horse should likewise be applied to any potential pack mule.

There are many positive aspects to mules. Their conformation is often a great help to a Long Rider packer because many mules have high withers. This helps keep the pack saddle in place, especially when travelling in mountainous areas. Mules are renowned for their stamina and strength, which generally allows them to carry a heavier load than a similarly-sized horse. Because of their hybrid vigour mules are less susceptible to colic, withstand hot weather well and enjoy a reputation for being hardy eaters. Many mules have a strong walk, an excellent sense of balance and enjoy a well-founded reputation for being extremely sure footed. The shape of a mule's hoof is slightly different than that of a horse. Mules' hooves are generally narrow and their feet are normally tougher than a horse's more oval hooves. The narrower hoof of a mule enables it to walk carefully across treacherous ground, a critically important asset when travelling. Mules are renowned for their keen sense of smell and will alert you if a strange animal is in the vicinity. Because of their mixed parentage, mules are normally sterile hybrids and are not distracted by mares in heat or amorous stallions. Unlike a horse, which generally retains a degree of independence, a mule is more apt to be a follower, which is why many of these animals are traditionally used in large military caravans.

However the mule has some serious disadvantages, especially if you are an inexperienced Long Rider. While mules can generally carry a heavier load than the same size pack horse, the hybrid mule is a stubborn animal that may balk. Mules are often described as being smarter than horses. This may result in an animal that is willing to challenge your authority or intimidate you. Though certainly capable of individual affection, as a rule mules seldom grant the same degree of trust to a human which a horse will. The result is that when he is challenged by unforeseen problems, a mule may be reluctant to respond to the Long Rider's commands as quickly as a horse will. This often results in an already grievous situation becoming even more complicated. While the horse has a musical neigh, the mule produces a harsh bray which has never been described as melodious. Mules dislike dogs and will often attack them. Mules are not available in many parts of the world. When encountered they are often more expensive than a comparable pack horse, with a good mule often selling for fifty percent more than his equine cousin. Many mules dislike being shod, a problem which needlessly complicates a journey. Last, but certainly not least, mules are potentially more dangerous than horses. Unlike horses, mules long remember an injustice and will carry a grudge against the offending human. Such resentful mules are known to bite their handlers. Even worse, mules are known to be vicious kickers. An offended mule will skilfully take aim and inflict a well aimed kick at the packer. Such kicks have been known to severely injure or kill people, so extreme caution is required.

If you decide to use a pack mule, do not be tempted to buy one of the exceedingly tall mules now favoured by many American farmers. These animals, though attractive, are usually bred from Belgian work horses and are too big for equestrian travellers. A Long Rider pack mule should be from 14¾ to 15½ hands in height and weigh from 1,000 to 1,200 pounds. He should be compact, stocky and have a short neck; short, straight, strong, and well-muscled back and loins; low withers and croup; large barrel with deep girth; straight, strong legs; and short pasterns and extremely strong hooves. In addition it is essential that pack mules should be gentle and have friendly dispositions. They should have no fear of man and be free of vices and vicious habits. They should walk and trot freely and boldly over varied terrain.

# Chapter 28 - Pack Horse Training

When you try to turn an out-of-shape pasture pet into a road horse, it suffers. When you try to draft an untrained animal into being a pack horse it can lead to serious injury or death. So if you're going to get it right, what do you do? The first thing is to avoid the danger of bad advice **Misleading Advice.** Earlier in this book I cautioned you not to accept advice from anyone who had not ridden a minimum of five hundred miles in a straight line, explaining that weekend riders do not understand the rigours and dangers encountered in an equestrian journey. Likewise, you should be extremely cautious about accepting advice from people whose packing experience is limited to guiding trail-riding tourists or participating in short hunting expeditions. While these professionals can relate to many of the primary equine problems encountered by Long Rider packers, there are some fundamental differences. Their pack animals are asked to carry very large loads. They travel over well known ground. They and their animals return home after a brief period in the field. Asking advice from such people is fraught with trouble. Long Rider packers travel light; move fast and they don't go home.

**Rule One.** Our concern as Long Rider packers is never to vindicate how much weight we can theoretically place on the pack horse. Our objective is to always protect the delicate health of our pack animals by travelling with a minimum of weight. It's not the kilometres that will kill your horse, it's the kilograms. Never overload the pack horse with a single ounce of extra weight.

**Fundamentals.** It's not easy being the pack horse. Not only does he always work harder than his companion the road horse, in case of an emergency on the trail the pack horse must also be able to operate using his common sense. With this in mind, when inspecting any potential candidate for the position of pack animal, be sure to ensure that you can lead him quietly while on foot, that he stands quietly while being loaded, and that he will travel alongside the road horse without biting or pulling back. Should any of these primary rules are violated your journey will be an ordeal.

**Tutoring for the trail.** Even if he has been previously ridden, a new pack horse is faced with a bewildering assortment of challenges. The creaking and swaying of the panniers may frighten even a calm horse. The weight of the load may throw his balance off. The bulky pack saddle no longer allows him to make his way casually between trees, around obstacles or along a narrow cliff side trail.

Instead the pack horse finds that he is carrying a great inflexible weight. Rigid panniers may poke him. Breast collars and breeching often scrape him. A crupper under his tail may frighten him. A lead rope pulls, rather than directs from behind like the riding reins he is used to. Is it any wonder that a horse might express his fright at this series of new intrusions? Because so many things can go wrong, you should choose a safe place to begin training the pack horse.

**Standing.** Your safety on the ground is immediately jeopardized if the horse is allowed to come too close without your consent or invitation. He can tread on your feet, smash you with his head or bite you. That is why it essential that a horse never be allowed to crowd you. Though you may decide to stand next to him, or demonstrate signs of affection such as stroking his neck, he must not be permitted to intrude into your space uninvited. First and foremost the pack horse must stand like a rock, not just when being packed but during the course of his normal working day as well. It is also important that a pack horse learn to come to a halt, and stand still, when the Long Rider stops his road horse and dismounts.

**Saddling.** Before the pack horse is ever fully loaded, it is critically important that he should be allowed to become thoroughly familiarized with walking about with only the empty pack saddle on his back. When he is accustomed to wearing the pack saddle, take him on very short training rides alongside your road horse. This allows him to become used to the feel, sound and smells associated with carrying the unburdened pack saddle on his back. Only when you are confident that he has no need to fear wearing and carrying the pack saddle can you carefully introduce him to the concept that low hanging panniers, or other luggage, will be placed on his back and may hang down along his ribs.

**Loading.** Instead of starting with hard sided panniers, which may frighten or rub him unexpectedly, you should begin by hanging two soft straw-filled bags off the pack saddle. Allow him to stand quietly, growing accustomed to this strange, low hanging, but unbreakable load. Then begin walking him calmly in hand. Always make sure that you stand well to one side so that if he becomes frightened he will not unintentionally injure you by shoving, running or jumping past you in a panic.

Lead him alongside, past or through objects which will touch the straw bags. To demonstrate how he needs more space than he is used to, walk him between two trees which provide six inches of clearance on each side. To accustom him to the unexpected sound of panniers scraping, walk him beside a barn wall .To build up his balance, walk him up and down a short steep trail. These exercises will build up his confidence, all the while reinforcing important new lessons; more space is needed to move safely forward, strange scraping noises emanating from the panniers are not life threatening and the sense of balance can no longer be taken for granted. When you feel he is ready, set off on a short training ride. But be ready to stop, halt, dismount, and calm the pack horse at the first sign of any trouble. If need be, drop his load and return empty, rather than frighten him. Next, substitute two hay bales in place of the straw bags. Though still unbreakable, they will teach him to accept a large firm load. Walk him through his exercises again, making sure to praise him upon his success.

Once the straw bags and hay bales have been accepted without trouble, take the next step, which is to carefully hang the empty panniers onto the pack saddle. It is often the noise, or unusual sensation of panniers unexpectedly scraping his ribs, which sends nervous horses into a panic, so proceed cautiously. Once the empty panniers are accepted without protest, once again walk the animal peacefully on a short lead rope. Always allow the new pack horse as much time as required to become accustomed to these strange new burdens.

Only after the pack horse has learned to stand quietly to be loaded, and will let you walk him with the pack saddle and panniers in place, should you begin to gradually add equal amounts of weight to both panniers. Training rides should be kept short.

The unaccustomed sounds of the gear being carried in the panniers might startle the pack horse. The result may be an impromptu rodeo on a narrow trail which sees your gear smashed and scattered. Even worse is when a panicked pack horse becomes a runaway, streaming gear behind him as he disappears into the distance. When travelling you must always ensure that any objects loaded in the panniers are padded, so as to diminish the sound of rattling or banging which might frighten an inexperienced pack animal. The training period is when you forestall this problem by intentionally placing a small tin can holding stones, or some other suitably noisy, small and indestructible objects in the bottom of the panniers. Walking the pack horse by hand, sooth his concerns when the noisy load begins to shake, rattle and roll. Repeat this procedure on your trail ride, using the noise to reassure the pack animal that any sound emanating from the panniers is of no physical or emotional concern to either of you.

Never rush any part of this training and make certain these exercises are accomplished slowly, so as to avoid frightening the animal.

**Leading.** Ideally the pack horse should walk along freely, maintaining a constant space of three feet between the rider's leg and his head. But it takes time and practice for the pack horse to learn to respect your personal space. Such training is vital, as a horse that invades your personal space is not demonstrating affection. He is attempting to dominate and intimidate you. That is why you must not confuse your feelings of emotional loyalty with any display of his physical bullying. Any invasion of your space is a strong indication of diminished respect. You have to establish that you are in firm control because the moment you introduce a pack animal into the equestrian travel equation you automatically diminish your own personal safety by half. This is due to two factors which do not arise when you travel with just your road horse.

A Long Rider normally sits erect in the saddle, with his eyes on the horizon, his shoulders square, his hands on the reins, his hips loose, his legs long and the balls of his feet resting lightly atop the stirrup. He and the road horse are a single unit moving in the same direction. But the pack horse instantly throws the Long Rider out of balance. This occurs when the Long Rider shifts the road horse's reins into his left hand and holds the pack animal's lead rope in his right hand. The effect is that the Long Rider's body is always slightly off centre, his balance is compromised and his attention is now diverted in two directions. He is literally a man in the middle. The true danger is that if a pack animal balks, and the road horse unknowingly continues to move forward with alacrity, the Long Rider can be pulled backwards out of the saddle without warning. Thus the lead rope becomes an instrument for your potential destruction if your pack animal is not properly trained to lead quietly.

Therefore, once the animal has been taught not to fear the pack saddle and panniers, the next critical part of his further education is to teach him to travel faithfully behind the road horse, not to pull back on the lead rope during the course of the day's travel and never to stop without warning. This training must be completed prior to your departure and the first part of such training begins on the ground.

Teaching the pack horse to follow the road horse correctly is a matter of practice and patience. Training should always be done at the walk. It is not uncommon for an inexperienced pack animal to show signs of confusion, or to hang back, when you and the road horse move forward. The first time this occurs you will feel the tension spring into the lead rope. If a stubborn pack animal is allowed to repeatedly pull back during the course of an entire day's travel, the pressure on your right arm and shoulder will become agonizing.

Begin by placing the pack horse's head close to your right leg. Holding the coiled lead rope in your right hand, urge the road horse to move forward slowly. Ideally the pack horse will follow the more experienced animal in front of him. If he continually balks, dismount. Wrap the lead rope up alongside the right side of the pack animal's cheek, running it over the bridge of his nose, down the opposite cheek and back under the halter. The lead rope will now encircle the pack horse's face. By placing the lead rope across the pack animal's nose in this manner, it will have been converted into a mild hackamore which will exert a slight pressure on the bridge of the nose. Remount, bring the pack animal up close to your right leg and set off again, making sure that the lead rope is kept sufficiently tight so that it exerts pressure on the animal's nose if he pulls back. This temporary hackamore instantly transfers a mild message to the pack animal. It is far better to follow along quietly, for should he decide to pull back the slightly uncomfortable pressure on his nose will be constantly applied until he learns to relieve it by resuming his correct position in line. Most horses are intelligent enough to take on the importance of this fundamental lesson and quickly learn to faithfully follow the road horse.

As with all things, there is a tender balance here too. While you wish to keep the pack horse close to hand, so as to not pull your arm out of its socket, equally you do not want him smashing the pannier into your leg or the road horse's flank. This is why it is imperative that you and your team practise leading until all of you are sufficiently well versed in this vital daily aspect.

With a well-trained pack horse, the lead rope should act as an indicator of direction transmitted from the Long Rider. When travelling along roadways, the pack horse should follow the road horse on the off side, so as to keep him away from traffic. The major exceptions are in countries where the cars travel on the left of the road, such as Britain, Australia, New Zealand and Japan. Never allow the pack horse to stroll along and then trot to catch up. The pace of the pack horse should always match that of his companion. If the pack animal becomes fatigued, do not enter into a tug of war with him. Dismount and rest the animals.

When leading the pack horse over level ground, there should be a constant, reassuring pressure running along the lead rope. When pack animals are led down short slopes, they should be discouraged from trotting. When confronted with steep slopes, the pack animal is given his head as much as possible so as to allow him to seek his own footing and maintain his balance. Pack animals should never be encouraged to jump over obstacles, such as logs and ditches, as this may dislodge the pack saddle or cast the panniers out of balance. If you encounter such a problem, proceed cautiously. If the terrain becomes rough or steep, you may decide to allow the pack animal to freely follow the road horse, as he can be caught as soon as the obstacle has been passed. However, you should have avoided placing you and your horses in such a precarious position to begin with.

**Straying.** Disasters hit you when you can least afford them. This is especially true in the mountains, where help is usually far, far away. Pack horses die when they fall off trails. They fall off trails when they stray out of line. They stray out of line because they're improperly trained before the journey begins. Most pack horses fall because they try to overtake the road horse. Their eagerness, curiosity or stupidity causes them to hit an unexpected obstacle, to lose their balance, to round a corner too quickly. Regardless of why, the result is that the unforgiving heavy load on their back is snatched by the force of gravity, and then, in a heartbeat, the pack animal is either falling through the air, or more likely, rolling down the mountainside. If he's unlucky enough to survive the fall, he'll be lying crippled at the bottom, in indescribable agony, while you're still perched on a trail high above, trying to figure out how to dismount from your scared road horse. That's what happens when a pack horse strays out of line! Never take inexperienced pack horses into the mountains, never take them along high, narrow trails and never allow them to stray out of line. If your pack horse isn't courteous, disciplined and smart enough to have grasped the life-saving meaning of this lesson, he doesn't belong on the journey – nor do you.

**Training Rides.** Most horses will soon realize what is expected of them in their new role as a pack horse. Given the proper training they learn to stand still while being loaded, negotiate between obstacles and not crowd the Long Rider on the trail. When these goals have been achieved, every effort must be made to physically condition the pack animal for the trials ahead. Such conditioning can be acquired by making training rides which require your pack horse to practise carrying a full load over varied terrain. This is also when you ingrain good discipline by introducing him to the wide variety of sights, sounds and smells which might startle him. This includes automobile traffic, blaring horns, noisy crowds, loud music, low-flying aircraft, train whistles, barking dogs and irritating children. Once he learns that none of these disturbances will cause him any pain or harm, his docility and good conduct will be assured. Additionally, the pack horse's sense of equilibrium must be encouraged. He should be challenged to undergo small trials which build up his confidence and reinforce his sense of balance. Carefully lead him across narrow bridges, along narrow trails, alongside streams, between trees in a forest, beside a traffic laden road, up and down a steep incline. He must walk along confidently behind you, following you without hesitation wherever you decide to lead. Never demand long trial rides from your unconditioned pack horse. Initial training rides should be short and then gradually lengthened as the animal's physical condition improves. Your goal is to have the pack animal ready to travel with a full load for five days a week.

**The Great Taboo.** I have chosen to include this information in a special section, so as to emphasize the dreadful consequences which may arise if you ignore it.

If you get lazy and wrap the lead rope around your saddle horn you have effectively tied your pack horse to your road horse. The consequences of this act of stupidity are dreadful and multi-faceted.

Should you wrap the lead rope around the saddle horn, the lightest punishment you can expect is that the pack horse will snap off the saddle horn if he suddenly stops. Should the lead rope be lying across the top of your leg when the pack animal balks, the rope will squeeze the top of your leg like a vice, effectively pinning you in the saddle, all the while a 1,200 pound pack horse is acting up or rearing behind you. Should you make the mistake of wrapping the lead rope around the saddle horn, and then let your hand rest on top, when the pack horse snaps the rope back, it will amputate your finger or thumb as effectively as a pair of surgical scissors. Should you be ignorant enough to dismount, and then tie the lead rope to your saddle horn, you have instantly placed the lives of both your horses in tremendous peril. That's what a criminally neglectful traveller did in the Sierra Nevada Mountains. When her road horse slipped off the perilous mountain trail, he pulled the pack horse to his death as well.

Never tie the lead rope to your saddle horn! Never wrap the lead rope around your hand! Never tie the lead rope to the tail of the road horse! Carry the lead rope in your right hand in countries where cars travel on the right. If you break this taboo, you and your horses may suffer severe injuries or die.

# Chapter 30 - Long Rider Packing

Packing horses requires special skill and unremitting care if the system is to be employed successfully. If you make a mistake it may result in serious injury. It is mandatory that you pay strict attention to the essential principles of packing, i.e. weight, balance, stability and pressure. No matter where you travel the load should always be as light as possible. No matter how many times you load your pack horse, the correct balance of the panniers is of paramount importance. Early detection of a problem may prevent injuries to your pack animal, which in turn will ruin your trip.

**The Dangers of Pack Saddles.** Sore backs are a plague which can cripple or even kill a pack horse. Before the Guild was formed nothing ruined equestrian travels more often than pack saddles. Do not think that a pack saddle has to draw blood to injure your animal. When the skin of an unconditioned pack animal is subjected to the unaccustomed pressure of a pack saddle, it is liable to be bruised by even moderate work. Once the animal's skin is broken, it will never heal thoroughly during the remainder of your journey unless you take an extended break. To reduce the already-high risk of injury to the pack animal's fragile withers and back, it is imperative that crude, improvised or antiquated pack equipment never be used on an equestrian journey.

**The Canadian Adjustable Pack Saddle.** The adjustable pack saddle made by Custom Pack Rigging in Canada has done more to reduce equestrian travel injuries than any other item in modern history. Because it is light-weight, strong, durable, inexpensive and can be adjusted to fit any equine, Long Riders have successfully used it on expeditions around the world. The adjustable pack saddle allows you to continually and accurately fit the pack saddle to the animal as his body changes shape. Because they are adjustable, one pack saddle can be fitted to the various sizes and shapes of horses encountered during an extended journey. This is a significant consideration for Long Riders, who may be forced by circumstances to change their pack animals as they cross through various countries.

**Saddle Pads.** Because of the dead weight bearing down on the pack horse's back, he requires a thicker saddle pad than the one you place under your riding saddle. A good pack saddle pad is usually twice as thick as a riding saddle pad.

**Panniers.** Because they are equipped in the rear with stout nylon loops, the modern hard-plastic pannier can be easily hung onto the adjustable pack saddle. This has largely eliminated the need for the long rope and hitches that was such an important part of 19<sup>th</sup> century packing. One of the other improvements of these panniers is that their smooth sides are curved to fit snugly alongside the pack horse's rib cage. This greatly reduces chances of the pack animal being wounded or rubbed by the load. The panniers also have closely fitting lids, which can be equipped with locks so as to protect your gear. Because they are water proof, the panniers can be taken through rivers with no problems. Long Riders have learned to divide the panniers into two separate units, the contents of which are also kept strictly segregated. One pannier should be marked with the letter P for provisions. Anything of an organic nature, including food, cooking gear, horse brushes and hobbles should be kept in this pannier. The second pannier should be marked with the letter E for equipment. This box contains anything which might potentially poison your food and water, including your lap top, camera, first aid kit, stove and fuel.

**Pack Scales.** It is essential that the panniers be as closely balanced as possible. Even the difference of a few too many ounces heavier on one side may pull the saddle off side. This in turn creates pressure, which causes saddle sores. Thus you must confirm the equality of the load's weight. To do this, you need packing scales. This tool costs very little and provides an accurate measurement every time it's called into service.

**Top Pack.** The top pack is a large square canvas bag which rests on top of the pack saddle's panniers. The problem is that this big luxurious space tempts you to fill it with paraphernalia, which adds to the overall weight the pack horse has to carry. The other drawback to top packs is that they raise the pack saddle's centre of gravity. Normally, the weight of the panniers ensures that the centre of gravity is fairly level with the top of the animal's rib cage. But a top pack places a hefty chunk of weight directly atop the pack animal's back. This in turn can cause the pack saddle to rock, become destabilized and pull the pack saddle off to one side.

**Lash Rope.** The lash rope is a long rope with a hook on one end. Though the length and diameter may vary, it is used to keep the panniers from swinging out of balance, or bouncing up and down when covering hard ground. A lash rope becomes critically important if you decide to use a top pack, as the rope will keep the canvas bag in place. The lash rope is placed over the top of the panniers and top pack and then brought underneath the stomach of the pack horse. The rope is run through the lash rope hook and then pulled gently to tighten it snugly under the horse's stomach. The rope is then tied off. Any excess rope is securely fastened to the pack saddle. Inexperienced pack horses may panic if the lash rope is pulled too tight or if a rope end is allowed to swing loose while travelling. So practise using the lash rope before your departure.

**Hitches and Knots.** If you use a lash rope, learn one standard hitch to secure your load. Regardless of which knot you choose, these are the rules regarding their use. Work quietly to avoid alarming the animal. Always keep the lash rope away from the pack horse's feet and legs. Form the hitch rapidly. Three minutes is sufficient time to complete any hitch. When completed, make sure all parts of the hitch are as tight as possible. Check to make sure the load is balanced before and after tightening the hitch. Always ensure that no part of the rope is fouled up on the pack saddle and that the loose end is secured.

**Breast Collar, Crupper and Breeching.** When you encounter steep terrain, there are three pieces of equipment which keep the pack saddle from sliding either forwards over his withers or backwards towards his tail, i.e. the breast collar, crupper and breeching. If the cinch, breast collar, breeching or crupper is fitted incorrectly, then friction and pressure will cause serious wounds, including having the animal's hair rubbed off, followed by severe abrasions. You should be able to fit one or two fingers under the breast collar and breeching, so as to confirm that it is not too tight. Because cruppers can cause a painful friction burn under the horse's tail, always ensure that they are fitted properly, and checked often during the day's journey.

**Lead Ropes.** The last piece of essential equipment for the Long Rider Packer is the lead rope, which should be eight feet long and an inch in diameter, so as to provide a strong and comfortable grip.

**Preparation of Cargo.** To begin with, don't interrupt the pack horse's breakfast until you've prepared his load for travel. Because every ounce counts, dispose of all surplus commercial packaging, placing food instead in tightly closed cloth sacks or sturdy zip lock bags. Telescope everything you can, so as to minimize the space needed in the panniers. Wrap anything breakable. Make sure any pots, or metal items that might rattle en route, are carefully padded. Don't mix food with poisons, i.e. keep provisions away from potentially lethal equipment and fuel. Place the heaviest items at the bottom of the pannier. Pack your cargo tight to make sure it can't shift when you're travelling. Try to roughly balance the weight of each pannier as you load it. When both panniers are loaded, use the pack scales to confirm their weight is evenly distributed. Also, not only do the panniers have to weigh the same; they also have to be balanced from front to back.

**Prior to Packing.** The goal of your morning packing is to close camp, load the horses, and set off, as quickly and efficiently as possible. But the morning's work cannot be hurried. In order to make this system work, you have to be disciplined and organized; otherwise your horses suffer because of your inefficiency. Though this takes practice, your goal should be to have your horses saddled, loaded and on the road in thirty minutes. Make it a part of your morning ritual to inspect your riding and pack saddles, including the girths. They must be clean of anything which might rub or injure the horse's sensitive skin. Carefully choose a level place where you will work. Lifting heavy panniers is hard enough without struggling to hoist them uphill onto a pack saddle or losing your footing when your hands are full. Before you begin saddling your animals, place their equipment in a neat pile behind where you plan to tie and work with them. Be sure you leave plenty of room between the horses, so that you can move between them safely. Also, make certain that neither horse can step backwards onto your equipment.

**Fitting the Pack Saddle.** Not only does the pack horse carry a greater physical burden, he is enclosed in more complex equipment, so extra care is always needed. Before saddling, use the saddle pad to smooth the pack horse's hair, front to rear, two or three times. Placing the saddle pad in the proper position is the first test of the day. The combination of constant movement, slick sweaty hair, loose girth and steep terrain results in the pack saddle slipping backwards during the day's travel. That is why it is a common mistake not to place the saddle pad far enough forward when you begin to saddle up. Place the front of the saddle pad one hand's distance in front of the rear edge of the shoulder blade. The result should be that about three inches, or one hand's width, of the saddle pad are left exposed when you place the pack saddle on the horse's back.

Always place the pack saddle gently on the horse's back. In addition to placing the pack saddle in the centre of the horse's back and far enough behind the shoulder blades, you must also ensure that it is not leaning to either side. Once the pack saddle is properly placed, lift the front edge of the saddle pad snugly up under the forks. This is to ensure that the pad is not riding on the horse's spine. A tight saddle pad can cause tremendous damage by rubbing off the hair, breaking open the skin and pressing down on the fragile spine. Lifting the pad also allows cool air to circulate along the horse's heated back.

Because the pack saddle covers such a large portion of the horse's body, fitting the girth properly is a vital part of your morning routine. A common mistake is to pull the girth too tight. This can induce a feverish sweat, interfere with breathing, cause galls under the girth, injure the back and leave the animal exhausted. Depending on the conformation of your pack horse, the girth is normally positioned approximately four inches behind the point of the horse's elbow. Learning to tighten the girth takes time and practice. The basic test is to draw it tight, until it reaches a point of resistance against the animal's body. Do not yank, struggle or apply too

45

much pressure. Also, be sure not to disturb the hair underneath the girth, as this may cause saddle galls.

With the saddle in place, place the breeching or crupper in its proper position. If you are using a breeching, make sure that there is one inch clearance between it and the horse's hind quarters. If a crupper is required, make sure that it is not too tight and lies at the base of the horse's tail. Next comes the breast collar. Place it above the point of the shoulder and make sure that it never restricts the movement of the front legs.

Now, with everything in place, walk around the pack horse and make a careful examination. If it all looks good, then give the girth a final adjustment, pulling it snugly into place. By adjusting the girth just before you leave, you decrease the chances of the load slipping to one side.

**Packing Up – Morning.** Your panniers should be already packed, weighed, balanced and ready to be slung on the pack saddle. If you are working in a team, have one person stand on the right side of the pack horse. They hold the pack saddle in place, while you lift the left pannier onto the pack saddle. With the first half of the load on, it is your turn to hold the left pannier up, keeping it from pulling the pack saddle off balance, while your friend in turn lifts the right pannier and secures it to the pack saddle. Both panniers should now be resting securely from the pack saddle, thanks to their sturdy nylon straps. Should you be required to load the pack horse alone, have both panniers sitting close by, ready to be instantly loaded. Lift the left pannier in place, then quietly but quickly move to the other side of the horse and hang the second pannier without delay.

**Distribution of the Load.** If you have decided to use a top pack, this is when it should be carefully lifted on top of the pack saddle and lashed into position. Never overload the top pack, as it can cause the load to tilt to one side or may damage the adjustable pivot on top of the pack saddle. Ideally the pack horse now has his load equally divided, with 40% on both sides and 20% placed on top. With this load evenly distributed, a robust pack horse should be able to carry one hundred pounds in the panniers and an additional twenty-five pounds in the top pack. The pressure from the load will also have been properly distributed over the weight-bearing surface of the horse's back. Many Long Riders like to cover the finished load with a top tarp. This can either be a regular piece of canvas which you tie into place or a specially made top tarp designed to cover your top pack.

**Get it Tight and Set it Right.** The art of good packing is not to overload the pack horse, to balance the pack boxes accurately and to secure the load so that it does not slip. You should begin your departure routine as soon as the road and pack horses are ready. First, give your pack horse a final once over and then check his girth. Next, before you mount the road horse, glance around your camp to make sure you haven't forgotten anything. Are your important travel documents safe? Have you confirmed the directions, have your maps handy and know which road you will be travelling on today? Have you visited the toilet before you swing into the saddle for the rest of the day? If you are travelling with a friend, don't swing into your saddle until they are also ready to leave. Then untie your road horses and mount at the same time. As soon as you are firmly in the saddle, turn your road horse in the direction you will be travelling, shift the lead rope to your right hand, and draw the pack horse close to your mount. You should now be ready to travel. Good packing and loading at the beginning means time and trouble saved all through the journey.

**Leading the Pack Horse.** In theory you can lead a pack horse over practically any type of country except heavy bush and swamps. While that's an encouraging thought, the first few minutes after you mount are often the most difficult. Once you're all under way, the lead rope becomes both a blessing and a burden. Always set off at the walk. Make sure your pack horse has taken his proper place slightly behind your road horse. The horse uses his head to maintain his sense of balance, as humans do their hands. If you hold the lead rope too tight, the pack horse cannot maintain his stability.

Keep the lead rope slightly taut. If you let it go slack, your pack horse may move to one side, bringing the lead rope under the road horse's tail. This will result in an instant rodeo. The lead rope should never be allowed to drag on the ground, become wrapped around your boot or get tangled under either horse's feet. Never place it between your leg and saddle. If the pack horse bolts, and the rope is under your leg, it will yank you out of the saddle. Hold it firmly in your hand, letting the slack rest on top of your leg. If you're riding in mountainous terrain, keep the lead rope on the downhill side.

Let me remind you again, no matter how tired you may become, never tie your pack horse to your saddle! This is the equestrian travel equivalent of playing Russian roulette.

**Breakaway String.** Traditional packers in North America sometimes tied the lead rope to the tail of their riding horse. The problem with this method, known as tailing, is that eventually all pack horses pull back. When this occurs you will end up with a riding horse that has a sore tail, if you're lucky, or even worse, your horse will have his tail snapped off.

If a situation arises where you are alone, but have to lead two horses, then you should employ what is known as a breakaway string. This is a light string, strong enough to keep your pack horse attached to your road horse, but weak enough to allow the pack horse to pull back and save himself if the first horse encounters trouble. The breakaway string is something you should keep where it can be reached in case of emergency. Never tie the breakaway string to the saddle horn or the tail of the road horse. Tie it in a large loop to a D ring on your saddle. With this looped string now in place, tie the lead rope to the riding horse with a half hitch, then guide your riding horse and pack horse in this temporary team fashion. Don't allow the pack horse too much slack. Give him enough of the lead rope not to trip but not enough to get into trouble.

It is also inadvisable to let your pack horses follow freely behind you. This practice is known as trailing. Because free roaming pack horses damage trails, the practice is illegal in many American national parks. Always keep your pack horse under close control.

If you encounter a problem, you may decide that it is better for you to dismount and lead your horses by hand. If so, never wrap the rope around your hand. If the horse panics the lead rope can dislocate your shoulder. If he slips off a trail he can pull you to your death. Hold the rope firmly but be ready to let go.

**On the Trail.** There are rules of the road after you've begun to ride. If you are travelling with a companion, you must be able to see and speak with each other at all times. On good ground the distance between riders may lengthen but when bad terrain is encountered, shorten up the distance and decrease the pace. If one person stops, so does your caravan. The person in the lead has a heightened sense of responsibility for those riding behind. If obstacles or sharp bends in the trail are encountered, then he must slow his pace to keep the group together. Never allow the horses to bunch up, as a nervous or irritable animal may kick out. Keep your distance between riders. Make sure you can always see the hooves of the horse in front of you.

**The Pace of a Pack Horse.** You must adjust the speed of your progress depending on the obstacles you encounter. If you are riding with a companion, and you come across a stream, sharp turn, road hazard, etc., the first rider must not proceed until all the horses are safely assembled. Otherwise the horses left behind may become upset at being separated and try to catch up with their companions. Similarly, if one of you needs to stop for any personal reason, then you should dismount and wait until he or she is back in the saddle.

**Taking a Halt.** Half an hour after you've started, plan to take a ten-minute halt to check and adjust the load. During the rest of the day, keep your horses moving at a steady pace, taking halts to rest the horses as and when the opportunity arises. When a halt is called for, be sure to move your horses well away from the roadside. If you are riding along a trail, move your animals off the trail so as to keep it clear for other travellers. Regardless of where you stop, be sure the location you have chosen is safe. Look for low hanging branches which could injure an eye, sharp objects which can slice open a leg or roots which can tear off a shoe. Then tie your horses up short, to make sure they cannot get tangled up. Unless you want to run the risk of having your reins destroyed, always secure your horses with lead ropes. Just because the horse is resting doesn't mean you can. Every halt demands a careful inspection be carried out before you can relax. Have the panniers gone out of balance? Has the top pack shifted? Is the lash rope still secure? Is the saddle pad still in place? Have the breeching or breast collar rubbed? If you decide to allow the pack horse to graze, care must be taken that the pack saddle doesn't slip forward onto the withers. Should the halt exceed thirty minutes, you should take the opportunity to off load and rest the pack horse.

**Trouble Up Ahead.** Equestrian travel, like life, is filled with dilemmas. That's why you have to mount a two-part defence against unexpected adversity. First, take every precaution. Second, when trouble arrives, and it will, stay calm. The easiest way to reduce the possibility of overt risk is to not wander off the trail. Should you lose your way, don't blunder ahead blindly. Dismount, secure your horses and scout ahead on foot. If you are travelling with a friend, one person should stay behind with the horses. Do not let stupidity, stubbornness or pride override common sense. If the trail appears treacherous, turn around, rather than risk the safety of your trusting horses. Your job is to be ever vigilant. Never take it for granted that the riding and pack saddles don't need to be adjusted. If either horse appears to be worried, pay attention and look for the cause of his concern. If you detect a problem, find a safe place to stop and resolve the issue immediately. A pack saddle can ruin a horse's back in an hour. Don't risk the animal's health and the outcome of your journey by neglect.

**Dangerous Trails.** Pack horses learn how to avoid knocking the panniers into trees, how to maintain their balance on narrow trails and how to step over obstacles. You may arrive at a stretch of trail that requires you to dismount and proceed on foot. Do not let the pack horse crowd you on the trail. Keep him well behind you. If you encounter rough country, slide your feet out of the stirrups and be ready to dismount quickly. If the trail looks dangerous, stop immediately. Never let your horses wander over to the edge of the trail, as it may give way. Train them instead to always stay in the centre of the path. If the trail starts to break away underneath your road horse, jump off on the uphill side. Removing your weight from the saddle might save his life.

**Packing Up – Evening.** Tomorrow's ride begins tonight. You must develop a system for stowing, checking and preparing your pack saddle and gear for the next day's ride. Not only does this reduce the chance of losing valuable equipment, in case of rain or emergency, it allows you to lay your hands on vital equipment in the dark without delay.

The first requirement at the end of the day's ride is to locate a safe place to off load and stable the horses. Once a safe location has been found, keep your horses together for safety's sake. While the road horse began your day, the pack horse now receives preference. Remove the panniers and loosen the girth. But do not remove the pack saddle. Exposing the heated area of a horse's back to cold air can cause injury. With the pack horse unloaded and standing easy, use a sponge to clean his eyes and nostrils with cool water. You can then offer him some hay, but no water for an hour.

With the pack horse eating quietly, loosen the girth on your road horse, sponge off his face too and give him a ration of hay as well. Once again, don't water him or remove his saddle.

While both horses are preoccupied and relaxing, scout your campsite. If you have been invited to put your horses in someone's barn, check to make sure there are no sharp items close to where they will sleep. If the horses are going to reside for the night in a strange field, check it for dangers. If you are pitching a tent, try to locate it close to the trail you arrived on. If horses become frightened in the night, they tend to run back in the direction from which they last travelled. Should you awake to the sound of horse bells rushing by your tent, at least you'll know in which direction to look for your horses in the morning.

Only remove the pack and riding saddle after the horses' backs have completely cooled. You can check by placing your hand underneath the saddle pad. If the back feels cool to the touch, then you can remove the saddle. This might take an hour or more.

# Chapter 31 - Caring For Your Horse

When we set out to become Long Riders, we enter into a life of adventure and adversity. We also undertake a serious duty to our horse.

**The Task at Hand.** Keeping a horse healthy and happy is a challenge. The difficulties increase when you ride into the unknown. Only a fool takes pride in dirt and disorder, thereby mistaking what he calls 'roughing it' for self-assurance. A real Long Rider is known by the way he maintains a strict regime of compassion, cleanliness and competence when dealing with his horse. The Long Rider must live for his horse, who acts as his legs, his safety, his honour and his reward.

Because you have chosen to take him into the unknown, the Road Horse relies on you, and not his home, to provide a much-needed sense of security. Though the horse is strong of bone and muscle, he is an animal of delicate constitution that is as liable to coughs and colds as any human being. A healthy horse gives little trouble if he is treated with ordinary care. Yet to ensure this his food should be of the best, his bedding should be kept scrupulously clean and he should always have a supply of good water. Though these are basic rules, they present daily difficulties when travelling.

**Your Horse Pays the Price.** One trait of the past was that the horse's owner tended his own stock so long as he was not ill or injured. One of the greatest dangers every Long Rider faces is the unforeseen need to involve strangers in helping feed, water and shelter your animals. After riding from the Arctic Circle to Guatemala, one weary equestrian traveller was invited to share dinner with a local minister. The hungry rider was urged to entrust his horse to the minister's servant, who accidentally killed the animal by giving him the wrong food. Never overestimate your allies. Never trust a drop of water, a bucket of grain, a syringe full of medicine or a night's accommodation to a stranger. You must always think of your horse first. You feed him before you feed yourself.

**Fair Play.** The horse never forgets injustice or error. His memory matches that of the elephant. He remembers everything, which explains how he can follow the exact route he took outward so as to find his way home. Patience and tolerance must always be uppermost in your mind. You can see what's on the inside of a man by the outside of his horse. When the road horse and Long Rider live together, the servant, like a mirror, reflects his master's qualities. To courage, energy, cheerfulness, and kindness, a horse responds with confidence, endurance, contentment and love.

# Chapter 32 - Securing Your Horse

When a Long Rider sets off into the unknown, there is no guarantee of a safe fenced pasture or a snug stable awaiting his horses that night. By contrast, the only thing you can depend upon is that after a long day of hard travel, your road and pack horses need water, food and rest, in that order. The problem is how to accommodate their needs, while maintaining a sense of security which will guarantee you're not afoot in the morning?

**Awake in the Night.** A horse only spends 12% of every twenty-four hours dozing. That's less than three hours a day. The rest of the time he's perfectly capable of getting into trouble.

**Different Options.** There are many ways to restrain your horse. Each has its drawbacks, proponents and dissidents. What you do depends on a variety of factors, including the horse, local accommodations and weather conditions.

**Hobbles.** Though hobbles allow the horse to take small steps, they restrict him from running freely. They can be constructed from rope, leather, nylon, burlap, rags, vines, anything soft and handy which can be used to prohibit the horse's escape. Never assume your horse has been trained to be hobbled. Untutored horses who suddenly find their movements restricted by hobbles will react differently. They may freeze in fear, bolt, rear or pull against the hobbles out of frustration. You must never place hobbles on an untrained horse, then let him loose, as he may panic, fall or injure himself. When you first put on the hobbles, keep a light grip on the lead rope and be ready to step forward and calm the horse. Give him ample time to practice moving cautiously. When he seems confident, drop the lead rope and step back a few feet. Increase your distance as he gains confidence and proficiency. Only when he can graze quietly, and move with self-assurance, can you leave him unattended in hobbles.

**The Picket Pin.** Another successful method of securing horses is to attach them to the ground. A strong metal stake known as a picket pin restrains the horse, while the long rope tied to his halter or leg allows him to graze freely. Many Long Riders are strong advocates of the picket pin system. Either a strong hammer or axe is indispensable when you try to drive the picket pin into rock-hard or frozen ground. The length of your picket rope is a personal decision, though Long Riders have noted that a picket rope which is fifteen to twenty metres long will provide plenty of room for their horses to graze. The thing to remember is that horses are far more likely to become entangled on a short line than a long rope.

**Training with the Picket Pin.** There are two primary reasons to train your horse to use the picket pin properly. First, if your horse lacks training he may wrap the rope around his leg while grazing and panic. If you're lucky he will only receive a serious rope burn on the back of his hock, a wound which may incapacitate him for several days. More worrying is when the horse lifts his rear leg to scratch and the rope becomes snagged under the rear edge of his horse shoe. Now he's caught with his hind leg up in mid-air, which can pull his tendons or cause him to fall and injure himself. In either case the rope becomes his instant enemy. But it gets worse.

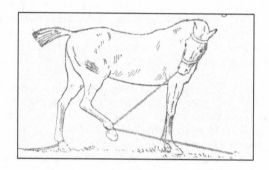

*When you attach the picket pin's rope to the horse's halter, you run the risk of the animal receiving a severe rope burn on his hocks.*

If your horse panics while grazing, pulls the pin free and runs away, this sharp steel object being dragged behind has been transformed into a deadly projectile capable of wounding you or blinding him. Always train the horse to graze on the picket pin before you start the journey. Whether it takes your horse a couple of days, or a couple of weeks, you must ensure that he is confident and capable of being attached to a picket pin without coming to grief.

**The High Picket Line.** The use of the high picket line is usually found in the western United States and Canada. There are strict environmental restrictions which must be followed at all times if you use this system. The basic concept consists of attaching the picket line between two trees and then tying the horse's lead ropes to the picket line. There are several parts to a successful high picket line, including the tree-savers, the knot eliminators and the actual rope.

The two nylon tree-saver straps are fitted around the bole of the two trees between which the picket line will be placed. These wide nylon straps, which have large metal rings at each end, prevent the rope from damaging the trees. It is not only time-consuming to tie your horses to a high picket line via a traditional knot, it also enhances the chances of a problem, should the animal get in trouble and you must quickly untie him. Instead of tying each lead rope to the high picket line, stainless steel in-line swivels, commonly known as knot eliminators, are placed at regular intervals along the high picket line to which the horses are attached. These swivels ensure that the animals do not twist the overhead picket line or become entangled with each other.

Where you decide to place the high picket line needs careful attention. The spot chosen should not have roots, stumps, rocks or plants underfoot which might trip the horses. How you position the animals along the high picket line is also crucial. Provide at least twenty-four inches between horses and take note of the animal's social order, placing the most dominant horse at the head of the high picket line and the most timid animal at the most secure end.

**The Trouble with Trees.** There are twin dangers when you mix horses and trees. Any time you tie a horse to a solid, immovable object, such as a tree, you place your animal at risk. If he panics, pulls back, and finds himself severely restrained by the halter, lead rope and tree, the combination could be injurious or fatal. If you must use a tree, then tie the lead rope to a break-away string to reduce the risk of injury. What is more common is that if you tie your horse to a tree, the animal will strip off the bark, devour the tender leaves, expose the roots by pawing, destroy the fragile undergrowth and leave a long-term scar on the landscape. Because of the damage done to trees by thoughtless horse campers, the United States Forest Service enacted a regulation which states that the owners of horses caught damaging trees are guilty of a federal violation and will be fined. The U.S. Forest Service now requires horse campers and travellers to use tree-savers so as to prevent the high picket line rope from cutting into and damaging the tree's bark.

**Electric Fence.** If you are travelling with a pack horse, then you might wish to consider using a portable electric fence kit, which can be fitted into the bottom of a pannier. This system is lightweight and runs on small batteries. A single strand fence will create a temporary pasture measuring 50'by 50, which should safely accommodate four horses.

**German Coupling Strap.** The German cavalry had a method of securing horses on a temporary basis. This system relied on a leather strap 412 mm long and 25 mm wide. It had a sturdy metal clip at each end. One clip was attached to the bit and the other to the rear of the second horse's saddle.

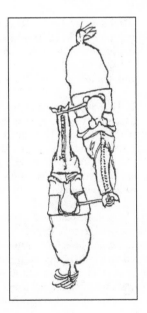

*The German cavalry used the coupling strap to secure two army horses.*

**Runaways.** If you fear losing your horses, don't allow all your animals to graze at the same time. Keep the most reliable horse tied close to camp, in case you need to ride out to find and return any runaways. Once they've had an hour or so to graze, many horses will have appeased their appetite and may become curious about what lies over the hill. You should anticipate this moment and be ready to bring them back to camp.

Horses that have learned to anticipate grain or salt will be more likely to follow you willingly so as to ensure their evening meal. Should a horse begin to run away when you approach, don't attempt to grab its lead rope and stop it. The power of a running horse will pull you off your feet and drag you across the ground. Even if a pasture is available, don't relax your guard. Always put bells on your horses. This will enable you to listen to the movements in the dark, and if they run away, be able to determine in which direction they fled. It is better to hear bells than count tracks.

If your horses have vanished, don't waste time trying to figure out how they got loose, concentrate on finding them. The first necessity is to determine where they went and most of the time the loose horses will have returned from the direction from which you travelled the previous day. If for any number of reasons your horses escape, the first thing to do is to circle your camp and look for outbound tracks.

# Chapter 33 - Grooming Your Horse

To keep the horse healthy, grooming must be done every morning and evening, with careful attention being paid to the horse's outward state at all times. The amount of grooming will depend on the conditions you encountered during that day's travel. The harder the day's work, the greater amount of care will be required to keep the horse's skin in perfect condition. The best way of testing if a horse has been well groomed is by passing the fingers the reverse way through the direction of the hair, particularly under the belly. If the horse is dirty, they will be covered with grey scurf.

Never saddle a horse that has not been perfectly groomed. Never conclude your day's travel with a hot horse.

If the horse is wet from rain, don't remove his saddle. Remove his bridle, replace it with the halter, tie him, loosen the girth, then rub him down with hands full of loose straw or a towel, using brisk friction to warm and dry him. In normal dry-weather conditions loosen the girth, remove the bit and bridle, place the halter on and then give the horse as much water as he will drink. When he has finished his drink his feet should be picked out to see that no stones have lodged in them.

Don't be in a hurry to unsaddle him. The sudden exposure to cold air, on the hot flesh under the saddle, is liable to cause injury to the delicate skin, nerves and blood vessels. Be patient and allow the back to resume its normal temperature. The time required will differ, depending on the climate, that day's work, your saddle and your horse. After having allowed the horse to relax, slide your hand under the saddle pad to determine if horse's back has cooled down. If so, then the saddle may be removed and any remaining sweat on the horse's back should be dried at once. It is a good idea to rub the back vigorously where the saddle sat, so as to restore the circulation in the skin.

Next, use a curry comb to remove loose hair, mud and any objects that become tangled in the horse's coat. Then employ a stiff brush to remove dirt and dust from the coat. Take note: you are attempting to remove dirt, mud, dust and insects, not the natural grease and oil which serves as a protector to the horse's skin and that which helps keep him warm. By stripping the coat of its natural oils, you leave the horse standing stark naked in the sun and rain. Always keep a sharp out for any type of saddle sore, horse bite or insect sting.

**Horse Hair.** Never cut the hair of a road or pack horse! Any horse needs the bristles on his nose. These feelers provide information to the horse in the same way a cat's whiskers do. The bristles on a horse's nose help him graze at night and to feel his way in the dark through unfamiliar surroundings. Removing them is akin to cutting off your fingers. You have removed the animal's sense of touch. To do so may appeal to a human's vanity, but it is a crime against nature. The hair which lines the external ear should also be allowed to remain untouched. Likewise, do not tamper with the hair around the pasterns, which acts as a shield against water that otherwise will enter the folds of the foot and cause cracks. Mane and forelock hair is vital to serve as a shield against excessive sunlight and harsh wind on the horse's eyes. Above all, it is absolutely essential, if you want to keep horses in good health and condition, that a road horse's tail should never be shortened or cut. By doing so, you deprive him of nature's protection against insects. Stables and pastures are excellent breeding grounds for flies. When the horse is required to stand in the open he must be equipped with his best defence, a long tail. If it is too short for him to reach his flanks with it, he will be kept in perpetual agony by his annoying air-borne enemies.

**Washing.** The washing of horses as a general practice is to be strongly condemned. The horse's skin contains essential oils and grease which protect the coat and flesh beneath. That is why travelling horses take no harm from the rain and may be ridden through water with impunity, because the natural greasiness and subsequent exertion of the journey keep up the circulation and warmth of the wetted skin till it is dry again. The only purposes for which the use of water, or soap and water, is necessary on the body of the healthy horse is for the removal of dirt stains which will not groom off, and for the occasional cleaning of the mane and tail and hoofs. If the legs and belly are covered with mud it should be left to dry and then be brushed off. Otherwise, washing of the body should be prohibited as a rule. Should it be necessary at any time to break the rule, the greatest care should be taken to dry the skin thoroughly, ensure the animal is warm and kept out of draughts.

# Chapter 34 - Watering Your Horse

Water is the life-blood of the journey. Yet Long Riders normally never carry it. According to the time of year, his size, and the difficulties of that day's travel, the road horse will need eight to ten gallons (45 litres) of water every twenty-four hours. Yet a single gallon (4½ litres) of water weighs ten pounds (4½ kg.). When every ounce counts, that is an impossible burden for a road horse. Plus, chances are that if you refresh your thirst from a canteen, you will overlook the equally dire needs of your parched horse. So if you don't carry water, what do you do and when do you do it?

**Why Water.** The importance of water to your horse's health cannot be over-emphasized. Water does more than ease a horse's thirst. He must, on average, consume ten gallons of water a day just to keep his various body functions operating properly. For example, six pounds (2 or 3 kg.) of hay passed into his digestive system will absorb 1½ gallons (nearly 7 litres) of the horse's saliva. And though he drinks ten gallons of water a day, only one gallon of liquid will normally be lost through urination. The rest of the water is absorbed into the horse's hard-working body. Thus, even in pleasant weather and easy country, horses must always be properly watered. When you factor in the additional challenges encountered on an equestrian journey, a lack of water can create a life or death situation for your horses. If horses are denied water, no noticeable effect may be seen immediately but over a long period it will tell and the horses will exhaust more quickly than a horse allowed free access to water.

**How much Water.** Water should ideally be fresh, pure, free from taste, smell and colour. Water should be at a temperature between 10 and 14 degrees Celsius (50 to 60 degrees Fahrenheit). You should attempt to water your horse at least three times a day. If the weather is warm, increase his daily watering to four times a day, minimum. Normally he will spend five minutes, drinking three or four gallons at each of these opportunities.

**Water in the Morning.** It is absolutely necessary that you not set out unless you have watered the horses. Although most horses are disinclined to drink early in the morning, especially in cold weather, every effort should be made to make them drink before starting that day's journey. This is critically important in countries where water is scarce, as this early-morning watering may be the only opportunity they have to drink for hours.

**Water at the Day's End.** Before you off saddle, every effort must be made to obtain your horses a plentiful supply of good, clean water. Stagnant water should be avoided if possible.

Since it is customary to pitch camp and groom before watering, this allows time to cool the horses thoroughly. Water drunk too fast is dangerous and can cause colic. That is why care must be taken at the conclusion of the day's journey. If you arrive at camp with a tired and thirsty horse, tie him, remove his bit and bridle and then loosen his girth. While he cools down, refresh the horse by gentling washing his eyes, face and nose with a sponge dipped in cool water. Then allow him a few swallows of cool, not cold, water. Don't let him over-drink. After he has slaked his immediate thirst, feed him some hay. Once he is cooled, he can have a long drink before his dinner.

If that night's water supply is supplied by a stream, places should be designated for drinking and cooking, watering animals, bathing and washing clothes. Be sure you water the horses upstream, away from any kitchen or bathing soap.

**Watering while Travelling.** Watering while travelling can be difficult. The Long Rider must be ever observant, pay great attention to the horse's drinking habits and remember "little and often" in terms of watering him.

Never pass up a chance to water your animals, especially on hot days. Never ride for more than four hours without watering the horses. A small quantity taken frequently is far better and more refreshing than copious draughts, taken before or after rest, and, more important than all else, far less dangerous.

Though it may appear tempting to ride your thirsty horse into what looks a cool lake or stream you should resist the temptation. First check that the footing next to the water is safe. If you are travelling in Africa, check for crocodiles before you approach with your horse. Regardless of what continent you are on, lead your horse to the water on foot, keeping him quiet and under control. Before you water the horses, remove the road horse's bit and loosen the girths on both the riding and pack saddles. Don't allow your horses to move faster than a walk to and from the water. Don't allow your horse to go any deeper into the water than is necessary to let him drink. Your horses should be watered quietly, without confusion. Don't rush them, letting them drink their fill. Never attempt to hold more than two horses at a time when watering. Do not let them crowd or push each other. If you are using pack mules, care must be exercised to insure that they do not lie down in the water and damage their loads. Horses should not be made to move faster than a walk for a quarter of an hour after a full drink. If fast work is required from your horses soon after watering, they should not be allowed to drink more than six to ten swallows.

**Water in Hot Weather.** Heat means the animals should be watered more often. Particularly in the summer, thirst tires a horse out more drastically than hunger. A horse may become placid after a heavy drink on a hot day. If the animal is sweaty and overheated when you stop to water him, he may be given a few sips to quench his immediate thirst. Then he should be walked slowly until he has cooled off, before being allowed to completely satisfy his thirst.

**Water in Cold Weather.** In order to maintain his normal body temperature, your horse must be encouraged to drink his fill. But his thirst is not as predictable as his appetite. That is why travelling on horseback in cold weather provides an additional difficulty, which is to provide your horse with a warm drink of water. There are two things to remember about horses and cold water. One, horses will seldom drink cold water freely. Two, drinking cold water can sometimes be harmful to horses. Thus providing him with fresh warm water and then con-vincing him to drink it can present a frustrating problem. No matter how much trouble he causes, giving your horse warm water is important, as if he drinks cold water he will use up precious body heat and valuable energy heating it internally. Cold water will also cause him to shiver, which reduces his vigour and drains his resistance to cold.

If cold weather is a factor, allow for extra time, rather than compromise your horse's safety by not allowing him the time needed to ensure he has had a long, deep drink of warm water before you set off across the cold landscape. Also, don't be tempted to think that snow can resolve your horse's need for fresh water. Regardless of how pure and moist it appears, snow leaves a horse dehydrated. Horses left without water in a snow-covered environment may die of exposure.

**Dangers of Watering.** If you get the sequence of watering and feeding wrong, your horse can die. It's that brutally simple.

The mechanics of a horse's stomach help explain why water can be dangerous. Unlike a cow, who is an herbivore equipped with more than one stomach so as to digest vegetable matter efficiently, horses are omnivores with only one stomach. Your road horse's stomach is equipped to hold two to three gallons of water. But the horse normally drinks four to five gallons of water at once. If you feed the horse first, then water him, the fluid passes straight through the stomach, flushing the food along with it into the intestines, where it often becomes lodged. The decomposing food, which cannot be passed, becomes gaseous, decomposes, causes unbelievable amounts of gastric pain, and often results in the horse dying a slow, agonizing death. Because of this deadly combination, you must always water the horse at least half an hour before you feed him, never after.

If you are travelling, and at least an hour has passed since the horse was fed, then the animal may be watered as usual. But there are pollutants to wary of. Be careful of water that may have been contaminated by pesticides that have been washed out of farmers' nearby fields.

**No Water.** Finally, what if you find yourself in a part of the world where there is no water? In cool weather, and if they have not been travelling hard, horses can drink only twice daily, as under such conditions they get a good deal of moisture from their grazing. Yet, if you find that you have to make camp without water, let the horses graze, but don't give them grain or any dry food.

# Chapter 35 - Feeding Your Horse

**Precious Food.** Diet has a large part to play in any equestrian journey. Before you set out on your journey, you must ask yourself these basic questions. What will your horse eat? Will you expect him to survive on grass alone? How much time will you allow him to graze every day? Will you give him hard feed? Where will you obtain it? Will the local population sell their own horse food in order to help you? Will you be forced to arrange for food drops in remote areas? Who will transport the food in such a case? Will you be required by cultural and climatic circumstances to give your horse food which you never expected?

If you ride in your own country, through a recognizable equestrian culture, then your horses may not encounter severe dietary challenges. But if you ride into a foreign country your road horse must learn to eat what is locally available. Thus what you feed your horse will depend largely on where you ride and what you can find. The good news is that horses are far more adaptable than most people realize. The bad news is that when Long Riders venture far afield, they discover that it can be nearly impossible to find adequate horse food of any description.

**Equine Digestion.** Unlike cattle, horses have a fast digestive process. Yet the horse's small stomach cannot contain large quantities at a time like that of the ox. It is normal for a horse to spend the majority of every day grazing, with small amounts of food taken in constantly and chewed slowly before being swallowed. The horse does not stop eating at night, preferring to spend part of each evening grazing instead of sleeping. This "feed little-and-often" point is one to remember, because as we know when our own stomach is empty, we feel languid. So does the horse. When travelling long distances, he must be allowed to eat every few hours as his small stomach must be frequently replenished. Otherwise he will lose condition.

**Amount of Food.** Because of his small stomach, a horse cannot eat very much at one time without impairing his digestion. On the other hand a horse has very large intestines; and bulk, such as grass or hay, is, therefore a necessity in his diet. Horses will thrive indefinitely on grass or hay if not worked too hard. But you cannot maintain a healthy horse if it is deprived of hay or other bulky matter no matter how much grain you may give it. Nor can a horse's digestion support an unlimited ration of grain unless a sufficient amount of bulk fodder accompanies it.

**Rules of Feeding.** Given that this is an international study, one must bear in mind that what works in England may be unacceptable in Ethiopia. For example, the question of feeding your horse grain will depend on what nations you ride through, as some equestrian cultures never practise this custom. Therefore, what must concern us are the rules of feeding which must never be broken no matter where you journey. First, feed hay or grass. Second, provide water. Third, feed grain, when circumstances permit. Fourth, do not work horses immediately after a full feed. Fifth, feed often and in small quantities during the day.

**First, feed hay.** Bulk fodder, i.e. grass or hay, serves as the horse's primary daily diet. If placed on grass, you must allow adequate time for the horse to graze. If fed hay indoors, leave the horse undisturbed while he eats.

**Second, water.** A horse drinks very rapidly and in large gulps. As this occurs, the water runs quickly through the gullet, stomach and into the small bowel. A serious danger arises when a stream of water passes through such a full stomach, as the water is capable of washing a considerable portion of the horse's undigested grain into his bowels. When this occurs, not only does this mean a loss of nourishment, it also raises the threat of indigestion, colic, and in extreme cases, death.

**Third, feed grain.** Never give your horse grain before water!

**Fourth, do not work horses immediately after a full feed.** Immediately after a meal the stomach and bowels are actually bigger than before as they are slightly distended by gases resulting from the digestive process. Allow the horse plenty of time to eat and digest his food before riding.

**Fifth, feed often and in small quantities during the day.** The equine digestive system is constructed to encourage a horse at pasture to spend most of his time leisurely grazing. In contrast a road horse learns that he has a short period of time in which to eat rapidly. Yet extreme care must be taken not to over feed the horse. He must be allowed enough time to consume his food quietly and thoroughly.

Horses should be fed bulk food in the morning and evenings, and be allowed to graze, as circumstances and time allow, during the day's travel. Also of importance, the horse should never be fed more than he will readily eat, nor should he be fed when very hot.

**Three Square Meals.** Ideally, a horse should have three feeds a day, the first at six, the next at eleven and the final one last thing at night. Of these, breakfast and dinner are the most important. The road horse that has not been fed and watered properly in the morning is not ready to travel, so make it a rule to give your horses their food two hours before you put them to work. Yet care must be taken. Horses receive slightly less food in the morning than in the evening because it is injurious for them to work when gorged with food. They also have more time to eat and digest their food quietly during the night. Don't miss any opportunity to try to feed the horse some hay, or a third of its grain ration, at lunchtime. The evening feed should begin with hay. After three-quarters of an hour, water the horse. Then give him his oats or grain.

If your horse misses a feed, do not give him a double ration as it may result in colic or another illness of the bowels!

When possible, feed the horse three meals – morning, lunch and evening, and dispense the food as follows:

| Ration | Morning | Lunch | Evening |
|--------|---------|-------|---------|
| Oats | One-third | One-third | One-third |
| Hay | One-fourth | One-fourth | Two-fourths |

**Emotional Concerns.** We have acknowledged the physical importance of keeping the horse well, but there is another element at play here; the emotional importance of the food.

When horses are placed in a long-term journey, they inhabit an environment where there are very few factors upon which they can rely. They awake in a strange place. During the day they are constantly exposed to frightening noises, suspect strangers and potentially dangerous animals. At night they are asked to sleep in a fear-provoking new location. Having been asked to inhabit such a worrisome world, is it any wonder that a road horse exhibits such intense loyalty to the Long Rider? During the day he provides the horse with a sense of protection and reliability. As the sun begins to drop, the Long Rider is the comrade who can be counted on to provide a reassuring evening meal. The longer the journey, the more emotional weight attached by the horse to his food.

That is why the building of confidence between horse and rider is imperative. Under no circumstances do the needs of the travelling horse come second. His well-being must always take precedence over yours. He must be first to be fed, first to be watered and must have the best bed available.

The foundation of this principle is trust. He must be convinced that in an uncertain world, full of chance and circumstance, you are the dependable ally who will always protect his interests. This need not mean that you must adhere to a slavish routine. The hardships of travel do not encourage precise time keeping. What matters is that the road horse knows that when he stops, you will feed him. Those who ignore this critical rule of travelling are more likely to risk an equine breakdown and journey failure than those who remain sensitive to the emotional realities which food represents to the travelling horse.

**Looking for Food.** When you travel you will learn that you face a serious nutritional challenge. Your journey cannot proceed without a well-fed horse. Yet regardless of your desire, it may prove difficult to keep the animal adequately fed. Thus, because conditions are constantly changing, keeping a road horse healthy is harder than maintaining an animal at home. That is why no opportunity to feed the horse should be passed without the animal being cared for. In order to accomplish this, you must develop a sharp eye for opportunity.

Because of its size and weight, hay cannot be transported by Long Riders. Your horse requires bulk food, even if its daily discovery cannot be relied upon. If you have a chance to buy hay, don't think twice. When an opportunity to graze occurs, it should become second nature to stop and take advantage of it. If you encounter a standing crop which will act as fodder, attempt to make a purchase. Empty nosebags should be kept full, no matter what the contents, so long as they are eatable. Cocoa, sugar and even meat may be made use of to help us keep up the balance of nourishment and the strength of the road horse.

**Who Feeds Your Horse?** There are three primary concerns involved with allowing someone else to feed your horse. The horse's food may be stolen. The horse may be given substandard fare. The horse may be killed because of negligent feeding.

If your table is not properly served you can complain. Your horse cannot. Don't trust the most honest face in the world in the matter of feeding your horse! A Long Rider should always feed the horse himself, rather than risk placing the animal in the care of another person. See the hay and grain put into the manger, and stay in the stable until your horse is done eating. Get your own dinner afterwards, for you are of less importance.

Do not trust to anyone to see to these matters but yourself, especially as regards the quantity and quality of the grain given, which should always consist of the best your money can buy. Otherwise it is very possible that you may pay for what you did not receive, to the detriment of your horse.

Why does this matter? Because the horse's condition is crucial on a long ride and you must monitor his appetite. The more he eats, the better his condition and the greater your chances of geographic success. To avoid the risk of deception, always tend to your own horses.

**Grazing.** Never pass up the chance to let your horse graze! You cannot expect a hard-working road horse to maintain his weight and condition if you only allow him to graze for a few hours in the morning and evening. Whether you are in an urban environment or in some hostile natural landscape, the rule remains the same. Because you never know where and when you will find good grazing, never ride by grass thinking that you will find better pasturage further down the road.

If you come upon good grass, stop travelling and let your horse graze for an hour or so. If the grass is rich and the camping fine, cease that day's journey early so as to allow your horse the chance to replenish his energy and rest. Also, whenever dismounted allow your horse to graze.

**Hay.** It is of great importance that the hay you buy be of good quality; if not, then no matter how much of it a horse eats, his condition will still be poor and his energy low.

**Oats.** Throughout the last few centuries, oats were the preferred grain feed for horses. Although many other grains are successfully used as horse food, wherever oats can be obtained they are universally acknowledged to be the best. As already mentioned, grass is the natural

57

food for the road horse and it will serve as the basis for his nourishment. Horses will instinctively choose the grasses which are good and nourishing. But one thing is clear; the hardworking road horse needs additional sources of energy and the Long Rider must learn to incorporate whatever energy-rich food is locally available.

Experience has shown that oats are generally speaking the best of all grains for horses. They thrive on them in the best possible manner. The amount of oats fed will depend on the condition and work rate of your road horse. Provided that a suitable quantity of bulk fodder, either grass or hay, is provided, the amount of oats may vary from 8 to 16 pounds (3.6 to 7.3 kilos) of oats per day, depending upon the size of the horse. Traditionally Historical Long Riders fed their road horses a gallon (4½ litres) of oats in the morning, half as much at noon and 1½ gallons (6-7 litres) at night, with all the hay that the animal cared to eat.

**Fruits.** Many places and cultures encourage horses to eat different beneficial fruits. This food source not only provides a horse with sugar, fructose and energy, it can add a welcome diversity to an otherwise boring meal. While it is common practice to feed horses apples, they also enjoy eating pears, figs, pomegranates, guavas, mangoes, papayas, paw-paw, apricots and dates. Horses quickly learn to drop the stones from fruit like apricots, dates, etc.

**Salt.** A travelling horse should always have access to salt. It purifies the blood, reduces disease and helps rid the horse of worms. When travelling in hot weather, horses, like humans, sweat out their body-salt. If not replaced, the horse will suffer from lassitude and weakness. Placing a teaspoon of salt in the horse's nosebag adds interest to his meal and helps him maintain this valuable mineral.

**Nosebags.** Many Long Riders use nosebags to feed their horses grain. If you decide to do so give all the feed bags at the same time so your road and pack horses don't get impatient.

Be sure the nosebag is properly fitted. If put on too long, it will make feeding difficult. Either the horse will throw his head back to fling the grain into his mouth, which of course means he will spill it, or he will put the nosebag on the ground, thereby dirtying the bag and its contents. If the nosebag is put on too short, the horse will get his nose in the food, which will also make feeding difficult. As soon as the ration is finished, the nosebag must be removed, otherwise if the horse tries to drink with the nosebag on, he could drown. Plus, if left in place the empty nosebag is often damaged and will be soiled by saliva and nose secretions. Even normal spittle will mix with the leftovers and result in a smelly, sour mess which ferments in the bottom of the bag, so clean the grain bag after each feeding as if it were your dinner plate. Otherwise the saliva, together with uneaten grain, may start fermentation. Turn it inside out and clean it with hay, grass or leaves. Wash it out and sun it when you can. If you don't use a nosebag, don't feed grain on the ground, otherwise your horse may develop sand colic. Place the grain on top of a flake of hay or a canvas tarp, then hold the horse by the lead rope until he has finished his meal. In an emergency, you may use a saddle blanket for this purpose. Place the grain on the top of the blanket, otherwise hair may become mixed with the food or grain which may irritate the horse's back when you saddle him.

# Chapter 36 - Shoeing Your Horse

**An Everlasting Dilemma.** The tradition of guarding horses' hooves did not simultaneously originate alongside riding. It was the advent of artificial terrain, such as cobblestones and gravel, which helped stimulate early man's research into equine foot security and even these initial attempts at horseshoeing were not practised for many centuries until after the horse himself was in general use.

**A Never-Ending Debate.** Miles mean trouble. How do we travel far and wide on our horse, while protecting its feet, not just from harsh terrain but from equally dangerous and incompetent farriers? Who do we believe when it comes to deciding if we should nail on shoes, put on boots or let the horse go barefoot? What sort of cultural traps await an unsuspecting Long Rider who seeks to have his horse shod in faraway countries? Realizing that your journey will be halted if the hoof fails, let us examine this problem carefully, using reason and history to try and find an answer. But first we have to investigate a debate which has raged for centuries. Do we send our horses out barefoot or shod?

**Barefoot is Best.** Let me begin by stating that history is on the side of barefoot horses. Genghis Khan led his cavalry to victory on barefoot horses. But times change and so did the perceptions of the horsemen alive in each age. When Napoleon invaded Russia in the summer of 1812, his Grande Armée was accompanied by an estimated 150,000 horses. These equine warriors departed from France after having been shod with 600,000 horseshoes, held in place by 4,800,000 horseshoe nails.

With such a conflicting equestrian history, it is no wonder that mankind became needlessly involved in a debate which continues to antagonize and distract horsemen today.

By the late 19th century a dispute was raging in Europe and the United States. It pitted barefoot believers against horseshoe disciples. The barefoot brigade challenged the horseshoe advocates to explain how man, (i.e. farriers equipped with horseshoes), could improve on what God had invented; that natural wonder, the horse's hoof? It was a good question, which went largely unanswered because with millions of horses working in cities, pulling and trotting across hard metalled roads, the majority of Victorian-era horse owners simply ignored the vocal minority who advocated a return to the past.

The argument largely disappeared until the late 20th century, by which time the majority of mechanized citizens in the United States and Western Europe had become increasingly out of touch with the day-to-day equestrian knowledge once possessed by their own mounted ancestors. This is one reason why many determined mustang fans took a militant stand against horseshoes. Yearning for what they perceived to be a more natural horse, these wild horse advocates routinely denounced the horseshoe as a token of impurity. In justifying their beliefs, these activists silenced reason and ignored any genuine criticism of the barefoot philosophy. When so-called authorities make blanket statements such as these they neglect to recognize or respect the customs of other equestrian cultures. They fail to realize that none of us have all the answers. Our culture and time constrict our knowledge. What works in the limited confines of our known existence may be completely wrong somewhere else.

Why does this matter? Because the horse suffers in silence when humans attempt to vindicate their personal pride and narrow national beliefs!

When it comes to equestrian travel, this is no mere parlour argument, for what goes under your horse's hoof will affect how far forward he moves. No one can deny that some extraordinary journeys have been made on barefoot horses. For example, in 1970 Scottish Long Rider Gordon Naysmith rode two barefoot Basuto ponies 20,000 kilometres (14,000 miles) from Africa to Austria.

But who's right? Do you set off barefoot or shod?

**Ancient Hoof - Modern World.** Barefoot advocates often rely on romance rather than science. They argue in favour of historical parentage, while tending to overlook modern facts. One typical commentator said, "How often did the Apaches shoe their Indian war ponies?" But 19th century Indian ponies weren't required to travel where today's road horse must go, were they?

The Australian Brumby and American Mustang, both of whom are free to roam on natural terrain, are often presented as examples of hard-footed horses that possess ideal hoof conformation. Freedom is not however an automatic guarantee of perfect hooves, as demonstrated by new research confirming that many wild horses have flawed feet. For example, when New Zealand's Kaimanawa wild horses were lately examined, it was discovered that hoof abnormalities were surprisingly common.

In its original natural environment, the hooves of wild horses were shaped and trimmed by the constant wandering needed to find grazing and water. Little changed when our ancestors first domesticated and rode the horse as mankind continued to reside alongside their horses in a grassland environment. Yet what happens when you take an animal designed to live on the clean dry plains and then confine him in a dung-filled stable? What adverse effects occur when you restrict his movements and pump him full of high energy food? What takes place when a horse is required to travel thousands of miles on abrasive modern roads? His hooves suffer!

As Long Rider history demonstrates, under certain circumstances a horse can work and travel without having worn shoes; but those circumstances are few and far between in this modern world. So what is the deciding factor: personal philosophy or geographic necessity?

**Let the Terrain Decide.** As Long Riders, we're trying to protect our horses, not advocate a cultural belief. When the Australian Long Rider Tim Cope set off to ride 6,000 miles from Mongolia to Hungary, his horses started without shoes. But after travelling thousands of kilometres Tim had to have his horses shod when he encountered rocks and roads. South African Long Rider Billy Brenchley was a professional farrier and a strong advocate of letting horses go barefoot when the terrain allowed. His goal was to ride across the African continent on barefoot horses. Yet after travelling 4,300 kilometres (2,600 miles) across the harsh terrain of Northern Africa, he too decided he had to put shoes on his horses. And who else used shoes? Gordon Naysmith! Though his Basuto horses made the vast majority of their journey barefoot, Gordon didn't maintain an obstinate prejudice against hoof protection when the ground became aggressive. When Gordon encountered harsh, stony country in northern Africa, he realized that there was some terrain which would destroy his horse's hooves if he chose to ride across it without protection. That is why he put shoes on his horses for part of the journey.

Tim, Billy and Gordon can be used as a measure for other Long Riders because their final decision, like yours, should always depend upon the terrain. You are not riding a wild horse or asking a feral horse to carry your pack saddle. Free-roaming horses such as these don't spend their days carrying hundreds of pounds on their backs or walking on hot modern roads.

In order to keep your horse's hooves healthy, you have to take a variety of factors into consideration. As a Long Rider, your first duty is to always err on the side of caution. If the way becomes rocky and rough, you shoe your horse or arrange to protect his hooves with boots or some other option. But if we are in trouble by leaving our horses barefoot, are we home free if we ask a stranger to hammer a metal plate on their feet? In fact, if you decide to shoe, your troubles may have just begun.

**Whom Do You Trust?** There is perhaps no question relative to the general well-being of the horse that has created more controversy than that of shoeing. Horseshoes are like religion. Everyone has an opinion on the subject – and many of them are mistaken. Every smith thinks he can shoe a horse better than any other farrier, and knows more than anyone else how it ought to be done. Yet horses are lamed and crippled daily by the bad shoeing of careless and ignorant farriers. So how do you protect your horse?

**Recipes for Disaster.** If we agree to have an open mind, and to use shoes as and when needed, what are the dangers to our valuable horses? There are three classic recipes for such a Long Rider disaster.

First, you ride into a country and are unable to locate horse shoes at any price because they do not exist in that culture. Not being able to find a horseshoe is nothing compared to the second problem, that of locating a competent farrier. Unlike the lack of horseshoes, this dilemma is not restricted to out of the way nations. There is a final common problem. You ride into a country that is equipped with horse shoes and has farriers, only to discover there is no one ready and willing to assist you.

Therein lies an extreme danger to a Long Rider's road horse. One of the major challenges encountered by today's equestrian travellers is the time, and luck, involved in finding a qualified professional farrier. Even if you locate a farrier, you should never be misled into thinking that the hard-won miles under your saddle will protect your horse's hoof from a knife-wielding knave. One equestrian traveller had ridden five thousand miles across the United States, when a so-called farrier cut his horses' feet so savagely the journey teetered on the edge of disaster. Even though there are thousands of extremely competent farriers in that country, in theory America would let an unlicensed monkey hammer a shoe on a horse, as there are no legal requirements prohibiting an ape from calling himself a horseshoer. This lack of official care stands in sharp contrast to Great Britain's Farriers Registration Act, which states that shoeing may only be undertaken by registered farriers who have completed an extensive course of training and then passed rigorous examinations. Likewise, France also insists that farriers, and their apprentices, are tested, licensed and insured. The horse world is populated by lying horse sellers and toxic trainers, but they quail in comparison to that trickster, the bad farrier. Therefore, when your horse requires to be shod, suffer no fools to touch him.

**Following Your Orders.** An age-old problem has been when the farrier attempts to make the foot fit the shoe. After finding a shoe of the right approximate shape, a lazy farrier will whittle and rasp the hoof so as to accommodate the horseshoe. Having cut away everything he can without drawing blood, he heats the shoe until it is red hot and then applies it to the bottom of the hoof in a boiling state. Nails are produced and the affected foot is now hammered to the iron plate. A critic once wrote, "As to farriers, it is useless talking to them. He works on the assumption that he knows better what the horse's foot should be than the Creator of the animal does, for they are never satisfied until they have altered the natural foot into a form of their own, which they think the right one."

While protecting the hoof is a noble aim, altering it to suit the farrier's fancy is counterproductive. Bad farriers are encased in selfishness, ignorance and prejudice. The health of the horse and the safety of the journey depend on you never allowing yourself to be bullied into silence by a farrier. If you are dealing with a licensed professional then you may assume there is a degree of scientific knowledge in evidence. However, if you are forced by circumstances to employ a backwoods blacksmith, you must never presume that though the farrier can observe the outside of the foot, he has any knowledge of its interior anatomy. Regardless of how educated he may be, when you take your horses to any farrier, in any land, make him follow your directions to the letter. If you suspect, for any reason, that your animal is being injured, order the operation to be halted at once. Better one poorly shod foot than four lame hooves.

**Cultural Problems.** It could be worse. In certain parts of the world the treatment afforded to horses in need of shoes involves a shocking degree of ruthless efficiency. Kazakhs, for example, routinely throw a horse to the ground, tie all four feet tightly together and then roll the animal onto its back. While several men keep the animal from struggling, the hooves are quickly cut and shoes nailed into place as fast as possible. Further east, the Chinese developed a method which is still in use. It involves placing the horse inside a strong wooden frame which has been driven deep into the ground. Once the horse has been pinned inside this chute, he is lashed securely in place. With the horse effectively restrained inside this wooden straightjacket, a farrier then sets to work.

**Do It Yourself.** Of course there is an alternative to tying your road horse between Chinese posts or letting an unlicensed hack hurt your horse. You can learn how to shoe your own horse. Because of the time, study and money involved, this isn't an option which many Long Riders pursue. But there have been some resounding success stories. Like any type of specialized equestrian knowledge, learning how to care for your horse's hooves is more complex than you might first believe.

**Heavy Shoes.** Regardless of who nails them on, there is a major drawback to horseshoes: weight. This may influence your trip in two different ways. The obvious issue is that an average horse shoe weighs from 1¾ to 2¼ pounds (0.8 to 1 kilo). So the idea of carrying the dead weight represented by extra horse shoes, nails and the tools required putting them on flies in the face of travelling light. This is especially true when you recall that it's not the kilometres which injure your horse, it's the kilograms.

But, though they provide protection, the shoes also deplete the horse's strength in a surprising second way. Medieval Islamic texts warned that one pound on the foot of the horse was akin to placing eight pounds on his back. The modern French Long Rider, Jean-François Ballereau, revised this formula in the 1990s, warning that a one kilo horseshoe drained as much energy from the road horse as seven kilos of dead weight. Therefore, it is critically important that you use the strongest, lightest shoes available, as an ounce on the foot equals about half a pound on the back.

Because they carry the majority of the weight, the front feet suffer the most abuse from rocky ground, so one alternative is to only shoe the front hooves when trouble arises. Many equestrian cultures, and Long Riders, have used this method with good results. In stark contrast, no culture only shoes the back feet.

Another point to be aware of is that some cultures prefer horse shoes which incorporate a large metal clip which is fitted deep into the front of the hoof. In theory this clip acts as a giant horse shoe nail, clamping the shoe firmly to the foot. Yet the hoof has to be cut back in order to fit the clip. This severely weakens the hoof wall. Furthermore, the clip adds weight to an already heavy shoe. Clips may be favoured by farriers but are seldom needed by Long Riders.

**No Hoof – No Journey.** In a world which is all too often obsessed with a horse's pretty appearance, the humble hoof is often overlooked. Yet hard hooves made history and you need them too if your journey is to succeed. The horse's hoof is akin to your fingernail, in that it grows continuously. This growth in turn demands that we provide adequate care for the horse's feet. So when do you do you shoe?

**When to Shoe.** Settled people determine when to shoe their horses by the calendar. The usual custom is to have the horse reshod every four to eight weeks, depending on the growth of the hooves and the wear on the shoe. But during the same eight-week time span that the pasture pet is grazing quietly, a Long Rider's road horse will encounter a host of challenges. This is why Long Riders learn to anticipate when their horses will need shoes and where to find them. Once you learn to estimate where and when you will need shoes, you can arrange for a farrier to be awaiting your arrival.

What you must never do is delay an appointment with the farrier. Don't procrastinate on this vital point of horse health or expect to find help miraculously awaiting you up the road.

**Long Rider Horse Shoeing.** It is critically important that before your departure your horse's hooves have been properly trimmed and the shoes fitted precisely. This is not a job that can be delayed, as a newly-shod horse may have tender feet. This is especially true if one of the nails has pricked him. Riding a sore-footed horse is irresponsible. Setting off on a journey with one is even worse. To ensure that his feet are in good condition, have your horse shod several days before you set off.

Regardless of how many horses you have, your morning begins with a careful examination of each and every hoof. Using a hoof pick and brush, look for stones, remove any mud, make sure the frog is clean and check for any signs of thrush. When the hoof is clean, confirm that the nails are tight and the shoe is snug.

If a shoe becomes loose during the day's journey, you will have to stop and remove it with care. Even if one or two nails have fallen out, simply pulling the shoe off with the remaining nails still in place may cause the nails to tear holes in the hoof wall as they are withdrawn. These large holes in the hoof wall will thereafter not hold a new nail very securely. When you have to remove a loose shoe, you must first loosen the ends of the nails and then carefully remove the nails so as not to damage the wall of the hoof. When drawing out the nails, check them separately to make sure there is no sign of blood or moisture on them.

Because the hoof is always growing, when the time comes to trim the horse's hooves, remember that many farriers blunder greatly by wielding their knives with happy abandon. You must ensure that the shoe fits the hoof. Never allow the farrier to cut the hoof to fit the shoe.

A horse's hoof is akin to a thick bamboo, in that its chief strength lies in the tough outer covering which protects the sensitive parts inside. Allowing a farrier to severely rasp off the outer wall of the hoof is as wise as removing the lids from the eyes. Likewise damage occurs if the bottom of the hoof is cut too severely. The ill-advised farrier who subtracts this part of the hoof is like a carpenter who cuts off the bottom of a post, which in turn weakens the pillar in the most essential way at the place where the greatest strength is required. Always keep trimming and rasping to the hoof wall to a minimum.

Likewise, don't allow the farrier to trim the frog severely. When horses walk, they do so from the heel to the toe, not from the toe to the heel. As they are walking the triangular-shaped frog comes into contact with the ground. This critically important portion of the hoof is designed to prevent slipping and concussion. Plus, unlike the insensitive hoof wall, the frog has nerves and can cause pain. Therefore the frog should not be touched if it is sound and firm. If it is ragged, then allow the edges to be lightly trimmed, otherwise the drawing knife should not be used. Neither should the sole of the hoof be interfered with except to remove the horn that has grown since the last shoeing. This should be done with a rasp, never with a drawing knife.

There are two types of shoeing, hot shoeing and cold shoeing. The latter involves nailing a shoe of the approximate size and shape onto the horse's hoof. Hot shoeing involves heating the shoe in a forge, then hammering it to fit the horse's hoof as closely as possible. Both require a degree of skill, with hot shoeing being practised in the Occident far more than in the Orient,

The construction of the horseshoes is also of importance. If the horse's hooves need trimming, but the shoes are still road worthy, then have them nailed back into place. Steel shoes are best, if they are obtainable.

**Making Shoes Last.** Don't think that just because you've managed to get your horse shod your worries are over. Harsh surfaces, hot roads, jagged gravel and ruthless rocks are all waiting to destroy your horse's hooves. This is a problem which has no geographic restrictions. Luckily Long Riders discovered a way to save their horse's hooves. They had a farrier place borium on the bottom of the horseshoes. Borium is a generic name for tungsten carbide crystals which. when embedded in a carrier material, provides a protective hard wearing shield to steel horse-shoes. This material is so strong that after Jean-Claude Cazade placed it under his stallion's shoes, the horse travelled 6,000 kilometres with only three changes of shoes. Another Long Rider, Robert Seney, rode his horse 3,000 miles across the United States using only one set of borium equipped horse shoes.

**No Loose Shoes.** Horseback travellers should avoid loose shoes at all costs. A loose shoe is dangerous. It is easily snagged off the hoof and very often takes part of the hoof with it. Unfortunately, loose shoes are all too common, especially for horses travelling on a daily basis on pavement. The tremendous repetitive impact will work the shoe loose in no time. The trick to avoiding loose shoes is finishing the nails properly. Most farriers will drive a nail into the hoof wall and then wring off the nail by using the hammer claws to twist off the sharp end of the nail close to the hoof wall. Do not do this. Instead, bend the nail over against the hoof wall and cut it off with nail cutters. Leave 1/8" of the nail projecting from the hoof wall. When all the nails are done in this fashion, they are then seated using a 'clinching block' or any other piece of flat metal. Carefully file away any burrs under the nail stubs, do not create a groove in the hoof wall or file away any of the nail, as this will cause weakening. The nail stubs are then softly hammered flat against the hoof wall, and the job is done (see diagrams below). Turning the clinches in this fashion (as opposed to cutting the nail stubs short and then using alligator clinchers) will not cause tearing in the hoof wall, and they will last much longer. There is no need to smooth the clinches with a file because this will occur naturally in a couple days. Long Riders using this method have had shoes stay tight for many months.

| Bend nail over | Cut nail leaving 1/8th inch and seat | Gently, bend over nail stub |
|---|---|---|
| | | |

**Boots.** There is a third option. You can use horse boots. As history proves, man has been strapping, tying, lashing and gluing various types of shoes, sandals, socks and boots on the bottom of hooves for countless centuries. This concept has always had its proponents and critics, with Long Riders once again having played a historically significant role in this field of equestrian hoof care.

One of the most spectacular equestrian journeys used rubber boots. During their historic 30,500 kilometre (19,000 mile) ride from the tip of Patagonia to the top of Alaska, Russian Long Rider Vladimir Fissenko and his companion, North American Long Rider Louis Bruhnke, used Easyboots with great success.

If you do decide to use boots while travelling, you must confirm that the boots are a proper size and fit for your horse's hooves. Once they have arrived, begin by having your horse's hooves properly trimmed, as a long hoof may affect the boot's fit. When his hooves have been prepared, tie your horse up safely and put the boots on carefully. If he has never worn boots before, walk the horse slowly, giving him time to adjust to the large objects on his feet. Once he has walked in a straight line, circle him slowly, being careful to watch for any sign that the boots may be slipping. Trot him and while you're running alongside listen to ensure that his footfalls sound even. While you're testing him, keep a careful eye for any signs of imbalance or distress.

Once you're happy with the fit, take a short training ride close to home. Stay on level ground, all the while paying strict attention for any signs of rubbing where the top of the boot comes into contact with the horse's sensitive skin. When one traveller detected signs of galling along the horse's hoof, he screwed a piece of soft rubber hose along the top edge of the boot to provide extra padding. When you return to the barn, check the horse's hooves and legs carefully. If everything appears to be well, then mark the inside of each boot with which foot it fits. Before you depart, be sure you practise putting the boots on and removing them. Better to make adjustments at home than on the side of a strange road.

One drawback about boots is that they are known to slip in muddy terrain.

**Hints.** Try to use horses with the same size feet as this will allow you use the same shoes. If you are travelling with more than one horse, it will make life much easier if they have similar-sized feet.

Regardless of who does it, you or the shoer, when the time comes to put on new horseshoes, expect to lose at least one full day of travelling.

If your journey is extreme and you feel you should carry one spare shoe, then it is recommended that you carry a hind shoe. Not only will it normally fit either hind foot, it may be adjusted relatively easily to fit a front hoof as well, whereas it is more work to fit a front shoe to a hind hoof.

Because of their weight, many Long Riders won't carry a spare horse shoe. However a handful of extra tough horseshoe nails weighs very little and can help when you're in trouble.

Regardless if you're carrying spare nails or not, if you detect any hint of lameness in your horse, stop and examine him immediately. There may be a stone stuck between the wall of the hoof and the side of the frog. Should you notice nails sticking out from the bottom of the shoe, then you can pull them out, being careful not to damage the hoof wall. If this leaves the shoe loose, then remove it.

If you lose a hind shoe you can still ride at a gentle walk. But keep off the hard road as much as possible. The rule is that if your horse loses a front shoe, dismount and lead him, even if it means a ten-mile walk to the nearest farrier. The equine foreleg is vulnerable to strain, so don't tempt Providence.

# Chapter 37 - Documenting Your Horse

**Paper Problems.** The bureaucratic troubles faced by Long Riders have not disappeared. In fact it has become more difficult to take horses across international borders. Being armed with the proper paperwork for your horses is of vital importance.

The necessary documents fall into three main categories. Certain documents prove the horse belongs to you. Other documents validate the horse's identity. The last group of documents confirms that the animal is healthy, carrying no communicable diseases and can travel without infecting other horses.

Obviously, the required paperwork needed to establish these three legal and medical principles differs from one nation to another. Mongolia, for example, does not allow any foreign horses to be imported, nor will the government authorize that nation's horses to be removed by travellers. So straight away these sorts of unflinching rules can ruin your travel plans. You must investigate the legal and medical requirements of every state and nation you plan to travel through. Many countries maintain an agricultural department, which deals with such questions. Only after you have obtained official clearance can you safely set off.

**Just Say No.** Just because officials in one country say "Bon Voyage," that's not reason enough to believe trouble isn't waiting to ambush you up ahead. What an official tells you in one country may not be accepted by their superiors further down the road or across the border. Though they are often well meaning, local representatives such as consuls might not be aware of border restrictions, visa requirements or recently-passed equine health regulations, which are known to their more informed colleagues in the border, passport or veterinarian branches of the national government.

This assumes that the government officials though ill informed actually do want to help you. All too often government officers don't care how far you've ridden. To them, your grand journey is only confirmation of your eccentric nature and a strong sign that your judgment can't be trusted. The result is that the officials obsess over your horse's paperwork. Any deviation from the rules means they might get in trouble, which in turn could result in them losing their jobs. Your progress thereafter becomes connected to their career and financial well being. In such a case, mild annoyance turns into official suspicion, which results in personal fear and concludes with professional hostility.

That is why when a timid official is in doubt about how to handle you and your horses; the fastest and easiest thing for him to do is to simply say, "No."

**Misplaced Trust.** In this mechanized age horses normally show up at national borders either in a truck or aboard an airplane. Papers are glanced at, because the horses are traditionally classified as valuable athletes, cargo or meat. They are no longer transport. They are instead transported.

In stark contrast, when you ride up unexpectedly atop your horse, perhaps with a pack horse in tow, you immediately present a problem, an embarrassment, a departure from the usual quiet running of the government official's office and department. In the majority of cases, these bureaucrats have never had an opportunity to deal with an equestrian traveller before. Your unwelcome arrival means extra work, more forms to be filled in, rules to be reviewed, veterinarians to be consulted, and worst of all, perhaps, the unwelcome interference of their department chief.

You are, in other words, someone who they want to get rid of. One way to do that is to reassure you that all your paperwork is in order, then hurry you down the road with a foolish smile on your trusting face, all the while they know, or suspect, that some other unlucky government border guard or official further along the line will be the one who has to break the news that your trip has come to an end because some form is not completed properly.

That is why the first lesson about paperwork is to never trust what appears to be well-founded and even well-meaning advice given by government employees stationed in another country. Accept this local help, by all means, as a good place to start. However, in addition, you must obtain the most up to date information directly from high-ranking authorities operating from legitimate offices located in the capital of the nation you are entering! These are the people who can actually authorize your horse's entry into that country. Once they know you are on your way, if you encounter a problem at the border, they are the ones you can telephone to ask for help and advice. If you avoid this step, you imperil your journey.

**A Plethora of Problems.** To put this complicated situation into perspective, let's not forget some of the other types of legal challenges waiting to ambush your dreams.

**Unrealistic Time Period.** Because most horses are now transported by motor, nations offer medical papers which are only valid for a specified time period. For example, many medical documents are valid for ten to thirty days. Yet it is the rare Long Rider, and the brief trip, which can travel across an entire nation in less than thirty days.

**Antagonistic Attitude.** Some nations are now requiring that any foreign horse receive a medical examination every ten to thirty days. That's fine, if you've just flown your million-dollar show jumper in for the Olympics and plan to be back home at your mansion at the end of the week. But it doesn't work for a slow moving Long Rider, does it? The German government, for example, insists that this medical inspection must be done by a nationally recognized government veterinarian. This means you have to find such a vet, arrange for him to meet you at some as yet undetermined place, pay for his services and any required lab tests, and then make sure the paperwork is provided to the home office in time.

**Official Confusion.** Don't be surprised to learn that the government's right hand doesn't know what its left hand is doing. Customs agents have one set of requirements. Border guards will look in your saddlebags for terrorists and contraband. National agricultural officers are frightened of allowing in diseased animals. Who reviews all these rules to find out which apply to your situation? Who finds out what papers will open the border and allow you across the country? Often, you do.

**Sexual Prejudice.** Because many nations are paranoid about sexually transmitted equine diseases, if you thought trying to take a mare or gelding across an international border was hard, wait till you discover how much more difficult it is to ride your stallion through a foreign country.

**What You Need.** Even though we are entering a legal jungle, let us investigate what sort of documents you and your horse may need. Let's start with various ways governments want us to prove who is the horse and who he belongs to; the Equine Identification Documents

**Breed Documents.** Purebred horses registered in the record books of an international breed are provided with documents from that breed's headquarters. Along with a photo or accurately drawn identification, this document presents the animal's detailed physical description, as well as his exact markings, specific colour, height, size, age, sex and details about the forebears. The name and address of the horse's breeder are also provided.

**Microchips.** An increasingly popular method of identifying horses is to implant a microchip in their neck. This is a tiny microscopic silicone chip which, when read by a scanner, not only provides the horse's identity number but information about his owner and home address. Microchips are effective because they can not be readily detected by thieves. All horses residing and travelling in the European Union must be microchipped.

**United Kingdom Equine Passport.** Beginning in 2005 Great Britain passed a law requiring all equines to be issued with a passport. This document clearly identifies the animal, describes its age, and provides information about its owner and residence. The equine passport must be kept up to date and the equine cannot be sold or legally transported without this vital document. Do not attempt to purchase or travel on a horse in the United Kingdom unless the owner can provide the passport.

**American National Animal Identification System.** Following the success of the British equine passport system, the American government instituted the National Animal Identification System (NAIS). Though still a voluntary program, it allows state and federal authorities to identify and track stolen horses. Once we can prove the horse belongs to us, what happens next? That very much depends on where you go.

**Travel between Countries.** Travelling with horses between countries ranges from relatively easy to completely impossible. Some nations, such as Great Britain, Ireland and France are less restrictive as there is a tripartite agreement between the veterinary authorities in these countries. Any privately-owned horse must still have a valid passport and an export license before entering the other countries. Likewise riding between Canada and the United States is fairly routine though the countries only allow horses to enter and exit via certain specified border control posts. Because of political hostilities, countries such as India and Pakistan do not allow horse travellers to take their animals across these national borders. Travel in certain countries, such as Russia, is drastically reduced to ninety days because of the short nature of the tourist visas offered to Long Riders. Mongolia will not allow horses to enter or leave. Horses are no longer allowed to travel in Antarctica.

Though the documents and regulations involved in allowing horses to travel over international borders vary, each nation will require entry and exit papers for each animal. Veterinary certificates stating that the animal is in good health are required. Customs declarations, such as the ATA Carnet, are often required to prove you do not plan on selling your horses after you arrive. Transit permits issued by the Ministry of Agriculture are strongly suggested. You must ensure that all of these documents are in the relevant languages of the countries you plan to travel through.

**Travelling in the European Union.** There are twenty-seven member countries in the European Union. To ride between EU nations, your horse will require an equine passport, export license and health certifications. But be advised that border crossings may prove to be difficult because the majority of equines cross them inside some sort of motorized transport. Because these animals cross entire nations rapidly, many health certificates are only valid for a limited time, so plan your border crossing carefully.

Though Switzerland and Norway are part of mainland Europe, neither nation is a member of the European Union. If you attempt to cross these borders on horseback you are departing the EU, which may have unintended negative consequences. For example, if a horse from the European Union resides in a "third country" for more than thirty days, the animal is automatically classified as a "non-EU horse." Should this occur while you are travelling, EU veterinarians will require you to obtain new health certificates and be able to prove to the EU border authorities that your horse poses no medical threat. Here again, this sort of problem requires careful advance research and plenty of intelligent reconnaissance on your part.

Should you be returning with horses to the United Kingdom from non-EU countries, DEFRA must be contacted in advance. In addition to accurate health records and blood tests, such incoming horses, and all their equipment, must be accompanied by an ATA Carnet issued in the horse's country of origin.

After you return to your home, keep all your equestrian medical documents carefully preserved, as local authorities may question the medical condition of your horse later on. And what sort of documents might they be?

**Export Licence.** If you are taking your horse out of Great Britain, ferry transport companies will ask to see the export license issued by the British government. This document, which is issued by DEFRA, documents the value and details of the animal.

**ATA Carnet.** This document demonstrates to custom officials that you do not plan to sell your horse after you have entered their country. The carnet also serves as a financial guarantee which offsets the need for you to pay import and export taxes on your horse, when you enter and leave a country. The carnet is issued by the Chamber of Commerce in your native country. Though it may not be recognized by some countries formerly allied to the Soviet Union, it eliminates the need for you to provide a cash deposit to the custom authorities of the non-European Union country you are riding through.

**Transit permits.** Obtaining transit permits for road and pack horses is complicated because the Ministry of Agriculture may require you to declare your route, explain how long you plan to reside in the country, and list the places where you will be staying. Acquiring the transit permit may largely depend on whether you can arrange for someone sympathetic in the local government to assist you in completing the paperwork, etc.

**United Kingdom Route Plan.** If you plan to apply to DEFRA for a United Kingdom Health Certificate for your horse, that office will require you to provide details regarding your planned route, which roads you plan to travel on, the time needed for your journey, etc. This information is entered on a form which you send to the DEFRA office, along with the application for a United Kingdom Health Certificate. Upon receiving your route plan, the DEFRA office will stamp your route plan and return it with your UK Health Certificate. You must keep the UK route plan with you during your journey, remembering not surrender it to any foreign officials. If any questions arise, DEFRA may require the route plan for inspection six months after the conclusion of your journey.

**Medical Documents.** Make sure that all your veterinarian certificates of health are in the language of the issuing country and in the one of the country of destination. This document certifies that an accredited veterinarian has examined your horse and found it to free of any diseases and all of its inoculations are up to date. The health certificate must include an accurate description of the horse. His age, sex, colour, markings, registered name and breed identification number must also be provided. The vet may also note where you plan to travel with your horse. The health certificate may not be valid for more than thirty days in some American states and certain nations. Confirm this in advance and carefully check in advance to ensure what blood tests are required by each country.

**United Kingdom Health Certificate.** Though you will not need a government issued Health Certificate to transport your horse between England, Ireland and France, other countries will require this document. To obtain the health certificate, either you or your vet should apply to the DEFRA office, though the document will be delivered to your vet's office. After the certificate is on hand, have your horse's medical inspection completed no more than 48 hours prior to your departure from Great Britain. The ferry company will want to confirm that your animal's health certificate is in order, but you will be allowed to retain the document. Be sure to protect this important document when you are travelling. Prior to your return to Great Britain, you will need to have a second health certificate issued from your country of departure.

**Vaccination record.** Whether you are travelling across state lines or international borders, Long Riders must have a vaccination record which confirms the horse is in good health and that all of his inoculations are up to date. For example, it is essential to prove your horse is not infected with the highly contagious and deadly equine disease known as glanders. Likewise, your horse must be vaccinated against tetanus, and flu. Certain European countries, such as France, require you to take additional precautions against piroplasmosis.

Check how long the vaccination record is valid for in the countries or states you will be travelling though, as the length of validity changes from place to place and in America, from state to state. Also, try to stay current about equine health conditions while you are travelling.

Though going across national borders is tough, taking horses across American state lines can also be challenging. You must determine what each state's medical requirements are in advance, so having the vaccination record up to date is the first step towards medical success.

**Coggins Test.** Having a valid Coggins test, proving that your horses do not carry EIA, is an absolute requirement in many parts of the world. The Coggins test was devised to detect the presence of Equine Infectious Anaemia. If a horse is found to be infected with EIA, even if the animal demonstrates no clinical signs of illness, he is quarantined for life or euthanized. The Coggins test, which proves that your horse is not infected with EIA, must have been done prior to your departure. State and national requirements vary as to how long the Coggins test is valid. Regardless, you must be able to present a valid Coggins test when you arrive at stables, campgrounds or other public equestrian facilities. Because it often takes weeks to obtain the lab results proving a negative Coggins test, you must allow plenty of time to have this document completed prior to your departure. Certain American states, for example Washington and Oregon, maintain reciprocal agreements, while other states demand additional information, such as the horse's temperature being recorded on the document.

**Brand Documents.** Branding a horse is an old method designed to identify the horse as the property of a person, place or organization, i.e. the owner, his ranch, or the national army. Traditional branding was done by applying a heated iron against the horse's hide. The more modern method of freeze branding uses liquid nitrogen to create a permanent mark along the top of the neck. This identity number is then hidden under the horse's mane. This identifying mark on your horse's body is noted on the brand inspection card. In addition to describing the actual brand, the document may also list the horse's other identifying features such as age, sex, colour, breed, microchip number and markings.

Travelling with horses in the United States and Canada will require you to be familiar with the brand card and ensure that your horses have this important document, even if they do not actually have a brand. Many American states employ brand inspectors to confirm that horses are not being stolen. To deter theft, brand inspectors inspect any horse which has been sold, has crossed a state line, or has been transported more than seventy-five miles within the state. When a brand inspection takes place, the brand inspector physically inspects the horse and documents and then issues a brand clearance which authorizes the transportation of the animal.

State brand laws vary widely, so it is imperative that you confirm the brand laws where you will be riding. For example, in western South Dakota you, as the animal owner, must have proof of ownership and obtain a certification from a Livestock brand Inspector before you leave that area. Failure to have your animal inspected is a misdemeanour and horse owners will be charged. Before you begin your journey, you should contact the brand control board in each state and request details.

The brand card becomes critically important once you cross the Mississippi river and continue to ride west. American state authorities will require you to carry health certificates, a Coggins test and brand inspection papers. When a brand inspector checks your horse, he will draw the horse's distinguishing marks on an outline of a horse pictured on the brand card. Notations are also made about the horse's colour, markings, age and sex. The brand inspector also confirms proof of ownership and ensures that the horse's health certificate is valid. After paying the brand inspector a fee, he will issue you with an official brand card or certificate.

State laws require that every horse have its own brand card. Because brand cards are valid until the horse is sold, brand inspections are usually done once a year. Some states offer a lifetime brand inspection which is valid so long as you own the horse. It is your responsibility to determine what the requirements are before you make your journey. Brand inspections and brand cards become of increasing importance when you ride your horse across state lines. Any time you see signs asking for animal identification, be prepared to provide your brand card to the local inspector. The United States Department of Agriculture may provide you with the most up to date information about brand requirements in each state.

**Hints.** It is the bureaucrats, not the bandits, who are your biggest challenge. This is why it is imperative that well in advance of your departure, you obtain all of the equine identity and medical documents which every nation, or each state, will demand of you. One potential source of information is a professional horse transport company: carrying horses across borders on a daily basis means they have to be completely up to date with each country's health and documentary requirements. You may have to pay a fee for their knowledge, but it would be money very well spent.

# Travelling Health Record

Animal's Name and sex

Birth date and place

Previous Owner

Date purchased

Colour and Markings

Normal weight

Normal respiration (at rest)

Normal pulse (at rest)

Inoculations (dates and vaccinations used)

Coggins Test (dates)

Travelling from

Travelling to

Statement of condition

Approval for further travel

Name, address and phone number of inspecting Veterinarian

# Section Three - The Equipment

## Chapter 39 - The Equipment - No more, No less

When it comes to equestrian travel, many original truths remain unchanged. One of the most important is how an equestrian traveller deals with the issue of equipment.

**Liberty and Luggage.** A sense of liberty comes when you swing into the saddle. To some degree you are freed because your world is now confined to what is stored in your saddlebags and on your pack saddle. One can be self-contained without having to be a Spartan but there are risks involved. If our journey is to be a success, not a button should be missing. Yet how do we achieve this freedom if we are burdened with excess belongings?

**Killer Kilograms.** When the English army invaded Abyssinia in 1867 they took 20,000 pack animals.

Long Riders can't count on such an extensive support system. They have enshrined an equestrian principle that is known, understood, and followed by all great equestrian travellers.

It is absolutely essential that the burden put on to the back of the road horse should be reduced by all possible means. The more you lighten the horse's load, the less liable he is to develop a sore back or give way to fatigue.

**Disregarding Comfort.** Weight is the greatest enemy of the road horse. To offset this danger, Long Riders have learned to leave out every luxury. When Howard Wooldridge rode "ocean to ocean" across the United States, he kept the weight of his personal possessions in his pommel and saddle bags down to 7.75 kilos (17 pounds). His list of equipment and possessions included such essentials as an extra pair of socks, a light-weight sleeping bag and a one-person tent. Carry only what is indispensable!

**Long Rider Lessons.** Learning how to pack your gear is one of the secrets of successful equestrian travel. This is not a new concept. Cavalry soldiers in the early twentieth century had their possessions restricted so as to provide the horse with as much relief as possible. The average load was 6 pounds 14 ¾ ounces in front of the saddle in the pommel bags and 12 pounds 13 ½ ounces behind the saddle in the saddle bags. The same rule applies today. To prevent pressure on the horse's kidneys and offset any chafing and friction on the hips, place as much weight as possible forward on the horse's shoulders and keep any weight behind the saddle as light as possible! Failing either of these, you will fatigue or chafe the horse.

**Tough and Light.** Equestrian travel is like mountain climbing. We don't use a lot of equipment but our lives depend on what we choose. When you're trying to cover miles, not influence a show judge, your goal should always be function not beauty. It is a safe rule to have everything three times as durable as you think necessary. Also, choose bright colours so as to make it easier not to forget anything when you're packing in the dim morning light.

**Buy the Best.** Every expedition has a budget but you must never succumb to the temptation to purchase second-rate equipment. Your horse's welfare always takes precedence over your bank book.

**Cultural Problems.** Don't take anyone's word that you can arrive in a distant country and find quality, affordable equestrian equipment. Long Riders have learned to their dismay that what passes as "good" gear locally would be considered horse killing junk back home. Badly fitting riding and pack saddles will injure your horses and ruin your journey, so ensure that you make the right choice in advance. Even if you have to pay customs duty to import your equipment, relying on poorly made local gear can be a painful experience for both you and your animals.

## Chapter 40 - Riding Saddles

Despite its fundamental significance, the purpose and mechanics of the riding saddle are often misunderstood. Before setting off, you need to be sure that what you place on your horse's back isn't going to undermine your chances of geographic success.

**An Understated Masterpiece.** The basic concept of the saddle has not altered for more than a thousand years. This is because the primary needs of today's horse and rider are no different than that of their ancestors. From a human perspective, the saddle has two main purposes. First, it provides the rider with a secure seat which allows him to offset the pull of gravity and move in rhythm with the speed provided by his mount. The saddle also provides the rider with stirrups. These two platforms enable him to remain in balance over the horse's centre of gravity. It also provides a vital service to the horse by evenly spreading the rider's weight over as large an area of the horse's back as possible.

**A Common Theme.** Despite the many variations mankind has devised, classic saddles share certain traits. The saddle has two arches, one in the front and one behind the rider. The front arch forms the pommel, the rear the cantle. Owing to the shape of the horse's body, the strain on the front arch is greater than that on the rear. Both front and back arches rest upon and are secured to two bars placed parallel to each other. The arches ensure the spine is not pressed upon. The bars distribute the rider's weight along the horse's back. The arch and bar are the twin themes upon which all great saddles are made.

**The Trouble with Bareback.** Why even bother with a saddle? When a bareback rider sits on a horse, the majority of the human's weight bears directly down on a small space on either side of the equine spine. This places all of the human's weight, many pounds per square inch, on a small portion of the horse's back. That pressure can damage sensitive tissue, bruise the muscles, injure the spine and harm the horse's kidneys.

To reduce equine injuries the rider's weight needs to be spread over the maximum number of square inches on the horse's back. By not placing a saddle on your horse's back, you place every bit of your weight on two pin-pointed spots on his back. Even if your horse does not receive an external sore on his back, you are doing him no favours by placing your weight near his kidneys and atop his spine.

**Basic Principles.** For a Long Rider saddle to work it has to adhere to basic principles. It needs to be as simple as possible, as complicated gear may go wrong in a sudden emergency. It has to be built for weight distribution, covering the largest possible bearing surface over the horse's eighth to sixteenth ribs. It needs a high arch which will allow a free channel of air to flow along and cool the spine. A rough leather seat gives a strong grip.

**Weight of the Saddle.** Long Riders find themselves in a dilemma when the topic of saddle weight is raised. A light saddle may offer too small a weight-bearing surface, which will encourage saddle sores. On the other hand, you must avoid an excessively heavy saddle. The answer is that the saddle must be large enough to carry the Long Rider's equipment, strong enough to withstand the rigours of the journey and light enough to do the work.

**Fitting the Saddle.** Saddles are like shoes. One size does not fit all. There are six rules which should never be forgotten when attempting to determine if a saddle fits.

1 – The withers must not be pinched nor pressed upon.

2 – The spine must have no pressure forced upon it.

3 – The shoulder blades must have free and unrestricted movement.

4 – The loins are not intended to carry weight.

5 – The rider's weight must be placed upon the ribs through the muscles covering them.

6 – The weight must be evenly distributed over a surface which extends from the shoulders to the last rib.

**Comfort.** The saddle must not only provide you with a sense of security, it must also be comfortable enough to allow you to ride all day long through various types of obstacles. Because of its significance, do not hurry to purchase a saddle. Sit in various sizes and styles to determine what suits and fits you. The seat of a saddle varies in length from 13 to 17 inches (33-43 cm) and a common mistake to purchase a saddle which is too large.

**Potential Problems.** The problem with purchasing a saddle prior to your departure is that it is very unwise to begin a journey with a new or untested saddle. A saddle can inflict an agonizing injury without drawing blood. If you do not carefully test your saddle well in advance, you run the risk of ruining your horse.

**A Basic Consideration.** What we must not do is to allow romantic notions or cultural allegiance to overrule mechanics and safety. Regardless of what our forefathers rode, there may well be far better, and safer, options available to a modern Long Rider.

**English Saddles.** The English saddle has several drawbacks in terms of equestrian travel. Unlike western saddles, the English saddle lacks either the raised pommel or high cantle which was designed to keep the rider in his seat at all times. The English saddle does not have a large weight-bearing surface. Nor does its small saddletree spread the rider's weight over the maximum number of inches available along the horse's back. Because many modern English saddles further reduce their overall weight by severely constricting the size of the sidebars, this prohibits the load from being properly carried. Thus, the sidebars may not cover enough of the horse's body to reduce the pounds per square inch for proper support during an extended journey. Also of importance, the English saddle was not traditionally designed to carry extra weight or equipment because it lacks the dee rings to which saddle and pommel bags can be fastened. Another point to consider in terms of long-term comfort is that English saddles use stirrup leathers that may pinch the rider's legs. This isn't to say that English style saddles have not been successfully used on many equestrian journeys. They have. But only if they were either reworked or designed to carry saddlebags. Even then, they provide little in the way of rider security and may compromise the horse's health if the saddletree is too small.

**Australian Saddles.** The Australian stock saddle took the basic design of an English saddle and then incorporated many of the best concepts of the western saddle onto it. The result was a saddle which demonstrates the best of both parents. Like the English saddle, the Australian offspring is fairly light weight. Yet like the cowboy saddle, the Australian has enlarged the bearing surface as much as possible so as to distribute the rider's weight. In order not to lose his seat during an emergency, the Australians added two bucking rolls to the front of their saddles. These padded additions provided the rider with a greater sense of security. Finally, because they were living from the backs of their horses, the drovers ensured that strong dee rings were added to the saddletree, so as to enable them to carry their gear. This compromise of cultures produced one of the world's best all-around work saddles. Comfortable and practical, it spreads the rider's weight, protects the horse's back and carries both their gear.

**Cavalry Saddles.** Traditional cavalry saddles can be very good for the horse and excellent for Long Riders, as they are immensely strong and practically everlasting. They are also easy to repair in the field. The problem is that they are no longer being made there are very few originals still available and the survivors may have not withstood the test of time. Before you buy a cavalry saddle, inspect it carefully. Look for cracks, splits or signs of distortion in the wooden sidebars. Examine the stitching in the leather, the girth straps and the rigging very carefully, looking for signs of rot or excessive wear.

**McClellan Saddles.** Thanks to countless articles, books and films, the McClellan became permanently associated with the dashing American cavalrymen who rode out west. While this makes for great television, it doesn't translate into good equestrian travel. From a rider's point of view, the McClellan provides a very poor support system, as the open gap between the sidebars must be ridden with care. While this is a grave concern for a Long Rider, the most damaging feature connected to the McClellan is how it adversely affects the horse's body. The sidebars on the McClellan are short and do not flare outwards. This results in the front of the saddle interfering with the movement of the animal's forelegs. Plus, the rear of the saddletree often places pressure on the horse's loins, digging into its body when in motion. Because a McClellan saddle is capable of causing serious wounds to the horse's withers and loins, Long Riders are strongly advised to choose another saddle.

**Randonnee Saddles.** Having carefully studied the original cavalry saddle, a French saddler named Aimé Mohammed set out to create a new saddle based upon the concept of the McClellan. His remarkable creation, the Randonnee saddle, has been one of the most important developments in modern equestrian travel. Unlike the narrow McClellan, the wider arch of the Randonnee does not interfere with the horse's freedom of movement, nor does it inflict wounds to the withers. The original narrow sidebars which caused so much trouble on the McClellan saddle have been widened to greatly increase the load-bearing surface, have been padded with thick wool felt and then covered with high quality leather. Another improvement was the removal of the McClellan's notorious open seat. While this open gap provided plenty of air flow to the horse's spine, its sharp edges presented a continual hazard to riders. The Randonnee resolved this problem by covering the seat with thick leather. The Randonnee has metal dee rings in the front and rear to which bags can be easily attached. Each saddle, which weighs only ten pounds (4½ kilos), has a high pommel and cantle which gives the Long Rider a deep seat and creates an excellent sense of security. Having provided many Long Riders with a trouble-free trip, the Randonnee saddle is recommended for any equestrian journey.

**Western Saddles.** There are several things to keep in mind when considering a western saddle for travel. Because the western saddle was originally designed to aid cowboys working cattle, it had options which would be a handicap for a weight-obsessed Long Rider. For example, cowboys took pride in a heavily carved saddle. While attractive, it is far easier to clean and maintain a saddle if the leather is unadorned. Also, there is no need to have the rear girth found on many western saddles. This second girth was designed to keep the saddle in place if the front girth snapped during a stampede. This flank girth is irrelevant for a Long Rider and should be removed. Another favourite option of the old-time cowboy was the large square leather skirt. They weigh more and prevent evaporation of sweat. If choosing to ride a western saddle, it makes more sense for a Long Rider to opt for the smaller, rounded skirts preferred by the Nevada buckaroos. Finally, the saddle horn was designed to anchor a rope while roping cattle. As Long Riders aren't in the business of chasing cows, the saddle horn is irrelevant except as a handle for mounting. Contemporary western saddle makers have taken note of the needs of Long Riders. One such example, the Tucker Saddle Company, has an excellent record of making western style saddles that protect the horse and provide comfort to the rider.

**Gaucho Saddles.** While the cattle-based equestrian cultures of North and South America share many similar traits, the adaptability of their saddles to equestrian travel is not one of these. The reasons for this are of importance to a Long Rider. The cowboy saddle relies upon a saddletree which distributes the rider's weight, keeps pressure off the withers and protects the spine. The gaucho saddle does not provide these critically important protections. While it is certainly of historical importance, and if used properly on short rides will not harm horses, this saddle is not equipped to carry saddlebags, is overly complex and can cause tremendous wounds to a horse's back. It is not recommended for Long Riders.

**Foreign Saddles.** Long Rider history demonstrates that many other types of foreign saddles have been successfully used. The most famous example was the Russian saddle used by Cossack Long Rider Dmitri Peshkov who rode from Siberia to St. Petersburg. But there are distinct disadvantages to picking the wrong saddle. The first problem that may arise is that you may not be comfortable riding in a native saddle unless you were born to it. For example, the saddles traditionally used in Mongolia, Tibet and China require the rider to sit very high over the horse's centre of gravity. At the same time they use very short stirrups. These saddles require the rider to sit on the horse in a way which is uncomfortable to a westerner used to long stirrups and deep seat.

**Treeless Saddles.** Equine vertebrae are fragile and easily damaged. A treeless saddle encourages weight to be concentrated in small, specific points directly above the sensitive spine. Of equal importance is the fact that a treeless saddle applies immense pressure along the spinal column. This restricts blood flow and encourages injury. A saddletree allows a channel of cooling air to flow over the horse's spine. Treeless saddles lack the ability to create or maintain this channel. Proponents of the treeless saddle argue that it does not restrict the movement of the horse's shoulders, conveniently forgetting that it allows the majority of the rider's weight to bear directly down onto the sensitive withers. Another disadvantage is that the treeless saddle can shift while in motion. This encourages the rider to over-tighten the girth, so as to compensate for the lack of stability provided by a saddletree. For marketing purposes, treeless saddle advocates are quick to tout the rider's comfort. They neglect to explain that the rider's ease is gained at the expense of the horse's safety. These alarming discoveries were confirmed in 2008 when the Society of Master Saddlers launched a thorough comparison between treeless saddles and those which used a traditional saddletree. Their findings were conclusive. The treeless saddle exerted pressure on the spine, produced localized pressure on the horse's body, induced soreness and eventually led to tissue damage. The unsuitability of treeless saddles was discovered by several Long Riders, whose horses suffered saddle sores due to the lack of a weight-distributing saddletree. The extreme rigours encountered during the course of an extended equestrian journey require you to provide your road horse with every possible advantage, before and during the journey. Therefore it is most strongly advised not to use a treeless saddle.

**Sidesaddles.** The sidesaddle is one of the most dangerous and disadvantageous pieces of equestrian equipment ever created. Yet today the sidesaddle is once again being described as a "romantic" way to ride, all the while its advocates remain reluctant to discuss the deadly side-effects associated with locking a human body into place alongside the left side of a galloping horse. The drawbacks include many dangerous disadvantages to horse and rider. Concessions to fashion ensured that the riding skirts are impractical for travel. Additionally, the sidesaddle is difficult to mount alone. Traditionally, a man could mount alone. Yet it took two men to help one lady get onto her sidesaddle. It also handicaps the rider in another way: communications. Unlike male riders a sidesaddle rider can not apply the pressure of her leg to the right side of the horse, nor give her mount any signals with her thighs, knees, or heels. Even worse, in severe cases female riders could not drop their hands in order to turn or stop a runaway horse. Because of its bad fit, grooms were known to girth a sidesaddle up so tightly that the horse had trouble breathing. A rider's longing for historical accuracy should never take precedence over the horse's safety. Just as women no longer bind their feet in the name of beauty, likewise there is no need to return to the equestrian past by incorporating the dangerous sidesaddle into equestrian travel.

**Buy the Best.** Beware of a clever sales pitch when shopping for a saddle. Never believe a salesman who says that a saddle will adjust to your mount or that a particular saddle fits a "normal" horse. Ensuring that the saddle fits properly is one of your first concerns. Regardless of whatever style of saddle you decide upon, buy the best. Cheap saddles are a mistake because your life is at risk if they break at a critical moment. When it comes to how much you can spend on a riding saddle, cut economic corners somewhere else but never purchase a second-rate saddle.

# Chapter 41 - Horse Equipment

Few things have changed since our ancestors formalized the basic requirements of equestrian travel. Yet every item is worthy of careful consideration, for mistakes are costly when the road is long.

**Local Bargains.** Before we investigate each of the vital components needed by a Long Rider, let us remember that unlike a weekend trail rider the equipment required to withstand the rigours of equestrian travel must be the best you can find and afford. Do not be tempted to arrive in a foreign country and think that cheaper local equipment will suit your needs. Even if you are lucky enough to locate an item which you recognize, local standards may not match your needs. That is why it is critically important for a Long Rider to purchase and test the necessary equipment prior to departure.

**Saddle and Pommel Bags.** One of the worst mistakes an equestrian traveller can make is to overload the road horse! That is why a primary goal of this book is to alert travellers to the ill-advised idea of placing enormous saddle and cantle bags on the back of your riding animal. Nothing is more likely to contribute to this fundamental mistake than the oversized saddlebags sold by American companies.

By providing saddlebags the size of suitcases, the rider is encouraged to dispense with the pack horse and overload the road horse.

As if this weren't bad enough, the creators of these American steamer trunk style saddlebags also urge the rider to place an immense cantle bag behind the saddle. This vast duffel bag is lashed directly behind the saddle's cantle. Not only does this add an obscene amount of extra weight over the horse's kidneys, it creates a safety hazard as it is very difficult for the traveller to swing into or exit from the saddle. This represents a serious hazard if the Long Rider needs to rapidly dismount in an emergency.

There are rules for saddlebags, just as there are for every aspect of equestrian travel. A saddlebag should be kept small. Place the majority of the weight over the shoulders instead of the kidneys. In order to ensure a safe ride, the saddlebags must be evenly loaded. Because of the constant movement of travel, never place sharp, hard objects on the side of the saddlebag that touches the horse's flanks, as this may cause pain and injury. Saddlebags should be made from tough light-weight material, have compartments, be securely mounted and rain-proof. Desensitize your horse to the sound of Velcro straps opening on saddle or pommel bags. Finally, place a strip of reflective tape on the back of the saddlebags so traffic coming up from behind will see you.

**Saddle Pads and Blankets.** The saddle pad is deceptively simple, yet tremendously important. It evenly distributes the pressure of the saddle and the rider's weight over the horse's back. It diminishes shocks and reduces pressure points. Because it is breathable, it absorbs sweat, while allowing air to circulate and cool the horse's back. It should be large enough to allow at least two inches of pad to extend around the entire saddle. When fitting the saddle pad, it should rest up inside the gullet of the saddle, so as to allow a channel of cool air to flow along the horse's spine.

**Stirrups.** Many people underestimate the importance of the stirrup, which accomplishes two fundamental tasks. It allows the rider to safely mount and provides a platform which helps him to maintain his balance during the ride. A lightweight metal stirrup swings away and is hard to catch if your foot slips loose. Long Rider stirrups should be heavy enough to make them easy to catch when the horse is in motion. The stirrups should also be wide enough to accommodate your riding boot. Finally, padded stirrups ease the pain in your knees which occurs after an extremely long day in the saddle.

**Girths.** While it is commonly known that saddles can injure a horse's back, the girth can also inflict wounds on your road and pack horses. Girth galls are caused by friction. Like the saddle pad, the girth should be non-abrasive, so as to reduce the chance of chafing while in motion. It should be soft, supple and dissipate heat. It must be easy to clean and quick to dry. Many Long Riders prefer mohair string girths, as they fulfil all these requirements. Though neoprene girths are easy to clean, they become hot, retain heat and induce sweating. Because of the rigours normally encountered during a journey, many horses lose weight while travelling. If your girth is too long, it becomes hard to adjust it properly. That is why many Long Riders use a 28" mohair girth, as it is a size which provides more adjustment.

**Breastplate and Crupper.** The breastplate and crupper are not usually required except when travelling in mountainous country, so many Long Riders dispense with the extra weight. However, in rugged terrain the breastplate and crupper are particularly useful, as the breastplate prevents the saddle from slipping back when travelling uphill, while the crupper keeps the saddle from sliding forward when going down steep trails.

The problem with both pieces of equipment is that they must not be too tight. There is nothing more distressing for a horse than to be harnessed up with either a riding or pack saddle held rigidly in place. An unyielding breastplate can quickly cause abrasions between the forelegs and cause saddle sores over the withers. A too-tight crupper will rub the root of the horse's tail, causing a nasty sore which resembles a rope burn. This type of wound is hard to heal and painful. For these reasons, the breastplate and crupper should be adjusted so that the saddle can move freely a few inches forward and back. Both the crupper and breastplate must be kept meticulously clean.

Should a horse make a false step, he uses his head to maintain his balance, much like a human uses his arms. For this reason a standing or running martingale should never be used on road or pack horses, for it affects the animal's ability to recover his balance.

**Bridles and Bits.** It is thanks to the bit and bridle that horse and human can achieve a subtlety of movement without the use of spoken language. The rider transmits his wishes via the reins. This in turn alerts the horse, via the pressure of the bit, to the needed change in speed or direction. The result is a silent symbiotic progress of two species. Bits have been successfully used since Kikkuli, the first recorded horse trainer, recommended them 3500 years ago. Yet there is a growing fashion in America and England to denounce all bits as barbaric. Advocates of what is called the bitless bridle ignore the fact that like any tool, bits can be misused. Nor is this modern version of the hackamore not without its faults too. When Irish Long Rider Caitriona Oleary tested a bitless bridle in 2011, she ran into trouble.

"The bridle worked great in the school and made it possible to perform very precise and smooth transitions and my first two canters in the field were nice and controlled. Then the horse realised that if she arched her head a certain way she could jimmy that little noseband up and she bolted across a field, round a corner and almost into a wire fence with me. I only stopped with the help of a man walking his dog and then dismounted and walked back to get a bridle with a strong bit."

Caitriona later realised that the bitless bridle had not been properly adjusted; as a result she lost control of the horse. "I had put the noseband too high, going for the look of a normal bridle. It only works if it's in a lower position where the nose is more sensitive."

Tragically, Caitriona died in 2012 after suffering fatal injuries during a riding accident in England. The runaway horse had been wearing a bitless bridle. However the coroner's inquest was not able to determine if this piece of equipment had malfunctioned or contributed to the cause of the accident.

What Caitriona sought, she said, was a happier horse. That is an admirable goal, one which Long Riders throughout the centuries have tried to obtain. Whether you go bitted or bitless is beside the point. Any equestrian implement can be cruel if misused. A Long Rider and a road horse have separate but equal needs. Horses do not respond well to force. In an ideal situation they seek emotional stability and physical comfort. Ask and they will give. But you cannot cross a continent on a horse who won't obey a simple command to stop or turn!

Likewise, a Long Rider's life is placed on trust when he swings into the saddle. Unlike ring riders, equestrian explorers often find themselves facing life-threatening challenges. When such an event occurs, the rider must be able to make an instant decision, so as to protect the life of both parties.

The issue, therefore, is how best to achieve this delicate balance of comfort for the horse and safety for the rider.

There are as many bits and bridles as there are equestrian cultures. Your challenge is to carefully judge what works best for you and your horse. What you must not do is fall prey to a cultural fad or condone cruelty. A traditional alternative to the bit is the hackamore. This system ignores the horse's mouth, preferring to use a noseband which is adjusted to lie just above the nostrils where the bone is thin and soft. A horse is very sensitive there, so responds well to commands. A hackamore is also good for travel because it allows the horse to graze and drink more freely.

**Halters and Lead Ropes.** The halter is one of those everyday items which is in constant use but seldom receives adequate consideration. It must be easy to put on, strong, flexible, simple to clean and fit well. Because it is seldom removed during the journey, it must not rub the horse or have abrasive parts which might injure him. Like bridles, halters were originally made from leather but this material is heavy and hard to maintain. That is why many modern halters are now constructed from flat sturdy nylon fitted with a steel ring and tongue in the buckle. Nylon halters can also be easily repaired.

Even though cotton rope is gentle on the hands, a horse can quickly damage it by dragging it on the ground, stepping on it, or rubbing it against rough surfaces. Marine grade synthetic rope is stronger, more durable and just as flexible as cotton. Climbing rope works well for equestrian travellers, many of whom choose a ½ inch diameter as it is easy to handle and tie. A lead rope should be eleven feet long. Many are equipped with a strong metal snap clip on the end, which allows you to instantly detach the rope from the horse in case of an emergency.

**Feedbag and Water Bucket.** Not only does feeding grain keep your animals in top condition, the sound of the grain rattling in the feedbag acts like a magnet and brings a horse running. Yet feed bags can be difficult and dangerous. Because of the mixture of saliva and grain, the bag must be washed frequently, otherwise it will ferment. A feedbag can also accidentally kill a horse. This occurs when the horse is done feeding and tries to drink. If the feedbag fills with water, the horse may drown. For this reason, a feedbag must have holes placed along the edge to allow water to flow out. The best option is the cavalry style mesh feed bag which is constructed from durable vinyl-coated mesh and comes with adjustable nylon straps. Not only does this eliminate the danger of drowning, the bag is constructed in such a way that the horse does not have to toss his head to reach the grain, which slides to the bottom of the bag and is in easy reach. The excellent style feedbag eliminates spills while remaining breathable.

Another item which is often overlooked is a collapsible bucket.

*The French have improved on this system by creating a collapsible bucket that cannot be tipped over by a thirsty horse.*

**Bells.** Bells are of tremendous practical value to a Long Rider. During the day bells provide a musical complement to your horse's gait. They transmit a reassuring message to passers-by that you have nothing to hide. From a practical point of view, bells alert pedestrians to move aside. Many riders who travel through heavily-infested bear country know that the sharp peal of a loud bell will help prevent a surprise meeting. This is especially important if you are travelling downwind, and a bear or another animal cannot smell your approach.

While bells are helpful during the day, they are even more essential at night. Chances are that some time during your journey your horses will take the opportunity to escape. For this reason, you should always bell your horses at night. The rhythmic sound of the bells allows you to hear the animals grazing peacefully during the night. Any sudden movement on their part will alert you to trouble. The soft sound of the bells during the night provides a comforting confirmation that your horses are grazing close by. That sound induces a sense of calm in you and the horses. You will learn that you can hear the bells even in your sleep.

If things go wrong, the sound of the bells will tell you what direction the horses are headed. Because a good bell can be heard for a great distance, it will also help you track the animals if they have been stolen. Plus, after a horse runs away, he may rest, or intentionally stand still so as to avoid detection. A bell will alert you to his presence in the dark. If you strap a bell around your horse's neck at night, make sure the strap is just tight enough so that it cannot get caught while he is grazing, or slip over his head. You should be sure to train your horse to wear his bells prior to your departure.

**Grooming equipment.** Though it is important to reduce weight whenever possible, keeping your horse clean is a priority. A curry comb, a brush and a strong hoof pick are necessities. Do not venture overseas without confirming that these items are available locally.

**Equine First Aid Kit.** Emergencies happen fast and are frightening. Make sure that you have bandages, antiseptic spray, an anti-inflammatory gel, a course of antibiotics if available, and a broad spectrum de-wormer.

**Caring for the Tack.** Neglected gear will always be a source of trouble and may well cause injury to you or your horse. Prior to your departure, the stitching on every piece of equipment should be carefully examined to ensure that no portion is giving way. One of your daily tasks will be to keep your tack as clean and dry as possible. Many Long Riders carry a small cleaning and repair kit with saddle soap, sponge, waxed thread, an awl, duct tape and a spare buckle.

# Chapter 42 - Pack Saddle

At the dawning of the 21st century an unreported revolution changed one of the fundamental aspects of equestrian travel. This occurred when Long Riders around the world began using the Canadian adjustable pack saddle made by Custom Pack Rigging.

*Until the advent of this remarkable piece of equipment, pack horses were routinely injured by outdated, ineffective pack saddles, such as this primitive pack saddle used in Guatemala.*

The sidebars of the Canadian pack saddle, which are made of unbreakable ABS plastic, are textured on the underside to grip the saddle pad and come in two shapes. One is flatter so as to fit mules, while a second type is designed to fit horses. Thanks to its adjustable nature, this pack saddle may be changed from one animal to another without refitting. The result is that the Canadian pack saddle can fit any pack animal ranging from a tiny Shetland pony to a massive two-humped Bactrian camel. This adjustability is important even if you use the same pack animal during the length of your trip, because it also allows you to alter the pack saddle to fit your animal's back as it changes shape during the journey. Able to withstand hardships, functioning in all climates, capable of fitting every type of pack animal, having nearly eliminated saddle sores, requiring no special training and affordable, this pack saddle has eliminated the need to use previous systems.

*The Canadian pack saddle is equipped with a wide mohair string girth that is attached to the saddle by nylon webbing, a combination that allows for precise adjustment of the girth.*

**Panniers.** The hard plastic panniers are curved to fit alongside the pack animal's rib cage. Each pannier is equipped with straps which allow it to be easily hung on each side of the pack horse. Unlike traditional pack saddles, this simplified system does not require a traveller to be an expert in handling lash ropes or tying complicated knots. The result is a pack saddle which can be easily loaded by one person. Another benefit is that when you need to ship your gear this system comes apart and can be compressed into a very tight package.

Available in brown, green or florescent orange, the latter colour works best for Long Riders because it can be seen easily by drivers when circumstances force you to travel along a busy road. It is also a very good idea to place reflective tape on both ends of the pannier to increase your visibility. Some panniers can be rigged into a table and one pannier always makes a handy stool in camp. If you are travelling through bear country, then you will need to obtain special panniers which are equipped with tops that cannot be dislodged by hungry prowlers.

**Pack Saddle Pads.** Because of the dead weight suspended from a pack saddle, great care must be taken when choosing a saddle pad. To ensure adequate protection against pressure points, a pack saddle pad must be bigger and thicker than a normal riding pad. A typical pack saddle pad is at least 30" x 40" (75 x 100 cm). Custom Pack Rigging offers an excellent selection of top-quality saddle pads. Some are constructed of soft, thick felt, which is lined on the top with smooth leather. These pack saddle pads are hard-wearing, soft, cool, and easily washed. Always avoid placing any type of abrasive material, such as canvas, against the pack horse's back and make sure the pack saddle pad is always kept scrupulously clean.

# Chapter 43 - Long Rider Equipment

A valuable Long Rider rule is "The more you know, the less you need." But how do we determine what we need? Since the dawn of that long ago day when the first human swung onto a horse and rode towards the distant horizon, equestrian travellers have needed a good reason for everything they wear. The goal of Long Riders is to be practical, not picturesque. The clothing worn by a Long Rider depends on the journey, the season, and the countries being ridden through. Because these factors vary, it is impossible to be dogmatic or specific. Yet some basic elements of equestrian travel have remained constant across the ages. Our duty then is to decipher what works when worn in the saddle.

**At Ease.** It has been said that there is no such thing as bad weather, only bad clothes. Because equestrian travellers have successfully ridden in every type of clime, ranging from minus 50 degrees in Siberia to well over the 100 mark in the Sahara, records indicate that proper clothing contributes to a traveller's success. When considering what to wear, everything should be avoided that may cause discomfort on horseback. Your sleeves should never be too tight or the easy movement which is so necessary to the arms when riding will be impeded. You should avoid wearing anything that may flutter in the breeze, for no sooner will your horse change from a quiet walk into a brisk trot than your clothing will begin flapping up and down.

**Culture or Comfort.** Though comfort is a necessity, what about the local culture? No matter where you find him, man is most comfortable in the clothes he wore by birth and tradition. Yet do we wear what pleases us or others? Are there repercussions if we place comfort over culture? Can we afford to disregard the animosity which our clothes might inadvertently inspire? Throughout history Long Riders have recognized the need to honour local tradition and harmonize with their surroundings.

**Shirts and Trousers.** As globalization advances Long Riders are aided by the fact that humans are increasingly donning more standardized clothing. Yet riding clothes must first and foremost be comfortable and functional. If you choose to wear western style jeans make sure they are not too tight. Long sleeved shirts can be rolled up in hot weather and provide additional protection in the cold. Many Long Riders have discovered that clothes made for mountain climbers offer waterproof protection and breathable comfort to horse travellers too. Some new clothes are created from cloth which has a built-in bug repellent. Everything you wear while travelling must be easy to wash.

**Vest.** The Long Rider has three places to carry gear – on his person, the riding horse and the pack horse. The best way to carry your personal essentials is to place them in a multi-pocket waistcoat or vest. These pockets can carry the small, lightweight items you may need quickly or in an emergency. The Kakadu Company in Australia makes a durable oilskin vest which has more than a dozen pockets.

Because you could accidentally forget your vest, or it might be stolen, you should always carry your most valuable documents in a small thin bag which you keep hidden under your shirt. This bag replaces the need for a traditional wallet, which might fall out while riding or create a large lump between you and the saddle. One aspect of clothing which should not be overlooked is safety. Because of the danger of heavy traffic, many Long Riders now wear reflective vests.

**Boots.** A fundamental rule was expressed by the U.S. cavalry, whose standard marching drill was "walk a mile, ride a mile." Road horse and Long Rider both benefit when you walk, as the animal receives a rest from carrying your weight and you do not become stiff from staying in the saddle too long. For this reason, Long Rider's boots must be comfortable enough to ride, hike and run in. Always break in your boots prior to departure.

**Hats.** Hats are critically important because they help moderate your body temperature. The tall crown provides insulation. The wide brim protects your face. A light-coloured hat will keep you cool. But a black hat retains heat and can be twenty degrees hotter than a white hat which reflects the sun. A Long Rider's hat should be equipped with a stampede string. This is a string that encircles the crown of the hat  Two small holes punched in the brim of the hat allow the string to hang down alongside either side of the rider's face. A small button can be slid up the two strings. This keeps the hat snug on the rider's head and ensures that it is not blown off in a wind or lost while galloping.

Though not strictly a hat, history has demonstrated the amazing versatility gained by wearing a turban. Not only does a turban allow you to merge into some local populations, it works well when riding through the desert as it provides excellent protection from sun and wind. Plus, by wrapping the tail of the turban around the lower part of your face, you retain moisture and protect yourself from damaging sunburn. Unlike a hat, a turban has many other uses. It can be unwound and used to lower a bucket into a deep well.

**Helmets.** Most people now equate riding helmets in terms of preserving their personal safety. There is an alternative school of thought which believes that wearing helmets encourages reckless riding by creating a false sense of inviolability and encouraging over-confidence. This line of thinking argues that safety zealots act within the framework of the law but outside the parameters of common sense. What helmet proponents seldom discuss is how it might actually contribute to injuries.

Don Andrews is a sports medicine expert who specializes in professional rodeo. He expressed a concern that adding the weight of a helmet to the rider's neck magnifies the snapping motion generated by a bucking horse or bull. "The solution isn't as simple as it appears. What we've found is that with helmets, we see a greater rate of spinal injuries. Whenever there's a force delivered, it has to be transmitted to another area. The helmet takes the force, but it transmits it to the spine. When you increase the load on the end of a lever, the head in this case, you're asking for a neck injury."

While helmets can provide a heightened level of protection, they were never designed to be a panacea which encourages irresponsible riding. A Long Rider should always strive to be in control of the horse. Despite everything, no matter what lengths you take to swathe your body in safety, riding will always be a risky affair.

**Gloves and Bandannas.** Gloves protect your hands from sunburn, prevent blisters caused by the reins and reduce the chance of injuries. Soft buckskin gloves are extremely comfortable – so long as they remain dry. When leather gloves get wet from snow or rain, your hands will feel like blocks of ice. Change to insulated, waterproof gloves as and when the weather dictates.

A large cotton bandanna is a versatile item. Besides protecting your neck from the sun, it can double as a washcloth, bandage or tourniquet.

**Rain Gear.** Encountering wet weather is unavoidable. What you must do is make a fundamental decision before you leave. Do you become soaked through and change into dry clothes later or do you deal with the elements before they strike?

Do not use a poncho! Regardless if the poncho is made from waterproof canvas, rubberized cloth or wool, don't take it on a trip. Because it is open ended, it will leave your arms and legs exposed to the elements. Being loose and floppy, it encourages a cold wind to blow around your body. Even worse, when a poncho begins to flap in the wind you will find yourself in the saddle, trying to pull the accursed bed sheet out from in front of your face, all the while your horse has decided to bolt. In such a situation, you're not wearing protection from the rain. You're draped in your shroud.

There are two safe alternatives for Long Riders; rain suits or rain coats. Increasing numbers of Long Riders are opting for light-weight, water resistant, Gore-tex rain suits made from highly reflective material. A jacket and trousers can be compressed and stored in a very small sack which fits into your saddlebag. Both should be bought oversized, so as to allow you to wear warm clothing underneath. This outer shell will not only keep you snug and dry; it will also help alert motorists to your presence on a dark and rainy day. Warm, waterproof gloves, with long cuffs, are also a boon on a wet and windy day.

**Staying Warm.** Your cold-weather gear should be designed to offset the season, not be a fashion statement. Walking beside your horse during part of the ride will help keep you warm. But once you're in the saddle your circulation will diminish and the cold will creep in.

**Chaps and Chinks.** There is a difference between leather chaps and chinks. Chaps go to your ankle, while chinks stop at your knee. Knee-length chinks are a derivative of and are associated with Nevada's buckaroo culture. Because a horseman has the most need to protect his legs from the knee down, chinks make no sense for an equestrian traveller. One drawback is that traditional chaps are secured by a sturdy belt that buckles in the back and a leather lace which connects the front of the chaps together. Cowboys were sometimes killed when their horse began to buck and the front of their chaps got caught on the horn of their western saddle. Even though becoming trapped in the saddle in this manner may be an unlikely problem, there are more immediate considerations. Because of the weight of the leather, chaps and chinks are both heavy, especially when the weather turns bad and they become soaked with rain.

**Sash.** The most useful but overlooked item from the horseman's original list of equipment is the long cloth he wrapped around his mid-section. Whether it was called a sash in English or a faja in Spanish, the result was the same. By wrapping himself tightly, from the bottom of his rib cage to his hips, the rider kept his internal organs in place, strengthened his lower back and fortified himself for extremely long distances. Central Asian horsemen, who wore a broad sash that was often fifteen feet long, claimed it gave them additional strength and offset nausea.

**Spurs and Crops.** Because road horses should be well trained, forward moving and emotionally stable, few Long Riders carry a crop. The long whip associated with dressage, is unthinkable. Likewise, the crop used during fox hunts, which allows a rider to reach down from the saddle and open a gate without dismounting, is equally unnecessary.

Though it is not a good idea to burden your hands, equipping your heels is another matter. Long Riders do not require their horses to act in an artificial manner. Theirs is a pragmatic approach, not an elaborate performance. Travel is usually about allowing the horse to proceed forward freely. The daily requirements usually consist of stopping on time and yielding at the correct moment. Yet because the world is full of dangers and trickery, you must be ready to meet physical chaos and emotional confusion. When this occurs, there is no time for your horse to contradict your commands. Nor must you try to coerce him into obeying. He must instantly respond to your commands to increase speed or turn sharply, otherwise you may both be lost. It is in such a moment that spurs come into play.

Spurs are not just a symbol of cavalier rank. Used properly they are an effective aid which can alert a horse to peril, encourage him to react and guide him out of danger. To be safely used without cruelty the rowels of the spur must be blunted or removed. Blunt spurs can bring a horse to attention, aid in steering him through a difficulty and do not harm.

**Compass and Telescope.** Carrying an accurate compass is a valuable and potentially life-saving bit of advice. It should not be confused with having a GPS, which is subject to mechanical failure. A compass, no matter how small, is ever alert. A small monocular can help your locate shelter and demystify the landscape.

**Knives.** There are two types of knives, fixed blades and folders. Both have their advantages. Each has been used by Long Riders. During the day a knife will be called into play for a variety of routine duties. Chances are you will have little warning when an emergency strikes. For this reason, you should never be far from your knife. Sleep with it close to hand, so if the need arises you can bound out of bed and put it to instant use.

**Tools.** You will be required to effect repairs, mend clothing or patch tack during your journey. There are several varieties of multi-purpose pliers now on the market. These square-nosed pliers can be used to withdraw a horse shoe nail, pick up a hot pot, pull a needle through heavy fabric or cut a wire fence. Like your knife, this is a small but important part of your gear which should always be on your person. Regardless if you are carrying a knife, tool, pistol or camera, you would be well advised not to strap it to your belt. Should you be thrown, you can break your hip if you land on the equipment. Carry your knife, compass, telescope and pliers in your vest pocket, not on your hip.

**Canteen.** The average cavalry canteen weighed nearly four pounds when filled. That is a great deal of weight to burden your road horse with. An experienced Long Rider will travel along a well-watered route. He will drink when his horse does. Full canteens, like lariats, belong on the open range as seen in Hollywood films, not on a Long Rider's hard-working road horse.

**Personal Items.** You have to consider that each item, no matter how small, still weighs something. While conditions will vary, depending upon country, topography and climate, these are the items which Long Riders have consistently brought in their saddle and pommel bags. Halter, lead rope, brush, curry comb and hoof pick. Toothbrush, toilet articles, soap and metal mirror. Sunscreen and sunglasses. Torch, maps, camera, diary and writing utensils.

# Chapter 44 - Electronic Equipment

Equestrian exploration is where tradition and technology meet.

**Laptops.** Long Riders who are riding within their home country may not carry a laptop computer, hoping instead that they can find internet access at a local library or in the home of a host. However, if you are bound on a long journey, one which will take you across international borders, then you may wish to consider carrying the most light-weight laptop currently available. If you make that decision, remember two things. Your equipment and your information may both be stolen. Thieves view travellers as walking wallets. So guarding your valuable computer becomes a primary task. Equipping your panniers with padlocks and then locking the boxes to stationary objects helps deter sneak thieves. However, there is a new threat to a Long Rider's writing – governmental intrusion and confiscation. Travellers entering the United States have had their computers confiscated or their information recorded without their authorization. Long Riders need to be aware that anything electronic can be confiscated, copied or destroyed by government agents. If you carry a computer, make sure your travel notes are regularly copied and sent home to offset theft or confiscation.

**Solar Chargers.** Many Long Riders generate their own electricity with the help of solar panels. Solar battery chargers convert sunlight directly into electricity reliably and silently without fuel or moving parts.

**Telephones.** Pay phones are increasingly difficult to locate and will soon be an obsolete form of technology. Also, considering how unreliable local telephone systems may be in some countries, carrying your own phone could an important consideration.

In addition to being able to summon help in an emergency, Long Riders have used mobile phones to maintain a safety network for their horses. During his ride from Mongolia to

Hungary in 2004, Tim Cope used his phone to obtain vital medical information from a veterinarian. "One of my most valuable contacts is a specialist horse vet in Australia. When something goes wrong I call her up and she talks me through everything. This can be very reassuring when the locals are telling you that your horse is finished and is going nowhere when in actual fact the injury or problem can be very easily treated."

Telephone technology has continued to progress since Tim's journey. Before setting off to ride from Canada to Brazil in 2012, Filipe Leite equipped himself with a multi-function iPhone. It didn't take long for him to realize how useful it was. "I have used the iPhone for the past eleven months. It wakes me up in the morning, tells me if I'm on the right road, allows me to share photos in seconds, and keeps me in touch with family and friends. It has an incredible camera, is super light weight and very durable."

**Sat Map.** Having access to the most up-to-date maps has proved to be of tremendous assistance to mounted travellers and the technology continues to improve dramatically. British Long Rider Elizabeth Hill had great success with a device known as the Sat Map. It equipped her with a treasure-trove of the most accurate maps, all of which were stored in a palm-sized device. The small Sat Map unit is easy to use and allows you to fine-tune your route on the move. It displays the map on a 3.5" colour screen and the battery lasts up to 120 hours in hibernate mode.

**GPS.** The Global Positioning System (GPS) uses a system of two dozen satellites hovering 12,000 miles above the Earth, each of which orbits the planet twice a day and beams back a constant position signal. American Long Rider Ed Anderson was the first to report success with a new GPS system known as the SPOT. Not only does it provide pinpoint geographic accuracy, it also allows the traveller to relay messages. Another valuable feature of the SPOT is the emergency button. It transmits the message, "I need help from friends," along with your location on Google maps.

**Misplacing our Trust.** Even though there are benefits to technology, a Long Rider would be well advised not to bet that batteries alone will save his life. An over-dependence on advanced technology can be a mistake for a Long Rider. Older, reliable tools and skills are still essential to an equestrian traveller. This was a lesson that American Long Rider Katie Russell learned during her ride through the rugged mountains of Montana. "Even though we had the latest technology, we relied upon traditional tools, like our axe, compass and ancient skills to keep warm and fed. So while technology is a help, it's not a solution," she warned.

**A Price to Pay.** Modern technology has created a world our great-grandparents could never have imagined. By pushing a button, messages fly through space, and then alight on another continent. Everything is faster and the world has grown smaller. Yet when the time comes for you to set off, you too shall still seek Grass, Water, Safety, Shelter, as did our forebears. That is why it is well to recall that one can be deceived into becoming overburdened by electronics and social services.

The last few years have seen an explosion of constant news, endless entertainment and limitless interaction with countless strangers who call themselves our "friends." What few realize is that there is a price to pay for being hooked to a relentless flood of communications. The power of these devices lies in their subtlety. One of the most precious things you will discover on the journey is a heightened sense of self. The quickest way to erode or destroy it is via the non-stop interruption caused by electrical devices and intrusive social networks.

Whereas early Long Rider websites supplied information about the route and the mission, modern social networks encourage people to become obsessed with themselves and seek constant feedback on their activities. Several recent episodes have demonstrated how equestrian travellers have bored the public with needless details about their daily existence. This deluge of travel trivia caused indifference and then antagonism amongst those who were subjected to this new type of spam. The result among readers was a loss of interest, then confidence, followed by antagonism.

Plus, any sense of mystery about the journey was slain in the cradle, as everyone on Earth knew what the person had eaten, seen, said, heard and thought during the course of the trip. Nor does it help when an emergency occurs, as then your disgrace is placed on public display for the entire world to see. Keeping in touch with your mum or spouse is one thing. Keeping your dignity is even more important.

Moreover, being exposed to constant internet stimulation means we panic when we find ourselves alone. Being alone is an important part of your inner journey. You should strive to break the cycle of noise which makes so much of modern life toxic. In addition to mere miles, coming to your own conclusions regarding issues which concern you is a priority. Instead of giving in to the pressure of supplying constant updates to stay-at-home pedestrians, you should explain your need to enjoy the contentment associated with riding your horse quietly. Your duty to others is conditional. That is why you should not let the allure of social networks to intrude upon the essence of your spiritual journey.

As Swiss Long Rider Basha O'Reilly warned, "Technology should be our ally, not our ruler. You can't explore your soul if you're obsessed with posting on Facebook."

# Chapter 46 - Support Vehicles

Prior to departing on an equestrian journey, many first-time travellers will have foreseen the possibility of enduring hardships and overcoming challenges. Few people realize that the idea of including a mechanized support vehicle into an equestrian journey is fraught with unexpected hazards.

**Keeping to the Safe Road.** There are two types of travellers; those who depart so as to arrive and those who journey in order to discover. Auto drivers belong to the former; Long Riders to the latter.

Mechanized travel is designed to maintain your sense of safety. Deviation from the itinerary is discouraged. Challenges are kept at bay. Fear and uncertainty are forbidden. By residing within the metal cocoon, the isolated driver watches the world pass by in a blur. Trapped by behind his windshield, the encased driver has a second-hand experience of life.

Once you venture onto a horse the world takes on a new perspective. Equestrian travel throws you into the environment. Your senses are brought alive as you see, smell, hear and touch the natural world around you. Being in the saddle brings you into constant touch with local people. You are not a robotized tourist, following the crowd from one mega-attraction to another. On such a rhythmic journey you are not obsessed with speed or competing against the clock.

In his poem, *Ode to the Long Rider*, American Long Rider D.C. Vision wrote, "From the saddle you will always get the entire sensual impact that fossil-fuel drivers in their boxes simply never find. There is an ancient natural heartbeat matched at this pace, where rider, mount, and environment discover their communion."

There are, however, occasions when the need to keep you and your horse alive require you to include a support vehicle.

**Transport by Necessity.** The vast majority of equestrian journeys do not require anything much more complicated than saddlebags and a pack horse. Yet exceptions do exist and sometimes equestrian travellers are forced by circumstances to employ the use of a driver and vehicle to overcome obstacles. Should your route demand that you include a vehicle on a permanent basis, there are a number of potential problems waiting to waylay you.

**Delayed Dreams.** The first consideration is that your progress may be postponed because of mechanical difficulties. This is what stopped the young American woman who had planned to ride "ocean to ocean." With her horse ready and her route organized, she had to reluctantly inform the public that a series of costly last-minute breakdowns to the support truck had left her with a horse and a dream but no trip.

**Insurance.** Some countries permit a foreign traveller to purchase a vehicle but will not allow them to then insure it. This proved to be the case in England, for example, where Americans can buy a vehicle but cannot obtain insurance. As their own insurance from home often does not cover driving through countries other than their own, Long Riders are left with an uninsured vehicle.

**Hostility.** Another drawback is that the vehicle can draw unwelcome attention or antagonise the locals. Canadian Long Rider Bonnie Folkins hired a robust UAZ all-terrain vehicle to help her cross northern Kazakhstan. While the vehicle proved to be a reliable success in the field, unfortunately it attracted an unexpected type of trouble. Because it was registered in Mongolia, local thugs in Kazakhstan resented its presence.

**Incompatible Priorities.** While expensive repair bills, high-priced petrol and costly insurance are all concerns, they don't stop as many equestrian journeys as the weakest link in this chain; the driver.

When you mix horses and support vehicles you are attempting to bring about a delicate balance between two competing definitions of time.

The road horse is a symbolic bridge between nature and the Long Rider. He draws you into the natural world without enclosing you as a machine would. The rhythm of his hoof beats echoes your heartbeat. Riding along quietly towards the horizon at three miles an hour slows down your body, clears your soul and places you in a solitary place of great contentment. In a world obsessed with haste, the first lesson your horse will teach you is to slow down.

By contrast, even as the Long Rider becomes part of the countryside, the driver of the support vehicle speeds through it. The automobile doesn't afford the driver a personal interaction with neighbours. It cuts him off from nature. Even worse, it also allows him to cover the daily distance travelled by a road horse in less than an hour. The result is that the driver reaches that day's destination in minutes and then spends the best part of the day trying to justify his decision to accompany the slow-moving horses.

No matter what country you go to, when you mix fast-moving drivers with slow-moving Long Riders, you often end up with quarrels and desertions.

**Conflicts of Interest.** Equestrian travellers are passionate about realizing their dreams. But people hired to drive a support vehicle have no particular allegiance to the Long Rider. What appears at first to be an easy job soon becomes a grinding bore to the driver.

**Deserting Drivers.** Sometimes the driver leaves you high and dry in the middle of nowhere. Other times you wish they would simplify your life by leaving. If you decide to employ a driver, the person should not be a timid, homesick, easily-bored safety-seeker.

**Love not Money.** There have been some splendid exceptions to the rule about lazy or disloyal drivers. The best drivers have been found among the ranks of those who were either family members or had a deep personal loyalty to the slow-moving Long Rider. An example of emotional support behind the steering wheel was demonstrated by Emma Brazier. When her friend Filipe Leite announced that he planned to ride from Canada to Brazil in 2012, the young woman didn't hesitate to help. When Filipe was forced to ride across a vast, drought-stricken portion of the western United States, Emma borrowed a car, found Filipe, and followed him to the Mexican border, all the while ferrying hay, grain and water to the horses. The experienced "Long Driver" offered a number of vital insights and suggestions to anyone considering using a support vehicle.

**Advice from Emma.** "The job of a driver is numbingly boring for the average person," she cautioned, because, "more often than not the driver is left with nothing but time." That is why finding the 'right fit' is everything," Emma explained. "I believe Long Riders in the past had negative experiences with drivers simply because they did not place enough importance on finding the right individual. If a Long Rider *chooses* to involve a driver, picking the right person to fulfil this role is as important as choosing the right horse. If the wrong person is chosen, then I believe the Long Rider will absolutely be abandoned and it is no one's fault but the traveller's," she wrote.

Above all she advised communication, patience and trust are all essential if the journey is to be a success.

Finally, Emma issued this warning. Even though Filipe had the additional help of a support vehicle during extremely difficult parts of his journey, he always kept the pack saddle equipped with his basic necessities with him at all times. This policy proved critically important when the vehicle Emma was driving broke down and Filipe was unexpectedly required to make camp at sunset. "This is a prime example of how a support vehicle can fail you," Emma said. But she added it highlights her last lesson. "Don't put all your eggs in one basket and plan for the worst."

**Good Advice.** So what traits are essential for a support driver? The person best qualified to answer that question is Peter Phillips, one of the most well-travelled Long Rider drivers alive today. He is married to the English Long Rider Mefo Phillips.

**Peter's Rules for the Road.** *What was your major concern before you set off to drive on the first horse journey?* Boredom and lorry breakdown

*Did you have an everyday check list before leaving the camp?* Yes – water, oil and fuel; power steering, fuel leaks, battery, tyres, lights.

*Likewise, did you have a check list before setting off in the vehicle every day?* I took every opportunity where there was access to electricity (such as a campsite) to charge up all the electrics.

*Because the riders travel at a vastly different rate of speed than the vehicle, how much time did you allow them to get on the road before you set off for the next camp?* That would depend on the route and terrain, e.g. a motorway journey would be very quick, but if say over mountains and down a gorge on a minor road it would take much longer, so I would try to judge it in view of that. The riders usually planned to ride for 7 or 8 hours maximum so I would plan my own journey accordingly. Sometimes I would stop en route to visit historical sites or to play golf.

*Were you the one who usually looked for a place to camp?* No. We believed it was more effective if the Long Rider with her charismatic horse asked would-be hosts if we could all stay.

*How did the Long Rider know where and how to find you?* We had mobile phones, and Mefo left me a note in the morning before she left to say where she hoped her destination for the day would be. I would get there before her and park on the outskirts where Mefo could not miss me.

*What did you look for in a camp?* Land that could be fenced off safely for the horses (we had a portable electric fence), and preferably where water was nearby.

*Because the riders are busy all day in the saddle, many drivers quit prematurely, citing boredom and fatigue. How did you offset these traditional problems?* You have to be self-contained, introverted, enjoy your own company and solitary pursuits like reading; visiting points and sites of interest. And have an ability to sleep at a moment's notice.

*What items would you consider to be of vital importance to keep with the support vehicle?* A good set of tools, battery charger, spare oil and water and hydraulic fluid, air pump for the tyres, spare bulbs, pieces of string, a hole puncher for adjustment to bridles etc, a cordless drill with more than one battery, a complete set of spare fuses, a bloody good torch, 30 books for the average trip, a bottle of whisky, a credit card, binoculars, lots of sweets that don't melt in the sun and a set of golf clubs.

*What papers/documents are of the utmost importance?* The horsebox papers and a decent map; notebook for entering expenditure.

*Because the riders are with their horses in the countryside, the driver is left alone for most of the day. How did you combat fatigue, frustration and loneliness?* Sleep! And lots of books.

*Any additional thoughts or suggestions?* Never underestimate the driver's need for privacy and space.

*What things would you tell other drivers to always do, always avoid and never forget?* Always do: check your vehicle very carefully every day; if you pass a petrol station and you're half full or less, always fill up because you don't know when the next one will be. Always avoid: driving down a street that's narrower than your vehicle; driving under a bridge that is lower than your vehicle's roof – if in doubt, get out and walk it first; getting into a situation you can't get out of (e.g. down a lane that's getting narrower and narrower). Never forget: you are there to provide support.

**Hints.** There are times when Long Riders have been forced to rely on a support vehicle in order to overcome short-term problems such as driving around traffic infested cities. But the inclusion of a support vehicle on a full-time basis complicates the journey on a financial, emotional and logistical level; most notably if an unsuitable person is employed as a driver. When the driver deserts, it is the Long Rider who ends up paying a high price for a mirage of safety. A support vehicle is a remnant of your past representing safety and modern comforts. In exchange for a feeling of convenience and security, you barter away your self-reliance and independence. Unlike other types of equipment, a Long Rider is better off only using motorized transport when circumstances, geography and climate offer him no other option.

# Section Four - The Challenges

## Chapter 46 - Courage and Common Sense

**No Guarantee of Safety.** When you cautiously announce you're setting out on an equestrian adventure, don't be surprised if someone warns you that no good comes of wandering far from home. But pedestrians have been urging Long Riders not to roam since time began. They prop up their argument by saying it's safer to stay in the village than set off on some foolhardy equestrian adventure.

What the nay-sayers overlook is how dangerous it is to be alive, no matter where you are. According to statistics, the leading causes of death are a variety of nasty diseases, followed by traffic accidents, falls, drowning and poisoning. Death by war trails all these. In fact danger is part of our everyday lives. Nor can Granny guarantee your safety even if you agree to stay close to her skirts and ride near to home. In 2011 beaches along France's Brittany coast were closed because of an invasion of poisonous seaweed. Nitrogen-rich fertilizers from nearby farmland washed into the ocean, encouraging the growth of seaweed. When this chemical-rich seaweed came ashore, it rotted in the sun and gave off hydrogen sulphide, a noxious gas with a foul smell. The toxic fumes proved fatal when an unsuspecting French leisure rider ventured onto one of the infected beaches. The horse was killed and the rider rendered unconscious by this uncommon menace.

Because equestrian travel is a portal to unforeseen challenges, Long Riders cannot afford to harbour a timid heart. To get somewhere, you've got to be willing to risk something. But how do we determine if we're taking a reasonable chance or acting foolhardy?

**Justifying Danger.** The Scottish Long Rider Robert Cunninghame Graham said, "Your true explorer must explore, just as the painter paints and the poet sings."

Yet ours is the first generation of humans to be uniquely under-qualified to become explorers. This was highlighted by a social study which cautioned that modern man can skin a client but not a rabbit. Urban dwellers, it said, exist "in a state of civilised imbecility" which has eradicated their sense of self-sufficiency and muted their courage. No journey can be accomplished without gambling our safety. The question then is what level of danger is justified? This is especially important in equestrian travel because when things go wrong it is usually the horse which suffers first. With the rise of industrial monocultures, equestrian folk wisdom has become a rare commodity. Because reality is intolerant of dreams, you need to be able to distinguish between an acceptable risk and a perilous obsession.

**Why we risk.** A series of related studies have revealed that the chemistry in our brains influences our decision to jeopardize our lives. The first discovery was made in the 1990s when scientists documented the existence of a risk gene. This behavioural coding affects the absorption of the neurotransmitter dopamine, which in turn affects how we react to stress and danger. The more accustomed we become to risk, the more likely we are to repeat a hazardous activity.

Yet this only explains a certain percentage of thrill-seeking behaviour. A later clinical investigation suggests the neurotransmitter serotonin also has an important part to play. This chemical which discourages impulsive actions could be in short supply in people who routinely imperil their lives. Testosterone levels influence personal decisions as well. Throughout history men have been more likely to risk their safety than women. This helps explain why more than twice as many men are the victims of drowning.

The life of a Long Rider is often filled with episodes which force one to deal with survival, not dwell on sentimentality. When this occurs, there is a balance between strong emotion and cold logic. When warnings are ignored, a heightened sense of self-esteem provides painful drawbacks.

**Fools Aplenty.** Exploration history proves that experience is a harsh teacher. For every medal winning hero there are many forgotten victims, some of whom were tremendously famous in

89

their day. Nor has the world of equestrian exploration been immune to people proposing to undertake equestrian journeys riddled with danger. For example, there was the American lady who foolishly wished to ride alone from Kabul to Peshawar, via the Khyber Pass. The Long Riders' Guild warned the would-be traveller not to attempt the journey and concluded by asking her to forward the names of her next of kin so the Guild could know whom to notify if she was murdered or kidnapped.

**Seeking your own grave.** Written on the tomb of a Knight of Malta are the foreboding words, *"Flecte lumina, quisquis es, mortalitatem agnosc."* This translates, "Bend down with your lighted candles, whoever you are, and acknowledge your mortality."

When disaster strikes, luck will often save a man if his courage holds. But some failures are never forgiven. The trap snaps shut when you've painted yourself into a self-destructive corner of your own devising. When this happens you realize you have risked your life and horses out of sheer obstinacy. Suddenly, with your breath racing and your soul about to flee your body, like all the other doomed explorers who have travelled this fateful trail, you realize that the press was wrong. You are no exception to death.

Never go searching for your own grave!

When you study the forthcoming information contained in this section you will discover a plethora of challenges. They may tempt you to think that the only constant in equestrian travel is disorder and danger. Precipitous mountain trails, life-threatening blizzards, disease-bearing insects and murderous thieves could all await you.

Trouble is what defines you in life. How you deal with it. How you overcome it. How you learn from it. How it makes you stronger, makes you better, makes you who you are. You don't out-run trouble; you weather it and ride on. That is why road-hardened Long Riders are apt to take things as they come, knowing that we are used to expecting the unexpected.

But remember, when in doubt – don't die from enthusiasm. A dream has no time frame. Better a disappointed Long Rider than a dead one.

# Chapter 47 - Mountains

Only those who have truly known fear can fully appreciate the rarity of courage.

Picture yourself sitting on your horse in a desolate, stony, forgotten corner of the world. Towering above you is a monstrous mountain which is unconcerned about your puny mortality. Everywhere you look above and below you is an unpopulated wasteland of sliding rock and unstable soil. Beneath your horse's hooves is an apology of a trail and he is trembling with fear. He is afraid to move on but unable to retreat. The reins are gripped so hard it feels like your fingers will snap. You daren't move a muscle in the saddle. Despite the cold wind tugging at your clothes, you're covered with sweat. You can feel the pounding of your heart in your throat because a heartbeat away is a drop into a bottomless void. You're one step from extinction, begging God to let you retrace your foolish steps. But it's too late for childish wishes. You've learned an ancient law the hard way. One false step and you will both perish. Mountains can look kind from a distance. Indeed on a clear day it seems they might never be anything but inspirational. Then you venture up close to inspect their secrets, and thanks to a series of minor mistakes, you and your mount find yourselves face to face with a mind-numbing peril.

**Suitable Horses.** Your chances of success are increased if you're riding a mountain-bred horse. It is unwise to take unsuitable horses into the mountains, as they lack the physical stamina or emotional experience needed to surmount these challenges. If you want to venture into the mountains, start by finding suitable horses.

**Season.** Next, pay careful attention to the time of year. After you have decided on your route, determine the best time of year to travel. Also, factor in the weather. If it changes quickly, you may find yourself in a snow storm. On the other hand, you may start that day's ride freezing but conclude it dripping with sweat.

**Distance.** How can we judge how far we can ride through the mountains on a horse? Success depends on knowing that the higher you go, the less far you can travel in a day. This formula can be used to judge mountain travel distance. Calculate the current condition of all your horses. Next take into consideration the weight on both riding horses and pack-horses. For example, if your pack-horse is carrying 100 pounds and your riding horse is carrying nearly double that, you can calculate the following:

1 hour for 5 or 6 kilometres on the map.
1 hour for 300 metres ascent
1 hour for 600 metres descent
1 hour for 400 metres descent if you have several pack-horses.

Included in this calculation are a few short breaks.

**Scouting Ahead.** A Long Rider in the mountains must expect the unexpected. Studying the maps prior to your departure provides you with an appreciation of the general topography. Once you are on the trail you must be ready to instantly alter your plan. Your decision to ride on always depends on current conditions. Moreover, if you seek information and advice from other travellers, keep in mind that it is easier for hikers to get through than equestrian travellers. They can climb over trees that will halt a horseman's progress. Deep snow may not impede them as it does a horse. So whereas it is fine to seek local information, judge the news in terms of equestrian progress. What you must not ignore are warnings.

**Bad Trails.** A lack of a trail may take your life. Another grave danger is trying to cut across country to increase your progress. If you attempt to undertake such a shortcut, you may find yourself marooned on a cliff above your longed for road. Staying on the trail is more important than making time.

**Gaining Ground.** It is also essential to remember the old golden rule of the Roman army engineers. "Height once gained is never thrown away." Don't ride your horses down and then back up the mountain. Prepare your route with care to avoid making your horse climb or descend unnecessarily.

**Delays and Detours.** All too often habit is stronger than reason. In a time-oriented society this translates into a lack of patience. But no matter what causes the delay, your guiding principle must always be compassion for your horse, not competition with the clock. When riding through the mountains you must be prepared to be delayed. When you encounter obstacles, the first thing to do is to accept that you are in for a postponement. Next, it is imperative that you stop and judge your options. Is it safe to dismount? Can you risk tying your horse and scouting ahead alone? Are you able to establish a safe manner to continue around a perilous obstacle? Should you retrace your tracks rather than proceed? Ultimately, the decision to ride forward or back depends upon your desire to protect your horse, not the desire to satisfy your ego! To make these tough decisions takes time, caution, patience and maturity.

**Riding by the Rules.** Nature is indifferent to our suffering. She neither loves nor hates us. Nor will she forgive our stupidity. Accidents can befall the most experienced Long Rider. But there is a difference between accidents and arrogance. No matter what they hear or read, some riders won't heed warnings. When such a person ventures into the mountains with horses, tragedy is sure to follow. Any time you break the basic rules of safe equestrian travel, especially when riding through mountains, your ignorance or obstinacy may destroy the horses. Tying your animals together is a primary example of foolish and reckless behaviour. Nor should you mistake tenacity for stupidity!

**Travel with Care.** If an emergency arises, and you find you must travel over a mountain which lacks a trail, there are two rules which you should never forget. You can take a horse either down or up a mountain. But asking the animal to travel across the slope sideways is a grim challenge, as loose footing may cause the horse to lose its footing and fall. Also, never lead a horse down a mountain which is too steep to climb back up.

**Riding Up Hill.** Steep hills and mountains require a Long Rider to relieve the horses of weight and help as much as possible. Before ascending you should tighten the breastplate and loosen the crupper if your horse is wearing one. It is suitable to ride uphill but never downhill! When required to ride uphill, don't lean back against the cantle. Minimize your weight on the horse's lower back and kidneys by leaning forward. This assists the horse to use his powerful hind quarters to travel uphill. If the climb is long, and the terrain steep, alternate by walking beside the horse. Always reward him with a long rein and allow plenty of rest periods en route.

**Riding Down Hill.** Even the most surefooted horse is at his most helpless when forced to travel downhill. In the wild an unencumbered horse may travel downhill relatively easy. But when you factor in a human and his saddle, the problem becomes enormously complicated. Two-thirds of all the weight of rider and saddle press down on the sensitive withers! This not only throws the load too far forward, it places extra weight on to the forelegs and cramps the action of the horse's shoulders. To release the horse from this unnatural pressure, you should always dismount and lead the horse downhill. Not only does this relieve the weight off his back, it allows refreshing air to circulate under the saddle and blanket. Before descending loosen the breastplate and tighten the crupper. If possible, you can aid the pack horse by placing some of the easily transferable weight from his load onto the saddle horse.

**Rest Stops.** There is no rigorous rule when resting your animals but there are guidelines. First, any time your horse is breathing hard and has worked up a good sweat, it's time to stop. Any time an opportunity arises to let them rest, call a halt. If the terrain is exceptionally mountainous, rest them ten minutes every hour, or even more depending on the altitude. Always stop at the top of a hill and let your horse get his breath. Never proceed without having first checked that the loads are secure. What is often overlooked is that it's hard work walking downhill too. This is especially true for your pack horse, which is required to hold back his heavy load. Though his fatigue going downhill may be less obvious, his need for a rest halt is equally real.

**Altitude Sickness.** Taking it slow and allowing the horse to rest is especially important the higher you travel because not all the dangers encountered in mountains are obvious. Altitude sickness affects both humans and horses. Known as puna in South America, one Long Rider described the symptoms as "giddiness, dimness of sight and hearing, headache, fainting fits, blood from the mouth, eyes, nose, lips and a feeling like sea sickness. Nothing but time cures it. It begins to be felt from 12,000 feet above the sea."

**Storms.** Travelling through the mountains is never easy. Bad weather can turn a tough trip into a precarious one. When it does, you have to be ready to act fast and alter your travel plans without delay.

**Traffic.** Travelling through mountains deep in the wilderness can be a life-threatening event. To truly test your nerves, try riding through the mountains on a road frequented by heavy traffic. You haven't known fear until you find a crag towering above your head, while badly driven trucks pass so close that their drivers can touch your hat. All the while a cliff is waiting a few feet way, ready to drop you into oblivion if your horse panics. Depending on which direction you are travelling, you may find yourself wedged up against the mountainside or peering down into a chasm. Regardless of what direction you ride, remember that heavy traffic often turns poorly maintained roads as slick as glass. Always check your horse's shoes or boots before venturing onto such a potentially lethal roadway.

**In Case of Emergency.** Pack horses and mules learn by experience. Even an experienced horse or mule can slip off a cliff.

If such an accident should occur, calm and secure your other horses before rushing to the rescue. If you can reach the animal, and he is lying down, do not rush to make him stand up. Speak to him calmly, reassure him, pat him and if possible, begin to quietly unsaddle or unload him. Check the horse for wounds. If he does not wish to stand immediately, he may be in shock. Give him time to rest and recover.

Even if the horse has not suffered any broken bones or serious injuries, he may be too exhausted to climb back up a steep hill or cliff. You may have to consider making a detour to rejoin the other horses. Once all the horses are together make camp as soon as possible, to allow the horse to rest. It is advisable not to travel the next day, so as to permit the fallen horse to fully recover.

*That is what happened to Harry de Windt. He lost his pack horse while crossing Persia's Kharzán Pass.*

## Chapter 48 - Deserts

Riding in the desert alters your previous conceptions. You will never know such weariness as when the heat rises in waves, while you and your horse plod towards water. In parching heat you struggle to reach the cool of an evening. You pray for a cool breeze. Though your body needs every atom of moisture, your clothes are soaked with sweat. Before you find yourself in such circumstances, it is good to recall this simple fact. If you make a mistake in the desert, you are apt to die a lingering and painful death.

**Desert Horses.** Regardless of where you ride, it is always wise policy to rely on horses that are used to local conditions. For example, horses and mules that are unused to desert conditions often fret on the sandy roads and rapidly weaken from drinking the saline waters. Being unused to the wide variations of temperature, they are also prone to suffer from the extremes of hot days and cold desert nights. Horses that are bred for desert work learn to drink as much as they can when the opportunity arises. The Danish Long Rider Henning Haslund rode one such animal across Mongolia in 1923. "My little desert horse Hao drank only once a day in the hottest weather and only once every third day in winter. When there was snow on the steppe he did not drink at all." Here again, thirst is better endured in hot climates by native horses which are accustomed to it, a fact that should be remembered when selecting animals for arduous journeys. Another point to consider is that a horse used to a soft environment lacks the heightened natural abilities of his tougher cousin who is bred for hard travel.

Because the scenting powers of an equine are ten times stronger than a man, a critically-important ability of the desert horse is his ability to detect water from a great distance.

**Careful Planning.** Horse and man alike can only live a few days without water. Yet remarkable journeys have been made by Long Riders in harsh deserts.

An inexperienced equestrian traveller should never enter the desert alone because the results can be disastrous! If you cannot find an experienced companion, you should proceed with the greatest caution. To begin with, it is vital that you gather all possible information about your route in advance.

Not only must you keep yourself abundantly supplied with water, it is critically important that you never leave one water station without a definite idea as to the location of the next.

Your motto in the desert should always be, One Water Hole at a Time!

It is a good general rule for a Long Rider travelling across arid country that when he happens to come to water, after not less than three hours travelling, to stop and encamp by it; it is better for him to avail himself of his good fortune and be content with his day's work, than to risk the uncertainty of another dry camp. Also, never trust the natives who assure you that water can be found further down the road.

Travel in the desert takes you away from traditional food supplies. From a practical point of view, this means that it is more expensive to ride through the desert than in other regions. A party making a deep ride in an uninhabited part of the desert will need to consider everything needed, even down to the smallest detail. This means that if the trip is to last for an extended period of time, enough food for each animal and enough provisions to last each person must be arranged.

**When to Ride.** Because of the risk of severe heat, you may have to alter your riding schedule. If you encounter severe heat then start your day at 3 a.m., ride until about 9 and then allow the horses to rest until 3 p.m., after which you can travel a few more hours. Even though horses have better nocturnal vision than humans, travelling through the desert at night is always risky. It takes horses longer to adjust their eyesight to bright lights, so use your flashlight with care.

**Desert Travel.** If you are unacquainted with the desert it will take some time to accustom yourself to its clear air. The resulting exaggerated detail can cause distant objects to look deceptively near. Don't be fooled into leaving camp without water or provisions to what appears to be a nearby hill without proper knowledge. Prior to your morning's departure you should study any landmarks in order to ensure they will be recognized from any point of view. If you are not following an unmistakeable trail, be sure to determine your general direction by compass, map, GPS and enquiry. To keep your line of travel true, ride toward and from selected landmarks. To accomplish this, check your compass bearing and then pick a distant object which corresponds to your line of travel. But take care not to only have one visual goal. If a man walks on a level surface, guided by a single conspicuous mark, he is almost sure not to travel towards it in a straight line. If he takes note of a second mark and endeavours to keep it strictly in a line with the first, he will easily keep a perfectly straight course. After marching to that goal, such as a tree or rock, recheck your compass bearing, choose another object and ride again. If you have studied the country carefully beforehand, you should have no difficulty in finding your way.

**Getting Lost.** However, if you have problems following a trail, get lost easily, or can't read a compass, there are safer places for you to ride. In case you think you are lost don't panic. Stop your horse and take the time to quietly consider where you've travelled and how you reached that point. It is amazing how a few minutes' contemplation may solve the riddle of where you are.

**Protection from the Sun.** Anyone who has journeyed for long distances across the desert in the same direction may recall how the sun was apt to burn them more severely on one side. When you become trapped in the sun, the backs of your hands burn and then swell like balloons. At all times except in midsummer – when the desert should be avoided – you must ensure that your clothing is suitable for both extreme heat and extreme cold. Desert riding may take you through heated valleys that lie at sea-level. But by the end of the day you may find yourself camped on an adjacent mountain, where the temperature may fall to freezing before sunrise. Being sunburned is bad enough. But being forced to shiver all night is even worse. Thus, be sure your clothes reflect as much heat as possible during the day and keep you warm at night. Wear a hat with a wide brim that is thick enough to exclude the rays of the sun. During periods of extreme heat, it helps to wrap a wet cloth around your wrists and to put a water-soaked handkerchief inside your hat.

**Surviving Sandstorms.** Sandstorms resemble a brown cloud on the horizon. As they rapidly advance, they suck up rocks and pebbles which will be hurled with terrific force at horse and rider. Prior to being hit by a sandstorm, you must prepare yourself and your animals to withstand the blast. Stop immediately and calm your horses. Search the ground for heavy stones or sticks that will mark your direction of travel. Despite the heat, don a heavy coat to protect yourself from the oncoming rock-strewn storm. After unloading the pack horse, hobble the horses, turning their tails towards the approaching fury. Many times men and horses lie down so as to endure more easily the rage of the sandy hurricane, which might last for hours. Regardless of how long it lasts, never loosen your grip on the reins or the pack horse's lead rope, as the animals are apt to panic in the noisy turmoil. The German archaeologist Albert Le Coq got caught in such a storm. He later wrote, "Woe to the rider who does not keep a firm hold on his horse's bridle, for the beasts, too, lose their reason from terror of the sandstorm and rush off to a lingering death in the desert solitudes." Chances are the storm will pass by without causing any more discomfort than making you swallow a lot of dust. But if you get caught out in such a situation, don't risk the safety of you or your horses by being foolish enough to think you can stay in the saddle.

**Making Camp.** Large campfires are luxuries that can be indulged in among timber or away from the beaten line of travel. In stark contrast, fuel is always scarce on the desert, especially in the vicinity of the better-known springs, where it has been entirely cleared away. That is why a wise Long Rider knows to gather brush, roots and dried animal dung long before he reaches the spring, so as to provide fuel for his camp fire.

**Endurance.** Long Riders who have to travel through sand will find it is very difficult on their horses. This will require you to walk much of the time. Sand and sharp stones will also wear out the horseshoes and your boots. Sand or not, desert travel beats down on an equestrian traveller and his horse.

**Carrying Water.** Anyone who has ever watched a cowboy movie may recall seeing the hero's horse carrying a big canteen on the saddle. Unlike a great many other cinematic mistakes, cowboys did carry water on occasion. But it wasn't an everyday occurrence. First, if they were riding on their home range, water was available from a nearby stream or at the bunk house. Conversely, if they were on a cattle drive, they drank from the same rivers used to water the stock or obtained a drink from the water barrel carried on the chuck wagon. Why didn't they carry a canteen as a part of their everyday equipment? Because water is heavy and unstable.

But some journeys cannot be done without carrying water. Steve Nott set off in 1986 to ride 29,000 kilometres (18,000 miles) around the perimeter of Australia. "Water is simply the key to travel in Australia," he wrote after the completion of his astonishing ride. Steve carried two army canteens. Each held slightly less than a litre of water. He allowed himself a half a canteen to brew a cup of tea for breakfast – the second half with Staminade (an electrolyte Australian sports drink) at lunch and the second canteen for evening camps if he had not reached water. A third canteen in the packsaddle was never touched until he had refilled the others. "That was my emergency one for retracing my steps if an expected water hole was dry." In addition to his own needs, Steve adapted a sensible Australian trick of hanging a canvas water bag around the neck of his horses. "In mid-summer a horse will drink up to ten gallons of water a day. So it is illogical to try and carry a full load in canteens. I had two neck water bags, which I filled when I was unsure about the country ahead. They each held 1½ gallons (4½ litres) of water, though some was always lost through evaporation."

**Drinking.** A point Steve stressed was that first-time travellers, and horses used to soft conditions, will need more water. Yet the practice of drinking water in excess of the amount needed to relieve thirst is a habit which should be strictly avoided. It places an unnecessary strain on the system and, if the water is alkaline, may result in illness that could have been prevented by foresight and self-control. It is unwise therefore to allow either the horse or yourself to drink to repletion until the end of that day's travel. "Both my horses and myself were conditioned to travelling on little water. This training allowed them to go longer between drinks," Steve explained.

It is advisable to drink heartily in the morning and at night and as little as possible during the day. A very small quantity of water will revive overtaxed horses. It should be given in repeated little rations rather than in one long draught. If the horse is very thirsty, allow him to rest for at least fifteen minutes after the first draught, before providing him a second chance to drink. If the amount of water on offer is scanty, say a pint or less, it is best to water the horses individually. If you put out a bucket, the first horse may receive an undue proportion or the animals may upset it in their eagerness to drink.

Horses can drink from a very shallow vessel if their bridles are removed. Taking advantage of this fact, small quantities may be poured into a shallow dish, from which they can drink. Offer the identical quantity to each horse in turn. You can calculate the amount of water by the horse's rate of swallowing. Twenty-five swallows indicates a normal thirst, while fifty swallows or more demonstrates severe thirst and dehydration.

**Bad Water.** Even if you're lucky enough to find this life-giving liquid, you shouldn't be naïve enough to think it will resemble the crystal clear ambrosia that springs from your tap at home. Travellers will often find springs choked by debris washed in by rain-storms or contaminated by the bodies of desert animals that have fallen in and drowned. It may therefore be necessary to dig out and clean a well or spring before you can drink from it. Also, owing to the intense heat of the desert there is a rapid and abundant growth of minute forms of animal and vegetable life in waters that are not too saline. All water should therefore be purified before drinking. There are now small, light-weight filters which may save a Long Rider from drinking bad water.

**Denied Water.** It seems obvious that when water is scarce its use must be carefully regulated so as to avoid any waste. What may surprise you is that this precious commodity has often been denied to many weary Long Riders and their thirsty mounts.

**Dying of Thirst.** Death by thirst is never swift but it is terrible. Delirium sets in. Stupefied by fear and suffering, the victim often tears off his clothes, which he feels are smothering him. In the final stage a man's eyes fill with light. This marks the beginning of the end.

**Treatment for Thirst.** Thirst hurts. This is because the membranes in a throat damaged by thirst become as stiff and brittle as sun-dried leather. People in this advanced state have difficulty breathing. Their breath will sound like the rattle of the dying. When a person's throat is contracted by severe thirst it is not easy for them to swallow the life-giving water they so desperately need. That is why the Libyan nomads learned not to try to make a rescued man drink water straight away. They hastily create a porridge containing lentils. This warm soup acts as a poultice in the victim's throat, softening the tissues sufficiently to permit him to swallow the water which follows.

# Chapter 49 - Rivers

**Death in the Water.** A river, like a king, obeys no law. You approach it with respect. You inspect it with care. You enter it with caution. Otherwise you may die.

**The Need for Caution.** Sometimes we pay a high price to satisfy our curiosity and see what others are merely content to read about. Any body of water, no matter how deep or wide puts a Long Rider at risk. A mighty river can present a fatal challenge. Because Long Riders still encounter rivers without bridges, the crossing of even fordable streams requires careful judgment and tremendous caution. The first thing to appreciate is how formidable water can be.

**The Power of Water.** In an age where the majority of people lead lives increasingly detached from nature, it is not surprising that many equestrian travellers underestimate the risk they run when trying to take a horse across a river. With the exception of television news programs, which delight in broadcasting footage showing out-of-control water sweeping away houses and trees, rivers are usually thought of as benign. Even a small brook flowing at a velocity of only five feet per second produces energy comparable to a man walking at a brisk four miles per hour. A river in full flood often roars along in excess of twenty feet per second.

Thankfully, horses are well designed to cross shallow water. Their narrow legs provide a small surface area against which the impact of the water can throw itself. Likewise, they have four points of balance which helps them stay steady so long as the footing is sound. Problems arise when the horse changes from wading across the shallows to swimming through deep water. The minute the horse loses his footing and begins swimming, the force of the water automatically attempts to drive the animal downstream in a manner akin to a heavy wind blowing against a sail. The faster the current, the harder the horse struggles to make any headway.

**Horses and Water.** Instinct has taught wild horses not to venture beyond the edge of the water when they come in search of a drink. Cunning predators lurk in the shadows, patiently waiting to attack any horse naïve enough to venture too deeply into the water. That is why, even though horses are generally good swimmers, they do not take baths. A vast expanse of water may alarm a horse. When this occurs, the animal can become confused. In an ironic rejection of not venturing too far into a stream for a drink, such a disoriented horse may unexpectedly launch itself into the water. But a Long Rider must be on his guard before his horse ever puts a hoof into the water.

**Training.** It is important that your horses know how to cope with water and cross streams prior to your departure. Although they are naturally good swimmers, some horses are afraid of water and will resist entering it. When in the water, such animals fight it and swim very poorly. You should introduce your horse to water quietly, coaxing him to wade through shallow water at first, the depth being gradually increased until he must swim. The goal is for your animals to swim boldly and freely. When training horses to cross a river every care must be taken not to frighten them. Choose a shallow stream with a hard bottom for their first test. If a horse balks, back him into water up to his hocks. When you turn him, he'll be more apt to enter the water willingly. But horses are just as apt to take fright and shy from a water-covered object such as a rock, as they do with similar objects on land.

**Finding the Ford.** If you are riding across a landscape filled with motorized vehicles, there is little chance that you will need to locate a suitable ford across a river. However, should your travels take you into territory where impoverished governments allow bridges to collapse, or chance forces you to ride across a river-infested wilderness, you will find yourself longing for signs of a safe way across dangerous water. In terms of a defining what makes a good ford, you are ideally seeking a shallow crossing with low water velocity. If you lack a map, you may often locate a ford by observing where houses have been built opposite each other upon either bank. Between them, you will find your ford.

**Dangerous Water.** Regardless of whether you know where to look for the ford or not, the first thing which occupies your attention once you reach the river is the state of the water.

*As this image demonstrates, if the river is running wild then it's not worth your life to try and cross it!*

When flooding rivers erode embankments, they tear out trees and hurl them downstream. Often times large branches, roots and other submerged objects are passing unseen beneath the water's surface. Glacial streams wash down large stones. Nordic waterways bring down blocks of ice in the spring. Perhaps the most dramatic example of a raging river was observed by South African Long Rider Ria Bosman. She was crossing Africa in 1970 when she witnessed an extraordinary spectacle. "When we arrived the Zambezi River was in flood. We saw herds of elephants come floating down the river!"

Never venture into the water if you suspect it may be hiding submerged dangers. Better to wait for the water level to drop.

**Reconnaissance.** The key to a successful crossing is a careful inspection of the river. In a perfect world you are seeking a shallow, calm, clear-running river which has firm footing and no boulders. But life's not ideal, is it? Never be in a hurry to enter the water. Take the time to halt your horse and ask yourself some basic questions. Study the surface. Can you see any dangerous tree limbs being swept by? Estimate the velocity of the water. Is it moving too fast for safety's sake? Look at the clarity of the water. Is the water muddy? If so, this will limit your ability to discern the footing. Estimate the width. How far might you have to swim? Examine the points where you will enter and exit the water. Are the banks clear of obstacles which might hinder or frighten your horse? Is the water safe further downstream? You don't want to cross if you might be swept into a logjam, smashed against big boulders or sucked into white-water rapids. Once you've made a personal inspection, if possible ask locals about the velocity of the current and the type of footing under the water. Do they take their animals across? Is this the exact spot where they cross the river? When was the last time a horse went through? Did it reach the other bank safely? Have horses or travellers ever drowned at this spot? Why?

If you find yourself without local advice, if muddy water prohibits you from seeing the river bottom, or you have any doubts about your horse's ability to cross securely, then you may have to scout the river on foot. Secure your horses and, using a stout stick to aid yourself against the current, cross the river with care. When you use a stick to support you crossing a strong current it is advisable to apply it on the upstream side as it will not be so easily washed away from you and is much easier to place for each step taken; you keep your balance better this way too. If you do topple and fall chances are your head will be upstream and feet facing downstream. It is much easier to regain your footing when you are in this position.

Rivers can be extremely noisy, especially when they are confined within canyon walls. If you are travelling with a companion, the noise of the rushing water may drown out your shouts to each other. So plan in advance what signals you may need to communicate with each other.

Once you walk into the river to scout it, your immediate objective is to determine the footing. A horse that is wading through shallow water may be able to manage rocky footing. Yet a fast current and bad footing may throw him off balance. Hard gravel generally provides the safest footing. Be extremely wary of sandbars and sandy islands which may appear mid-stream. Quicksand often forms on the down stream side. After estimating the strength of the current, exit on the other bank. Is the ground soft and boggy? Are there overhanging branches which may impede your departure from the water? If your reconnaissance concludes the river is dangerous, do not attempt to cross it!

**When to Cross.** There are always two time periods to consider when crossing rivers; seasonal and hourly. Seasonal considerations appear if you attempt to cross a mountain river too early in the year. Glacial torrents are fed by snowmelt. This renders them treacherous in the early part of the year, when ice and stones are flung down stream. Additionally, snow-fed streams are more dangerous in the late afternoon. As the sun melts the snow, the water rises and the velocity of the current is greatly increased. As a rule, it is best to cross snow-fed rivers early in the morning, when the current is weakest. Events upstream may influence your safety. It may not be raining where you are; however a rushing wall of water could be headed downstream without your knowledge. If you are riding downstream from a major dam, beware of runoffs which may release a large unexpected volume of water. In such a situation, it is best to try and confirm that no runoff cycle is planed. If the river looks flooded when you arrive, it is best to delay crossing it until you can confirm your safety.

**Where to Cross.** It's not enough to arrive at a river and boldly announce you're going to cross it. The selection of the site for a crossing is a matter of consequence. Because careful observation will provide clues to the hidden nature of the water, a wise Long Rider learns to read the river before he ever steps down from the saddle. The water is willing to provide you with clues. Spiralling water often indicates submerged obstacles or strong currents, either of which should be avoided. Smooth, clear water is the safest. By throwing a piece of wood into the river, you will gain an idea of water's velocity. By studying the movement of the wood on the current, you may detect deep water.

Because a swift current erodes the stream bed, fast-moving water often indicates the undetected existence of a deep channel. To complicate the problem, you should not attempt to cross within a bend in the river. If you enter the water from inside the bend, you may find it has a smooth sloping stream bed. Only a fool would trust it. What should concern you is the fact that the water's velocity is greatest on the outside edge of a bend in the river. There the additional power often cuts deep into the bank. This erosion leaves a deep hole in the river bed. Additionally, because of the increased current, not only will the water be at its deepest at the very moment when you are desperate to exit, you will find that the stronger current has sliced away the sides of the river bank, leaving it nearly vertical and making it difficult to exit from the river. For all these reasons, never attempt to cross at a bend in the river!

**Preparing the Ford.** Never take your horse through a ford until you have thoroughly reconnoitred it.

The entrance to and exit from the water must be good, particularly the exit. The ideal is a gravel bottom with an even slope. A muddy bottom may cause the horse to struggle and become trapped. Extracting a horse from a bog on dry land is difficult enough, but trying to rescue a thrashing animal ensnared in muddy running water is a nightmare. Spend the time to confirm the footing. If necessary, prepare and improve the banks of the ford prior to riding into the water.

**One Horse at a Time.** Never rush the river! Four times more lives are lost in water than in fire. You should always take your time and do things properly. A fundamental mistake is trying to cross a river with too many horses. Choose the most emotionally-dependable animal to cross first. Be sure the other horse is securely tied and that he can see you for reassurance.

**Riding Across Shallow Water.** If you have examined the stream and determined that you can ride through the shallows, allow the most experienced horse and rider to go first. Give a thought to what might happen if your boots fill with water or if your clothes become wet. If your boots fill, they may help sink you. Heavy clothing may become a shroud.

**Focus on the Bank.** When the Swiss Long Rider Ella Maillart was exploring the Pamir Mountains, she was forced to cross a rushing river. "I had the queer sensation of being carried downstream, the land opposite appearing to swim away from me. But, having traversed rivers in Persia, I knew the danger of becoming giddy and falling helplessly into the torrent; therefore I kept my eyes on some fixed object and not on the swirling water."

What Ella experienced is the strange sense of dizziness which sometimes strikes people and horses who stare at fast moving water while they are trying to cross it. Looking at swirling eddies creates a spinning sensation and causes you to lose your sense of balance. This impression is strengthened if you pull your feet out of the stirrups and perch on top of the saddle. Stay in control. Focus your attention on the far bank. Direct your horse with confidence towards the spot where you want him to head.

**If You Fall In.** Far too many people underestimate the river and overestimate their horse's ability to stay on his feet. That helps explain why more people and horses drown than any other cause of death associated with trail riding. They're killed from over confidence. The moment you arrive at the river, you should be asking yourself, "What will I do if I fall into the water?"

When things go wrong in the river, the consequences can be swift and merciless. That is why you should never ride your horse into strong running water unless you can swim! Even if the water is initially shallow, a strong river can knock you off your feet or out of the saddle, then drag you under. If you can't swim, you won't survive. Don't diminish your chances of survival by crossing upstream of hazards such as low-hanging trees, waterfalls or rapids. Before you enter the river, make sure you've studied the water downstream and confirmed that nothing will hinder you from swimming to safety.

No matter how well you plan your crossing, a situation may arise when you have to leave the saddle and hit the water. If your horse starts to lose his balance, kick your feet clear of the stirrups and slide out of the saddle before he rolls on top of you. If you go into the water, your first priority should be your own safety. Always exit on the downstream side of the horse! If the water is shallow, you may be able to stand, grab the reins and walk to the shore. However, if the water is deep, or the current is rapid, point your feet down stream, then concentrate on swimming to shore. You can always set about catching your horse once you're back on dry land.

**Preparing the Riding Horse for Deep Water.** Should the occasion arise when you have to swim across a river, your riding horse must be prepared to face the challenge.

There are two primary concerns prior to his entry into the water; removing weight and becoming entangled. The safest thing to do is to remove his saddle and send it over by raft or rope. This will allow you to take him into the water wearing nothing but his bridle. If the saddle must be worn into the river, start by checking the girth. Make sure it is tight enough to ensure that the saddle cannot slip under the horse's stomach while swimming, but not so tight as to restrict the horse's breathing, as he has to remain buoyant and swim freely.

A horse cannot swim if his head is restricted by a tie-down or martingale. Not only may he drown from this restrictive equipment, his legs may become entangled. Before swimming across, make sure there are no lead ropes or straps which might restrict the horse from lifting his head clear of the water or that can foul his legs. Likewise, you do not want your reins trailing in the water, as they may become entangled in the horse's legs. Tie a knot in your reins prior to entering the water. To give him every assistance, you should ideally ride the horse into the water wearing nothing but his halter. Make sure the lead rope is looped around the neck, tied off securely and isn't long enough to entangle his forelegs.

**Swimming with the Riding Horse.** The horse is a powerful natural swimmer and is capable of carrying a human alongside for a considerable distance. Despite the horse's natural ability to swim, you must provide the animal with encouragement and never hamper his movements. When afloat, the horse's head is the only part visible, the body being just below the surface, and the tail awash behind. To aid his crossing, you must remove yourself from his back once the horse begins swimming. If you remain on his back, your weight sinks the horse's body lower into the water. This increases his effort and may interfere with his ability to keep his nose above water; it also raises his centre of gravity, increasing the chance that the current flowing against and under his body may roll him over.

Ride your horse into the water, ensuring that he is headed in the right direction. Once he enters deep water, and begins to swim, slip off his back on the downstream side.

Never venture in front of a swimming horse as his flailing forelegs may strike you. The safest place for you to be located is alongside the horse's downstream shoulder. By grasping the saddle horn and floating alongside quietly, your body acts as an outrigger which counteracts the current's efforts to roll the horse over on his side.

You do not direct your horse with the reins once he has begun swimming! Once he is under way, if you pull the reins backwards, the horse may throw his head up, which may cause him to roll over in the water. For this reason, you should let the reins or lead rope lie along his neck at the first possible moment. To guide your horse across the river, use your free hand to splash water on the side of his face. This will help you maintain your direction by heading him up or down river. If you lose your grip on the saddle horn, then catch the horse's tail. If you follow behind in this manner, be careful that his hind legs do not kick you.

**Preparing the Pack Horse for Deep Water.** Regardless if you are swimming the road or pack horse across, allow both animals the chance to drink before fording a stream. Otherwise it might stop and try to drink in midstream, thereby losing its footing.

Although horses generally are good swimmers, pack animals should not be swum while loaded. Not only can their legs become entangled in the girth or breeching, a soaked pack saddle is very heavy. Even if they remain dry, loads make the pack animal top-heavy. A combination of a swift current, water deep enough to shove against the body and poor footing may cause the animal to lose his balance, fall over and drown.

You must use extreme care when determining how you will transport gear across the river. When you have to swim your pack horse across the river, the animal should be unloaded and unsaddled as close to the water's edge as possible. If you cannot locate a boat, you may have to construct a raft or use an inner tube to transport your heavy gear across the river. Do not risk your pack animal's life by asking it to combat the current, maintain its balance on unstable footing, and carry your luggage to a distant shore.

100

**Aim Upstream.** If you attempt to swim straight across a strongly-running river, the powerful current will carry you past your landing place. To offset this danger, you should enter the river upstream of where you wish to land. Even if they are wading, the constant pressure of the water causes horses to tend to drift downstream. This downstream drift becomes especially pronounced if the animals are swimming across in a strong current. To correct this drift and to make your landing at the appointed spot, aim your horse at a 45 degree angle upstream to offset the current. This also gives your horse a better sense of balance if he is wading and lessens the impact of the current against the horse's body if he is swimming.

**Horses Towed Behind Boats.** Extreme care should be used if the chance arises to tow your horse across a river or lake. If you don't know how to tow a horse properly, you may quickly kill him! If an occasion arises when you must tow your horse behind a small boat, use extreme care. Make sure the lead rope cannot slip and choke the animal in transit. If the animal is unwilling to enter the water, back him in or splash water on his hind quarters. Once he begins to enter deeper water, proceed to row slowly, allowing him to follow close by. Do not pull on the lead rope. Keep a steady pressure on the rope so as to confirm the direction he is to follow, all the while you quietly urge on the horse with your voice.

**Landing.** The horse never stops swimming because he doesn't know how to float. If you have swum the river together, get back on as soon as the horse touches the ground. Make sure you keep the horse moving when he emerges. Under no circumstances should he be tied up as long as he is wet. After fording a river, you should stop and see if you can let the horse loose. If you do, he will instinctively trot, roll, and dry himself without catching a cold. The entrance and exit of a stream crossing, as well as the ford itself, may be treacherous ground. In a spot like this your horse could lose a shoe; as soon as you have safely crossed, halt and examine the shoes.

**Keeping Dry.** Depending on the climate, elevation and time of year, swimming in cold water is a shock to the system. When you emerge, even though you may be shaking with cold and breathing hard, your responsibilities will demand instant action. Add the anxiety of trying to protect the lives of your horses while keeping your personal possessions from being washed downstream, and you have one of the most stressful situations a Long Rider may encounter. That's why it is best to face the facts. If you encounter a deep river, you should plan on getting wet. If you can change into dry clothes so much the better.

**Rescuing a Horse in Water.** Horses, like humans, may panic in the water or be swept away by a strong current. Trying to rescue a horse from the water may put you at extreme risk.

The safest methods of rescue should be attempted first. If the horse is swimming, offering it verbal encouragement or letting it see its equine companions may entice the animal to swim to security. Unless you are an expert with a lasso, it is not recommended that you try to throw a rope over its head. Chances are if you miss the horse will become more frightened and swim away. If time and circumstances allow, you may try to extend a pole with a looped rope on the end in order to try and snare the horse or saddle. But care must be taken that you are not dragged into the water.

If you can remain out of the water do so, as entering the water to attempt a rescue either by swimming or using a boat increases the danger. Should a boat be available, you might be able to row out and induce the horse to follow your to safety by offering it grain in a bucket. But great care should be taken if you grab the horse by his bridle or halter. He may struggle to keep his nostrils above water. Even if the horse reaches shore, if it has taken water into its lungs chances are a case of pneumonia may develop.

Because moving water can draw heat out of the body 250 times faster than air, stress and hypothermia will have an effect on the horse's chances of surviving after he emerges. Cover the horse with a blanket to prevent hypothermia and allow him to rest.

# Chapter 50 - Jungles

Regardless of where the jungle is located, it represents an alien environment to the horse.

**Harsh Reality.** The majority of urban dwellers lead lives devoid of physical danger and hardship. It is impossible for them to relate to the risk and reality of riding through one of the infamous jungles which have lured in Long Riders. If you were to ask such a naive urbanite to describe a jungle, he might think of Tarzan, swinging gracefully through the mighty tree tops, co-existing peacefully with the surrounding animal kingdom, at one with Mother Nature, all the while a soundtrack provided by soft bird calls plays soothingly in the background. As Long Riders have learned to their horror, trying to cross a jungle on horseback doesn't match the Hollywood fantasy. Temperatures soar to 100 degrees Fahrenheit in the shade. Insects suck your blood and drive you mad. Leeches lurk in the swamps you must wade through, waiting to feast on your water-soaked flesh. Vampire bats gorge on your horses at night, leaving them too weak to travel in the morning. There is a shocking lack of food for you and the horses. The undergrowth is so dense you can't move. The humidity makes it difficult to breathe. It can be, as one Long Rider described it, a "green hell."

**The Pantanal.** There are wicked and boggy places in many parts of the globe. Australia, for example, hosts crocodile-infested coastal zones. Likewise there are the jungles of Central Africa, with their infamous horse-killing tsetse flies. Yet few Long Riders have had occasion or need to venture into either of these wilderness areas. Because of their close proximity to the great equestrian cultures of the pampas, it is the two great jungles of Latin America which have usually either stopped or threatened to kill equestrian travellers in the past. The larger of these is the Pantanal.

The Pantanal is the world's largest wetland. In contrast to the Florida Everglades, which covers 10,000 kilometers, the Pantanal encompasses 240,000 kilometers and sprawls across Brazil, Bolivia and Paraguay. The allure of the place is perhaps partly explained by the fact that the area is home to the largest concentration of wildlife in all of the Americas. As a result of the combination of topography and climate, seasonally-flooded grasslands and various types of forest provide an ideal habitat for jaguars, monkeys, tapirs, anteaters, snakes and more than four hundred bird species.

Filipe Leite rode across the Pantanal in 2014 during his two-year journey from Canada to Brazil. He was shocked at the extent of the area's wildlife. The Brazilian Long Rider also discovered that an environment which is good for birds doesn't mean it will be suitable for horses. Filipe noted that the landscape was so water-logged that he would sometimes have to ride 50 kilometres (31 miles) before he would find a spot to camp. But there were worse things than mosquitoes lurking in the wetlands. Filipe and his horses rode through country that was heavily populated by jaguars. Because these deadly big cats had a reputation for killing cattle and humans, local ranchers warned Filipe to be extremely vigilant as otherwise his horses might be attacked.

**The Gran Chaco.** The Gran Chaco is the name used to describe the Paraguayan portion of the Pantanal. It has attracted Long Riders both past and present. The Gran Chaco is sparsely populated. Because it is located east of the Andes, and sits along the Tropic of Capricorn, it endures some of the highest temperatures on the continent. In the rainy season, locals ride horses that are specially adapted to the flooded environment. Yet ironically, because of its high mineral content, much of the underground water is not fit for stock to drink. So a lack of suitable water is the stumbling block associated with this area. Because its borders were ill-defined, Bolivia, Argentina and Paraguay fought over the area in the past. Despite its current political calm, it is still a place of soaring temperatures, rampant insect life and potentially lethal animals. As bad as the Chaco may be, its neighbour further north is worse.

**The Darien Gap.** The Darien is a jungle of the most dangerous sort which divides South America from her Central American sister. A nearly trackless maze of muddy tangles, the hellish Gap not only splits Panama from Columbia. but it has effectively stopped all equestrian travel from moving north and south since mankind reintroduced horses back to the Americas. The province of Darien lies along the eastern edge of Panama. The majority of the area is rainforest wherein rare settlements huddle along the rivers. On the other side of an invisible border, Columbia's Atrato River pours its waters into impenetrable swamps. Regardless of which side you're unlucky enough to find yourself on, the Darien boasts one of the world's highest rainfalls. With the exception of a few rough roads near the villages, there is no consistent trail through the morass. Thus, although the Pan-American Highway extends from the top of Alaska to the bottom of Tierra del Fuego, it is halted on either side by the Darien Gap.

**Going Hungry.** It may surprise you to learn that in a vast jungle you and your horses may often go hungry. That is because the environment does not encourage the growth of grass. Nor is it easy to locate foodstuffs. So before venturing in, be extremely confident that you and your horses will have enough food to enable you to complete your crossing.

**Insects.** Sinking into mud, hacking your way through thick undergrowth, pouring sweat and going hungry might sound like mild challenges. But they're not the worst threats facing a jungle rider. That dubious honour is reserved for the insects which drive horses and humans mad. Mosquitoes, gnats, ticks and flies are a constant plague. But there are worse things waiting to hurt you. For example, the Darien Gap is home to stinging caterpillars and inch-long black ants whose bite hurts like hell for hours. Because of these various insect threats, never lean against anything, sit down or put your hand on top of something without checking first.

**Jungle Travel.** Unexpected things occur when the raw power of a journey drives you further than you believed you could go. Because the jungle can conjure up so many deadly challenges, it is crucial that when an emergency occurs you not allow the sudden onset of fear to undermine your confidence. This isn't to say that you won't be frightened. It means that he who survives is the one who anticipates, then controls, his fear when it eventually appears.

A journey in a jungle can resemble a fragment of hell. If circumstances force you to enter into such non-horse-friendly country, be sure to take the extreme heat into account. Always start as soon as it is light. Be prepared to go on foot, leading your horse with care. If travelling in heavy undergrowth, carry a machete. Also, because of the many negative factors involved in jungle travel, be aware that there is a limit to the time you can expect your horses to survive in this hostile environment. Lack of food, savage insects and inadequate water have traditionally combined to give horses three months maximum before they become seriously ill or die.

# Chapter 51 - Quicksand

One of the horse's oldest and deadliest enemies is still with us. God help you if you should encounter it.

**An Ancient Adversary.** Some of the greatest Long Riders of all time have fallen prey to quicksand, mud and bogs. Aimé Tschiffely had 2,000 miles under his saddle when quicksand nearly got him. Thurlow Craig was the wisest jungle rider who ever rode a trail but he nearly lost his horse to the mud. Donald Brown survived a winter's ride across the Arctic Circle but almost lost his horse in a bog. Roger Pocock, who rode the Outlaw Trail alone, remarked on this evil. "I have seen so many horses piteously downed in mud holes that I understand why they act cautiously as they approach wet ground."

Nor should you be merely concerned for your horse's well-being, because other Long Riders have nearly been entombed. After having ridden half the length of California, English Long Rider Joseph Smeaton Chase and his horse, Chino, were suddenly fighting for their lives in a patch of coastal quicksand. With no help for miles, Chase had a gruesome thought. "As I struggled a horror of the event flashed over me and with it the thought that no one would ever know what had happened to me, for there would be no trace, no clue. That horrible sand would close over me, the roar of the waves would go on unbroken; I should simply cease to be."

How then do we avoid being held relentlessly by this death trap of the ages?

**A Brush with Death.** You need to realize that even an experienced Long Rider can come to harm. But even if you're forewarned, what if caution isn't enough? What if you find yourself without a road, surrounded by miles and miles of trackless marsh and quicksand?

**Quicksand.** Death by drowning comes in a variety of nasty ways. One of them is quicksand. Quicksand is a pervasive threat which can be found on riverbanks, near lakes, along stream beds, down river from islands located in mid-stream. Quicksand is a mixture of water, sand and clay. Movement along the surface causes the mixture to become unstable. Once it liquefies, anything unlucky enough to be on top begins to sink. How far down you go depends on its density and how much you thrash about, as struggling redistributes the mixture with heavier clay and sand moving downwards, while upper layers are liquefied. The good news is that research indicates that it is impossible for human victims to sink into quicksand much beyond the waist – but it is equally impossible to pull someone out once they are stuck. A heavy, glutinous layer forms, which prevents the victim from being drawn further in but also prevents their escape. But horses aren't humans, are they? And you can't reassure them with soothing words after you've misled them and they're thrashing for their lives as a result, can you? Quicksand, mud, bog. No matter what you call it or what shape it takes, the first thing to remember is, trust your horse.

**Saved by Instinct.** People often joke about horses being afraid of only two things, things that move and things that don't. Though they react without words, their deep-seated wisdom is plain for all to see. A case in point is the horse's ancient instinctive fear of boggy spots and their remarkable ability to use their olfactory sense to judge the nature of swampy ground. This ability to scent the ground for danger was demonstrated by Aimé Tschiffely's Criollo, Gato.

"Much to my surprise the ground became boggy, but wishing to save time and distance I continued straight towards a cut in the mountains. I knew this was the way we had to go towards Cuzco. The horses had already waded through soft puddles that gurgled in a very unpleasant way, and when we came to a broad strip of water which appeared to be traversing the plain from side to side, Gato, whom I was riding, refused to move further. The water was only some four inches deep, but the horse stopped with the stubbornness of a bad-tempered mule, and when I hit him with the lead line he reared up and snorted like a bronco. I tried every means of persuasion to make the horses enter the water, but all my efforts were of no avail. Presently I saw an Indian in the distance who seemed to be shouting and waving his arms whilst he came running in my direction. When he was near enough I heard him calling to me in broken Spanish to stop. He told me that this was a very dangerous place and that we would meet with disaster if we entered the treacherous pool. He then guided us to a spot far away and put us on a safe trail. Gato had taught me a good lesson, and I never interfered with him again when he refused to step on a doubtful piece of ground. The good old boy had not forgotten the lessons he had learnt in his youth whilst roaming over the plains of Patagonia and the instincts of the wild horse had warned him that danger was lurking below the innocent-looking water."

**Reconnoitre.** You should never venture into any type of marshy ground unless it is absolutely impossible to avoid it! Such treacherous terrain does not allow either the horse or rider to relax for a second. Before advancing, it is always best to check with a native. But take care. Because bogs are hard to detect, even local knowledge may not be up to date. Reconnoitre your route on foot with the greatest of care. If possible, mark it. Never hurry! The time you spend scouting a safe route is minimal compared to the hours you will spend trying to free your horse from a bog. If the ground is even slightly suspect; stop! High, dry ground is always preferable to sloppy meadows, stream beds or coastal trails. Always avoid the risk of taking your horse into such an area by either riding above or around them.

**Moving Ahead.** It happens fast! When riding in treacherous terrain, don't hesitate to lead your horse on foot. If you are travelling with a pack horse, take one horse at a time across dangerous ground, walking steadily and never stopping. When a horse feels himself sinking, he will try to plunge forward in an effort to find firm footing. This often drives his legs deeper into the mire. If you can ride him to safety, stay in the saddle. If he begins to sink, get clear of the saddle. Be careful that he doesn't panic and jump on top of you. Stand to one side if you have to lead him to safety. If the worst happens, and your horse becomes bogged down, then everything changes.

**Rescuing a Trapped Horse.** There is a growing awareness of what is now termed "large animal rescue." Horses residing in urbanized environments topple into swimming pools, fall into abandoned wells or become bogged down in muddy creeks. When such a catastrophe occurs, uniquely trained fire-fighters respond with an assortment of specialized equipment. One of the most common accidents occurs when horses become trapped in deep mud. As the animal struggles, his exertions cause him to sink deeper and deeper. In time he will become exhausted and drown in the mire. Extracting a horse from such a muddy trap is difficult and dangerous work, the result being that rescuers themselves are often injured by frightened horses. An additional worry is that ill-trained rescuers may inadvertently strangle, injure, drop or kill the horse. Thus the situation is fraught with peril unless the rescuers are expertly trained and properly equipped.

But what does a Long Rider do when he is miles from help? How do you react if there is no cell phone to call emergency services? Can you save your horse if you lack specialized rescue equipment?

**Calm and Caution.** Should your horse become bogged, your immediate concern will be the need to balance speed against caution. If you become trapped in a lethal tidal zone, you will be in a race against time. But rapid movements and frantic struggling decrease your chances of escape. The vibrations turn the relatively firm ground into more quicksand. Slow movements will help stop such an adverse reaction. Unless the tide is coming in, you're going to have to be patient and careful, as it could take hours to free your horse. Try to remain calm as your assess the situation, otherwise your fear will encourage the horse to panic.

**Safety.** If your horse becomes trapped, don't automatically wade in to rescue him! Your immediate concern is that you not become ensnared in the mire too. Assess the situation quickly. Check to make sure the water or bog isn't hiding additional hazards. Even the calmest horse becomes incredibly dangerous if he feels himself sinking. As he struggles unsuccessfully to reach solid ground, he will become unpredictable and shake with fear. Act calmly. Move toward him slowly. Reassure him quietly. Allow him to regain his breath. Do not approach him directly from the front! This is the area where you will be exposed to the most danger as he may strike out, bite or hit you with his head. Make your way towards him at an angle and be extremely careful moving around his back legs as he may kick you in his haste to escape.

**Remove the Weight.** If he is trapped, your initial priority is to remove the weight of the riding or pack saddle without any delay. Before making your way to the horse, immediately dispense with anything heavy on your own person. Be aware that shoes, especially if they are equipped with flat, inflexible soles, create suction as you attempt to pull them out of the mud or quicksand. If you are wearing heavy or rigid boots, change them for light shoes or go barefoot so as to enable you to free your feet easily. To help keep yourself from becoming trapped while you unload the gear, make use of anything nearby which you can use as a flotation device; a tree limb, a piece of wood, an old ladder, anything which helps keep you afloat. Once you reach the horse, remove everything except his halter and lead rope. If you can't loosen the saddle's girth, don't hesitate to cut it or anything else binding the equipment to the horse. When you are removing the equipment, remember to breathe deeply. Not only will deep breathing help you remain calm, it will also make you more buoyant. Keep as much air in your lungs as possible while you are working.

**Don't let him drown.** Once the horse is unloaded, your immediate goal is to keep him alive. That means don't let him drown. Even though a horse's body is reasonably buoyant, his head is heavy. The longer he struggles, the greater the difficulty he will have keeping his nostrils above the surface to breathe. This will become even more acute if he is deeply mired, as he may be at risk of asphyxiating from the pressure placed against his ribcage. Stay calm, and while you talk to him quietly, place something which floats under his head to keep his nostrils clear of the water. This may be a chunk of wood, a piece of equipment, anything which will provide him with the vital support needed to rest his weary head above the mud.

**Dangerous Amateurs.** If you are lucky enough to be able to summon help, do not let enthusiastic amateurs complicate the situation by inadvertently injuring or killing your horse. It would never occur to a paramedic to tie a rope around an injured human's neck, wrists or ankles and then drag them free from a wreck. Yet when a horse becomes mired, many people quickly try to grab some portion of the animal's body and begin pulling. The results are often devastating. Well-intentioned but naïve rescuers may instinctively tie a rope from the horse's halter to a tractor or four-wheel-drive vehicle. They do not understand that when you apply

105

traction to a horse's head, his natural reaction is to resist the pressure and pull back against the rope. Not only can the pressure from the rope cause nerve damage, the combination of an unbreakable halter and a powerful vehicle may decapitate the animal! Do not pull on his head! Do not use his tail or legs as handles! The only safe way to extract him is via a carefully positioned lifeline.

**Securing a lifeline.** When confronted with a horse lodged in deep mud, professionals employ a thick, wide webbing strap (as seen in the illustration below) which they carefully place around the horse's body prior to lifting him to safety.

But you won't be carrying a convenient thirty foot long length of four inch wide webbing, will you? That's why you will almost certainly have to make do with a rope. That option presents you with an immediate problem, as if you're not extremely careful the thin rope may cause serious injury.

Now stop for a moment to imagine what has happened. One moment you're riding along wondering where you will camp that night. Ten minutes later you're up to your chest in life-threatening mud. Your beloved horse's eyes are bulging with fear. You're both shaking with cold and scared to death. He can't talk but you can and you're trying not to curse, to cry, to panic. With all that going on, imagine that now you have to secure a lifeline to your horse.

To do that you need to stand close to his left shoulder, facing him. Shove the rope down through the mud in front of his chest. The loop has to go between his front legs. It emerges on the left side of his body behind his foreleg. Then you pull the loop up out of the mud. Now you carefully lay the rope across his back just behind the withers. After you carefully make you way to his right shoulder, you once again shove the loop down into the mud. This time you pull it between his forelegs again, ensuring that it emerges in front of the horse. Now the horse has a rope encircling his body behind the withers, under the sternum, along his ribs and emerging from between his front legs. Professionals have a specially designed tool called a "Nikopolous Needle" which they use to work the wide webbing down through the mud. If you're lucky, you might be able to tie the end of your rope to a short, strong limb so as to make it easier to force it through the mud. Once the rope is safely around the animal, you can tie it securely to a nearby tree, if there is one, so as to keep him from slipping deeper into the mud. Now the real struggle begins.

**Dangers of Suction.** Your enemy is the suction which has swallowed your horse's body and keeps him trapped. Thick mud creates a vacuum so powerful that its destructive force is hard to comprehend. If the suction is not cancelled before rescuers attempt to pull the horse free, the animal may be severely injured or killed. Animals trapped in shallow mud have had their hooves pulled off! Horses have been cut in half by helicopters who pulled them free without first counteracting the deadly suction! You have to break the suction to free the horse!. Professionals use hoses that force compressed air or water down alongside the horse's body. These help break the mud's grip. Your options will depend on what tools and help you can muster. What matters is that you recall this threat and break its deadly grip on your horse before you begin to use the rope to pull him to freedom.

Regardless of how you go about it; pace yourself. Since this can be a long process, exhaustion will be your worst enemy. Take breaks and speak to your horse to calm him. Despite the hair-raising accidents which nearly ended their lives, there are no known episodes wherein Long Riders or their horses died by drowning in quicksand. So remain calm, stay positive and be patient.

**Breaking Free.** One of the most reliable ways to free the animal is to shift the horse onto his side, then pull him to freedom via a sideways drag. Aimé Tschiffely used this method to rescue his guide's horse from the river's quicksand. "Whenever a horse sinks into quicksand hind legs first, it is of no use to try to pull him out from in front, but to save him one has to pull in such a manner as to make him fall on his side. This frees his hind legs and gives him buoyancy, and then one can usually rescue him." By tipping the horse over onto his side, you increase the body surface area in contact with the mud. This not only assists you in pulling him across the mud, it incorporates the skeletal strength of his torso to reduce injury.

**Emotional Concerns.** When your horse's life is at stake there is no room for sentimentality. Only a concerted effort is going to free him. If he becomes too exhausted to assist, allow him to rest for a few moments, before you try again. Shout if you must. Hit him on the rump to encourage him. But don't let him surrender.

**Free at Last.** After you've waded in to save him, stripped off the gear which might drown him, managed to secure the lifeline around his body, and pulled him to freedom, don't forget that he may injure himself in his desire to break free of the mud or quicksand. Most horses will react violently when their feet finally touch hard ground. In a desperate effort to free themselves they may scramble up the bank. Make sure the horse doesn't shove you aside or injure you at the last minute. Have your knife ready to cut the rope if necessary. As soon as he has emerged, walk him forward until you are convinced he is on safe ground. A horse's body temperature often drops quickly when he is immersed in mud. After having endured such a stressful incident, keep him warm to prevent hypothermia. Be sure to check that the mud has not sucked his shoes off.

**Hints.** Unlike riding through a jungle or over a mountain, both of which might be avoided, quicksand or mud may take any Long Rider by surprise. But there are basic rules which will decrease your chances of encountering such a fearful danger. *Avoidance* – Treat any type of wet ground, such as river banks, marshes or beaches, with extreme suspicion. Always be on the lookout for any clue which indicates false footing. *Caution* – Quicksand and muskeg cannot be detected by looking for them from the saddle. Never advance unless you are absolutely sure the ground is safe for your horse! *Scouting* – If you suspect the ground, stop and scout ahead on foot. Carry a long, strong pole to test the ground in front of you. *Safety* – If your horse becomes bogged down, don't compound the problem by rushing into the mud or water without having assessed the situation for dangers. *Don't think it is quick* – It often takes professionals six hours to extract a horse from deep mud. *Don't think it is clean* – Before this dangerous and complicated rescue is ended you will be covered in filth.

# Chapter 52 - Environmental Hazards

Any would-be equestrian traveller has enough common sense to know that certain types of geography represent various levels of challenges. The previous chapters on mountains, deserts, rivers, jungles and swamps provide abundant evidence of these types of traditional dangers. Yet modern Long Riders must not forget that there is a new type of dangerous geography, one which our mounted ancestors could not have imagined and never encountered. Deadly man-made hazards, including radioactive landscapes, lethally polluted water, and disease-causing air now pollute sizeable portions of the planet which have traditionally been connected to equestrian travel. To ignore these hazards is not only naïve, it could be potentially deadly. What must be borne in mind is that a political decision made decades ago can not only diminish the chances of a modern journey's success, it could also have an extremely adverse effect upon the health of horse and rider.

Staying away from busy urban centres is an obvious solution, as no Long Rider willingly engages with man-made problems like traffic and air pollution. Likewise no one is going to willingly ride through a red-hot nuclear zone. The problem is that there is a surprising lack of recognition accorded to the radioactive or toxic chemical sites associated with former defence industries and test ranges. Because many years have elapsed since these facilities were operating, knowledge of their danger, or even existence, has increasingly been overlooked except by those locals too poor to emigrate. Becoming aware of these environmental dangers is part of your planning.

Complicating the problem is that these sites are scattered through some of the most important horse travel locations on the planet, such as Russia, Kazakhstan, Kyrgyzstan, Ukraine and Uzbekistan. All of these countries not only have populations which have suffered enormously because of intense assault on their environments, but in addition, because of their equestrian pasts. these nations continue to draw the interests of modern Long Riders. Before setting off on a journey through these portions of the former Soviet Union, Long Riders would be well advised to educate themselves about any potentially deadly environments which may be awaiting their arrival.

**The Aral Desert.** The Aral Sea, which covered 68,000 square kilometres (26,300 miles), was one of the four largest lakes in the world. In a vain hope of increasing the economic output of Uzbekistan's cotton fields, Moscow decided that the water from the two major rivers could be better used if they were drained into irrigation canals instead. The idea had two flaws. First, because many of the canals were poorly built, an estimated 75 percent of the water evaporated. Even worse was to follow; a lake that was once the size of Scotland eventually shrank by ninety per cent. The surface area of the Aral Sea has become so reduced that the shore lies around 150 kilometres (95 miles) from its previous location. The legendary inland sea is no more. In its place is a contaminated wasteland known as the Aral Desert and God help the Long Rider unlucky enough to try to cross this toxic ground. As the water receded it left an estimated 40,000 kilometres (25,000 miles) of former sea bed exposed. The loss of so large a mass of water contributed to the onset of severe desertification, which in turn altered local temperatures, making regional winters colder and summers hotter. To make matters worse, this huge plain is covered with salt, noxious chemicals and powerful pesticides. These substances are blown by strong winds and spread to the surrounding areas. Local inhabitants suffer from liver, kidney and eye problems attributed to the toxic dust storms. Other serious public health problems include high rates of cancer, lung diseases and a frightening type of drug-resistant tuberculosis.

**The Zone of Alienation.** Late on the night of April 26, 1986 an explosion ripped through the building which housed the fourth reactor at the Chernobyl nuclear power plant. The roof disintegrated and the walls buckled. Many years later witnesses recalled seeing a strange glow radiating from the direction of the Soviet Union's secretive nuclear facility. The red light, they said, looked like it was rising straight from Hell. In a way they were right, for mankind had unleashed a demon into the environment. There is now a specially designated Zone of Alienation which encompasses a 30 kilometre (19 mile) exclusion sector around the destroyed Chernobyl nuclear reactor site. It is administered by the Ukrainian Ministry of Extraordinary Situations.

**Polluted Polygon.** The Soviet Union controlled fifteen separate republics from 1922 to 1991. At the height of its power the vast empire ruled 22,402,200 square kilometres (8,649,538 miles) of territory. Hidden deep within the communist kingdom was Semipalatinsk, a super-secret nuclear test site. Located in the north-eastern corner of Kazakhstan, this polluted Polygon (military zone) presents a major geographic hazard to modern Long Riders. From 1949 to 1989 the Soviet Union carried out 752 nuclear explosions there. The blast from a single 130 kiloton nuclear explosion created an enormous crater which later filled with water. Fifty years later Lake Chagan is still radioactive and utterly devoid of life. The Republic of Kazakhstan declared its independence from Russia in 1991. Like Ukraine, with its polluted Chernobyl legacy, Kazakhstan also inherited an environmental time bomb from its former Soviet masters. An estimated 300,000 square kilometres (186,000 miles) of Kazakh countryside, inhabited by two million people, had been polluted by radioactive fallout. Once one of the most enigmatic and restrictive places on earth, the surrounding countryside suffered tremendous damage and large swathes of land are still contaminated. Parts of the Polygon have been declared safe to visit, while other portions are still banned. Checkpoints are maintained to deter intruders. The few authorized visitors are required to wear protective clothing and must be insured. Long Riders should avoid making a journey near this part of eastern Kazakhstan, as contamination continues to severely affect the local environment. The Chagan River, for example, contains a hundred times more radioactive tritium than the recommended limit. Nor can grazing be assumed to be safe, as the government has banned all agriculture in contaminated parts of the country.

**Poisoned Landscape.** When the newly-formed republic of Kyrgyzstan declared its independence, it proudly described itself as "the Land of Horses and Free Riders." What the politicians in Bishkek did not acknowledge was the notorious Mailuu Suu uranium mine. And who can blame them? When Soviet scientists detonated their first nuclear device in 1949, the uranium came from the mountains of Kyrgyzstan. For more than fifty years the town of Mailuu Suu housed the industrial complex that supplied the uranium used by the USSR in its immense nuclear arsenal. The legacy of the Soviet era was the creation of two million cubic metres of radioactive waste. Efforts were made to bury some of the poisonous material underground. These level patches are now favourite places for children to play on. Women often graze their animals on the grass growing from the contaminated soil beneath. Not everything was buried. Vast amounts of polluted material were simply bulldozed into convenient canyons. Years later the radioactive goose is coming home to roost. With uranium now leaching to the surface of the ground above the radioactive dumps, malignant cancer and birth defects are twice as high among the residents of Mailuu Suu as the rest of the Kyrgyz population.

# Chapter 53 - Storms

A Long Rider learns to live with the weather, not to fight it!

**Coping with the Weather.** While it is impossible to avoid bad weather on a long journey, many people are surprised to realize how capricious the climate can be. As Emperor Napoleon Bonaparte said, "We're all victims of the climate."

**Horses and Weather.** When hail the size of hen's eggs is hammering your hat, snow is falling in mid-summer, it has rained for weeks on end or lightning is threatening to turn you into a crispy fried treat, you may shake your fist at the wrath of the elements. It's one thing for a determined Long Rider to grit his teeth and vow to ride on. What you must not forget is that weather will age a horse more than it does a man! That's why you must never neglect to observe what's happening in the sky above you.

**Watching the Weather.** Throughout the ages man has looked for clues to how the weather was going to behave. Some of these signs were considered standard wisdom until the advent of the 20th century. This special folk lore was often passed on from generation to the next via easily memorized rhymes such as, "Morning dry, rain is nigh. Morning wet, no rain yet."

Other ditties used a horseman's tools to remind him to keep a sharp eye on the weather. "When ropes hold tight it's going to rain. When weather's fair, they go slack again." Keen observation had taught them that humidity rises before a storm. This causes the fibres in hemp rope to swell and knots to tighten before a rain storm.

Nor were the horses ignorant of the weather. They normally graze facing downwind so they can smell any predator which may be upwind of them, all the while keeping an eye open for anything which might try to sneak up from downwind. Knowing this, early Long Riders used this poem to explain how a horse reacted to the changing weather. "Tails pointing west, weather's the best. Tails pointing east, weather's the least." Here again, observation was confirmed, as a strong east wind often indicated the approach of wet weather, while a west wind meant fair weather. Rain does not hurt horses, as the natural grease in their skin renders it waterproof. But in cold, wet and windy weather, horses turn their tails to the wind, so as to gain some minimal protection. This same cold wind will degrade their condition, unless they get extra food.

**Riding in the Rain.** The rain falls on the just and the unjust alike.

When English Long Rider Mary Bosanquet was making her way across Canada in 1939, she had plenty of time to mull over the miseries of being wet. "Rain doesn't matter when you know where you are going. But where there is absolutely no certainty of getting feed for the horse or dry clothes for oneself, the effect on morale is considerable. If one gets down to walk, the saddle collects water like a pond. If one does not walk one grows numb with cold."

The longer your journey, the more unpredictable the weather may be. Wet conditions not only wear down a Long Rider's morale, but they also cause leather saddles and gear to rot and encourage sores to form on the horses.

**Thunderstorm.** Being wet can be demoralizing. Being caught in a severe storm can threaten your life. Thunderstorms are created when cold air crashes into warm moist air. The result can be a dangerous storm which springs up with very little warning. A sharp-eyed Long Rider will learn to detect the signs of this approaching menace. At night a halo around the moon confirms there is moisture in the air. This may lead to troublesome weather the next day. Once the sun is up, rainbows are a sign of the increased humidity needed to spawn a thunderstorm. Clouds also carry clues. If they are moving in one direction it reveals the passage of air from a high pressure area to a low one. If they begin to scatter in various directions, it may confirm a serious weather pattern is approaching. Should they become heavy and dark, an intense storm may be forming. Strong winds are easily discernable and loud thunder is a certain clue. Thunderstorms carry more of a threat than merely getting you and your mount wet. Strong winds can cause limbs to break off trees. Hail may hammer your horses if you can't get them into shelter.

**Flash Floods.** Being struck by hail is bad; being swept away in a flash flood is worse. This type of destructive occurrence typically occurs in desert or semi-arid environments, when a brief but immensely powerful surge of water, usually caused by short heavy rainfalls, triggers a flood of water to flow either over the surface (sheet flood) or down a normally-dry stream channel (stream flood). Such destructive floods often take place in countries which have areas of long, narrow drainage. Wild storms in Mongolia, for example, often cause flash floods to strike. Disaster struck Alexander the Great during his march across the Balochistan desert. He and his large army unwisely set up camp in a canyon. A roaring flood swept down the canyon, drowning many people.

You must be extremely cautious if a thunderstorm strikes while you are riding along a dry creek bed or within a deep canyon. Though the weather may not appear dangerous in your area, heavy rains further away may provoke a flash flood which appears without warning. Rain falling into these narrow channels collects and can rapidly trap you. You must be prepared to evacuate such a dangerous area without delay!

**Underestimating the Danger.** There are many inconveniences and threats attached to a severe storm. But none is more deadly or frightening than being struck by lightning. The majority of people do not associate riding and being struck by lightning. If the sky looks a bit cloudy, they might pack a rain coat and then set off without giving it another thought. Such a light-hearted group of riders recently departed on the north island of New Zealand. They were near the crest of a hill when a violent electrical storm took them by surprise. Lightning struck the last rider, instantly killing him and his horse. The other riders were treated in hospital for symptoms of shock. Perhaps in their naiveté they failed to realize that lightning kills more people than any other weather-related hazard? Learning how to avoid this deadly danger is of critical importance to a Long Rider.

**The Power of Lightning.** It is hard to grasp the destructive force of a lightning strike. Because the intense heat from a massive bolt can reach temperatures of approximately 50,000 degrees Fahrenheit, lightning has been known to burn a hole through a church bell and melt chains into iron bars. Because the deadly current can contain 100 million electrical volts, it has cooked potatoes in their fields and killed vast herds of animals in a single strike. What's even more alarming, an average of 1800 thunderstorms rage across our planet concurrently. These storms create a hundred lightning strikes every second - lightning hits our planet nearly nine million times a day.

**Defining Lightning.** Lightning is formed when a thundercloud becomes polarized. When this occurs a tremendous electrical connection is created between the positively charged clouds and the negatively charged base. Ultimately the charge becomes so immense that it overwhelms the capacity of the air to behave as an insulator. The resulting lightning bolt may then be dispensed entirely within a single cloud or be transmitted on horizontal lines between clouds. Even though the planet is generally negatively charged, a positive reaction is produced when negative ions in the base of a cloud provoke a positively charged electrical reaction, or shadow, on the earth below. Such a positively charged shadow not only overcomes and climbs any obstacle in its path, including mountains, trees and towers; in an effort to connect the flow of current between itself and the cloud above, it will blast up a streamer of power from the highest points on its surface. The instant this streamer connects with a descending pulse of current, the primitive circuit is complete. The result is a white-hot bolt of lightning which snaps towards the sky. Thus, notwithstanding an illusion of our eyesight, the majority of lightning strikes are racing from the ground up to the clouds above. Regardless of which way it's moving, lightning is fast. An average bolt racing along at 3,700 miles per second carries 300,000 volts of electricity over a few milliseconds. The good news is that the chances of being struck by lightning are rare. So the first thing to do is determine how close it is to you and your horse.

**Judging Distance.** To calculate the proximity of this danger, you need to listen to the clap of thunder, which is caused by the rapid heating and expansion of gases within the lightning channel. Whereas an average lightning bolt races across the sky at 224,000 miles per hour, a thunder clap proceeds at the slower speed of sound, which is one mile every five seconds. Consequently, by timing the pause between the lightning flash and the subsequent thunder clap, you can make an accurate estimate how far you are from the centre of the storm. As soon as you see the lightning bolt count, "one thousand one, one thousand two, etc." until you hear the thunder clap. Every five seconds places you a mile away from the storm centre. Thus, a ten second delay between observing the lightning and hearing the thunder means you are approximately two miles away. Lightning rarely strikes from more than six miles away. This means that if the time between observing the lightning and hearing the thunder clap is less than thirty seconds, you are less than six miles from the storm's epicentre. If that's the case, you need to pay immediate attention and prepare for evasive action.

**Avoiding the Danger Zone.** A lightning strike usually entails three or more strokes. Because it only takes an ordinary cloud a minute to recharge itself, the lightning can send out a rapid series of strikes. The quickest way to protect yourself is to immediately avoid any place which is likely to become a compelling target for a lightning strike. Remember what happened to the unfortunate New Zealand rider who was struck on the mountain? If you find yourself riding atop a peak, alongside a ridge or across a highly exposed promontory, make your way down without any delay! Keep in mind that lightning is not only attracted to a high point, it also tends to strike moving targets. A Long Rider sitting atop his road horse presents a perfectly lethal combination of these two attractions!

**Taking Cover.** Perhaps a primitive message deeply implanted within our DNA makes us instinctively seek shelter under a tree when the sky explodes? Regardless of where that alluring instinct originates, ignore it or you may perish. Never seek shelter under a solitary tree, as any tall object which stands above the surrounding countryside is automatically a prime target! Even an exceptionally tall tree located among a surrounding canopy of other trees may be hit. A herd of cattle was slain in Uganda when lightning struck the tree they were sheltering under. Should you find yourself riding through woodland, seek shelter in the undergrowth or among a stand of shorter trees. A recent discovery has proved that even the type of tree you're near may heighten your chances of survival. A common belief among old-time range riders was that lightning was more likely to strike a tree with rough bark. A smooth barked tree, they alleged, was safer. Scientists have now confirmed that lightning is less likely to strike a smooth tree and, if it does, the resulting explosion may not be as deadly. Another major threat is open water, damp ground or any type of natural drainage. All of these conduct ground currents, which will allow the lightning to travel along the surface directly towards you. Stay well away from wet ground or water! Finally, though it may seem obvious, never remain close to any type of metal structure, along a metal fence, near metal pipes, equipment or railroad tracks.

**Protecting the Horses.** The moment you've found the safest place to stay, set about securing your horses. Never tie them to metal picket pins, wire fencing or a steel railing. If you decide to tie them to a tree, make sure it is not the tallest one. Space the horses far enough apart that they can see each other, but if they become frightened cannot spin, kick or crash into their companions in a panic. As soon as they are secured, move the saddle, pack saddle, bridles and any metal gear away from them. Be sure to retain the saddle pad, as it will help provide you with important protection in the forthcoming emergency.

**Drop the Metal.** With the horses tied, choose a spot where they can see you, then set about removing anything metal from your body which might attract a lightning strike. Immediately remove metal objects like watches, rings, necklaces or spectacles that can conduct a fatal electrical charge. It may seem obvious, but never use a mobile phone as it increases the risk of lightning striking you directly in the head. Place your phone, any other electrical devices, and any metal objects, including tools from your pack saddle and metal tent poles, in a protected pile well away from you and the horses.

**Protect Yourself.** Though it is tempting to huddle together in a group, your safest option is to spread out, as this minimizes the risk of multiple injuries. Don't lie down or curl up into a foetal position. Place the drier side of your saddle pad on the ground beneath you, then crouch down on your toes with your feet close together. Don't sit on your hands, as they conduct lightning more effectively than your buttocks. Use your hands instead to cover your ears to offset the danger of having your eardrums shattered. By lowering your profile, placing yourself on the insulating saddle pad, and assuming a small protected position, you have reduced your chances of being struck by lightning. Don't be in a hurry to leave this relatively safe location. Until the thunder cloud departs, lightning can recur every minute. Even if your companion is struck, take great care before going to his aid, as there have been multiple cases where survivors rushing to attend a victim were themselves all struck and killed. Though it is equally distressing, if one of the horses is struck, do not risk your life by leaving your safe position! Most horses struck by lightning are killed. Those that are not slain are often knocked unconscious. There is no special treatment. Your primary objective is to stay alive until the lightning passes.

**When Lightning Strikes.** Though the chances of being struck by lightning are extremely low, the physical and psychological repercussions are often devastating. Victims reported that prior to being struck their skin tingled and their hair stood on end. The bolt of lightning that strikes the body and flows around it is described as the external flash over. The intensity of this charge is so great that if the victim's body is wet from sweat or rain, the moisture will be turned to steam. This tremendous charge is also capable of causing the victim's clothes and shoes to explode. As can be imagined, when such a gigantic electrical charge passes through the body, the internal organs are often injured. Most deaths occur from a heart attack, though the most frequent injury is rupture of the ear drum. Many victims also suffer burns. Other symptoms include confusion, numbness, seizures and amnesia.

**Waiting out the Storm.** Your first line of defence against becoming a lightning strike statistic is to always keep a sharp eye on the weather. If you encounter an unexpectedly severe thunderstorm, take immediate evasive action by evacuating any high ground and avoiding places which may attract lightning. Once you and the horses have found the safest shelter possible, be prepared to wait for the storm to move on. Plan on getting wet, being cold and exercising a great deal of patience. Also, be prepared to deal with upset horses. Thunder may scare them. Lightning close by will certainly terrify them. If they break free during a lightning storm, do not risk your life by trying to catch them! Always wait until the severe weather has receded before you begin your search and continue your journey.

112

# Chapter 54 - Cold

**Comprehending the Cold.** When American Long Rider Colonel James Meline rode across the American prairie during the winter of 1866 he survived a storm so cold that "even my memory froze." How can you relate to those words, as you sit reading this book in the warmth of your comfortable home? What do you think when I tell you that it gets so cold that metal snaps, that your teeth break from shattering together, that you're driven so mad with despair that you tear off your clothes and burrow into the snow? You see these words on the page, but your body doesn't feel the pain of what they mean.

**Horses in the cold.** Horses have the ability to resist extremely cold temperatures.

*For example a Long Rider witnessed this Yakut horse being ridden in Siberia. The thermometer registered minus 64 degrees Fahrenheit (minus 53 degrees Celsius).*

**Defence Against Cold.** To understand why horses die in the winter, we must first appreciate how their body normally functions. A horse's average body temperature ranges from 99 to 101 degrees Fahrenheit (37.2 to 38.3 Celsius). The outside temperature affects the horse's core body temperature. The colder the weather, the greater the chance that Nature will hamper the animal's natural ability to maintain the constant core body temperature needed to protect vital organs and life processes. As the cold increases, so does the horse's corresponding need to create the heat needed to protect its life. The creation of this heat is derived from the energy gained by digesting calories. No food, no heat! No heat, the vital organs die! Every decrease in the temperature is linked to a corresponding need to increase the horse's food supply. For example if the temperature stood at 30 degrees Fahrenheit, a horse weighing a thousand pounds would normally consume 15 pounds of hay per day. If the temperature dropped to 20 degrees, the hay supply must be enhanced to 17 pounds so as to provide additional raw energy to the horse's beleaguered system. It is also recommended that horses be fed grain to augment their energy needs.

**Drink or Die.** It isn't just a lack of fodder that can undermine the health of horses. They can also be injured if they become dehydrated. A horse will normally consume one gallon of water per 100 pounds of body weight, i.e. a 1,000-pound horse will consume 10 gallons of water per day. Even though it is critically important to keep your horse hydrated, as temperatures fall, the less likely it is that the horse will want to drink. Horses prefer water with a temperature ranging between 45 and 65 degrees Fahrenheit (7.2 to 18.3 degrees Celsius). When the water temperature drops to 32 degrees Fahrenheit (0 degrees Celsius) the horse may only drink between 1 and 3 gallons of water. At a time when you already have your hands full, a reduction in the horse's water consumption, combined with an increase in his forage consumption, will amplify the chance of colic.

113

Another danger is when a horse is required by circumstances to eat snow in order to reduce its thirst. This is counter-productive for many reasons. Ten times as much snow must be consumed to meet the horse's daily need for water. The calories needed to consume the snow and convert it to water drain off the vital energy needed to maintain core body warmth. Depending upon circumstances, you must attempt to provide ten gallons of water for your horse to drink per day. It should be free of ice and ideally warm enough to entice the horse to drink.

**Natural Defence.** Because the horse's hair functions as an efficient insulator, his heavy winter coat is his first line of defence against the cold. For this reason, horses travelling through cold climates must never be clipped or trimmed. Their coat must be allowed to grow. Nor should the hair in their ears or along their fetlocks be trimmed, as the onset of cold air causes the hair to stand up, which in turn helps the horse to trap and retain vital body heat. A horse has so small a stomach that he routinely spends seven hours a day working to get sufficient grass. As far north as fifty degrees of latitude, Nature provides the horse with seven hours of daylight even in mid-winter. Northward of that he needs beard bristles to aid him in feeling and selecting grass in the darkness. Southward of that, if he is hunted by wolves or tigers, he needs a few bristles for night grazing except in cloudless regions where there is always starlight. The extreme sensitive-ness of his face compels the horse to stand with his buttocks turned to the gale, tail tucked, head down. Problems arise when the coat becomes wet, as once the hair lies down it loses its insulating capabilities. Do not be misled into thinking that a long coat automatically ensures a warm and healthy horse. The most accurate assessment of the animal's condition is obtained by a careful feeling of the condition and fat found over the horse's ribs.

**Struggling to Stay Alive.** Travelling with horses during the winter is a difficult and dangerous task. Choosing horses that have a natural ability to tolerate extremely cold weather is a criti-cally important first step. If possible, the animals should be fed and fattened before you set off, so as to encourage the accumulation of fat which will later insulate the body and provide energy with the onset of colder temperatures. Even if you take these precautions, it is very difficult for horses to maintain their body condition if asked to travel through extremely cold weather. As a result of wind, wet and cold, most horses will lose body weight regardless of how carefully you care for them.

Just like you, the horse must maintain his core body temperature to survive. If he lacks the food and water needed to stay healthy, hypothermia will set in. When exposed to constant cold, the result can be a lower body temperature which causes the animal to shiver violently. As his body struggles to replenish the heat that is being lost, his movements become slow and laboured. In an effort to focus remaining resources on keeping the vital organs warm, the horse's surface blood vessels will contract further, causing the horse to stumble or appear confused. As the internal temperature continues to decrease, further physiological systems falter and heart rate, respiratory rate, and blood pressure all diminish. Walking becomes impossible. Eventually the animal's cellular metabolic processes shut down. Hypothermia has played a role in history. It was responsible for wiping out entire armies. For example, Napoleon lost an estimated 200,000 horses during his disastrous winter retreat from Russia. If your horse is unlucky enough to be afflicted with hypothermia, handle the animal with care. Warm him with blankets but do not rub his body. When his horse became cold and exhausted, Roger Pocock mixed sugar in the water. "The carbon is fuel which enters the blood and so becomes exposed to oxygen in the lungs, where its burning produces the heat which warms the body." Any type of shelter, no matter how rough, which provides protection from the bitter wind and helps keep him dry will increase your horse's chances of safety. If a three-sided shed is used, the open side of the shed should be opposite the prevailing wind.

**Wind Chill.** Regardless of which winter-time country you decide to ride through, your safety will depend on paying special attention to the threat of wind chill. As cold air passes over you, it amplifies the loss of warmth from your body in the same way that blowing on hot soup cools it down. The wind chill temperature is always lower than the actual temperature, which means that relying on the thermometer to gauge your safety may be misleading. In order to accurately calculate the temperature, and thereby estimate the level of danger, you must always remember the wind's negative effect. Thus, even if the thermometer "only" reads 35 degrees Fahrenheit, if the wind is blowing at 25 miles per hour, the wind chill factor causes the air to feel as if it is 8 degrees Fahrenheit. Great care must be taken if you are travelling through strong winds, as they are connected to serious winter weather health hazards, including the onset of hypothermia. Wind chill also increases the likelihood of frostbite.

**Frostbite.** As the outside temperature drops to 0 degrees Celsius (32 degrees Fahrenheit) or colder, the body's blood vessels begin to constrict and transfer blood away from those parts farthest from the heart. This constricted blood flow is designed to protect the vital organs and preserve the body's core temperature. Unfortunately, a reduced blood flow results in the eventual freezing and death of the skin tissue in the threatened areas. Extremities such as the fingers, toes and nose are all commonly victims of frostbite. In addition to wind chill, wet clothes and extreme cold also help bring about this injury. Long Riders in the saddle must take great care to avoid frostbite. There are four degrees of frostbite, each of which has varying degrees of pain. Extreme cases result in the tissue breaking away and the digits to be lost. Emergency treatment for frostbite requires placing the victim in a sheltered area, removing wet clothes and keeping him warm. Do not administer alcohol.

**Saddling with Care.** Travelling in extreme cold requires a Long Rider to give careful thought, not just to obvious considerations such as the weather, but to the small details of daily life on the road. The amount of time and additional care needed to saddle up in the morning is an excellent example. Saddling up is never easy matter when your fingers are stiff and painful with the cold. Serious weather will require you to wear gloves to protect your fingers from frostbite. But wearing gloves will compel you to carefully study your equipment, so as to determine how easily you can handle it when your hands are covered and clumsy.

Your choice of equipment is also affected by the temperature. For example, it is common for cheap plastic rope to freeze. This makes a nightmare out of trying to untie a tethering line. Higher quality mountaineering rope stays pliable in cold weather, allows you to handle knots, dries quickly and is easy to grip. To help diminish the chances of leather freezing, be sure it is well oiled. Avoid using plastic tack on your reins or bridle, as plastic may stiffen and break when frozen. Give particular consideration to the bit. Never put a cold bit in the horse's mouth! When the icy metal comes in contact with the warm, sensitive flesh of the horse's mouth, it may cause it to split and tear. Test it by touching it with your exposed fingers. If it burns you, it will harm him. You must always warm the bit by breathing on it, placing it under the arm of your coat or rubbing it with your gloved hands. Test it to make sure the metal is safely warmed before you put the bit in the horse's mouth or it will hurt him. Likewise, metal stirrups may cause you an equal amount of grief in cold weather. The metal transmits an amazing amount of cold into the rider's feet.

**Riding in the Cold.** Getting warm before you set out is an important part of a cold morning routine. Providing a brisk grooming will produce the heat needed to stop your horse from shivering. Always make a point of warming your feet before mounting, as it is much easier to keep the circulation than to create it. Once you're in the saddle, the area which receives the most cold is the legs. Captain John Codman rode from New York to Boston during the winter of 1887. He devised a way to stay warm in the saddle. "Double the blanket, and leaving just enough to go under the saddle, allow most of it to fall over the horse's neck until you are mounted. Having mounted, pull the remainder of it over your legs. This rug will keep you warm in the cold."

During the course of the day, you will find occasions to dismount and walk alongside your horse. A good way to warm your cold fingers is to place them between the saddle and the horse's back. Another small tip to help your day go easier is to make sure your pack horse is wearing a bell. By listening to the bell's gentle, consistent ringing you don't have to turn around in the saddle to know that your pack horse is following closely behind.

**Hidden Dangers.** Cold weather demands that you take every precaution, otherwise a life-threatening situation may suddenly arise. Never set off unless you are confident that you can reach that day's destination or an alternative source of safety en route. Because bad weather might trap you, always make sure you have enough warm clothes and food to survive an unexpected storm. Once you've begun riding be extra careful with orientation, especially if it begins to snow, as distances and dimensions become distorted.

If you encounter deep snow, stop and take time to carefully calculate the depth of the snow and its quality. A single horse can push through dry snow up to three feet deep, but not for long. If you are travelling with a companion, let each rider take a turn riding in the lead to open a track through the snow. But remember, deep snow can hide a great number of perils. In Mongolia and Tibet, snow treacherously conceals the marmot holes. Horses which step in them frequently stumble. If possible, always stay on an established trail. If you encounter deep snow, dismount, secure your horse, then proceed cautiously on foot, probing the snow with a long thin stick so as to detect any hidden holes, treacherous crevices and menacing precipices. It pays to be suspicious of snow bridges, as the warming of the sun may have weakened them. Probe them on foot before riding over. Always pay keen attention to the dangers of an avalanche. Large drifts of wind-driven snow are extremely unstable. If you suspect the snow pack lying on the mountainside overhead is dangerous, do not proceed.

**Horse Hooves and Snow.** Even though the chances of you encountering an avalanche are slim, once you venture into a snowy environment there is one problem you will certainly encounter. Winter time riding will require you to pay extra attention to your horse's hooves. It is very common for snow to become impacted under the animal's feet. This can lead to injury and lameness. As is always the case when discussing the topic of allowing horses to travel either with shoes or without, there are valid considerations for both points of view. The deciding factors should be based on the condition of your individual horse's hooves, the type of ground you will be covering and the amount of snow you expect to encounter. In either case, there is no guarantee that your horse may not come to harm. Your goal is to arrive at a conclusion based on logic and evidence, not dogma and emotion, then provide the horse with as much protection and assistance as possible.

Now that the great herds of wild horses which once roamed across the snowy Central Asian steppes are a thing of the past, with the exception of Mongolia's Przewalskis, there are very few wild horses residing in harsh winter climes. Consequently, when we consider the idea of allowing our horse to travel barefoot through the snow, we must not put too much stock in Mother Nature. Generations of interaction with man has resulted in horses whose natural protection and abilities have been diluted. We should therefore carry out a careful examination of our horse's hooves before making a decision on how the animal proceeds.

Individual hooves vary as much as human feet. Some are naturally balanced, blessed with dense hoof horn and possess concave soles, all of which help reduce the chances of snow becoming impacted under the hoof. Other horses may be less fortunate. Their hooves may have a flat sole, which provides poor traction and brittle hoof horn, which will break on the rock-hard ice. Keep in mind that the hoof's growth is dramatically reduced during the winter, slowing to half its spring rate. This reduction in growth can adversely affect the horse's hooves if you subject him to travel over surfaces which are abrasive, i.e. ice, snow-covered rock and gritted roads. By riding the horse barefoot, you expose the hooves to increased abuse.

This isn't to say that metal shoes are the automatic answer. In fact, they offer a specialized set of problems. It's easy to forget that the hard hoof is actually a sensitive, fragile, living part of the horse's body. Just as the metal bit can burn the susceptible tissues of the horse's mouth, the cold metal of a shoe transmits freezing temperatures to the hoof. Plus because metal contracts in the cold horse shoe nails have a tendency to shrink in cold weather leaving the shoes loose. Despite these drawbacks, horse shoes offer protection to the hoof during its dormant period of growth, and if properly equipped, they also provide much-needed traction. Normal steel horse shoes can become dangerously slippery in winter conditions, as the combination of smooth metal and ice is a sure recipe for a horse to lose its balance and come crashing down. A number of methods have been devised to offset this danger. Adding borium to the bottom of a shoe provides the horse with an extremely hard material which digs into ice. Duratec horse shoe nails are another alternative, as their extra-large heads also provide traction on slippery surfaces. Caulks are small tungsten carbide studs which act like crampons. They can either be screwed in or driven on. Providing your horse with extra traction becomes even more important if you ride through mountainous terrain, where the animal will have to dig in if he is to proceed. It is not advisable to use rubber shoes, as they harden in cold weather and provide less traction than either a natural hoof or a winter-time shoe.

**Snow Balls.** One of the problems involved with equestrian travel is the need to foresee possible negative events. When the weather is freezing, and you're hunched over in the saddle desperately trying to stay warm, you're going to be praying for a roof and a meal. The last thing you will want to do is stop your cold horse, crawl down and knock grapefruit-sized balls of ice off his hooves. But the chances are that's exactly what you will end up doing, as the alternative is even worse.

It's important to understand that a horseshoe provides an ideal setting for snow and ice to become securely lodged. This occurs when the heat of the horse's sole melts the snow, which in turn causes the slush to freeze onto the cold metal horseshoe. The result, known as a snowball, consists of snow, ice, mud and manure. This compacted mess causes an amazing number of complications. Walking on a snowball may throw the horse off balance, which may cause him to suddenly slip and fall. Even standing on a snowball is extremely fatiguing for the horse's muscles, tendons and joint ligaments. Because of his decreased stability, the horse may wrench a fetlock. These frozen blocks can also cause severe pressure on the sole and bruise the frog. Even though borium and studs increase a horse's traction on slippery ground, they are useless if the shoes are not touching the ground. Thus, added traction does not automatically also prevent the build-up of snowballs.

There are two effective defences against snowballs, one is state-of-the-art, the other home made. The Mustad Company offers a unique No Snow pad. This air cushion compresses when the hoof is on the ground. When the hoof is raised, the cushion pops out the accumulated snow. The pad, which is applied before the shoe is nailed on, may decrease the horse's traction. These pads work well when the horse travels through deep snow. An old-fashioned, low-tech remedy is to lubricate the horse's soles with grease, Vaseline or non-stick cooking spray. This is a temporary measure, which will not last long. If you find you need to make use of this tactic because of an emergency weather situation, dry the sole of the hoof before applying the oil or grease. But take note. The rougher the conditions, the shorter the amount of time this remedy will last. While such an old-fashioned solution may serve in a pinch, unless your horse is equipped with snow pads you will learn that the hoof pick will be your indispensable and constant companion. Some Long Riders have also carried a small hammer, which they found was effective for knocking out the snowballs and scraping the hoof clean.

**Frozen Rivers.** Crossing a frozen river on horseback is a specialized hazard, one which requires caution and patience. If you make a mistake count yourself lucky if you only come out wet, as chances are that either you or your horse may drown.

Never take your horse onto a frozen river unless the ice is at least ten inches thick!

Because ice quality is unpredictable, do not attempt to cross a frozen river too early in the winter season. If you cannot determine the thickness of the ice, remain patient. Your best option is to stay safely on shore. Unluckily, dangerous ice isn't obvious. But you can detect certain clues as to its thickness and safety. For example, ice formed over a moving body of water, such as a river, is always more dangerous than ice formed over a still body of water, like a lake. Also, ice with bubbles is always weaker than clear ice.

Never ride over a frozen river without having first scouted it on foot! Use a long pole to help sound the ice as you progress cautiously. Once you have confirmed that the river appears to be safe, remove anything heavy you may have been carrying, then lead your horse across on foot.

Even though people fall through the ice every year, there are no known cases of Long Riders and their mounts crashing into a river. Should you and your horse fall through simultaneously, things will happen very quickly. The moment you feel the ice breaking, concentrate on saving your own life. Do not panic. Even in near-freezing water, people generally have at least five minutes to extract themselves from the water. The effect of the freezing water on your body will immediately cause you to begin hyperventilating. Keep your head above water, stay afloat and swim away from the flailing hooves of the horse. Concentrate on normalizing your breathing so as to ensure that you can summon enough energy to get out of the water. The strongest ice will generally be that which you were on just before you fell in. Try to make your way to that edge, looking for the ice which appears to be thick and intact. Using your elbows and arms, pull yourself out as far as possible. Chances are you won't be able to extricate yourself totally, but the water running off your upper body will help lighten the load. Once you are as far forward as possible onto the ice, kick your feet as you would if you were swimming, while you use your arms and elbows to push and pull yourself out of the hole. Once you're out of the water, don't stand up. Because the ice may be weak, you must distribute your weight. Crawl several feet away from the hole before you risk standing up. Retrace your footsteps to a point of safety. Because of the onset of hypothermia and death it is essential that you begin efforts to get warm. Change clothes immediately, otherwise you will begin to freeze. Start a fire and seek help for the horse.

**Preparing for a Cold Camp.** The way you conclude a cold day in the saddle is very significant. A horse can withstand severe cold but it is absolutely imperative that it not be made to sweat! You must gauge the day's ride so as to ensure that the horse arrives calm and dry. Select a place which is free of snow and offers the best protection from the wind. Position the horses with their tails to the wind. When you dismount, loosen the girth but do not remove the saddle! Sudden exposure to cold air will cause the horse's hot back to be afflicted with the onset of severe saddle sores. Depending on the severity of the temperature, you should be prepared to leave the saddle in place for at least two hours. During this time the job of the saddle changes. It now serves as a fundamental blanket which will allow the horse's sweaty back to gradually cool. Remove the bridle and tie the horse by his lead rope. But do not allow him to eat or drink! Cold water can have a deadly effect on a hot horse, as it drains off vital energy needed to keep the internal organs warm. Tim Cope nearly had a disaster when he allowed his horses to drink too quickly on a cold winter's day in Kazakhstan.

"If you give water straight away their body temperature will drop rapidly and they risk sickness. One time I had no choice but to give water from a well at the end of a day because I had to flee the village to find a campsite. The horses all began to shiver immediately and looked very sick. In this scenario it was important to keep on moving and warm them back up," Tim explained.

Once the horses are tied, allow them to rest quietly. Check the horses by sliding your hand under the blanket to see if their backs are still sweaty; once they have completely cooled, you may unsaddle, water, feed and grain them as usual. Should you be caught out during severe weather, you must make an effort to keep the horses warm and dry. If you are travelling with three or more horses, then you can resort to the practices used by the Swedish cavalry. First they covered the ground with spruce or pine branches to provide insulation for the horses' hooves. During the course of the night, a soldier would continually move a horse from the middle of the picket line to the outside of the line. This rotation allowed the horses in the middle to stay warm, and diminished the time any one horse was exposed to the extreme cold experienced on the end of the picket line.

**Keep Moving.** In extreme cases, you may be forced to continue moving, otherwise you and the horse run the risk of freezing to death. This happened to Baron Fukishima when he rode across Siberia. He had to frequently dismount and clear the ice from the horse's nostrils and eyelashes.

"During an eleven day stretch it never got warmer than minus 20. It was probably colder but the thermometer didn't go below that degree."

**Hints.** Even though mounted man has been riding through winter weather for centuries, an apprehension runs through our subconscious like a deep genetic code. If you underestimate the cold, its power will break you. If you treat the winter with contempt, the elements will slay you and your horse. Know your limits! Proceed with caution!

118

# Chapter 55 - Heat

There are two types of hot weather riders, those who are prepared and those who are surprised. Regardless of where you ride the sun has no respect for you or your horse. If you venture out into it without caution, you are putting your lives at risk.

**Horses and Heat.** Because horses stand dry heat better than damp, humidity is always a concern. But dry heat or not, the amount of exertion a horse is capable of undergoing is affected by other factors. For example, more often than not the danger of riding in hot weather will be compounded when circumstances force you to travel alongside a paved road, as the asphalt reflects the heat straight up onto you and your weary mount. Even under normal conditions the act of locomotion only requires about 20% of the body's raw energy. Much of the remaining energy is transferred into body heat. Here's where your worries begin because this heat builds up in the horse three times faster than in your body. Like us, the horse will lose some heat via respiration. The problem is that the shape of his body, and its larger percentage of heat-generating muscle, reduces his ability to dissipate heat through the evaporation of sweat. Thus, though you are travelling together, his ability to dissipate heat is seriously reduced compared to yours. In a word, even though the climate may not be causing you undue stress, the horse will suffer more than you do. To add to your concerns, if your horse is not acclimatised, has a thick coat, or is overweight and unfit, he will sweat all the more. This in turn will cause his body to work hard just to cool itself down.

**Water.** The first line of biological defence is water. Like all other living organisms, water is an essential element without which your horse cannot survive. But a horse doesn't just drink water. Nearly 70% of his body is composed of this life-giving liquid. Most of it is concentrated in the individual cells of his body and acts as a vital component in his blood. Additionally, his internal organs, principally his large intestine, serve as a fluid reservoir which may hold up to 16 gallons of water. Thus, water will account for about 660 pounds (300kg) of the body mass in a 1,000 pound (450 kg) horse. Horses on average drink about a gallon (4½ litres) of water per day for every 100 pounds of body weight. Therefore a thousand pound horse should be consuming ten gallons a day. However, it's not unusual for a horse to drink more than it needs. The daily requirements will depend on a variety of factors including heat, humidity, how heavy his load is and how far you have travelled. Under stressful conditions a horse may increase his daily water intake by as much as four times the minimum amount. Your job is to provide him with every opportunity to replace his body fluids and restore his depleted electrolytes. Never withhold water, as every drink, no matter how small, works in his favour.

**Sweat.** Where does all that water go? Part of it is lost in vast amounts of sweat. It is not unusual for a Thoroughbred running one mile in two minutes to produce more than two gallons of sweat. The quantity of water your horse loses will depend on the temperature, humidity and how hard he is working. Regardless of the exact amount, as the animal sweats it loses precious water and the body salts known as electrolytes. Because a horse's sweat is hypertonic, it contains a higher proportion of salts than blood does. Should water be lost and electrolytes not replaced, the horse will become dehydrated. But long before that, it has become thirsty.

**Thirst.** Because sodium is more concentrated in the human bloodstream, the signal to relieve thirst is dispatched quickly. This crucial signal acts more slowly in a horse. Consequently, even though a horse may have a lost a large amount of water by sweating, his body will not immediately acknowledge thirst. A dilemma then arises because even though you have provided water, the horse's body has not recognized that he is dehydrated and thirsty.

**Salt.** Like water, salt is an element which all animals need in one form or another to survive. Because it helps balance cell fluids and retain water, horses and humans cannot live without it. In fact they both crave it. Most horses will consume small but sufficient amounts of salt if it is made available on a daily basis. They will not routinely overindulge. However the amount of salt needed and digested varies between horses and is affected by extenuating circumstances. A horse will consume about one ounce (28gr) of salt per day, if he is not working hard or being exposed to hot weather. As soon as he starts to sweat heavily, additional attention must be paid to his need for salt, as excessive sweating requires an increase of 1% to his normal daily ration. As travelling horsemen we need to be keenly aware of how important salt is to our horse's health, especially in hot weather, all the while realizing that this vital element may be hard to find and difficult for your horse to digest. Is there a solution? Normally, your horse would be allowed to consume the amount of salt his body desired and needed. This delicate balance would vary from day to day, depending on his work and the weather. But if he is being bedded down in a different place every night then this normal routine won't work. Depending on what country you ride through, you should obtain and carry a small amount of livestock salt. This has additional trace minerals and is not as pure as common table salt. However, should this not be available, then you may have to use what you can find. When it comes to providing the salt to your horse, you can mix his small daily requirement with his grain ration. Another method is to sprinkle his hay with water, then sprinkle on the salt and rub it into the hay. Adding a small dash of salt to the horse's water has also been used effectively.

Too much salt can be deadly. Yet scientists have confirmed that a horse's body will still be working to recover lost salt the day after intense exercise. So a delicate and careful balance is required. Also, pecking order may be a factor if you are feeding, watering or offering salt to more than one horse.

**Dehydration.** Horses and humans normally lose water on a continual basis in the form of sweat, urine and faeces. Ordinarily this liquid is replaced by consuming more water. Serious danger sets in when a horse loses so much fluid in the form of sweat that his body's fluid levels become out of balance. The serious condition known as dehydration occurs when the horse has lost an excessive amount of water, usually brought on by a combination of factors including heat, humidity and exertion. Because the onset of equine dehydration can be very dangerous, it is essential that you identify the symptoms as quickly as possible.

Despite the urgency, an immediate problem arises due to the fact that dehydration is difficult to detect. A dehydrated horse will sweat less than normal. Because of his loss of liquids, he will also urinate less frequently or not at all. His flanks may look caved in. His eyes may appear to have sunk into his skull. His extremities will feel cool. His pulse will be fast and weak. More obvious still will be his loss of strength and an increasingly weakening condition. When these symptoms take affect, total exhaustion is soon to follow.

But there is much more to be worried about than simply the animal's deteriorating performance. His life is at stake! Severe dehydration will cause the horse's heart-rate to raise dramatically, as the reduced amount of fluid in the animal's blood vessels forces the heart to pump ever harder in order to send blood through the weakening body. As the condition worsens the horse may collapse and then die. Horsemen have traditionally relied on an ancient analysis to detect dehydration. Known as the skin pinch, this test relies on the fact that under normal conditions the horse's skin is elastic and pliable. To perform a skin elasticity exam, you gently pinch the skin on the horse's neck and observe its reaction. If the skin quickly returns to normal you know the horse is safely hydrated. Should the skin collapse slowly, or even worse remain erect, you can assume the horse is dehydrated. The longer the skin remains erect before going flat, the more severe the dehydration. Like other non-scientific tests of this kind, the results can be inaccurate and confusing, particularly as the elasticity of the skin varies from horse to horse. Yet even if you are unable to determine exactly how severely dehydrated the horse may be, skin tenting is a strong indication that the body fluids are dangerously low and the horse's safety has been seriously compromised.

**Treatment.** When considering the severity of what may happen to a dehydrated horse, you will understand that prevention is by far the best option. On the other hand equestrian travel is filled with unforeseen hardships and hazards, so if you are forced to ride in hot weather you should take every precaution.

His body cannot dissipate heat as efficiently as yours can. This means you will have to ensure that you keep him as cool as possible. Even if you do not think the day's travel has been too severe, dismount and loosen his girth. Because moving muscles dissipate heat, walk him slowly and stop him in the shade. After you come to a halt, don't be tempted into thinking that giving him a big bucket of ice cold water will solve the problem. In fact you must not over water the horse. Because his body is lacking essential electrolytes, the horse's body will not interpret an excessive amount of water as a life saver. Mistaking the water to be excess fluid, the kidneys flush it out via renal excretion. This not only removes more of the critically low electrolytes from the system, in a perverse act of nature it increases the animal's state of dehydration. To add to your worries, allowing an excessive amount of water may also induce colic. The proper treatment is to offer a hot horse sips of cool, not cold, water at frequent intervals.

Also, consider the depletion of electrolytes in the horse's system, as animals that are sweating heavily can lose up to 50gr of these vital minerals per hour. Even though salt, potassium, calcium, magnesium, phosphates and sulphates all have a fundamental role to play, caution must be used when providing a dose of electrolytes to a horse. If too large a dose is administered, the animal's weakened body will mistakenly direct critically needed water to the upper intestinal tract so as to dilute the influx of electrolytes. This serves to enhance the effects of dehydration. Providing electrolytes to a dehydrated horse is akin to obtaining veterinary help. The country where you ride will largely determine what medical options you have. Should you know in advance that you will be travelling beyond the call of medical assistance you may wish to prepare for a hot weather emergency by purchasing a tube of electrolyte paste. This two ounce dose is squeezed into the horse's mouth. The absorption begins immediately, lasts for two hours, and restores lost minerals.

In addition you can help cool him further by softly spraying or washing him with water. Use a sponge or rag to wash down the large blood vessels inside his legs, stomach and neck. Don't let water rush into his ears. Wash his face carefully, being sure to moisten inside his nostrils.

**Riding in the Heat.** There have been occasions when an equestrian traveller has knowingly set off to ride across one of the world's hot spots. For example when Major Clarence Dalrymple Bruce found himself riding across "The Devil's Plain" in Tibet during the summer of 1905, the temperature in the sun was 130 degrees Fahrenheit (55° Celsius). Yet it had been known to reach 158 degrees!

When you create a combination which includes a sweaty, tired, weakened horse, match him with a weary, drooping rider, then place them both on a busy road which is populated by fast traffic - you're looking at a potentially lethal problem. This isn't to say that you can't travel if the sun is blazing. But if you do decide to risk it, then you need to radically restructure your daily routine in order to enhance your safety. The first thing to remember is to never ride during the hottest part of the day. This is the most dangerous thing you can do. When the weather's hot, always travel early and late. You should be moving down the road at first light. This means getting up in the dark, feeding the horse breakfast, tacking up and swinging into the saddle a few minutes before the sun rises. You should allow two hours prior to sunrise to make this system work.

Prior to your departure, prepare yourself and the horse for what lies ahead. If your horse has pink or sensitive skin, then apply zinc oxide cream to prevent sunburn. Protect your own face and hands. Otherwise they will burn and blister. Wear long sleeves, a large hat or a turban.

In temperatures up to 100° Fahrenheit (37° Celsius) you should always be out of the saddle and in the shade no later than eleven a.m. This will allow you and the horse to rest, decrease sweating, stay relatively cool and reduce mental stress during the worst heat of the day. Never mount again until the worst of the heat has passed, which usually occurs by late afternoon.

Do not ride if the temperature exceeds 100° Fahrenheit (37° Celsius)!

Regardless of the hour, when you ride through great heat do not move faster than a strong walk. Six hours in the saddle, at four miles per hour will still allow you to travel an average of 24 miles a day. If possible, wash the horse with cool water as soon as you stop. If water isn't available, be extra careful about pulling the saddle off too quickly. The horse's back will be very hot, so you have to give it time to cool naturally. Loosen the girth but only take the saddle off once the back is no longer sweaty.

121

**Riding at Night.** Well, you must be saying, if it's so bloody hot during the day then I'll outsmart the sun and ride at night. Wiser Long Riders than you thought of that idea long ago. What they learned was that this is a dull and dangerous option. To begin with the horse's natural hour to sleep is between 1 and 4 a.m., not to mention what such a move will do to your own biological clock. Another consideration when riding at night is that one has the sensation of sitting very high above the ground. Finally, because nothing can be seen, distances seem enormous and hours stretch into eternities. If your life depends on it, then use this option with an exceeding amount of caution. Otherwise, ride in the daylight when you and the horse can see where you're going.

**Hints.** If you've never experienced truly life-threatening heat it's hard to realize what it does to you. It's not until you feel the air burning as you breathe, your skin frying, or your mind reeling that you begin to comprehend what a deadly foe the sun can be. You cannot beat the heat. You can only outwit and outlast it. Your geographic goal isn't going anywhere. You're supposed to be enjoying yourself, not suffering in the saddle. If things don't feel right, always put the safety of you and your horse before any kind of trick which your ego might try to play on you. If you suspect that the health of either you, or your horse, is being compromised, then stop that day's ride immediately. If you suspect that your safety is at stake, reschedule the ride for a cooler part of the year.

# Chapter 56 - Bridges and Tunnels

As many Long Riders have learned, things can get very bad, very quickly, on a bridge. It's going to be you and your horse against the river. So learning everything you can about bridges is of great importance.

**Taken by Surprise.** Never let the bridge surprise you! If you've studied your route in advance, don't take if for granted that you'll just trot across the bridge. Most maps are flat-faced liars; the bridge may have been washed away or be in terrible condition.

**Where to Cross.** Depending on what country you find yourself in, the choice of bridges will influence the progress of your travels. Many nations don't have numerous bridges. This may force you to ride hundreds of miles out of your way to cross a hostile river.

Other countries are blessed with bridges and finding them presents no problems. For example, there are more than 40,000 bridges in America. The problem is that not all of them are horse friendly, nor will the authorities permit you to cross with your animals. Take the mighty Mississippi River for example. It's one such obstacle which offers a variety of options and it proves that even if you've found a bridge you may not have found an answer. If you find yourself at the top of the American nation, then you may cross over the Mississippi River via Minnesota's Lexington Bridge. Travel further south to the bridge at LaCrosse, Wisconsin and you'll find yourself sharing a span that routinely sends 9,000 cars a day over the river. The Burlington Bridge in Illinois only allows trains. Further south you might consider Louisiana's Horace Wilson Bridge until you learn about its notorious daily traffic jams. This is why most Long Riders going "ocean to ocean" decide to cross "the big muddy" at Cape Girardeau. Located in the state of Missouri, this puts a Long Rider in the centre of the country. Of course just because it makes sense on paper doesn't mean it's going to appeal to you when you ride up and finally inspect it in person.

**Legalities.** So what do you do when you're face to face with the mighty Mississippi or some other enormous waterway? Obviously you're not going to swim it. Chances are there isn't a ferry. This will almost certainly require you to cross via a bridge. So what's the first thing you check? You give a thought to discovering if it's legal to take your horse over. Some American state transportation departments require you to apply for a permit before taking your horse across. The 5,000 foot long Tacoma Narrows Bridge in the state of Washington is one such example. Because it is one of the longest suspension bridges in the nation, not only do you have to obtain permission from the state government to continue your journey via the bridge, you also have to arrange to have a highway patrol car follow behind with its light flashing. Other states are not as lenient. It is illegal to take a horse across the three-mile-long Golden Gate Bridge which spans San Francisco Bay in California.

**When to Cross.** Any time you share the road with cars it becomes a perilous situation; but never more so than when there is a drop of hundreds of feet to the water below. After consulting with the highway patrol or local authorities, choose a day and hour to cross which will place you amidst traffic that is as light as possible. Sunday mornings are ideal times to cross normally-busy rivers.

**Inspection.** To reduce the risk of nasty surprises, never cross the bridge with your horse without first walking over it. Carefully inspect the bridge before you attempt to take your horse across. Walk its length. Shake the rails. Study the traffic.

**Determine the Footing.** Your first concern will be with the footing underneath the horse's hooves. Countries subject to cold weather often construct the bridge flooring out of see-through metal. These strong steel grills allow the snow to melt and fall into the river below. A problem may arise when an inexperienced horse encounters this steel flooring. From the horse's point of view, it seems he is being asked to walk on air over a river he can see flowing beneath. That is why you may think yourself fortunate if you find a bridge whose surface is covered in asphalt. After all, the horse will probably not realize that this stretch of road leads him over a river. Whether the footing is steel or asphalt, a terrible peril may arise the moment a horse steps foot on any bridge. Horses have gone into a panic and bolted when the loud sound of their metal horseshoes hit the metal bridge.

**Lead the Horse.** Lead your horse across the bridge on foot. Before starting out, take a moment to make sure that everything is tightly cinched and tied down. The last thing you need is something to start flapping and frighten the horse half-way over the river. Once you're sure your gear is secured, do not rely on the fragile reins. Use the lead line and halter so as to provide you with the maximum amount of control. When you come to the bridge, allow the horse time to make sense of the situation. Stand to one side when he first steps on. Do not to let him bolt. Hold him tightly, but stay calm and act confident. If he becomes frightened, remain relaxed and speak to him in a low voice. The words do not matter so long as the tone is soothing. Depending upon the construction of the bridge, do not stray too close to the railing. The last thing you want is to be thrown over the edge or jammed against the railing. Once you're moving, don't stop. If your horse trusts you, he will follow. Your aim should be to make it across without any delays.

**Flags and Escorts.** There are two good ways to protect you from surly drivers. The best is to arrange to have an escort vehicle follow behind you and the horses. Any time you find yourself involved with traffic, it's a good idea to alert them to your presence as soon as possible. One way of doing this is to carry a red flag. A 24" long pole, with a red flag attached, can be easily carried either behind the cantle of your saddle or in easy reach on top of the pack saddle. As you lead your horse with your right hand, hold the red flag out with your left hand as a warning to drivers.

**Swinging bridges.** Never attempt to take horses over a swinging bridge unless there is no alternative! If you should be unfortunate enough to find yourself facing such a situation, there is no room for error. When you reach the bridge, stop and tie the horses securely, then unload them. Carry your equipment across the bridge in small loads. This not only ensures that your gear is safe, equally importantly; it will allow you to inspect the bridge with the utmost care. Pay special attention to the deck. If there are gaps in the flooring; place stones in or around the hole. This will alert the horse to avoid that hazard. If a horse loses his balance, shies, or falls through a hole in the deck, his actions may cost both your lives.

Before you attempt to take your horses across, give a thought to their mental abilities. The horse who is the least likely to panic will be the first across. But don't ignore the emotional needs of his stay-behind companion. Tie the remaining horse so that he can observe the first horse make the crossing. This will diminish the chances that the horse left behind will begin screaming if he can't see his friend. Don't attempt to use the bit and bridle for this situation. Replace it with the head collar and lead rope. Lead the horse to the bridge and then allow him to assess the situation. Chances are he may sniff the deck or look at the bridge with suspicion. Once he's had a good look, walk him onto the bridge gradually. Once he has all four feet on the bridge, stop to let him gain his balance. Then begin to proceed steadily, slowly and calmly. Don't pause to look back. Stay ahead of him. Keep your free arm out from your body to discourage him from trying to pass you. Never let the lead rope drop, as he may step over it.

**Tunnels.** Horses don't like tunnels. Why would they? To their mind, it looks like the terrifying end of the world. Even though the horse is only relying on his instincts, your logical mind will have alerted you to the very real dangers that actually lurk ahead. The amplified noise, the blinding headlights rushing at you, the cold water dripping down from the ceiling, all combine to turn a trip through a dark hole into an equestrian version of Russian roulette.

Like bridges, it pays to scout ahead. The majority of tunnels have been built to accommodate motorized traffic, and therein lies a host of dangers. Depending on how long, tall and well-lighted the tunnel is will determine if you lead the horses through one at a time or travel in a group. If you do decide to travel together, try to arrange for a vehicle to follow behind with its lights flashing. Not only will this provide you with protection, the vehicle's headlights will illuminate the road ahead. Should there be two of you, and if the tunnel is narrow, consider sending your friend on ahead on foot. Once he is on the far side, he can halt traffic entering the tunnel from the other direction. Unless you can see the ceiling overhead, you will be in danger of cracking your head in the dark or being swept from the saddle by a low-hanging pipe. It's always safer to walk your horse through a tunnel.

**Hints.** Bridges and tunnels present a variety of potentially lethal hazards to the horse and rider. Extreme care must be used with dealing with both obstacles. The importance of patience on the part of the traveller cannot be stressed enough. Scout ahead and obtain legal permission if required.

# Chapter 57 - Gates and Cattle Guards

Several countries, notably the United States and New Zealand, are known for the number of locked gates scattered across their landscapes.

Travellers in the American west often encounter what are known as a "cowboy gate." It is constructed by stretching three to five strands of barbed wire across several evenly-spaced lightweight posts. The gate is secured at either end by being loosely attached to sturdy posts driven into the ground. While the barbed wire fence running in either direction is held firmly in place by embedded fence posts, the light-weight cowboy gate can be disengaged, rolled back, and then replaced.

Care must be taken when opening a cowboy gate, as when the tension is released the gate may collapse onto the ground. This creates a deadly tangle of barbed wire which can quickly trip and seriously injure a horse.

Never attempt to deal with a barbed wire cowboy gate with one hand, while you hold the horse's reins in the other. Dismount and secure the horses before proceeding.

The proper way to handle a cowboy gate is to disengage it from the adjacent fence post. Holding the flexible gate; swing it back in the direction of the embedded fence. Be sure the gate is leaning firmly up against the fence and that you have created the widest possible opening, before you bring the horse near the barbed wire fence.

American ranchers and New Zealand stockmen can become hostile if you neglect to treat their gates with respect. If the gate is open, it might provide the only access to precious water in that area. Or it might be closed to ensure that stock do not become mixed up. Whether it is open or closed, it is imperative you leave the gate as you found it.

**Cattle Guards.** The name differs from country to country, with Australians calling them stock grids and American preferring cattle guards. Regardless of how you describe them, they are one of the most deadly modern obstacles a Long Rider will encounter.

Do not ever try to cross one with a horse!

Invented in 1915, it is a brutally effective way of prohibiting animals from passing along a road. This obstacle consists of a deep hole in the ground which has been covered by a grid of metal tubes. Though strong enough to allow a vehicle to pass, the gap between the tubes is wide enough to trap an animal's leg should it be unwise enough to step on the cattle guard. These obstructions, which are often found at the boundary between private and public lands, serve as an alternative to a gate which would have to be repeatedly opened.

Cattle grids are widely used in Canada, Australia, the United States and the United Kingdom. Horses who fall into a cattle grid often suffer serious accidents, which can result in the animal being euthanized. In 2012 one woefully ignorant amateur horse traveller tried to ride his horse across a cattle grid in Texas. The resultant wound required law enforcement officers to shoot the injured horse on the spot. Even if the horse is not severely injured, it may be necessary for a veterinarian to be summoned without delay. The horse should be tranquilized and then an acetylene torch will have to be employed to cut the horse free from the bars.

In theory highway departments should provide a safe gate or access next to a cattle grid. If you encounter a cattle guard on a public road, search along the wire fence until you find a gate. Be sure to close it, so as to ensure that no stock escape after you've passed through. But private land owners are under no obligation to facilitate your progress. If you can't locate a gate, you may be forced to consider temporarily removing the wire. Sometimes staples can be pulled from fence posts. This will allow you to push the wire down to the ground and then walk your horse over. If you have to cut the wire, pull the loose ends together and splice them with a piece of spare wire, so as to create an effective barrier. But don't ever tamper with a fence unless you are in a serious situation. Land owners will take a dim view of finding you wandering gaily across their land, after you've cut your way onto their pasture. If you encounter a cattle grid and cannot gain entry on either side, do not under any circumstances attempt to jump your horse over this lethal obstacle! Seek help or turn around.

# Chapter 58 - Traffic

**Riding in an Urban Age.** This book contains the advice of a host of knowledgeable equestrian travellers. Their wisdom was carefully gathered from hundreds of sources. It was then diligently recorded to assist you and enlighten posterity. Locked in these pages is the key to surviving a number of hazards, many of which may appear to be obscure. What is under discussion in this section is not an avoidable danger, like jungles or mountains. Nor will it take you by surprise, such as an attack by animals or bandits. Traffic, in one form or another, tests every Long Rider. The menace represented by traffic is a multi-dimensional conflict whose implications continue to impact every equestrian traveller's life and safety.

Horses and mechanized traffic originally shared the road. In those early days it was safer to ride near cars for several reasons. There was a great deal more horse traffic. There were fewer motorcars and they seldom exceeded a speed that would today be considered faster than a crawl. More importantly, the drivers knew and respected the needs of horses. Today it is vastly different. As the number and needs of cars grew, an increasingly urbanized society created a never-ending concrete jungle to accommodate them. Thus one remorseless hunger fed another. The result was that natural surfaces dramatically diminished, replaced by slick roads, which in turn encouraged the building of even more motorized transport. This combination of faster cars and more roads created the final portion of this dangerous recipe. As the majority of mankind slipped further away from any personal equestrian experience, there was a dramatic rise in aggressive motorists.

**By the numbers.** Dealing with bad drivers is nothing new. For example, Julius Caesar banned chariots during the day to relieve congestion in ancient Rome. Nor did the problem abate. By 1720 traffic fatalities from "furiously driven" carts were the leading cause of death in London. As the 20th century came to a close, it was a rare Long Rider who hadn't encountered the problem and only a diminishing number of remote places were free of traffic. A glance at the numbers will reveal that things don't look encouraging for equestrian travellers eager to avoid aggressive motorists. As you might expect, the number of cars varies widely from one nation to another. If you're anxious to avoid traffic, then ride in Mongolia which only averages one car for every 1000 people, but avoid the Netherlands which has 196 cars per square kilometre. Thinking about riding in search of the Old West? Then think again. The United States has 116,203,000 cars, roughly 478 cars for every 1000 people. The country is paved from top to bottom with 4,374,784 kilometres (2,718,364 miles) of roads. Even worse, the nation leads all other countries in terms of deaths caused by cars involving pedestrians or animals.

**Dangerous Drivers.** Because motorized transport has become so widespread, we are often too fixated on reaching our goal to give much thought to the complex social problems associated with driving. The majority of people travel alone in privately-owned vehicles. These become extensions of their personal space where in addition to driving they eat, drink, listen to music, talk on the phone and reflect on issues of personal concern. Encased within, two things often happen to drivers. They become alarmingly selfish. Equally worrying, they behave as though the vehicle makes them anonymous. As a result, being wrapped in a car encourages many people to perpetrate acts of aggression which would be unthinkable in a face-to-face encounter. Herein lies a conflict that was never foreseen by the inventors of the automobile. Driving is by necessity a highly social affair, one wherein the assumed urgency of everyone's personal journey must interact smoothly with the equally important needs of others. Unfortunately, mixing personal desire with the greater good of the community doesn't bring out the best in most people. The result is that numerous drivers behave as if the road belongs to them alone. Likewise, rules of polite engagement, such as speed limits, are often scoffed at, being seen as nothing more than a guide for less skilful drivers. The final straw is that the faster a person drives, the harder it is for his senses to react to risk.

**A History of Motorized Aggression.** Ironically, compared to mankind's murderous past, violent deaths are now relatively rare when viewed by historical standards. Fewer people may be dying in wars but more of them are marooned inside their automobiles. Studies reveal that an average American spends 38 hours a year stuck in traffic. As the influence of the automobile grew progressively stronger, traditions and courtesies of the past were forgotten. Drivers became increasingly impatient. Roads became impossible to cross. Collisions between horse and motorized transport increased. The result was that the course of equestrian travel history was repeatedly affected.

**Dying in the Saddle.** Perhaps, you think, this danger isn't as serious as I suggest? In which case allow me to share a couple of grim reminders of your own frail mortality. A glance at the news revealed a recent example. Janet Teeter of Salem, Massachusetts, was riding her Peruvian Paso along the side of the road when they were struck from behind by a man driving a pickup truck. Even though the impact killed the horse and wounded the rider, sheriffs declined to issue a citation against the 23-year-old driver.

While all deaths are equally tragic, one in particular sent shock waves of grief through the international Long Riders' Guild community. Christy Henchie and Billy Brenchley had set off to ride from the top of the African continent to the bottom. After crossing the northern deserts, and floating their horses down the Nile River on a barge, the determined travellers pushed on.

Though they emerged unscathed, death caught up with the unfortunate Long Riders in Tanzania. On January 8, 2013, an out-of-control bus struck the pair and the onlookers following them as they walked with their horses through the small village of Isela. The impact killed Christy instantly. Billy, suffering from a broken leg, crawled to his fiancée; but it was too late. The accident also killed two villagers and injured many others. The driver was fined $154.

When informed of Christy's death, New Zealand Long Rider Ian Robinson shared this thought. "I think what is going through the mind of every Long Rider who hears this news is the same for all of us 'That could have been me.' We have all had at least one brush along the road with reckless, careless or downright insane drivers."

*Christy and Billy had ridden through Tunisia, Libya, Egypt and the Sudan, when they first encountered aggressive traffic in Kampala, the capital of Uganda, as seen in this photo.*

**Horses and Traffic.** Horses and humans have a great deal in common. History has proved that a fear of on-coming traffic is one such case in point. Because we understand what we are looking at, it is easy for us to dismiss the horse's fear of cars. As rational beings we realize that the car isn't going to consume us. Even a horse which is usually steady can take fright around cars. So how do you go about protecting yourself from this global menace? You start by recognizing the peril you are facing.

**Steel versus Bone.** Should two motorists become involved in a minor crash, they have the luxury of determining who was at fault after the accident. But equestrian travellers can seek no such comfort, as even if the blunder lies with the other party, all too often they or their horse are seriously wounded. When you ride in traffic, it's not enough to be innocent. Your goal is to stay alive!

The way to do that is to prevent an accident. But you must understand that the odds are stacked against you. When you swing into the saddle and head out onto a busy road, you have effectively pitted your 1,200 pound equine vehicle against hundreds of massive chunks of motorized metal which are moving in your direction at very high speeds. What happens when two cars collide? The law of physics favours the heavier vehicle. So what are your chances? The average small car weighs 2,000 pounds (900 kg.). A four-door model weighs more than 3,000 pounds. A pickup truck hits the road with 4,500 pounds, while a big SUV tops them all at more than 5,000 pounds. But they are not your worst nightmare. A semi-trailer truck is 8.5 feet (2.5 metres) wide and 13.5 feet high. When authorized to haul triple trailers, it can weigh up to 129,000 pounds. Given that the odds are in favour of the driver, you need to study ways to avoid getting killed on the road.

**Training for Traffic.** To begin with, no matter what country you find yourself riding in, do not ever venture near a busy road on an untrained horse. Aggressive drivers have no nationality. They are merely bullies encased in a steel cocoon. So your best initial defence is to avoid them. Next, give a thought to your horse's emotional state. A highly nervous horse cannot be relied upon in an emergency. A horse that is unfamiliar with traffic should not be exposed to this danger. Also, consider how stressful an environment a city can present to an unprepared horse. To his way of thinking the large buildings resemble a box canyon and make him feel surrounded. Loud noises, honking horns or even the echo of his hooves on an empty street are all unnerving.

It takes time and patience to produce a traffic-safe horse. This isn't a process you should attempt to do once you're under way. It is critically important that you devote enough time prior to your departure to allow your horse to overcome any fears of moving traffic, loud motorized vehicles and unexpected lights. Unless you have raised the horse yourself, chances are the

127

horse you have purchased for the journey may be an unknown quantity on several levels. Finding out his tolerance for traffic is a critically important test.

Your first challenge is to determine what his fears are. Does all motorized traffic frighten him? Or he is only afraid of noisy vehicles? Do tall vehicles throw him into a panic? Do motorcycles alarm him? Do cars passing on the left scare him more than on the right? Is he terrified when vehicles approach him head-on or when approaching from the rear? If he takes fright, how does he react? Does he jump into the traffic lane, spin in one direction or try to bolt? Before you set your sights on the horizon, you first need to determine the answers to these life-threatening questions.

Should your horse prove to be traffic-shy, then you must set about exposing him to these modern sights and conditions, all the while building up his confidence. These sorts of miles are hard won, and you must constantly change the elements which test your horse. For example, even if your mount doesn't shy at a passing car, but jumps into on-coming traffic because of some invisible demon, then you're not ready to travel.

The horse has the muscle but you have the brain that makes the decisions which ultimately protect the two of you during the trip. This means that at the end of the traffic training, he has to completely trust you. When you bring him to a halt, he has to stand rock-steady. Should you urge him to turn swiftly or move aside quickly, he has to respond instantly. Don't venture into the traffic if you think your life is at stake because your horse won't follow these simple commands, can't be trusted not to face traffic bravely or will panic in the face of motorized aggression.

**Horns and Whistles.** Your horse must have impeccable road skills, and you had better have nerves of steel, before the beginning of any journey which will include encounters with hostile traffic. But even a steady horse is liable to become frightened if he is exposed to the intentional blast of a truck's air-horn. Many drivers have outfitted their rigs with air-activated deer whistles. When mounted to a vehicle, car or truck moving at 35 miles or faster, the deer whistle makes a sound that warns deer, moose, elk, antelope and kangaroos of the approaching vehicle. In theory the whistle alerts the wild animal, which assists with accident prevention. In reality, it scares the hell out of horses caught along the road.

**Stay Afraid.** Your first line of defence is to remain constantly vigilant, or as Shakespeare wrote in Hamlet, "Your best safety lies in fear."

**Rate the road.** Next, don't anticipate any respect from the overlords who build the roads. Traffic engineers view Long Riders as irritants who disrupt the smooth flow of motorized traffic. The traveller's physical need to share the road is not acknowledged. They are either dismissed in reports or degraded to the position of "vulnerable road users." It's not just the width of the road which should concern you. The death rate on rural roads is two and a half times higher than on larger interstates. This increase in crashes has been linked to poor lighting, high speeds, driver fatigue and drunk driving. Regardless of what causes the wrecks, medical help is usually nowhere near. Being shoved to the edge of the road by antagonistic engineers is bad enough. But it gets more complicated. The majority of drivers are not expecting suddenly to see a horse looming at them through the windscreen.

**Uncertain Sunlight.** You could be forgiven for believing that because you are riding a large animal alongside the road, drivers will quickly spot you and take evasive action. You would be wrong. A recent study confirmed that most pedestrians make the mistake of believing that drivers can see them twice as far away as the motorist actually does. In fact, most drivers are unaware of your existence. Because driving has become such a boring activity, they are often day-dreaming, drinking coffee or chatting on their mobile phones. They're not expecting to see a horse. Nor did they hear your approach. Suddenly their reverie is broken by the realization that they're on top of a massive animal and its startled rider. If the sun is shining in the driver's eyes the risk of a collision is instantly increased.

**Watch the Weather.** Things are bad enough on a sunny day. Don't decrease your chances of survival by riding along a busy roadway in weather which lowers the chances of fast-moving drivers spotting you. Your chances of survival are also diminished if you are riding a dark horse and wearing dark clothing. Anything reflective which can be worn on you or the horse increases your chances of survival.

**Age and Sex.** So you're riding along a busy road atop your carefully-trained horse. What have you forgotten? Who is driving towards you? Anyone can become impatient and dangerous while driving. However, age and sex will influence the chances of who may hit you. Younger drivers are involved in more accidents than their elders, with the probability being that a young man is 100 times more likely to be killed in traffic than a middle-aged woman. There are other alarming facts connected to male drivers, all of which should concern you. On average more men drive than women. Men are more likely to kill someone else in a fatal accident. They tend to wear their seat belts less than women but are consistently more aggressive behind the wheel. Thus, when you're studying the traffic, look at who's behind the wheel.

**Alcohol.** As if you didn't have enough to be concerned with, there is another worry; alcohol. With the exception of motorcyclists, drunk drivers in pickup trucks are most often involved in fatal accidents. Men are twice as likely to drink and drive as women. When this occurs, the combination of alcohol and testosterone can create a unique danger.

Luckily, there are a number of practical ways to protect yourself and your horse.

**Riding in Traffic.** Avoid riding in fog or snow. Don't let blinding sunlight render you invisible to drivers. Use reflective clothing on you and the horse to augment your visibility. If conditions are poor, wear a head-torch or mount a light on the edge of your stirrup.

If there are two or more in your party, always ride in single file. Put the most reliable horse in the lead, maintaining at least one horse-length between riders. If you're travelling with a pack horse, keep him on the inside, well away from traffic coming up from behind. Sit tall in the saddle. Never ride faster than a walk through traffic. Proceed slowly and carefully on a paved surface. On the off chance that a lane has been provided for horses, use it. But do not be tempted to ride in a bicycle lane.

It is more likely that you will find yourself on a road designed for automobiles. If so, then ride on the correct side of the road. Stay as far away from the traffic as the road will allow. Scan the ground ahead for signs of broken glass or debris. Pay careful attention if you find yourself between the road and a drainage ditch, always keeping your eyes open for a possible escape route. Take great care if you have to cross a busy road. Travel across the road at a right angle to ensure that you make the shortest possible crossing. Always look in both directions, twice, before setting off. Never start off unless you are sure you can make it all the way across. You do not want to get stranded half-way or become separated from your companion. Cross as quickly as possible, at the walk, so that normal traffic can resume without any delay. Ride defensively. Make it a habit to study the traffic, searching for signs of potential trouble before it takes you by surprise. To reduce the chances of aggression, make eye contact with the drivers as they approach. Don't hesitate to wave in an effort to slow them down or to remind them to keep their distance. If you must change directions, use hand signals to alert the drivers in advance.

**When Trouble Comes.** Things get complicated fast with horses. Not only can they see that giant wall of menacing steel fast approaching, they will base their decision to stand or flee on your reaction to the emergency. If they feel you tense with fear, you're both lost. Should trouble arise, you must hold your nerve. It's easy to say, "Stay calm," but that's what you must do. You must breathe deeply and keep your muscles relaxed. In such a tricky situation the greatest disadvantage of the rein is that it serves as a telephone wire that carries the vibrations of fear straight to your mount. If you want to steady your horse's nerves, it is always better to speak to him in a low pitched quiet voice. This allows him to conclude that his concerns are groundless.

If your horse becomes frightened, and time allows, dismount and lead him out of danger. Sadly, it often happens that a Long Rider on a main road has to instantly make up his mind when faced with a crisis. In such a case, he has to transmit a message, and the horse must react, in the blinking of an eye. When riding in the country, a gentle spur is fine to encourage a horse to travel in one direction or bring him to attention. But all too often horses learn not to respect a spur without a rowel, as the rider tends to hammer away with these blunt instruments.

Don't just look for aggressive drivers. Keep your eyes roving up ahead so as to spot merging cars, dogs on the loose, children playing or anything which might frighten your horse and cause him to jump into on-coming traffic. Be ready to move away from any type of potential danger without a moment's hesitation.

**Legal Riding.** Despite the fact that you're only travelling at one-horse-power per hour, many governments classify you as a non-motorized vehicle which is required to obey the laws of the road. Because regulations vary between nations, it is your responsibility to determine what these rules are in advance. Some laws are obvious, based upon common sense, and apply everywhere. For example, you must ride with traffic on the correct side of the road, so as to place your horse in the same lane as the traffic coming up from behind you. Equally importantly, you must stop at traffic lights and obey traffic signs.

**Hostile Cities.** Official opposition to Long Riders is increasingly encountered in a growing number of cities across the world. First determine if it is legal for you to ride through the city. If it is, then there are a number of ways to strengthen your chances of a successful transit.

Don't arrive at the edge of a large city and hope to ride through on the same day! Plan to rest the horses on the outskirts of the city while you scout ahead. When the horses are safe, enlist the aid of a local citizen to drive you along the best route through the city. Search for the quietest way. Take your time. Scout it carefully. Inspect any problems you might encounter along the way. Be sure to look for landmarks that will help you determine how far you've travelled. Confirm that there is time enough to cross it in one day. Don't conclude your reconnaissance without knowing where you and the horses are going to spend the next night. After such a stressful day in the saddle, you don't want to seek shelter after sunset.

Choose a day of the week which will have a diminished amount of traffic. This is usually connected to the prevalent local religious observations. To help your horses remain calm in traffic, don't grain them the night before. Start at first light, so as to give yourself as much time as possible before the morning rush hour begins. Before leaving, double check all your equipment. Make sure the girth on your riding saddle is snug and that the pack saddle is properly balanced. So as to alert drivers, be sure you use any reflective leg wraps or blanket you might have for the road horse. Likewise, if you have reflective tape, be sure you place it on the back portion of the pack saddle's panniers. Keep your short flag with its reflective banner close to hand during the ride. If you have a reflective vest, wear it.

Once you're under way, don't be tempted to trot. Walk your horses. You need to exude confidence to them and to passing drivers. Keep your eyes constantly moving, always looking out for loud trucks, looming buses and aggressive cars. Even if your horses are trained for traffic, be prepared to stop immediately. If you are halted by police, respond politely. Because of the shock of seeing you, don't expect adults in an urban environment to make eye contact or come to your assistance. But be prepared for children to follow behind, making trouble, throwing stones or hurling insults. Regardless of what occurs, focus on reaching the far side of the city before nightfall.

**Re-route.** You can avoid traffic almost anywhere, if you know where to go and are not in a hurry. The only exception is in mountainous districts where there may be only one pass and consequently only one road. Unlike encountering an unexpected bog along a trail after a rainy day, you will have had plenty of advance notice that a major urban centre is looming in front of you. Consequently, there is no reason to be taken by surprise. You should have instead made every effort to re-route your journey around these equestrian nightmares. On rare occasions a geographic necessity may force you to cross a city. If this is the case don't hesitate to hire someone with a truck and trailer to drive your horses through this hostile environment.

**Police Escorts.** It is a good idea to enlist the aid of the local police before attempting to ride through an intimidating city or traversing a dangerous stretch of road. In some countries it is required.

**Riding on High Alert.** Having made eight journeys in the USA, totalling more than 20,000 miles, Bernice Ende has evolved a series of ways to help decrease the chances of encountering any accidents in traffic. Before she "merges" with traffic she goes through several deliberate steps. She dismounts, and takes a few minutes to have a drink of water and something small to eat because "it will help your mind." The next step is to check the cinches on the riding and pack saddle. She always makes sure the panniers are tightened down. Then she pulls her hat on tight. Bernice then remounts, gathers up and shortens the reins and the lead line to the pack horse, then proceeds to ride on "high alert." She suggests that Long Riders develop strong anticipatory skills. "It's important to anticipate any potential problem and quickly assess the situation". The position of the Long Rider's body is also of strategic importance. "Ride with your ears! Keep your head lifted up. There should be a slight twist to the torso so you have a constant look on traffic in front and back. Keep your legs long and your heels buried deep in the stirrups." The actions and position of the horses is also of great importance. "Pull the horse's heads slightly together and hold them steady. Watch your horse's ears for signs of trouble." Try and slow down traffic. "You can help aid the traffic by using your ears and your eyes and height to help drivers. Flag them around if it is safe or signal to them, 'No or Wait.' Be active in the saddle but always stay focused." If a car slows down and wishes to pass, Bernice waits until she has reached a safe place, then she tips her hat or waves in thanks to the driver to let him know he can proceed. One thing Bernice made sure to pass along was a warning which other Long Riders will appreciate. "Don't knock over the mail boxes with the packsaddle panniers."

**Stop the Traffic.** Never assume drivers are going to do the right thing. Instead be prepared for them to honk their horns, shout abuse, refuse to surrender the lane, throw rubbish or even try to hit you with their car. In such a situation visibility is paramount. You may not be able to curtail their aggression but you can guarantee they see you. You should never enter a traffic zone unless you are armed with a two-foot long pole which has a brightly coloured flag attached to the end. Florescent material is best, but failing that use red cloth or anything which can attract the driver's attention.

Now, you must seize control of the road! The strategy is to use the first car possible as a blocker vehicle to stop all the traffic behind it. You must use the entire lane. Do not try to be nice and ride on the edge. Take the whole lane!

Long Rider Howard Wooldridge is a retired policeman who used this technique during his journey across the USA. He explained, "To put the strategy into use, dismount. Wait for a break in traffic. Take an aggressive stance with both legs spread, one slightly ahead of the other. You and the horse take a small step onto the lane, thrust your arm out at the vehicle, make eye contact with the driver and put your hand up in the universal 'stop' signal. If the driver slows down, use both hands to indicate he should continue to slow down. Move the horse another step into the lane, showing you want the lane. When you are convinced that the driver is going to stop, either mount up or begin running alongside your horse for as long as the dangerous stretch of highway lasts. If the driver does not slow down, back up your horse and try again with another driver."

Women are more likely to stop then men, at least in North America. Don't be embarrassed to put this extreme measure into practice if you feel your safety is being compromised.

**Accidents.** Should an accident occur, avoid confrontations with motorists, especially in the United States, where many drivers carry guns in their cars. Obtain the help, advice and protection of local police officers.

**Becoming a Distraction.** Your sudden appearance is going to come as a delightful surprise to a great many people. They will be eager to meet you, to learn about your trip, ask where you are going and perhaps offer their hospitality. The problem arises when you stop to chat on the side of the road. Traffic accidents have occurred when inattentive drivers glanced at the Long Rider and then rammed into another vehicle.

**Hints.** Always ride defensively. Never expect the driver to see you, move over, slow down or act courteously. Avoid riding on national holidays because of the increased risk of drunken drivers. If you encounter a dangerous place filled with heavy traffic, ask a local if there is an alternative route. If not, then be patient and wait until the traffic dies down before proceeding. Should the situation require you to ride in heavy traffic carefully check the horses, saddles and gear before proceeding.

Remain on the alert, listening and looking for signs of trouble. In an emergency be prepared to stop traffic and enlist the aid of a motorist to use their car to protect you and the horses while you proceed.

# Chapter 59 - Transportation

As many Long Riders have discovered, because of the vagaries of equestrian travel, an occasion may arise when you have to transport the horses either in-country or across international borders. The methods used have included railroads, ferries, ships, trucks, trailers and aircraft. Regardless f you're moving horses inside a state-of-the-art jet or across the steppes in the back of a rickety truck, it is critically important that the horses arrive in good condition at their destination. The value of fit horses cannot be estimated in terms of mere money, especially when you consider that if they arrive in poor condition they will be kept off the road until they have recovered. That is why you should give careful thought to learning how to ensure your horse will travel safely on a boat, truck, plane or train.

**Transport by Rail.** The practice of moving horses by rail reached its climax during the Second World War, with armies on both sides of that conflict routinely transferring large numbers of animals to the front lines. Because the veterinary corps oversaw this branch of military operations, there were surprisingly few equine injuries. Traditional rail transport is still available in some countries. Should you find you have to resort to moving your horse by rail, the safeguards set in place by previous masters of transport should serve as your guide.

The prelude to using a railroad is to determine if the line requires your horses to have a veterinary health certificate or medical inspection prior to departure. Once you have confirmed and followed these requirements, you must pay careful attention to the train schedule and routing. But this mode of transport allows you no initiative once you're on board. You are dependent on the goodwill of the train administrators to reach your destination. While it can be comfortable for the horses, trains present a terrible danger for equestrian travellers. There have been cases when travellers and their horses have been placed inside a rail car, only to be side-tracked and forgotten. It is essential to be able to open the door from the inside, otherwise if the train is abandoned for any reason, and you can't get out you and the horses may die!

During the days when trains routinely transported horses, the company was responsible for keeping specially-constructed cars in good condition. To reduce the chances of communicable diseases, these cars were cleaned and disinfected between shipments. Though the cars differed from one country to the next, they were usually equipped with tether rings and their floors covered with sand to reduce slipping. Because the rail company may no longer take such obvious precautions, you must not allow your horses to be loaded into a railway carriage until you have made sure there are no holes in the floor. The base of the vehicle should be sprinkled with sand or small gravel to prevent the horses slipping; on no account should straw or any flammable material be used for this purpose.

Your horses should be watered before departure and be unsaddled. Care should be taken that their halter and lead ropes are in good condition. To make sure the horses do not become excited or obstinate, it is important that loading should be carried out without noise or violence. The first horse to enter the rail car should be the quietest available. Walk in front of the horse, holding the lead rope at its full length. Lead the horse as if it is being taken into a stall. Walk confidently and don't look back when moving up the loading ramp. Load any troublesome horses last. Once the horses are all on board, they should be given hay as soon as they are tied up.

Never depart without having carefully discussed the journey with the rail staff, both at your point of departure and with those who will travel on board. Determine when the train is scheduled to stop. Find out if it will be possible to disembark the horses so they can be allowed to walk and roll. Don't expect comfort. The noise inside a rail car is shocking. Because of its lack of springs, it will shake, bump and rattle you severely. Also, be sure to carry a battery-powered torch, as the inside of the car will become pitch black after dark and the train is liable to depart without notifying you. Unless you have made an arrangement with the conductor, do not risk leaving the train even to fetch water. To reduce the chances of an emergency, be sure you carry food and water for the horses. Because of the risk of loss or theft, never allow your saddles and equipment to travel apart from you and the horses.

**Transport by Ferry.** The back country is still filled with an odd assortment of floating vessels. These range from crafts that are pulled across the river by a rope, to more sophisticated motorized transport. Your first challenge is to board your horses safely. If the ferry operator is used to transporting animals, then the ferry may have an accessible ramp. But do not be surprised if these nautical non-horsemen attempt to lift, shove, cajole, bribe or bully your horse aboard. This is your first concern, as horses have been seriously injured while loading. If luck is with you, and you've encountered a flat-bottomed ferry, then begin the loading by leading a quiet horse on first. Small ferries toss about, even if the current is not too strong. Prior to departing, ask the captain to set off carefully so as to give the animals time to adjust. If you find yourself on a more traditional craft, one which allows you to stand alongside on a flat surface, do not tie your horses to the ferry. Stand to one side, hold the lead ropes firmly and face them in the direction you will be travelling. If the ferry is exceptionally small, place yourself in such a way as to partly block the sight of the water rushing close by.

Should the ferry be manpowered, then chances are you may enjoy the journey across the water. But any time the vessel is motorized, you must exercise even more caution. If a horse panics and falls into the water, allow him to swim away rather than risk coming in contact with the dangerous propeller. If you are riding in Europe or Latin America you will encounter cross-country ferry systems that require careful thought and investigation. England, for example, has ferries departing to France, the Netherlands, Ireland and Spain. Large international ferries also depart from Chile. Ferries in the European Union require horses to be transported inside a horse box or trailer. International equine transport companies can move your animal country to country. This is an expensive service and must be booked well in advance. You might also arrange to hire a truck and trailer. If you opt for this method, remember that the ferry company will charge you by the vehicle's overall length. Hence, a truck hauling a trailer will cost more than a horsebox.

Regardless of where you're sailing from, check with the authorities for delays or severe weather. Many captains will not permit horses on board if they know the passage is going to be exceptionally rough. Should you be allowed to walk your horses onto a large modern ferry, remember that the loading ramp moves up and down, so as to accommodate the ship's movement in the tide. This floating floor immediately presents your horses with a challenging entry. Plus, because modern ferries often have slippery metal flooring, slick steel horse shoes may cause your animal to slip and fall, especially if you experience a rough crossing. To provide their horses with additional traction, some Long Riders used duct tape to cover their horse's hooves in an old inner tube. Whether the ferry is a computer-driven marvel or a simple back country vessel, it pays to treat the ferry hands with courtesy because your horses are almost certainly going to mess up their clean decks before docking.

**Transport by Ship.** Horses should be fed and watered as soon as they are on board. If conditions and weather permit, walk the horses on the deck twice a day. If the horses soil the deck, clean it up immediately. Injuries en route seldom occur and are usually connected to a horse that falls during rough weather. In the event of a horse being thrown down, untie his lead rope so as to loosen his head. Next, pull his fore feet out in front of him and place something against them to give him leverage. It is important that he have traction when he attempts to stand, so scatter sand on the deck to prevent slipping. He should now be able to rise with ease. But if he struggles and cannot rise, be sure he cannot strike out and injure the horses on either side of him.

Upon arrival at the port, horses cannot be disembarked before the local veterinary officer confirms the animals are not infected. Horses that have been at sea for some time are apt to fall on their knees once they are placed ashore. To decrease the chances of such an injury, if horses were unloaded via a sling, sand or straw should have been spread on the wharf. Another, far more dangerous, method of unloading from a ship was by swimming the horses to shore. When in the water a horse's range of vision is so limited that he cannot see a beach until he is very close to it. As a result, horses become confused, and instead of heading towards the safety of the beach, swim towards the open sea and drown. To prevent them from swimming out to sea, on-shore horses should be kept at the landing point to attract the attention of the swimmers. Small boats should also be stationed in the water to help keep the horses on course.

**Transport by Truck.** If you're reading this book in North America, Western Europe or Australia, then chances are you've been raised in a culture which automatically connects the concept of personal equine transport with the use of a horse trailer, or a float as it's called "down under." You may not realize that a great percentage of the world does not move horses in this manner. In fact horse trailers have never been seen in many countries. For example, should you find yourself riding through the Ukraine, you may catch a glimpse of a horse being hauled in the rear of a passenger car. Riding through Africa? Don't be surprised if you observe horses travelling cross country in the back of a sturdy Land Rover. Both these examples demonstrate how inventive horse owners can get when difficult circumstances arise. They should also alert you to another vitally important transportation fact: when you're riding overseas you should appreciate the availability and low cost of local trucks.

**Driver Requirements.** Many countries do not observe the same type of regulatory controls which you might consider normal; such as requiring the driver to pass any type of driving test or obtain a driving licence. That is why, before loading or departing, you must take the time to ensure that the driver and vehicle meet certain basic safety standards. It might seem obvious but your first consideration is confirming the driver is sober. Does he have the papers proving he owns the truck? If insurance exists in the country where you're travelling, is the vehicle properly covered? Once you've determined that the driver and truck are legally prepared, be sure you agree on the cost of transporting the horses. Be cautious in terms of paying the driver. Offer to provide half of the amount on departure and the rest upon a safe arrival. Make sure there are no hidden costs, such as fuel or meals, which will cost you extra after you're under way and unable to re-negotiate. Don't depart until you and the driver have discussed and agreed upon the route. Have an agreement about where the truck will stop for rest breaks, how long it will be off the road, and whether the horses can be taken off for water and exercise. Also, to reduce the risk of the horses being thrown off their feet, make it abundantly clear that the driver must drive around corners slowly and not brake too hard. Ask for a receipt, write these agreed-upon conditions on the back and then ask the driver to sign or make his mark. Keep this vital paper, along with the documents connected to the horse's ownership and health, close to hand while you're travelling.

**Truck Requirements.** Once you're convinced the driver is reliable, move on to the truck.

Your first concern is the truck bed. Make sure there are no holes in the floor. Once the truck is moving, your horses are going to be working hard to maintain their balance. To help them, it is vital that you provide good footing. Sand works best. If circumstances dictate that the floor is covered with straw, or anything flammable, then take extra care that no one smokes near the truck while the horses are aboard. Next, go over the truck walls carefully, making sure there are no bolts or metal protrusions which might cut the horses. Don't forget to check the tyres. Find out if the driver is carrying a hydraulic jack and a spare tyre. Confirm that all the lights, front and back, are operating correctly. Chances are you won't be able to check the engine and brakes, but ask the driver to confirm that they are working properly. After you're confident that the truck is as safe as possible, set about loading the horses. No loading ramp may be available. In such cases, the driver will back the vehicle up against a ledge, a loading dock or an accessible hillside. Choose an emotionally reliable horse to be the first one to be loaded. Once he walks on, the others will likely follow quietly. But take great care when boarding the horses.

Some might be tempted to jump on. If this occurs, a horse could be crippled if his leg falls through the gap and he becomes trapped. Face the horses towards the front of the vehicle. Be careful how tightly you tie the lead rope. They will quickly learn to steady themselves by using the taut rope to maintain their balance.

In such a situation, always travel with the horses yourself. Once they're under way, most horses settle down quickly and travel quietly. If you are travelling a long distance, then plan to stop and unload them, as they will need to drink, urinate and stretch their muscles. When the driver stops for a break, make sure the truck has the emergency brake firmly set and the vehicle has been left in first gear. So as to ensure the truck can't accidentally roll, instruct the driver to either block the wheels or to turn them up against an obstacle.

**Transport by Trailer.** To reduce the chances of an accident, you must exercise caution when loading and moving horses in a trailer. Start by inspecting the exterior. There must be air vents along the side and the roof to allow plenty of fresh air to circulate. Confirm that the brake lights and turn signals work properly prior to departure. If hauling at night, interior lights must be provided and working. Make sure the hitch is in good shape. Also, be sure the vehicle is equipped with safety chains to ensure the trailer stays hitched to the pulling vehicle. There have been horror stories about trailers which became unhitched. They went off the road, spun into on-coming traffic or even passed the pulling vehicle. Don't put the horses at extra risk. Check the chains. The tyres must be in good shape, adequately inflated and showing no signs of dry rot. Test to make sure that all doors operate properly.

Next, investigate the interior. Check that the floor is sound. The trailer should be equipped with rubber mats to provide traction to the horse. Most two-horse trailers provide an area seven feet long and two feet wide to accommodate each animal. The first consideration is to ensure the trailer has enough height and width to accommodate your horse.

Once you have confirmed the trailer is ready for travel, give a thought to how you load your horses. Because of the ramp's great weight, take care to stand to one side when you lower or raise it. Always make sure the ramp is sitting level and supported evenly. It might seem obvious, but never ride a horse into a trailer. If you lead your horse into the trailer, always make sure that you leave yourself an escape route – pass the lead rope through the side-door and then direct the horse to enter. If you are only transporting one horse in countries where they drive on the right, load the horse in the left stall. In countries such as England or South Africa, where one drives on the left hand side of the road, a single horse should be loaded in the right stall.

Always tie a horse with a quick-release knot or use a lead rope equipped with a safety snap. The rope should be attached to the trailer at chin height. Make sure there is no excess rope which the horse can walk on. Once the horses are secure inside, close the tailgate and raise the ramp immediately.

Horses can come to grief when travelling in trailers. If a horse panics it has been known to jump through the small window or side door in the front of the vehicle.

You must schedule rest stops every four hours so as to permit the animals to drink, graze and stretch their legs. Be extra careful when unloading. Never unhitch a trailer with a horse still inside, as the vehicle may flip backwards. Always release the lead rope prior to unloading. Because the horse may back out quickly, stand to one side. After your arrival, be sure to allow the horse time to recover from the journey.

**Transport by Airplane.** Transporting your own horse by means of a modern airplane is going to require a tremendous amount of time, patience, planning, money and luck. It cannot be stressed enough the need to verify the competence of the flight company. How long have they been flying? Have their airplanes been inspected by the government? Have they transported horses before? Do they have special facilities and procedures on board to ensure the safety of your horse? Do they provide qualified staff to monitor the horses in flight? Will they fly the horses direct, or will there be a layover? If the plane stops before your final destination, will the horses be landed in a third country? Does such a stop require additional documentation? Will they provide you with the names and contact details of someone who has previously flown their horses via this airline? The charge for flying horses is astronomical. For example, in 2010 it cost between $5,000 and $10,000 to fly a horse across the Atlantic one way, not including the additional charges levied by medical authorities. Regardless of where you're flying, determine how the airline must be paid. Do they require a deposit? Do you have to pay in local currency? Will they provide a refund if the flight is cancelled or they do not live up to their side of the bargain? Once you have obtained a quote for the cost of flying your horses, compare it to other airlines. But flying horses can be a nerve-racking proposition. Consequently, the deciding factor should never be cost but safety.

**Border Bullies.** Your next hurdle will be to confirm the health and quarantine requirements demanded by the countries on both ends of the flight. I cannot stress enough how important it is for you to verify these health regulations. Do not take anyone's word about these critically important rules! Ask to see them in writing. Even more importantly, authenticate the requirements by speaking to the health authorities at your point of arrival. This may entail a telephone call or a series of emails, but confirmation at the other end is critical. A well-meaning consular official who works in your country of departure may quote you one set of rules, but upon your arrival at the next country, local government authorities may inform you that despite your best intentions and efforts you have not followed proper protocol.

**Quarantine.** Prior to an international flight, horses are routinely placed in quarantine. The length of the quarantine varies from 72 hours to 30 days. This will involve multiple visits by the veterinarian, blood tests, and assorted extra medical expenses. Requirements for stallions are even more stringent. After a great deal of delay and money, you will eventually be rewarded with a health certificate which authorizes your horse to begin his journey on to the airport.

**In the Air At Last.** Obviously, moving a horse from one country to another requires a tremendous amount of careful planning. But even when you've got the precious health documents in hand, your concerns are far from over.

If you're flying via a major commercial carrier, chances are your horses will end up inside a Boeing 747. However, it's a long road to the airport. Be aware that your departure date is flexible. Equine flight companies arrange for a shipment of horses all going to the same international airport. Only after they've located a suitable number of equine passengers, and all these horses have passed their quarantine requirements, will the company official ring to say that your flight is confirmed. This leaves you in a state of anxiety, as the time spent waiting for the flight to fill varies.

Once you've been told that you're leaving, horses travel to the international airport by a large commercial lorry that delivers them to an isolation stable located close to the airplane. It's not uncommon for the horses to spend the night in this holding facility prior to flying the next day.

When the time comes to load your horse, he will be led into a metal air stall, after which the back will be closed. Three horses usually make up a full load inside this strong steel container. Though they have a limited space to move, the horses are now safely confined and protected within a box that can be moved by the staff. The air stall can be lifted onto the plane or pulled into place using a series of metal runners.

Reputable equine air companies provide a professional groom to travel with the horses. This person's services should be included in the price of transit. The groom is on board to make sure the horses are fed, watered and safe. Should the horse become a concern to the flight crew, the groom is trained to administer a tranquilizer. The vast majority of horses fly quietly. However, if an animal panics and threatens the safety of the plane, he will be euthanized immediately. To reduce the chances of an accident, it is wise to remove your horse's shoes before the flight. No matter how well you have prepared, regardless of how many health hoops you have jumped through, despite the extraordinary amount of money you have spent, when you set off to fly your horse from one country to the next, you must be prepared for unbelievable obstacles to appear suddenly.

**Stress.** There is a variety of reasons which may induce stress in travelling horses. It is important that you identify and minimize their effects.

Whenever possible, loading and unloading a horse into a trailer should be done in daylight hours. It should be done quietly, even in the face of difficulties. The next step is to study the horse's transportation environment, paying special attention to his thermal and physical comfort, as each of these can induce severe stress. Transporting a horse in cold weather should never be undertaken unless you have carefully considered the season, the outside temperature and the length of the transit. Extra care should be taken with the management of the horse's diet, so as to ensure that sufficient fodder is provided en route. Many animals become sick during or after shipment because of improper ventilation and heat. Heat and humidity are causes for serious concern. A horse dissipates his body heat through sweating and respiration, which in turn generates a significant amount of moisture and heat. To minimize thermal stress, schedule your departure time to avoid travelling during the hottest part of the day. In extreme heat, limit the duration of the trip and stop to check the horses frequently. A dark-coloured enclosed trailer is generally 15 degrees hotter than the outside temperature. Thus, it is critically important not to park for long periods, as the horses may suffocate in this oversized oven. Another source of environmental stress is toxic air generated from vehicle exhaust fumes or the build-up of ammonia from urine. Because of the need to keep the horses supplied with cool, clean air, you must ensure that the truck or trailer is properly ventilated but draughts should be avoided. Others stressors include the emotional anxiety caused by separating a horse from his usual companions or aggression directed towards him by strange horses in transit. Prior to your departure, consider how you can reduce the impact of all of these negative influences in your horse's travel experience.

**Feed and Water.** Extremely hot weather may decrease the horse's appetite. But one of the easiest ways to offset stress is to make sure the horse is offered a meal once he is boarded. A hearty meal not only offers the horse something which will divert his attention from the journey but will ensure that he arrives well fed. If a manger isn't available, then offer hay in a net. Make sure the net is tied securely and is placed high enough to ensure that the horse cannot paw or step on it. Because of limited air flow in a trailer, shake the hay thoroughly before departure, otherwise the horse will inhale dust or mould in the tightly-confined space. Don't overlook the problem of your horse becoming dehydrated during transit. Some horses will not drink because the water tastes or smells different from what they are used to at home. You should still offer water every few hours.

## Chapter 60 - Borders and Bureaucrats

**Sailors Home from the Sea.** There is a fundamental difference between the receptions afforded to humanity's two legendary types of travellers. A sailor and his ship are traditionally welcome in any port. While there are of course rules to follow in a harbour, the sailor and his ship have been greeted throughout the ages by other sea-loving people, who in turn admire the sailor's bravery, respect his courage, and welcome his money. History has taught the sailor that hospitality is always looming on the horizon. That sense of camaraderie, bonhomie and jovial welcome stands in stark contrast to the cold hostility which equestrian travellers have endured throughout the ages. For unlike a harbour, which is usually inhabited by other sympathetic sea people, border guardians are antagonistic by nature to a horse traveller. They are sentinels of a settled community whose collective national identity is opposed to the entrance, and existence, of a mounted nomadic traveller. The job of a bureaucrat is not to welcome but to turn away. They're not interested in your tales, nor do they long for your money. They maintain the historical prejudices established by those legendary pedestrians, the Greeks, that anyone mounted is a barbarian, uncivilized and untrustworthy. Sailors aren't perceived as a threat by the authorities because those nautical wanderers don't journey deep into the country and upset the populace. Thus the concept of arriving at a border on horseback is diametrically opposed to sailing into a harbour.

**Good People, Bad Government.** What's ironic is that whereas it is true that you can't tell a book by its cover, likewise you can't judge a people by their government. If the horse is the key to the village that opens people's hearts, he is also the spark that ignites authoritarian aggression. This explains why Long Riders are continually taken by surprise by the hostility they encounter at borders. It's not the citizens who oppose the progress of a Long Rider; quite the contrary. It's the government. They are obsessed with control and dominance. They rule because they have the ability to monitor, tax, imprison and intimidate their citizens. Their power is based upon their subjects remaining placidly in place. Your approach on horse awakens people's longings to travel, explore, escape and lead a fuller life. The people admire your courage, envy your freedom and open their homes to you. These are dangerous ideas and your journey is a cause of concern to those who worship power.

**Invisible Threats.** International frontiers have been constructed to act as obstacles designed to make those who want to enter a country feel they are violating its sanctity by their unwelcome arrival. And those are the friendly ones. Because Long Riders journey on every continent except Antarctica, they are liable to find themselves up against some of the world's most politically hostile boundaries. The cause of the conflict may be an indistinct memory, but all of these contested borders share one thing in common. You don't want to find yourself and your horses stuck on either side of any of these hellish no-man's lands. Nor are they confined to one continent. If you hope to get your animals through, then you have to learn how to master the formalities of cross-country border crossing.

**Battling the Bureaucrats.** For countless generations travelling horsemen simply disregarded borders, preferring to ride where their hearts led them. Nowadays settled people have invented jobs which nomads could never have imagined. This has brought about the rise of an increasingly hostile mindset, one which defines you as a hazard. People who are obsessed with rules and are paranoid about security view any violation as not only a national menace but a threat to their personal career. If a rule is defeated, they could be the one who suffers the consequence. Not wanting to risk their retirement benefits, they take the coward's way out. They obstruct your progress instead of invoking the anger of their superiors. Dealing with bureaucrats will test your patience and may ruin your trip. Nor can you expect to receive any sympathy. English Long Rider Mary Bosanquet summed up the problem in 1939 when she wrote, "I know it is vain to reason with the minor officials of a government department, for one might as well endeavour to explain oneself to a teapot."

**Expect Delays.** During his ride through the Himalayan Mountains in 1873, British Long Rider Andrew Wilson travelled through various kingdoms. Though the names of the nations have changed, the hostility of the bureaucrats remains the same. When Wilson pressed the officials to explain why they were hampering his progress they answered that they were not bound to give reasons, they were simply obeying orders. By the time his journey concluded in Afghanistan, Wilson had developed a deep loathing for these men whom he deemed the devil's agents. "Bureaucrats," he concluded, "are men of cunning but not of courage." Little has changed and few things have improved since then. In fact there are more rules, restrictions, laws and paranoia now than at any time in human history. That is why the first thing you need to comprehend is that a display of impatience isn't going to make the locals work any faster. So take a deep breath and prepare to endure.

**Degrees of Difficulty.** Should you be forced to take your horses across an international boundary, circumstances will dictate the ease with which you progress. What lies ahead varies. You may find yourself stranded between two countries, not allowed to ride on and prohibited from returning. Your horses may be wrongly classified as wild animals. You may face unfair expenses ranging from minor robbery to high-level corruption. Long Riders have been ambushed by, and eventually overcome, all these dilemmas. But before you encounter any of them, you must first arm yourself with a Long Rider's most powerful diplomatic weapon – patience.

**Timing Your Arrival.** Arriving on horseback unannounced at a border is sure to raise eyebrows and inspire a few headaches. To improve your chances of receiving a friendly recaption, it's best to visit the border station the day before you wish to cross. Introduce yourself to the officials and try to determine who is in charge. Explain the importance of your journey to

138

the boss. Make sure you show him any letters of support and newspaper stories which will help your cause. If you've got the media on your side, be sure to drop the hint that reporters may well arrive to film your smooth departure to the next country. Go over the paperwork and procedures carefully. Confirm how long you can expect the process to take, what costs are involved, and ensure that all your papers are in order. Ask what time would be convenient for you to cross the next day. If no specific appointment has been made, plan to arrive at the border between 9 and 10 in the morning. This should have provided the border guards with enough time to process all of the lorries that have been parked and waiting all night to cross the border. Never attempt to cross a border on a religious or national holiday!

**Worshipping the Rules.** To one degree or another every country is now enslaved by this type of monstrous bureaucracy. At a border the rootless Long Rider runs head on into the fierce guardians of a hostile tribe. Regardless of their native tongue, these motorized pedestrians are used to routine and worship predictability. Your sudden appearance throws them into a panic. When this occurs, your identity doesn't enter into the equation because you're no longer a person. You're a problem.

And there's another dilemma. Lacking any equestrian credentials, such officials aren't concerned if you ride into their country on a fiery chestnut-coloured Thoroughbred and depart on a docile dappled-grey Shetland pony. What matters to them is if you have the required red stamp in your passport and the compulsory blue stamp on the animal's exit permit. Such blind allegiance to procedure becomes a ceremony which cannot be altered, regardless of the emotional cost to others.

**Armed with the Facts.** Keeping your chin up in the face of unwarranted hostility is a wonderful philosophy, but your journey stands a far better chance of success if you've done your homework.

No matter how tedious it is, your first challenge is to define what paperwork, signatures, quarantine requirements and veterinary authorizations will be required before you arrive at the border. If you're not ready, you're never going to cross! Times have changed so dramatically that most border guards only see horses when they're being transported by truck or trailer to a meat-packing plant or a competition. In such a situation it is common for veterinarians stationed at the border to issue travel documents which are only valid for ten days. That may provide plenty of time for a truck driver to deliver his load. Yet a Long Rider is rarely going to transit across a country in a little more than a week. That's why if you arrive unexpectedly you can count on ramming into panic and prejudice. You can expect to be asked a load of inane questions, starting with why you would want to suffer on horseback when you could travel in the luxury of an air-conditioned car? Regardless of your best efforts to defend your odd choice of transport, don't expect to be taken seriously by short-tempered and impatient border guards. To them you're just a rich, foreign eccentric. Like Pontius Pilate, they'll wash their hands of you by passing you over to the national veterinary. That's when your troubles really begin.

**A Misplaced Word.** Sometimes it's not enough to be brave or even resourceful. Sometimes you just have to be lucky. Deliberate deception is one thing and nowadays it is rare. Far more common is when an equestrian journey is brought to a halt because a minor typographical error neutralizes an official government document. Tim Cope had ridden 6,500 kilometers (4,000 miles) when he reached the border between Kazakhstan and Russia. Having obtained what he thought were the proper documents, Tim was shocked when he was prohibited from riding into Russia because the document he carried stated the Long Rider was authorized to travel "with" horses, i.e. via a truck or trailer, not "on" horseback. The journey had been stopped at the cost of a word! What occurred next was a nightmare of long-distance phone calls, international emails, a flurry of faxes and an unprecedented wave of equestrian diplomacy. Friends from many countries rallied to Tim's support. The head of the Kazakh Ministry of Agriculture telephoned his colleagues in Russia and petitioned them to allow the equestrian traveller to enter the country. The Long Riders' Guild sent a letter to the Russian Federal Government, reminding their country's leaders of that nation's historical links to the equestrian exploration community. Despite everyone's best efforts, things looked grim. With eight hours left on his

Kazakh visa, the telephone rang and Tim's equestrian dreams were saved. The Federal government of Russia had issued a special permit allowing Tim Cope to "ride" his three horses into their country.

**Play It Safe.** As Tim's case illustrates, it's not enough to have the correct documents. You must make absolutely certain that the paperwork authorizes you to RIDE your horses into the country.

Also, it is important to note that during his journey from Mongolia to Hungary, Tim estimates that he spent four months stuck on various borders, all the while attempting to process documents for his animals. Because of this, all of his visas from Mongolia, Kazakhstan, Russia and Ukraine had to be extended at least once.

And consider your return. One Long Rider's journey home was delayed because his travel papers neglected to include the words "and back," meaning he was allowed to leave his country but not return.

Be sure that you do not arrive at a border unprepared. Always have the documents translated exactly making sure that every single word is accounted for prior to your arrival. In order to safeguard this precious information, scan in your documents and email them, either to yourself or a trusted friend. It also pays to email yourself a copy of your passport, any vital documents and a list of important contact details, including addresses, phone numbers and email addresses.

**Border Guards.** Arriving at a busy international border can be a nerve-racking experience. Having ridden through the quiet parts of a country, suddenly you'll find yourself an unwilling occupant in a portal to the worst of the modern world. Prepare yourself. There will be cars filled with impatient motorists, monstrous lorries belching exhaust and crowds of people peering at you. In addition to keeping the horses calm, your job is to stay relaxed and not lose your temper. Most border guards will be professional, polite and intrigued. They'll also realize what a stressful situation you're in. Treat everyone with courtesy. Explain who you are, how far you've come and why your ride is important.

Even if things don't turn out as planned, remember to respect the customs of the country. It won't help your cause if you brag about how much more efficient things are in your country. Never denigrate your hosts or denounce their country. Praise what you can and confide your true feelings to a diary.

**Bewildered Vets.** You might be forgiven for thinking that if you need an answer you could ask an expert, in this case the veterinarian official in charge of authorizing your horse to enter his country. If so, you're often going to be disappointed and delayed. Why? Due to the fact that these government-appointed guardians routinely deal with horses which arrive by motorized transport, the medical certificates, injection confirmations, etc., they issue are only valid for a brief duration. Since travellers on horseback are a rarity, veterinarians seldom know what kind of papers are required for horses that need more time to transit across a country. More times than not low-level veterinarians stationed on remote borders are neither qualified nor willing, to issue an opinion authorizing foreign horses extended access to their nation. The result is that while the frustrated traveller fumes at the border, the vet sits quietly in his office, praying the problem will ride away in the direction it came from. Consequently, Long Riders across the world have found to their dismay that confusion reigns and every office has a different story.

**Pay to Ride.** While expecting to pay for hay and horseshoes, inexperienced travellers are surprised to discover there are hidden costs waiting to attack their carefully-protected funds. Some charges are genuine. Others come about because the traveller is envisioned as being a person of privilege ripe for the pillaging. This attitude is nothing new. Savvy locals have been swindling travellers since Moses visited Egypt. Nor has the practice diminished in the internet age. The Indian tourism board only charges their citizens 40 rupees to see the Taj Mahal but foreigners pay 750 rupees. When confronted with this discrepancy, Indian tourism officials defend the policy by saying that foreign travellers can afford it. When it comes to horses it pays to learn what the average correct price for the region is. And pay you will, for transit permits, vet checks, vaccinations, health certificates and photocopies.

*During his 10,000 mile ride from Canada to Brazil, Filipe Leite encountered intense governmental opposition. He was required to pay large amounts of money and was forced to provide dozens of documents at each border. This photo shows the paperwork demanded by the government of Costa Rica. After having finally gained entry into that country, Panama refused to grant Filipe permission to enter. He had to fly his horses to Peru in order to continue his trip.*

**Corruption.** Dealing with small villainies is a common complaint among international Long Riders.

Pay-offs infect a country to differing degrees. It is extremely rare to find police in the United States who harass travellers for a bribe. Less lucrative countries employ underpaid police who routinely supplement their meagre income by squeezing money out of citizens and travellers. In Kazakhstan police have stopped Long Riders, demanding to see proof of horse ownership and threatening to levy an unofficial fine on the spot. When the cops are crooked, it's not surprising that the locals are also on the take. Money-hungry citizens have even tried to charge Long Riders for badly-needed directions.

Such is the way of the world. The problem is when graft gets out of hand and corruption threatens your trip. German Long Rider Günter Wamser has seen plenty of borders and out-witted his share of corrupt officials. He recommends travelling to the border a few days prior to arriving on horseback. Once at the border Gunter would confirm what type of documents were needed and verify the procedures to be followed. Regardless of this visit, when Gunter arrived on horseback many border officials would say he was missing vital documents. Of course, by paying a bribe the problem could be quickly resolved. Gunter always refused. Instead he picketed his horses and waited until the officials agreed to play by the rules.

Dealing with a government official may be frustrating, and not everyone is who they say they are. Several Long Riders have been waylaid by fake policemen. Wherever you are, always require a policeman to produce photographic identification. If he continues to demand to see your papers, insist on accompanying him to the nearest police station. Be sure to explain that you will release your passport to his superior officer after having received an official receipt.

Should things go wrong at a border, don't be shy about contacting the local media. Newspaper editors and television reporters are always curious about Long Riders arriving in their town. If they suspect that a corrupt or inefficient bureaucrat is involved in an embarrassing situation, reporters will take a sharp interest in reporting on the incident.

**Entering Illegally.** As any Long Rider can tell you, life's not fair. Perhaps you've been told you can enter a country and then the officials change their minds. Maybe they've authorized you to come in but not your horses. Perchance you've been told the way can be smoothed if you'll agree to pass some cash. Given all these tales of being chased, hassled and threatened, is it any wonder you've become frustrated and impatient. After all, you've tried to play the game

141

according to the rules. When the other side keeps moving the goal posts, who could blame you for being tempted to consider quietly slipping across a hostile border? There are a lot of traps waiting to lure an unwitting Long Rider to his destruction, and this is a deadly siren's song that has uncomfortable results.

After having walked with his two pack mules across China and Tibet, the British equestrian traveller Daniel Robinson found himself alone in the Himalayan Mountains. Winter was fast approaching and his supplies were perilously low. So Daniel decided to head south towards warmer weather. Shortly after he crossed into India without a visa, he was captured and sentenced to ten years in prison. Luckily, Daniel was eventually released with the help of the Long Riders' Guild and an international coalition of friends. But let Daniel's experience be a warning. If you're caught, you'll be lucky if they only confiscate the equipment and expel you from the country. If unlucky, you'll go to prison and the horses will be destroyed. No matter how easy it looks, regardless of how tempting it feels, don't break the law and ride into another country unless you have been authorized to do so!

**Stallions.** If you have a stallion, everything becomes ten times more difficult. Expect to pay extra to cover the costs of expensive medical tests designed to confirm that the male breeding animal is not carrying any type of sexually transmitted diseases. Plus, there is the additional concern that while these tests are under way your journey may be delayed for more than a month while the horse is kept under strict quarantine. That translates into extra cost for you in hotel bills, etc., while you cool your heels.

**ATA Carnet.** Because officials are obsessed with papers, it pays to have powerful documents to assist you. The ATA Carnet is one such influential item. Carnets are often referred to as "merchandise passports" for boomerang freight, since all goods listed on the document must return to their country of origin; the merchandise in this case being the horses. This international export-import document is used to clear customs in 71 countries and territories without paying duties and import taxes on items that will be re-exported within 12 months. By presenting an ATA Carnet to the border guards, you are demonstrating that you have no intention of trying to sell the horse and avoid paying customs.

**Equestrian Allies.** Your chances of success are always improved if you've chosen to ride in a foreign country that has an existing equestrian culture. By contacting active riders in that nation, you may experience the warmth and hospitality which can be found amongst the international brotherhood of horse-humans. But obtaining equestrian support may be more of a necessity than you suspect. Some countries, such as Russia, insist that you establish these equestrian credentials before you will be allowed to enter the country. Other Long Riders have requested and received official invitations from the national Equestrian Federations of Ukraine, Belarus and Russia. However negotiating with these agencies is time-consuming, there is no guarantee of success, and even if you receive the invitation the host governments are still prone to change the rules regarding invitations.

**Friends in High Places.** Having friends in the barn is one thing. Being able to whip out an official document that puts the fear of God into a bureaucrat's jaded soul is another. Such rare paperwork has been used by a variety of Long Riders, past and present, with remarkable results. Modern Long Riders have also sought out high-level documents which establish their diplomatic credibility. Before venturing into war-torn Sudan, Billy Brenchley obtained a letter from Yasir Arman, the military commander of the Sudan People's Liberation Movement. The powerful document helped Billy resolve many problems, including dealing with quarantine issues and keeping aggressive underlings in check.

**Deadly Mistakes.** You have two sets of border guards and national officials to contend with. Having successfully appeased one set of administrators, many Long Riders forget that those in the next country may have a surprise or two up their sleeve. This can include enforcing medical requirements which might injure your horses.

**Stopped by Disease.** Sometimes, no matter how many documents you managed to obtain, regardless of what high-powered individual has befriended you, and in spite of how worthy your mission is, events conspire against you. This is especially true if your horses are infected with a contagious disease. When animals are imported from one country to another, there is the possibility that diseases and parasites can move with them. For this reason, most countries impose strict animal health regulations on the importation of horses. A vast number of horses in South and Central America are carriers of the mosquito-borne disease known as piroplasmosis. Once a horse has this illness, his blood carries the disease for life. The danger here is that a mosquito in the USA can bite an infected Latin horse and then transfer the disease to the unprotected American equine population. While already very bad in South America, the disease has spread north into Mexico. Thus Mexico has recently begun prohibiting many horses from Central and South America from entering. The United States, on the other hand, has had an incredibly strict law in place since the mid-1970s in regards to the entrance of infected horses. In a word, all horses attempting to come north are stopped at the US border stations, where they must undergo rigorous testing. If infected, the horses are banned from entry. If discovered on US soil, they are immediately destroyed. There have been a number of Long Riders who came to grief because of this strict American law. The good news is that contending with a deadly disease rarely happens. Most Long Riders instead find themselves dealing with a plague of petty rules, searching for a border crossing authorized to deal with horses and longing to interact with a sympathetic human being.

**Closed Borders.** Some countries will not allow horses across their borders. The reasons for this abject refusal include cultural considerations, war, greed and politics. This equine censorship has severely restricted Long Rider plans. A border blockade stopped Long Rider Magali Pavin from continuing her journey from France to China. Her progress was halted by a decree issued by the President of Turkmenistan forbidding foreign horses entry into that country. India completely forbids any of its horses permission to enter Pakistan. No one has successfully ridden through the Khyber Pass, which links Afghanistan and Pakistan, in more than forty years.

**On the Other Side.** Crossing an international border is one of the most stressful challenges of any equestrian journey. The horses may view it as just another day. But you must recognize the tremendous emotional pressure you will be under. Do not plan to cross a border and then put in a full day in the saddle. Arrive at the border. Stop and Camp. Confirm your paperwork. Cross. Stop and camp nearby. Proceed the following day.

**Hints.** Should your ability to proceed be seriously hampered, you may have to load your horses and drive them across the border in a truck or trailer. Before exiting a country it is wise to turn all of your small bills and loose change into food that either you or the horses can eat across the border.

Borders don't recognize dreams. The historical antagonism felt by sedentary cultures towards nomadic individuals still exists and rigid rules are enacted so as to discourage or turn back equestrian travellers. Many Long Riders will find themselves encountering some aspect of this hostile and tradition-encrusted portion of the population. Patience, perseverance, courtesy and luck are needed when dealing with these rule-minders. If you would overcome and outwit them, then you must be informed and prepared for every possibilty. Remember that the loss of a word or the changing of a phrase may slay your journey. Confirm, verify and then re-check every document. Expect delays. Arm yourself against deceit. Ignore pleas for bribes. Don't give in to the temptation to violate a border.

# Chapter 61 - Natives

No matter where you travel, every Long Rider is intensely involved with the local populace.

**Realism versus Romance.** How do we decipher a traveller's on-going need to understand other cultures? Where is the dividing line between strutting bully and passive crème-puff? How do we keep our mind open to new ideas, without revealing our personal disgust at the actions of our hosts? What happens when we find our emotional moorings pulled free because a sacred trust has been destroyed by natives?

The first thing to realize is how much we humans have in common. Throw aside the social trappings, ignore the yearly income, overlook personal transport, reject religion, don't go near the kitchen and what do you find? People around the world love like you do. They fear for their children's future. They weep over the loss of their parents. They starve, scrape and sacrifice to help the next generation live more productive lives. They long for peace, enjoy music and are capable of great romance – just like you.

They are also capable of participating in acts of incredible savagery. They perjure themselves to gain an unfair advantage. They break sacred oaths and cheat on their romantic partners. They tolerate cruelty, enshrine stupidity, squander liberty and worship ignorance. In a word, they are similar to much of mankind; capable on the one hand of tremendous compassion yet unable it seems to rise above the sordid bloodshed which has plagued our species since Cain slew Able. Balancing the romantic and realistic views of other people is an important part of any journey.

**Encouraging Isolation.** What is often overlooked is that the rise of large-scale transportation, either by road or in the air, has exacerbated the problem of isolation. Highways urge humans to speed along within steel cocoons, either through the clouds or above the tarmac. Ignored along the way are the many small towns which once marked the staging places where horse travellers stopped every few miles for rest, food and news. Those who never venture out of this speed-obsessed rut have little chance to study the slower daily lives of the inhabitants residing in obscure corners. It is hard to participate among a nation's people if you only observe them after you've disembarked at the airport and taken up residence in an air-conditioned hotel room. Pampered tourists never voluntarily undergo the dirt, hardship, discomfort and delay which an equestrian journey routinely entails. The tourist's privileged but sterile view of life is far removed from the everyday poverty, bizarre discoveries, and joyful living which Long Riders consistently encounter.

**The Key to the Village.** There is another tremendous emotional difference between a tourist and a Long Rider. The former is usually armed with great wealth. The latter, though often poor, is accompanied by a powerful ally. The Horse is the key to the village, no matter where that village may be. All people instinctively react with sympathy, courtesy, curiosity, kindness and trust to a Long Rider because of the symbolic animal at their side. Most of the world still views the horse as a confirmation of the rider's nobility of character. That is why it is so vital not to abuse the gift of trust bestowed upon you by total strangers.

**Approaching a Village.** It doesn't matter if you're in Albania or Alabama; you're always better off contacting the local inhabitants rather than trying to hide your presence. People are naturally inquisitive. When they observe you, they will want to investigate your unexpected appearance. If you choose to camp without making contact, your desire for privacy may be misinterpreted as mischief. With few exceptions natives are friendly. If they are treated correctly, strangers quickly turn into kind-hearted allies who can provide shelter, share food and warn about dangers lurking up ahead. Even though the topography will influence events, it is better to ride towards a village or home slowly. This gives the locals a chance to observe you from afar. Don't be in a hurry. Halt your horse in plain view and allow them the opportunity to approach and start a discussion. Don't worry. Chances are you won't be alone for long.

**Excited Locals.** American Long Rider Thomas Stevens made an interesting observation when he rode across Russia in 1898. His appearance startled the placid existence of the Czar's subjects. "So uneventful is the life of these people that the appearance of a stranger on horseback, dressed differently from themselves, is an event of portentous possibilities."

Time has marched on, so the appearance of an equestrian traveller has become even more of a rarity. This helps explain what happened when Billy Brenchley and Christine Henchie arrived in Uganda in 2011. Their horses ignited a social storm. It didn't take long for the Long Riders to discover that the majority of Uganda's 32 million people had never seen a horse.

For reasons still unexplained, the country's equine population was wiped out in the 1960s during Idi Amin's reign of terror. Thus the arrival of the Long Riders electrified the countryside. Schools emptied out as hundreds of children ran out to shout questions to the Long Riders. "Is that a kangaroo? Does it grow horns? Why doesn't it have cloven hooves? Which one is the female? Does it eat people? Can we eat it? Is it true your horses used to speak Arabic but now they speak English?"

144

Nor is this sense of confusion confined to the young, as in many countries adults struggle to understand why a person from a rich country would choose to travel "like a poor man" with an animal, when air-conditioned motorized transport is available. As Long Riders past and present have discovered, their arrival not only ignites a sense of brotherhood among fellow equestrians, it also provides a charming distraction to many people.

**Seeking Shelter.** The horse may deliver you to the door but it's up to you, the mounted diplomat, to negotiate for what you both need. Horsemen can appear threatening and arrogant if they remain in the saddle. To put your potential hosts at ease, never speak down to pedestrians. Dismount and make an overture of friendship. If you have arrived in a village, ask to meet the leader, headman, chief, mayor, alcalde, sidi, pasha or effendi. Should you stop at a private dwelling, seek permission from the owner.

Inspiring confidence is critically important in the early stages of the discussion. If you are armed, don't intentionally display your weapons or make any sudden movements which might alarm the natives. Fear inspires hostility, not hospitality. Nor should you appear frightened. Act confidently and use common sense.

Even if you can speak to the leader, it will save valuable time if you present the one-page letter which explains in the local language where you are riding and why. Once the host has had time to read the document, ask for what you need. Never demand it. State your business simply and frankly. If no one understands your language, use the Long Rider Equestionary to clarify your requirements. It is important that you appear friendly, polite, patient and honest. Remember to smile frequently. Once the ice is broken, don't be surprised if you become an object of intense curiosity. Remain patient and courteous. Speak of your journey with modesty, as no one favours a braggart.

**A Good Guest.** Once you have been invited to stay, make an attempt to befriend everyone, regardless of their social class, economic station or educational status. Be it rustic peasants or bejewelled nobles, everyone has an interesting, humorous or tragic story to share. Be generous with your time. Express an interest in local affairs. Ask for advice. Seek out history. Relish discoveries. Your sincere willingness to learn will open the doors to hearts otherwise closed to a more indifferent traveller. In return for such generosity, don't hesitate to show photographs of your family, home and nation. Be entertaining. Tell stories. Sing songs. Offer advice. Share a kind word. Volunteer to help. However you manage it, strive to enrich the lives of those who have shared their home with you, a stranger. Offering to pay for food and shelter is a sensitive subject. Most hosts will turn down your proposal. However, many families make silent financial sacrifices to host a traveller; so don't be shy about suggesting that you might make a reasonable financial contribution for the food and shelter you have received.

**Mutual Respect.** It's not all sunshine and roses out there. Whereas your horse may open doors, there is an equally strong chance that your journey may be viewed with immense cynicism by people who are struggling to stay alive. Many nations retain a deeply ingrained sense of global injustice against westerners. Likewise the citizens of poorer countries may harbour a sense of personal antagonism because they were denied the educational and political benefits you enjoy due to your country of origin. These deep-seated hostilities may manifest themselves in a variety of ways, ranging from personal rudeness to official animosity. The granting and receiving of respect is one of the intangible elements of a journey, one which can affect your daily happiness and could colour your overall chances of success. The dark days of colonialism are behind us. Travellers no longer appear with a large safari and attempt to impose their beliefs upon the locals. This is never truer than for a lone Long Rider for whom adapting an attitude of respect enhances his security among an otherwise sceptical populace. Greet people courteously. Do not be quick to take offence, as customs considered rude in your culture are harmless elsewhere. For example, it is an accepted practice in the Sudan for people to snap their fingers to gain one another's attention. Several nations believe it is the height of rudeness to sit with your feet pointing at another. Practise civility and polish your manners.

**The Opposite Sex.** Nations adhere to radically different views on a variety of topics. A case in point would be the principles which rule the intimate part of a people's lives. It would be a mistake to believe the outdated notion that natives lead an unrestrained sexual life. Regardless of their geographic diversity, families, tribes and nations everywhere are held together by codes of moral conduct. Sometimes these social edicts are well known. For example, wearing shorts is considered extremely provocative in many countries. Other times it may be difficult to determine an unwritten code of moral conduct. Case in point is the Buddhist belief that it is vulgar for a woman to place her hands on her hips. But relations among members of the opposite sex is an important consideration even among the most primitive people. Any breach of sexual tradition may result in strict, even violent, repercussions. That is why it is wise to determine what behaviour is sanctioned by ancestral custom or religious practice; for though a breach of etiquette may not be actually punishable, you should regulate your behaviour with extreme care. You do not wish to be victimized due to a misunderstanding.

**Privacy.** The aura of strangeness is one of the reasons Long Riders are routinely denied a basic level of privacy. People are fascinated by the wanderer. They crowd round the horse, stare in disbelief, are eager to hear the stranger speak. Cultural conflict often results because of a double standard. As a traveller, it is vitally important that you respect the privacy of your hosts at all time. Do not enter a house unless you are invited. Be careful not to embarrass the opposite sex during their bath or toilet. You, on the other hand, should expect no such consideration. Some cultures do not look upon privacy as a privilege. They pity the person who is alone. Another worrying concern is that your personal hygiene can be of the greatest possible interest. Many cultures do not realize that you have a different set of needs. They are too naïve to realise that you desire privacy during hygiene. Mild curiosity from a handful of villagers is one thing. Being overrun by a crowd is another. German Long Rider Esther Stein was almost asphyxiated by a mob of natives while riding through Tanzania in 2003. Nearly 2,000 people trailed her for miles. Despite her pleas for privacy, they were intent of following her into the bush when she attempted to relieve herself. What you should bear in mind is that your presence inspires an intense reaction from simple people. If you cannot evade this problem, you must brace yourself and learn to endure it.

**Religion and Taboos.** It has been said that horsemen and theologians are both intolerant. Believe my faith and ride the horse after my fashion, they say. Whereas you may be able to arrive at a peaceful resolution involving equestrian issues, don't be fool enough to tamper with local religious beliefs. Your world view may differ sharply from that of your host, who may regale you with heart-felt stories involving belief in witches, shamans, giants, fairies, talking mountains, enchanted wells, miracle cures, deadly curses and other manifestations of superstition. Many times it may not be enough to merely display respect for local religious beliefs. It is also critically important to avoid trespassing on sacred ground or breaking cultural taboos. One common mistake is to photograph or draw people without their consent. Many traditional cultures maintain a strong objection to having their likeness, which they consider as part of themselves, taken from them. It can be a dangerous mistake to photograph women in Islamic countries. Always seek prior permission, otherwise your actions be may perceived as a threat.

**The Power of Praise.** Learn to listen patiently, and without offering the least contradiction, to the religious and political opinions of your host, however different they may be from your own. In this diverse world of ours, it is always recommended that instead of finding fault with the customs of a place, and telling the people that your ways are a thousand times better, you should commend their food, admire their dress, praise their horses and overlook their lack of manners. Providing more praise than they deserve is neither criminal, insincere nor abject. It is but a small price to pay for the goodwill and affection being bestowed upon you.

**Language.** Memorizing even a hundred words will permit you to converse on a variety of important subjects. Every effort should be made to learn how to express yourself in a simple and direct way. Do not be concerned about making mistakes in grammar or pronunciation. The way to master a language is to listen carefully and speak boldly. Besides, locals appreciate your efforts and will be eager to assist you. Regardless of where you ride, language is always going to be an important part of your journey. This is why it is worth remembering that standard tourist phrase books will be of limited help to a Long Rider. Such books will be able to teach a traveller how to say hello, goodbye, thank you, please, yes and no. But don't expect them to know the words for barn, horse shoe, hay or saddle. Nor can you expect vital equestrian terms to be known by natives who lack an equestrian culture. If you are puzzled over an equestrian term, use the Long Rider Equestionary to explain your dilemma to the locals.

**Food and Drink.** Long Riders know that if you want to lose weight, go on a gruelling equestrian journey. The combination of grooming large horses, lifting heavy saddles, riding long distances and walking several miles a day produces lean, strong, vigorous individuals who routinely report losing dozens of pounds. Hard riding often incurs a feeling of nagging hunger. The problem is that much of the time there is precious little to eat. Sometimes the countryside may be unable to provide you with a large meal. Yet there is a cultural aspect to this equestrian weight-loss programme as well.

Long Riders cannot afford to be fussy about what they eat because it is not uncommon for travellers to encounter items on the menu which are so repugnant that remaining hungry takes precedence over eating. When these occasions arise, you must be equipped with a cast-iron stomach; otherwise you may offend your hosts. Equestrian travel includes tales of Long Riders who have gobbled down pigeon's eggs preserved in chalk, lotus seeds, stag's tendons mixed with sea slugs, goat and turnip stew, camel heads and salted pigs fat, and then washed it all down with coffee spiced with pepper.

It gets worse if you're a strict vegetarian. Because of the protein-rich diets favoured by many cultures, Long Riders have tried to avoid meat by living on bread, yoghurt, noodles and tea. But the availability of these items influences the chances of success.

There is, however, another, far more common culinary conflict which might send you spinning; the practice of eating horse meat. The majority of North Americans consider the eating of horse flesh a social taboo nearly as reprehensible as cannibalism. Across the Atlantic the consumption of horse flesh by Europeans is influenced by politics and religion. Whereas Englishmen won't touch it, Italians enjoy horse sausage and Belgians are fond of equine steak. Yet horse meat does not constitute a large percentage of the national diet in any European country. In contrast, the Yakut equestrian culture in Siberia raises, rides, and eats their horses. Further south in Kazakhstan, equine flesh is as important to the national diet as the Thanksgiving turkey is to Americans or roast beef is to an Englishman.

Regardless of what's on offer, don't be surprised if you're presented with a large serving. Many cultures do not use forks or chopsticks. Some cultures prefer to eat with their right hands from a communal bowl. Others place individual servings on large leaves.

The other culinary consideration is the consumption of alcohol. Countries such as Saudi Arabia maintain draconian laws designed to suppress the ownership and drinking of alcoholic beverages. Mongols on the other hand take great pride in consuming vast amounts of the drink known as kumis, which is made from fermented mare's milk. Even if the law permits you to drink, as a Long Rider you have a more immediate concern. Drinking large quantities of alcohol with the locals may place you and your horses at risk. If your hosts pressure you to drink, do so with extreme caution, carefully gauge how much you've had and do not give in to peer pressure to consume too much.

**Demanding Gifts.** Differences in dishes are one thing. Encountering dramatically diverse views on basic social concepts is another. Long Riders, past and present, have described how surprised they were when Mongols asked to be given valuable objects as "gifts." According to this practice a Mongol may appear suddenly and ask to be presented with anything and everything in the traveller's camp, including his horse, equipment and clothes. The posing of this bold request doesn't generate the slightest hint of shame. On the contrary, the native is often aggressively insistent that the traveller hand over the desired object without delay. Long Rider reactions have ranged from bewilderment to outrage. What needs to be remembered is that Mongol herders inhabit a society which condones such behaviour, that this is a common practice and you are not being singled out. Mongols believe that if an individual voluntarily gives away an object, he will have occasion to ask for something in return. This spirit of generosity provides an important social safety net on the often hostile and desolate steppes.

Respecting any type of local tradition is fine, to a point. But giving away irreplaceable equipment or a beloved horse is not an option for a Long Rider. The issue then becomes how to acknowledge this local custom, without being fleeced by it. Long Riders have learned two simple tricks to offset these greedy demands. First, outbid the original request. If a Mongol asks for your saddle, demand he give you his yurt in exchange. Another tactic is to explain that the requested object was a family gift. It is therefore quite out of the question to part with it. Protecting your possessions shouldn't discourage you from being charitable. Many Long Riders carry sweets, candies or small gifts which they present to hosts and their children. Such generosity offsets the idea that you are mean spirited. It also reinforces the contention that your horse and equipment are a matter of life and death to you.

**Abusing Hospitality.** That is why it is vitally important that you take a careful, albeit quiet, note of your host's surroundings. Regardless if they are rich or poor, never overstay your welcome. Don't use their phone, food or any personal item without prior permission. Treat them with the utmost respect. Express your sincere appreciation. Always offer to pay. If you have food, share it. Give gifts, however simple. Clean up after your horse. Have your hosts sign your visitor's book. Promise to inform them when you have completed the journey.

**Hints.** One of the powerful elements of equestrian travel is the often intense feeling of a solitary revelation. You can't take comfort from the other members of a tour group. There's no one there to hold your hand. It's you, your horse and a disturbing discovery. Long Riders are not missionaries sent to pass judgment on their neighbours. Their goal is to venture deep within the emotional context of a country and learn how other people live their lives.

# Chapter 62 - Guides

Interacting with the natives is one thing, employing them quite another. There is nothing worse than an undependable guide and there is no way of ascertaining their unreliability beforehand! But you can take precautions. The inclusion of a guide and interpreters complicates matters, as strangers introduce an unknown factor into any expedition. Yet as the actions of these people will influence the welfare of the horses, a few remarks on this aspect of equestrian travel are required. In the days before an all-seeing satellite could beam down geographic secrets to your GPS, the success of an expedition often involved finding and hiring talented scouts. Moreover, a lack of native help was often interpreted as meaning the "sahib" was too poor to warrant respect. Like any section of humanity, there are heroes and villains to be found amongst those you hire.

**Whom to Hire.** Don't expect to just show up in a far-flung part of the world and recruit the first honest, hard-working, thrifty, sober, modest, clean, multi-lingual person that you find. To begin with, you need to determine what sort of work is required.

If you lack critically important geographic information, then a guide is needed to help negotiate your way through local challenges. A person who is familiar with equestrian travel will appreciate the need to follow routes which are suitable for horses. He may also be able to warn you about toxic plants in that region. But do not rely on his expertise once he has ventured beyond his locality. Finding a way through the mountains takes skill. Being able to speak a multitude of languages takes brains. One member of the party must understand the local language, otherwise you may not be able to find water, understand directions or comprehend warnings. This has been the traditional job of the interpreter. Many Long Riders have realized that without this vital linguistic skill, the success of their expedition is at stake.

**Delegate Authority.** Should circumstances demand that more than one person be hired, then appoint a sirdar, or head man, who is responsible for the actions of the others. This person of authority carries out your commands, oversees the security of the horses and answers directly to you.

**Clear-Cut Rules.** Problems arise when people from various backgrounds are thrown together for long periods of time. Civilisation teaches us to conceal our irritation with others. Yet the slow pace of an equestrian journey invariably reveals the best and worst qualities of those involved. Words cannot express what a living hell a journey can become if your companions turn out to be ghastly villains. Expeditions succeed when everyone knows their job and pulls their weight! Anyone hired to accompany you should know that in addition to their normal responsibilities, they will be expected to maintain discipline, share camp duties and do everything possible to promote the expedition's success. Failure to do so will result in dismissal and loss of wages. While allowances may be made for minor infractions, the one exception is disloyalty.

**The Contract.** I once participated in a conversation about the availability of hay which involved questions and answers being passed along through a mangled verbal chain of English, Pashto, Urdu and Kalash. Given the linguistic challenges involved in such a simple task, imagine trying to express yourself in a foreign language to a hostile policeman asking how much you promised to pay your guide or explaining to a suspicious judge what the guide's duties were. When you factor in the cultural differences which will influence the outcome of any argument involving angry native help, you can see why it makes sense to draw up a contract that protects you should a misunderstanding arise. Do not agree to depart with any type of native assistance unless you have a signed agreement that describes all the details regarding pay, duties and penalties. If the guide/interpreter can't sign his name on the contract, have him apply his thumb print to the document as a mark of affirmation. Here is an example of a standard agreement.

"I, the undersigned, forming an expedition about to explore the interior of _____, under Mr. ____, consent to place myself, horses and equipment entirely and unreservedly under his orders for the above purpose, from the date hereof until our return to _____, or, on failure in this respect, to abide all consequences that may result. I undertake to use my best endeavours to promote the harmony of the party and the success of the expedition. In witness whereof I sign my name. Read over and co-signed by the leader of the expedition.

In addition to the information suggested above, be sure the contract also specifies how and when the guide will be paid.

**Payment.** Successful alliances are premised on mutual interest. In this case, you need help and the locals can offer services. Don't be naïve enough to think that just because someone can't read or write he isn't a shrewd businessman. Plenty of Long Riders have learned the hard way that natives have a keen eye for profit. Nor is this rapacious eagerness to plunder travellers restricted to the forlorn parts of the Earth. Greed resides in every country. It doesn't matter if it's Abyssinia or Arizona; unscrupulous inhabitants view the arrival of a Long Rider as a rare occasion to enrich themselves at the traveller's expense. When dealing with guides, interpreters or any native help, take it for granted that sharp practices will be used against you at every opportunity! Expect to be asked to pay twice what is customary for goods and services. Establish the local rate and then offer half this amount. When the guide demands more, gradually adjust the amount higher until you arrive at a small percentage above normal. If you do not agree to pay the going rate, it will cause discontent and encourage theft during the journey.

Never pay the full amount in advance. Guides and hired help who have received their money before departure have been known to steal equipment and abandon their employers soon after the expedition is under way. Pay a small amount on departure and the rest at the conclusion of the journey. Stipulate how the money is distributed in the contract. Many countries have a long tradition of baksheesh. This is not the same as the western concept of tipping someone who has done an exemplary job. Baksheesh is a Persian word that describes a custom whereby someone rudely demands payment for no services rendered. Do not be victimized by the hired help into giving baksheesh! Presenting a small gift at the conclusion of the journey is a far better practice.

**Handling the Horses.** A great many people have been around horses but few know how to protect them when travelling. To ensure there are no misunderstandings, make sure that anyone who works for you clearly understands your orders about the horses. On no account allow anyone else to make decisions about the horses' feeding, health or welfare. Never authorize them to shoe the horses without your knowledge or permission. Make sure everyone knows that if anything goes wrong, you are to be informed immediately. Keep a careful eye on how they load the pack horses. Never let the guide, or a local horseman, set the pace. Guides are eager to go home. Local horsemen ride in a hurry, not realizing that at the conclusion of their brief spell in the saddle your horse still has a long journey ahead of it.

**Obtaining Directions.** Should your guide become lost or confused, there are a variety of reasons why you may not be able to obtain accurate directions from the native inhabitants.

They may find it hard to understand your motivation. When exploring the jungles of Brazil in 1799, Alexander von Humboldt was asked, "How is it possible to believe that you have left your country, to come and be devoured by mosquitoes, so as to measure a land not your own?"

They may not comprehend vast distances. When Swedish Long Rider Sven Hedin was travelling through the dreaded Lop Nor desert in 1900 he asked how far a faint road went. The local replied, "To the end of the world and it takes three months to get there."

They may not know how to judge distance according to your standards. Alternative measurements include the Thai kabiet, the Russian verst or the Chinese li. The English furlong refers to the length of the furrow in one acre of a ploughed open field. The Persian parasang was the distance a caravan could travel in an hour. The Brazilian league was the distance a horse could walk in one hour. The Roman mile was the distance of one thousand paces, while the kilometre was based on the meter, which was defined as one forty-millionth of the polar circumference of the Earth. The Japanese ri was based on the length of a baleen whale bone and the Finnish peninkulma was the distance a dog's bark can be heard in still air.

They may only know the immediate area. In 1995 Swiss Long Rider Basha O'Reilly attempted to obtain directions to a nearby Russian village. A local woman said, "Don't know. I've never heard of it." Turned out the hamlet was five miles away.

**Making Decisions.** As these examples illustrate, directions obtained from locals should be treated with suspicion. The majority of people either do not know the topography or cannot relate to your slow speed of travel. To diminish the chances of becoming lost, always seek to obtain the most accurate and up-to-date information regarding your route. Armed with this knowledge as a back-up, you can trust your guide to steer you to the next destination. But do not ask him to make decisions which involve parts of the country he is not acquainted with. He may well swear that he knows how to reach that place, when in reality he is hiding his lack of knowledge for fear of the results should he be found out.

A guide's actions will be influenced by local custom. This may include an inability to arrive at a quick decision. The pace of many cultures is much slower. Judging time may not be defined by hours. Alternative systems rely on the observation of physical objects. For example, when one Long Rider asked the time required to reach a village, he was told, "As long as it takes to smoke three cigarettes." When another traveller attempted to learn how much time a task would require, the answer was, "As long as it takes for a leaf to wilt."

Decision making will also depend on the temperament of the guide, the observance of any local holidays, the avoidance of taboos, and ensuring that the departure occurs on a favourable day.

**Drawbacks.** Just as there are rules regulating your actions as a guest, those whom you hire also have obligations and special needs. Any time you involve another person in your geographic journey, you complicate your emotional life. Thus, a guide may well solve one problem but create another. Whereas it is wise to consult and consider the opinions of those hired to help, as the expedition leader you are ultimately responsible for financial, legal and ethical issues connected to the journey. You are therefore entitled to express the final word on any decision.

**Disrespect.** The guide is paid for a service which you cannot control in advance. He may be knocked out of commission due to bad health or have to return home because of urgent family obligations. Taking another person's personal life into consideration is fine. But care must be used when guides, or anyone hired to help you, exhibits any signs of emotional antagonism or contempt. This problem has arisen repeatedly in Mongolia and Russia, when local men were

150

hired to guide expeditions led by female Long Riders. In these cases the native men were arrogant, dismissive of the Long Rider's knowledge, antagonistic to compromise and ultimately mutinous. You need to learn to draw a line between pampering the help and bullying them. If you treat them too leniently, they will become insolent. Drive them too hard and they will desert. The right way lies between these two. Treat anyone you hire with kindness and courtesy. Do not be disrespectful or mock them. Do not force them against their will to do more than the work they are paid for, but make sure they do that properly. If you make a promise, keep it. Be a little friendly and chat with them if you wish to, but the moment a man presumes on you doing so, stop it. Grant your trust and seek out their opinions. But do not allow anyone to take liberties or believe he is invaluable. Require respect! Do not hesitate to dismiss anyone who is incompetent, cowardly, surly or discourteous.

**Handling Hostility.** If you're sitting in the safety of your home, you may well be saying to yourself, "I would never be fool enough to hire such a villain." But you fail to appreciate the fact that the potential guide isn't likely to be an obvious, scowling, scarred cutthroat. He is more likely to be a cunning rascal who uses his smile to emotionally disarm you.

Don't be taken in by a disguise of fundamental decency, otherwise you will find yourself riding down a lonely road wondering what to do, how to proceed and what the repercussions may be if you fire the guide. Never allow the guide to over estimate his importance! He has far less interest in the success of the expedition than you, so cannot be counted on to imperil himself on your account. Do not confide your secrets to him, as they are sure to be shared or sold later to your disadvantage. Take a strict view on alcohol and never tolerate drunken behaviour. Should a crisis arise, be sceptical if asked to accept a sacred oath. If a man does not speak the truth, he will not swear it either! To discern his honesty, look straight into another person's eyes and hold their gaze. A great deal can be told by the way the suspected party reacts. The guilty take alarm easily.

Relying on a distant legal system won't provide you with immediate protection in camp. Threatening a guide may provoke him into attacking you. Defuse the tension by adopting a frank, joking but determined manner. Never let your nerves get the better of you. Always show more confidence that you really feel. Do not involve yourself in a physical fight! Nor should you curse the person or verbally dishonour his family, tribe or nation. A physical injury may heal, and eventually be forgotten, but an emotional insult is rarely forgiven.

Even though your own problems may be of tremendous immediate concern, do not forget that your actions will leave an impression that will affect other Long Riders. Whenever possible, resolve your differences peacefully, rather than leave behind any irreparable wounds.

# Chapter 63 - Attacks

Just as you wouldn't venture into deep water without knowing how to swim, similarly you should not set off on a journey without realizing that not everyone wishes you well. You cannot afford to ignore the danger which always attends: that deadly predator known as man.

**The Trouble with Travel.** Horse travel has always been a hard business. Regardless of all the soothing talk about this being a global village, those of us who have ridden out there can tell you that the world is a vast and lonely place still filled with dragons, superstitions, and some extremely horrible people. Being a Long Rider will teach that you don't need to look for trouble on a journey. It often finds you.

**Conflicting Philosophy.** To understand the risks you must first acknowledge the diversity of our species. Making a journey on horseback isn't guaranteed to endear you to the locals. Chances are they will not have been raised with the values you hold dear. Their nation may take a sceptical view of travel.

**Eyes Wide Open.** What happens when the siren song of the journey calls? All too often our restless blood has awakened a longing to see what lies hidden far away. Armed with a belief in peace and understanding, we set off in happy anticipation, never realizing that sooner or later we will cross an invisible line. On one side remains everything you knew, including the law.

On the other side a wide range of problems await your arrival. These vary from the mild discomfort of listening to the ravings of a madman to the danger of being hunted by fanatics bent on your destruction. People who have spent their lives sheltered by kindness, truth and honour do not automatically recognize the base treachery which can dominate the lives of others. The ugly reality is that a Long Rider cannot afford to be naïve. Never think you're an exception. No matter how pure your heart is, you too can become a target of aggression!

How do we balance protecting our lives against becoming cynical? We start by realizing that there are different types of dangers.

**Territorial Males.** Just as a Long Rider needs to keep a keen eye on the weather, he must never lose sight of the human factor. Aggression, stupidity and violence are not restricted by geography. Generally you can expect to encounter three basic types of antagonism: hostile individuals, aggressive tribes and belligerent nations. Women have rarely attempted to harm or kill equestrian travellers. That's not to say that women haven't tried to murder Long Riders. Yet it is usually the male of the species who is going to attack you. This frequently occurs when he feels you have infringed upon his territory, invaded his private space or threatened to consume his precious resources. Male hostility is increased when alcohol is involved. Long Riders have noted how young men in Kazakhstan, Tuva and Russia have reacted aggressively. In such cases unemployment and cheap vodka can quickly spark an incident which turns mild curiosity into overt aggression. If by chance you are unlucky enough to venture into the wrong place, be on the alert, keep a low profile and remember that you may be viewed as fair game.

**Antagonistic Tribes.** Sometimes it's not just a couple of bullies who are spoiling for trouble in the pub. Long Riders have also encountered hostile tribes who harbour a community-wide distrust of strangers. The more cut off the locals are from outside influences, the more bigoted, ferocious and intolerant they become. In 1977 English Long Rider Christina Dodwell's horse was stolen and its front legs were cut off by Turkana tribesmen in Kenya. In 2002 American Long Rider Mike Winter was forced to spend the night hiding in the woods to avoid detection from hostile locals residing in Kentucky's Appalachian Mountains. As these episodes demonstrate, some societies still distrust strangers, fear new ideas and hate change.

**Deadly Nations.** At the dawning of the 21$^{st}$ century it is standard practice to view Tibet as the beautiful mountainous homeland of spiritual Buddhist monks. Given the peaceful teachings of His Holiness, the Dalai Lama, it is easy to understand why the Tibetans are commonly associated today with the benign influences of Buddhist philosophy. What few remember today is that in spite of its current peaceful reputation Tibet has the dubious honour of being the country where Long Riders were repeatedly murdered and savagely tortured. Some of the most astonishing and dangerous horse journeys ever undertaken came to tragic conclusions in what was once known as "the hermit kingdom."

Another deadly area is the Andes Mountains, where Long Riders have been attacked by Native Americans who have a fear of the Saca Maneteca, a white-skinned demon mounted on a horse. In the 1920s Aimé Tschiffely was forced to use his guns to defend himself against such an attack. In the 1980s the Russian Long Rider Vladimir Fissenko was almost beaten to death by rock-wielding Indians who mistook him for this superstitious monster. And in 1995 the Polish Long Rider Tadeusz Kotwicki was also savagely attacked by Andean Indians.

**Stone-Throwing Children.** Luckily for Long Riders, being mistaken for a demon isn't a routine occurrence. Being pelted by an angry swarm of stone-throwing children is a more common danger. The results can range from mild annoyance to serious bodily injury.

Usually a Long Rider can integrate into a community peacefully. Establishing trust with fellow adults quickly follows. That time-honoured tradition is killed in the cradle when you and your horse are subjected to an unprovoked attack by feral children bent on your humiliation and retreat. The majority of the children you encounter will be anxious to meet you. Only a few will be intent on hurling stones, bottles and abuse. A contributing factor will be the attitude of local adults. In certain countries grown-ups turn a blind eye to the activities of stone-throwing children. As a result of adult apathy, the children quickly learn they are at liberty to behave as badly as they want.

Stone throwing usually occurs in rural areas or on undeveloped roads where ammunition is readily at hand. When attacks happen in an urban setting it is usually at the edge of a town where fewer adults are in attendance. If you see children gathering to attack, try to defuse the tension by looking straight at them. Then smile, wave and greet them in the local language. Should they ignore your offer of friendship and begin picking up stones, don't forget the intimidating presence of your horse. Ride up to them and ask what they're doing. Like most bullies, even pint-sized pedestrians think twice if you act self-assured. With luck your confidence may make them regret their actions and begin to act friendly.

Should they press home an attack, look for adult help without delay. The moment you see grown-ups, try to converse and connect with them. Ask them if they approve of their children acting this way? Remind them of the religious and cultural edicts which state that travellers are to be treated with honour and respect. Remain polite, but if you feel seriously threatened, inform the adults that if they don't intercede at once to protect you and your horse, you will file a formal complaint with the nearest government agency. The best defence though is to take heed of local politics. Beware of cultural and religious influences. Watch the ground for stones. Keep a keen eye on the kids. Act confidently.

**Sexual Assault.** Lady Long Riders may not be avoiding Tibetan bandits nowadays, but they're still being tracked, hunted and harmed by predatory males. French Long Rider Magali Pavin was one such example. Prior to setting off in 2002 to ride from France to China, Magali armed herself with a small electric stun gun. Unfortunately it had been damaged while travelling. Of course the Romanian man who attacked her had no way of knowing that. All he saw was a solitary foreign woman who had pitched camp close to his village. That night the rapist broke into Magali's tent and attacked her. In the ensuing struggle Magali defended herself with a knife. The enraged Romanian responded by breaking her nose with an iron bar and nearly beating her unconscious. Despite her wounds, Magali made use of a moment's respite to escape. She jumped on her horse and galloped into the village, where she found protection.

Women riding alone in foreign countries have noted that sexual harassment increases near cities with western influences. Any time alcohol is readily available, the risk of being harassed and threatened intensifies dramatically.

Even though rape is one of mankind's original crimes, an added element of danger was introduced in the 21st century. Lady Long Riders would be well advised to shield their exact location from cyber-stalkers. These sexual predators can use the traveller's blog or Facebook account to monitor the traveller's movements and plan an attack. This happened to a woman who was sexually assaulted a month into her journey. After reading the traveller's blog, which described how she was rowing a small boat 1,500 miles on Lake Michigan, the rapist was able to pinpoint the victim's location. He waited until she was in a vulnerable location, broke into the cabin of her boat, identifying her by her full name and then raped her. When you make efforts to get attention, you don't get to select the people who pay attention! Keep your exact position private, so as to lessen the chances of assault.

While it always pays to remain extremely vigilant, when riding solo you must exude a sense of supreme self-confidence. Depending on which country you choose, it is also a good idea to have something close to hand to defend yourself with. Several solo lady Long Riders have opted to protect themselves with knives or pepper spray.

**Robbers.** Robbery is the act of taking something by force. But, like any occupation, there are degrees of dedication to the trade. Chinese robbers would usually allow you to retain your underwear to enable you to reach the nearest village with a modicum of decency. But in Tibet, they shot first and robbed your corpse. There are still dangerous places where everything you do must be considered carefully. One thing you must think about is how you will react if you're robbed. Many robberies are spontaneous. They are usually perpetrated by men who grab a chance to enrich themselves quickly at another's expense. Alcohol is often involved. Should you find yourself facing robbers, try to restrain your fear. Move slowly. Smile. Act polite. If possible, pretend to misunderstand what's happening by acting friendly and offering to shake hands. Sometimes the impulse to rob you may evaporate and be replaced by embarrassment. Be extremely careful about reacting in an aggressive manner, as this may turn robbery into murder. If things turn bad, focus on staying alive. Nothing you own is more valuable than your life!

**Kidnapped.** Being robbed is usually a short discomforting experience. Being kidnapped can last months or years. Mexico, India and Iraq currently lead the list of global hot spots. Phoenix, Arizona is America's kidnapping capital. Unlike-a-spur-of-the-moment robbery, kidnapping is often a carefully-constructed crime.

**Avoiding Conflict.** So what precautions can we take against stone-throwing brats, robbers intent on stealing our underwear and kidnappers anxious to wring every dollar out of our weeping mothers? In order to decrease the chances of you becoming a plucked pigeon you should enact basic safety standards in every country, no matter how benign it may appear to be. First, don't place loyalty to your route before allegiance to your life! You're not driving along a well-lit interstate highway, one which provides a security phone every few miles so as to assist stranded motorists. You're riding alone in a big and often dangerous world. If you encounter or are warned about serious hazards alter your plans or you may lose your life.

Next, even if you're not being chased by the Taliban, avoid riding in perilous places. Crime festers in cities. Attacks and robberies are often perpetrated nearby. Ride well around any place with a bad reputation. Don't reveal your life story to dubious strangers! Should a suspicious character ask where you are bound, tell him the nearest town is your immediate goal and that upon arriving you will be the guest of the police who are expecting you. Never leave your financial life in a saddle or pommel bag because if the horse runs away or is stolen you are ruined! Protect your most precious valuables by keeping them hidden under your clothes in a thin cloth or leather bag. A comfortable cord should allow this little bag to rest under your arm, so as to be nearly undetectable.

Also, travellers through the ages have learned that it pays to look poor. Be careful not to advertise your wealth. Not only does carrying expensive equipment burden your horse, it also excites the envy of criminals. If you have cameras, cell phones, laptops, wristwatches, etc., keep them out of sight so as to reduce the possibility of theft.

**Exercise Self-Control.** Every country has its fair share of rude people. But equally true, all nations have angels of mercy dwelling there as well. Whenever possible, allying yourself with a sympathetic local, even for a short distance, may help offset the formation of trouble. But if you find yourself alone, then take care how you react if you're verbally attacked. Whether the situation is mildly annoying or utterly life threatening, always try to keep your emotions under strict control. However difficult it is, don't react aggressively to vocal provocation. Ignore taunts. Don't respond to racial slurs. Disregard verbal aggression. Don't plead for privacy. Don't try to explain what a good person you are, how you're raising money for a wonderful charity back home, that you love God, Mom and apple pie. Safety means space. Remain silent and ride on.

**Retain Control of the Horse.** It's one thing to ignore an insult. But your life is in jeopardy the moment assailants are allowed close enough to seize control of your horse. If things get dodgy, always remain in the saddle! Not only are you safer, you can make an immediate escape. Sitting high on a horse provides you with a psychological edge over pedestrians. But that advantage is neutralized if a stranger gets close enough to grab the horse's reins. Suddenly you're no longer in control. In fact you've been effectively imprisoned up in the saddle. Always be aware of the safety space around you and your horse. If anyone attempts to come close to the reins, or to move up alongside your stirrup, warn them off by signalling the horse bites.

**Mounted Danger.** It is just as vital to maintain your security against mounted threats. On the trail offer a friendly greeting to all strangers. Consider a failure to respond as suspicious. It is a point of honour to give clear trail directions when asked. Be wary of anyone who is unwilling to offer this basic courtesy. Always halt a safe distance away from a mounted stranger! If there is cause for suspicion, keep the stranger in front of you while speaking. Never reveal your travel plans to strangers. Pay strict attention to the activities and backgrounds of anyone who attempts to ride, travel or camp near you. Should any person, regardless of shabby or genteel appearance try to force himself into your company, outride him if you can. Do not permit a stranger to ingratiate himself and then ride close beside you. If an unwelcome person attaches himself, look for another traveller and keep pace with that person until you reach a place of safety.

**No Gun, Big Smile.** The topic of riding with weapons is reserved for a separate section. What you can always use to your benefit are the social skills which turn any potentially harmful confrontation into a pleasant meeting. Never underestimate the power of friendship. A smile can defuse a tense situation. Laughter may neutralize anger. A sense of humour places peril into perspective. Act modest, approachable and affable.

**Alcohol and Aggression.** Being friendly is recommended. Drinking with strangers is not.

Alcohol abuse is a serious problem in many parts of the world. People may appear friendly when they start drinking, but they can become abusive and violent if the liquor keeps flowing. The best defence against alcohol-inspired aggression is not to expose yourself to the threat. Don't ever drink with a stranger whom you have met in the open. You can't afford to have your senses clouded or your reactions slowed. Don't ride with or camp near people who are drinking. Alcohol sparks acts of spontaneous stupidity. Don't allow the people you have hired to help you drink! Alcohol encourages abuse and apathy.

**Fleeing for your Life.** Even if we adhere to the philosophy of "tread softly and travel far," menace may still find us. In wild countries your life will depend on your ability to recognize danger and to extricate yourself quickly. Though conditions will differ depending upon circumstances, there are certain basic rules we can rely on to help increase the chances of shaking off our pursuers and saving our lives.

Take a route that won't allow cars to follow. Remove the bells off your horse's bridle to help disguise the sound of your retreat. In case you've had trouble during the day and feel the need to hide your camp that night, never halt next to water. Give your horses a long drink and then ride a considerable distance to confuse your pursuers. If you are following a beaten path or well marked trail, select a place to turn off where the ground is too hard to show hoofprints. Never stop until after sundown in order that people on your track are unable to pursue you with ease. Stay out of sight. Camp away from roads where a car's lights can be used to spot you in the dark. After you've halted, never allow any hammering or loud talking in camp. There's no time to make plans after you're under attack. Discuss what you will do and where you will meet should you be forced to flee. If you fear robbers, take time to protect your valuables. Dig a shallow hole; place the majority of your money within, replace the dirt, then build a small fire atop the hole. Next morning, brush away the ashes and retrieve your treasure. Should you fear for your life, keep a strict watch all night. If you are travelling with a companion, take turns standing guard. Agree to stand watch in a secluded position away from camp, in the direction from which your attackers might arrive. Relieve each other every hour to insure against falling asleep. Because of the horse's superior sense of smell, his acute hearing and his keen sense of danger, don't forget to rely upon your equine comrade's ability to detect danger before you can. Watch his ears to see if they prick up in the direction of a strange noise. His nostrils will flare wide if he smells something suspicious. Pay attention if he becomes restless. If you suspect an attack, don't be taken by surprise. Keep your horses saddled, tied close by and ready for instant flight. Don't delay fleeing if you're faced with a flight-or-fight situation. Should a chance to rest present itself, a person who may need to quickly ride for his life sleeps most safely with the horse's head tied to his wrist by the reins. The horse, if he hears anything, tosses his head and jerks the rider's arm. Because the horse is a careful animal, there is little danger of his treading on you while sleeping. Preserving your life is the primary consideration. Abandon the equipment if it enhances your chances of survival.

**Spies on Horseback.** Robbers and rapists share something in common. They are private citizens whose illegal actions harm a Long Rider. Should you be unlucky enough to meet either class of criminal, you can count on receiving the assistance of the police. Espionage is different. You're not the victim. You're the criminal. The police won't help you. They'll hunt you. The laws which normally protect your civil rights may be quickly suppressed by a country which views your quick capture, the immediate restriction of your liberty, the suppression of your journey, the denial of your existence and your long-term imprisonment as being beneficial to national security.

Danish Long Rider Henning Haslund was arrested in Russia in 1923 and accused of being a capitalist spy. During her ride across Canada in 1939 Mary Bosanquet was accused of being a Nazi spy, scouting Canada prior to a German invasion. English Long Rider Donald Brown was making his way south from the Arctic Circle in 1954 when Finnish police arrested him on suspicion of being a communist spy. Gordon Naysmith was insulted and injured in 1971 when Tanzanian soldiers mistook him for an Israeli spy.

The average man has no clear idea of how to determine who is a spy. But they take delight in the idea of catching one. Regardless of which government snatches you for spying, protests and resistance are met with rough treatment. Requests to contact the embassy or to use the telephone are often refused.

**Hints.** How a nation reacts to a traveller varies greatly. What a modern Long Rider must remember is that other countries are under no obligation to treat him with respect, demonstrate kindness, exercise tolerance or extend forgiveness.

# Chapter 64 - Arrests

You may smile at the thought of risking your neck in some bit of mounted foolishness but your courage will fade if you are arrested for breaking the law. Long Riders have been captured by cops for a variety of reasons, including politics and crime.

**Hostile Governments.** When the Soviets confirmed that Henning Haslund was just a wandering Long Rider in search of a hot meal, they released him. After the Finns confirmed there were no photographs of the airport on Donald Brown's film, they released him. After the Tanzanians confirmed that Gordon Naysmith was Scottish, not Israeli, they released him. Those episodes are connected to our collective cultural past, one wherein the definition of a spy was understood by all. In those days it was a man in a trench coat sneaking across Berlin's Check Point Charlie with a roll of micro-film hidden in the heel of his shoe. But times have changed, as has the political climate and the definition of a foreign agent. It's no longer enough to just empty your camera to prove your innocence. These days you are more likely to be charged as a terrorist. Aggressive governments are anxious to maintain a strictly-controlled environment. They find it difficult to believe that equestrian travel is a benign activity. If you're not a tourist travelling in an automobile along a well-established route, it is often assumed you're an involved in sabotage, spying or spreading political dissent.

**Political Prisoners.** New Zealand Long Rider Ian Robinson wasn't merely arrested. In 2004 he was hunted across Tibet, imprisoned and then deported by infuriated officials of the Chinese army of occupation. "I tried to play the innocent tourist and argued to be allowed to continue. But my horses were confiscated and I was driven 200 kilometres to Naqu by jeep. There I was fined and ordered to leave Tibet. That night I escaped. I smuggled myself out of town in a car to a small monastery, where I managed to buy two more horses. I was just about to set off when the police found me again. This time I fled on horseback and was chased for hours by the police in their jeep. Luckily it had just snowed. I headed to high ground too steep for the vehicle and vanished into the hills." Ian rode for three more weeks, during which time he avoided even the smallest settlements in an effort to elude the police who were hunting him. After three months in the saddle he had ridden more than 2,000 kilometres across most of Tibet when he was discovered on the shores of Laky Gyaring Tso. He was arrested, his horses impounded and his passport confiscated. Then he was fined and expelled by the country's Chinese conquerors.

**Under Arrest.** Should you find yourself under arrest, rely on your brains, not your emotions.

Don't anger your captors by verbally attacking them or ridiculing their country. This will only compound the danger you're in. Respond politely to questions by providing your name, country and the reason you're making the journey. Act confident and relaxed if you're questioned.

Never admit to having committed a crime, even if was unintentional. If you're a Member of the Long Riders' Guild, mention that fact and provide the names of important people who support your journey. Assure the arresting officers that a mistake has been made, that you won't hold a grudge against them for doing their duty, that it's important your journey be completed and that releasing you promptly will help convince your supporters worldwide that it was all an innocent mistake. Explain that unless you are released political leaders and the press will be informed of your false arrest.

**Tortured.** Travel is a beguiling mistress who never willingly reveals the vengeful side of her nature. She has two faces. The majority of Long Riders only encounter the kind one. But I would be remiss in my duty if I did not admit that during the long life of this book a handful of you will unfortunately meet the face of terror. There is no need to pretend that some countries are not brutal and repellent. Nor does it help to compare the enlightened polices of the country you voluntarily left against the cruel practices of the nation who has captured you. These are countries who nurture cruelty in the cradle. In the worst possible case, serious men will attempt to bend you to their wills with more than hard looks and rough words. They will enforce any number of devilish deeds on your mind and body. Should this be the case, nervousness is a luxury that a Long Rider cannot afford. As hard as it sounds, it is necessary to remain clear headed in the face of what is to come. The problem is that people, like cables, have a breaking point. Only Hollywood pretends that people don't crack under torture. Given enough time, men who are dedicated to evil, and proficient in their dark trade, can make you say and sign any-thing. When professionals set out to torture you, there comes a time when the only thing you can control is what you think. You will experience more than just pain. In time there will be a complete erosion of confidence. Regardless of what they do, you must reach inside and find the courage to continue living! My own narrow escape being tortured and imprisoned in Pakistan proves that every minute of survival brings a chance of a reprieve.

**Imprisoned.** Trouble is capable of taking many forms. Being imprisoned is one of the worst. It is a solemn moment when you're torn from the saddle and placed behind bars. Hearing the cell door slam shut strikes cold fear into a heart which is steeled against traditional physical dan-gers. Nor are you the first. Along this hard track, as far back as history can be traced, other men and women have ridden, been imprisoned and despaired. Marco Polo and Cervantes likewise bore the scars which came from being imprisoned. The Scottish Long Rider Don Roberto Cunninghame Graham was imprisoned in Morocco in 1897. Regardless of what jail, prison or labour camp you are tossed into, quickly make an ally of a person who is well-versed in the ways of that penal institution. On such chance meetings and thin threads hang the fate of travellers. It was thanks to such wise old prisoners that I was able to survive in a repellent Pakistani prison, until I was found innocent and released. Should the paradise of your journey be turned into a desert full of sadness, don't expect diplomats and lawyers to come rushing to rescue you!

**Diplomats.** Once upon a time an English Long Rider knew that merely mentioning the name of Prime Minister Palmerston was enough to strike fear into the hearts of citizens of other count-ries. Nowadays all that is changed.

An episode of the British television programme *Yes, Prime Minister* highlighted the new policy of doing nothing.

"What happens in an emergency?"

"Then we follow the Four Stage Strategy."

"What's that?"

"It's the standard Foreign Office response in a time of crisis. In Stage One, we say nothing is going to happen. Stage Two we say something may happen but we shouldn't do anything about it. In Stage Three we say that maybe we should do something but there's nothing we can do. Stage Four we say there was something we could have done but its too late now."

That dark comedy only confirms the fact that gone are the days when Prime Ministers had the backbone to defend you. Nor should you waste your time thinking that your nation's ambas-sador or his staff are going to rush to your defence. Diplomatic support is like honey on the elbow: you can smell it, you can feel it, but you cannot taste it – and you should never expect it. Once you establish contact with embassy employees, your first priority is to sign a privacy disclosure. This authorizes the embassy to pass on all relevant details about your arrest and imprisonment to your family and the press. The embassy may provide you with a list of lawyers. Here again, don't put too much stock in being quickly rescued.

**Lawyers.** Should your journey require you to ride through a perilous country, you must remain vigilant. This includes not counting on someone else to be there when you need help. The best defence is common sense and awareness. Do not be tempted to bestow your trust too quickly on a lawyer, solicitor or barrister in a foreign country. Several are of no more use than a tooth-ache. Even worse, there are many cynical members of the legal trade who make a cold-blooded profit from the misfortunes of travellers. There have been numerous cases where criminal gangs in league with the police have set up unsuspecting travellers in a compromising situation. The victim's family is quick to hire a sympathetic-sounding lawyer who has promised to use his local influence to bring about a "rescue." Once the foreigner has been squeezed for every cent, he is allowed to depart. The lawyer then divides the loot among the criminals and police. Even a portion of such a fee may represent up to a year's wages in some impoverished countries. Should the case go to court, the barristers can be counted on to engage in phoney adversarial combat. This is a trade that will place profit before honour. Their freedom is not at stake. If your life is compromised, they still get paid and go home richer for the experience. Despite all the fine talk about serving justice, this is a profession that has often been steeped in treachery. You would do well to reserve your trust, and watch your bankbook, when dealing with the members of the legal profession.

**Surviving the Impossible.** These are the events which create memories that hurt forever. It may appear that the long ride has drawn to an end, in which case your mind may be tempted to become clouded with humiliation, fear and grief. But a defeat of this nature can awaken us to how precious life and liberty really are. There are only a handful of living Long Riders who have survived prison. They all know what it means to enjoy the glorious feeling of freedom.

Should a serious misfortune befall you, circumstances will demand that you allow yourself one spasm of despair. Then you must put all traces of self-pity behind you and meet your adversaries with a brain of ice and a heart of fire! Lost though you may be in the dark bowels of some pitiless prison, the armour of your soul is protection against the ills of life. Take refuge in the knowledge that no misfortune, however grave, cannot change within the hour. Other Long Riders have found that hope shines even in the darkest portions of our lives.

**Hints.** Do not ignore your intuition. If in doubt, check it out. Though it is important to be realistic about the dangers which might affect your journey, it is equally true that most trouble never materializes. You will be pleasantly surprised to learn that the mother tongue of many strangers is "horse."

# Chapter 65 - Guns

Times have changed. When Genghis Khan visited other countries he thought nothing of using his weapons to impose his imperial will on the inhospitable residents who opposed his unex-pected arrival. But in this day of paranoid national governments, ever-alert security systems and increasingly hostile sedentary societies, the chances of you riding anywhere heavily-armed have dramatically diminished. That is why, even though the decision to carry armament is a personal one, the choice ultimately depends on a variety of factors.

**Reason not Romance.** The first of these is the need for common sense. Like every object carried by a Long Rider, you must be able to justify the weight of the weapon in question. Guns are heavy. When Japanese Long Rider Baron Fukushima set off to ride from Berlin to Tokyo in 1892, he carried a .44 calibre Smith & Wesson revolver and 50 cartridges. But he never used it during his 14,000 kilometres (8,700 miles) ride. Like that previous generation, we too have to determine if we even need a weapon.

**A Mounted Misconception.** Shooting accurately is a skill like any other. Knowing how to do it well is commendable. Of equal importance is the ability to maintain and clean the weapon. But once we acknowledge the need to point and polish the pistol, what do we use it for?

Straight away we can dismiss another Hollywood myth; the need to shoot a horse with a broken leg. Nearly every gun-related message sent to the Long Riders' Guild by would-be travellers concerns the need to shoot a horse with a broken leg. What people don't realise is how remote a possibility this is. In fact, if it's horses with broken legs that worry you, then don't look at the world of equestrian travel for examples. Despite the millions of miles ridden by Long Riders on every continent, including Antarctica, there is not one known instance of a horse breaking its leg and being shot by an equestrian explorer! Not one. Did it ever happen? Maybe. Will it happen to you? Not likely. Why? Speed, safety and sensibility.

A number of factors separate equestrian travellers from the competitive horse industry. Unlike racing, which is obsessed with speed, Long Riders achieve the majority of their miles at the walk. By reducing the speed, equestrian travellers dramatically decrease the risk of injury. There are two other unsuspected elements involved in shooting a horse with a broken leg. Knowing how and where to shoot a horse is more complicated than you suspect. Finally, in this age of astonishing personal communication, the ability to quickly contact qualified medical personnel diminishes the need for you to personally exterminate a wounded horse. For the vast majority of modern Long Riders, a vet armed with a lethal injection is only a phone call away. Thus, carrying a gun for the sole purpose of being able to dispatch a horse in the unlikely event he breaks his leg is not recommended!

**Hunting and Hunger.** This raises the possibility of carrying a gun so as to supplement your diet by shooting game while travelling. There are a handful of American Long Riders who are uniquely qualified to hunt while they travel. In addition to being skilful back-country equestrian travellers, they are also actively involved in the "mountain man" community. These exceptional Long Riders practise special skills, including the ability to successfully hunt various types of game with black powder weapons. The thing to keep in mind is that these singular travellers possess a set of highly honed skills which most modern humans lack. If you know how to live off the land like your forefathers, then carrying a gun for hunting is justified. But before you burden your animal with the weight of a pistol or rifle, make a careful check of the hunting regulations in the areas where you will be travelling. Being a hunter is one thing, hunting legally is another.

**Animal Action.** This brings us to consider the need to carry firearms as a defence against attacks by wild animals. This book has a special section devoted to that topic, wherein the likelihood of animal attack is discussed in depth, according to species and country. Without delving too deeply into that topic prematurely, we can arrive at several conclusions about the need to carry a firearm to ward off dangerous animals. The majority of journeys will not place you in close proximity to wild animals that are interested in eating you or your horses. There is of course one final reason to carry a gun; to protect you against that deadly predator, man. But this, as you will see, is a far more complicated issue.

**To Arm or Not To Arm.** It takes a lot of courage just to set off on a long ride. You have to summon up the pluck needed to ignore the dire warnings of sceptics who believe death lurks around the first bend in the road. You must find the bravery needed to set off into the unknown with no guarantee of success or even arrival. Thus, in one way the moment you depart your emotional courage has already been confirmed. But that's one kind of valour. Encountering people who mean to do you harm is another issue. Which brings us back to the old question; do we carry weapons to defend ourselves?

This was a lesson well known to the last generation of Long Riders, who often rode armed. And their guns weren't just for looks. If you crossed them, they might kill you. For example, because of the immense danger encountered in Paraguay during the 1920s, Welsh Long Rider Thurlow Craig always carried a Colt .45 single-action revolver. Being constantly armed helped him survive numerous journeys through the jaguar-infested Chaco jungle and several political revolutions. Of course it would be easy to say those were turbulent times and that the days of savage turmoil are behind us. Sadly, mankind may have climbed down from the trees but he's still a deadly threat. Perhaps similar circumstances might arise during your journey? If so, you need to consider the practicalities involved in being armed.

**Bad Vibes.** First, there are serious social drawbacks. Chances are you won't bump into a gang of bandits. It's much more likely that the vast majority of people you encounter will be kind, courteous, curious and hospitable. No matter how friendly they may be, the problem is that our actions and appearance reflect our aims and our beliefs. And no matter how you spin it, an armed man exudes violence. Imagine for a moment what it would feel like if an intimidating stranger suddenly rode up to your house. Sitting up there on his horse, he stares down and asks for hospitality. It is unlikely that he will be greeted enthusiastically because guns don't encourage smiles or conversation. Most land owners will be distrustful. Women who are alone usually won't allow an armed stranger to dismount. The result is that the gun you're carrying to protect yourself has encouraged suspicion and hostility among the people whose friendship you need.

**Precious Paperwork.** The political landscape has changed dramatically since the violent birth of the 20th century. In an age when sceptical governments insist on fingerprints and biometric eye scans to confirm your identity, obtaining authorization to ride armed can be extremely difficult.

**Arrested.** While you might expect nations to view gun ownership differently, it may surprise you to learn that bureaucratic hostility can be experienced by merely crossing a state or provincial border within the same country. At the time of writing, the United States is an example of how conflicting gun laws have resulted in Long Rider arrests. Many states require a pistol to be carried in the open. Others have ruled that is illegal to carry a handgun in a saddlebag. Some states demand that private citizens obtain a special permit before they can carry a concealed weapon. But in Arizona anyone over the age of 21 can carry a concealed weapon without a permit. Regardless of where you carry it, once you ride into the neighbouring state your local weapon's permit may no longer be valid. Several states require an armed person to carry a valid hunting licence in game country. Other states will allow you to carry certain types of weapons, so long as you're not hunting. Many national parks ban all firearms. And we don't have time to consider the countless city restrictions against guns. Sound confusing? It is a Byzantine web of torturous laws that can bring your journey to an unhappy ending and has resulted in several Long Riders being arrested.

**When Trouble Arrives.** Regardless of what country you decide to ride in, let us assume you believe the situation warrants carrying a firearm for protection and that you've taken care of the legalities. Now what?

There may be no stories of road horses breaking their legs, but there are plenty of tales of Long Riders being scared to death by horrific humans. Bullies and bad men aren't restricted to any one nation. They lurk in all corners of the globe and it may be your reluctant duty to deal with them. That doesn't mean you have to charge towards certain destruction.

What may surprise you is that even if you're carrying an assortment of lethal guns, concerns about your safety won't disappear. Packing a pistol may help reinforce your courage. Yet if you allow fear to undermine your sense of serenity, no gun is big enough to keep your confidence intact. That is why it is unwise to put all your faith in a weapon. Any enemy can analyse such obvious strength. Should you find yourself up against foes, it's not the absence of fear which matters. Every normal person will feel afraid. What counts is your ability to hide that fear from antagonists. At such a critical moment, deception is your initial weapon. You must make your opponents hesitate, so as to try and calculate what they cannot see. Thus, your first line of defence is never a gun. It is making an opponent respect you because of your display of unwavering self-confidence.

**Being Shot At.** When tempers flare, one way of disarming your opponent is to get him to start talking. Once he begins, the more vociferous he becomes, the sooner he will talk himself out. After the first laugh you can usually walk away in safety.

If luck is against you, your opponent may start shooting. To be shot at in a wild strange place is a very different proposition than from being faced by soldiers engaged in a collective conflict. They can seek safety with their comrades. Medics hover nearby to dispense comfort. To be fired at when all alone and far from home is a very different proposition.

Aimé Tschiffely endured such a challenge. He was riding through a deep, narrow canyon in 1926 when a robber began shooting at him from above. Tschiffely quickly found cover and then retreated. "Did I feel fear during that ticklish experience," Aimé wrote. "And How, as the Americans would say."

**Shooting Back.** If extreme violence is going to be useful, it has to be carefully chosen and made not out of passion but with a sense of cold calculation. In such a situation international law often classifies the action as having been committed based on "anticipatory self-defence." The law may declare it legal to defend your life, but it is foolish to fight for money. Never stake your life for the sake of a handful of possessions or even your horse. Employ your pistol only to protect your person! A time may come when you have a split second to weigh the advantages and disadvantages of your actions. Don't pull your gun unless you intend to use it to fight in self-defence. When guns come into play, it's best to accept the probability of death, yet fight for your life to combine the realism of your situation with the optimism needed to help you survive.

If you are fleeing for your life on horseback, and have need to shoot your pursuers, hold the reins firmly in one hand, then rest the barrel of the pistol on your bridle arm to steady your aim. Aim at the centre of your opponent's body. In each bound of the horse, the moment when his forelegs strike the ground is one of comparative steadiness, and is therefore the proper instant for pulling the trigger.

Should you suspect that your camp may be attacked; a handy trick is to hold your pistol in the crook under the knee when squatting down next to the fire. It is handy in case someone steps out of the dark and orders you to reach with both hands. You can do so, but with your pistol coming into play as you stand.

In exceptional circumstances, you may feel the need to employ armed guards. Keep in mind that the strength of any escort should be in proportion to the level of danger. Better to employ a single man who can keep his head during trouble than an armed rabble. A bad shot eats no less than a marksman.

**Legal Consequences.** Merely having a gun isn't enough. To be effective, it must always be close to hand. But even if your blood is as cold as a snake and you're capable of shooting another human being, there are legal implications in killing someone. Disregarding any ethical issues, it may be true that in some desolate corner of the world where there is no civil law, each man is a nation unto himself. Yet those places are increasingly few and far between. In contrast, every nation, however primitive, maintains a system of civil legislation and authorizes violence on its behalf. A nation drapes a man in a uniform. After feeding him an intoxicating diet of patriotism, the nation calls this individual a soldier and then orders him to kill strangers for the good of the state. The nation not only condones this killing, it legalizes and encourages it. The duty of a policeman may likewise force him to kill in the service of the state. Whether it is the military or police, these individuals are authorized to commit socially sanctioned homicide. Long Riders have no such luxury. If you execute someone you are in serious legal trouble. Therefore a traveller who enters into a state of war with local citizens must be prepared to face the gravest consequences. In addition to the legal costs of defending yourself, certain countries present an additional challenge. Even if you win in court, there may be lethal tribal implications waiting to ambush once you re-emerge. In Pakistan, for example, Pathan blood feuds last for generations. In such cases, the family members of your assailant will be honour bound to seek revenge against you.

**Horses and Guns.** Keeping in mind the type of serious trouble which might induce you to draw a weapon to defend yourself, consider your horse bucking in fear at the unexpected sound of a gun going off over his head. The last thing you need at such a moment is to be thrown or left afoot when your horse bolts in panic. That's why it is one thing to include weapons in the trip; you must ensure that your animals are part of the programme. As history has repeatedly demonstrated, horses can become accustomed to every type of gun fire, ranging from small calibre pistols to modern cannon fire. However, shooting off an untrained horse is a certain recipe for trouble. It takes time to train an untried animal to tolerate the sound of weapons discharging and the smell of gun smoke.

**Weighing the Evidence.** There is no point in denying the reality of danger. Long Riders face up to its existence and accept it. As so often happens, however, once you recognize the likelihood of peril, and do not run away from it, the menace seldom materialises. Thus on an obvious level, because the weapon is never used the majority of the time, it ends up becoming a burden which the horse carries for no reason. When it comes time to consider carrying a firearm, compile a list of all the possible reasons which might tempt you to do so. Next to each of these reasons, place an equally honest appraisal of how likely such an adverse situation might actually occur. Chances are the perceived risk won't match the actual reality.

**Hints.** If you feel the need to ride armed, never leave your weapons on the horse when you dismount and walk away. Carry them so as to prevent theft and to keep them from being turned against you.

To offset the attendant difficulties connected with dispatching opponents with guns, Long Riders have protected themselves instead with a wide variety of less lethal options including pepper spray, machetes, whips, sling shots and even firecrackers.

# Chapter 66 - Horse Theft

Many things have changed since our ancestors began to ride thousands of years ago. But one tragic act links us to the past. Stealing a horse is still a calamity with terrible repercussions. To learn how to guard against this crime it is necessary to understand that horses are stolen for a variety of reasons, including greed, revenge, tribalism, transportation, hunger, prestige and a desire for fame. Regardless of what motivates the culprit, the horse is a prime target in every country. But in an age when the majority of humans are transported by car, why steal a horse? The answers are ageless.

**Money on the Hoof.** A lust for profit has always stalked the shadows of the horse world. Because they can be quietly sold, stealing horses remains a profitable business. According to one estimate, at least 40,000 horses are stolen in the United States every year. This explains why this ancient crime has continued into the modern age. Horses are still an easy source of cash for thieves interested in short-term profit.

**Aggression and Alcohol.** Centuries before people played the video game, *Grand Theft Auto*, drunken thieves were taking joy rides on pilfered ponies. Alcohol-inspired aggression certainly isn't restricted to one part of the world. Like other errors in judgment, mankind is quick to drink too much and then act foolishly in a variety of countries. Whichever country you ride in, the availability of alcohol influences the likelihood of your horses being stolen.

**Cross Country Thievery.** History proves that through the ages men have routinely proven the depth of their courage, both to themselves and their enemies, by undertaking various types of testosterone-inspired audacity. One traditional manner of confirming courage was to steal your neighbour's horses. Because of the fear of reprisals, steppe nomads do not normally heist horses belonging to an immediate neighbour. Yet they think nothing of travelling long distances to steal horses from distant strangers, especially if they belong to a different ethnic tribe. Animals belonging to such unknown people are considered fair game by brave-hearted horse thieves.

**From the Trail to the Table.** There is another reason to steal a horse; to eat him or sell him for meat. Either reason has devastating consequences for a Long Rider. Any Long Rider making a journey in parts of Europe, Kazakhstan and Mongolia, needs to remember that a horse can be quietly stolen and quickly sold on the meat market by villains. Hence you must exhibit the greatest caution in these areas.

**The Cost of Celebrity.** There is a final reason your horse might be stolen; because he's famous. A valuable horse is always more likely to be stolen, even a Long Rider's horse. That's what happened to Mancha, the most renowned Long Rider horse of the 20th century. Aimé Tschiffely recalled how his famous horse was stolen in Mexico due to its celebrity. Luckily the horse was quickly recovered. Even if your horse isn't the celebrated Mancha, you too need to appreciate the fact that unscrupulous people may wish to steal the horse because of the reflected glory associated with your journey.

**Geographic Influences.** In the past, geography influenced the occurrence of this offence. Stealing horses was never a major social dilemma in Europe for a variety of reasons. In contrast to the highly mobile nomads of Central Asia, there was very little movement among the European population, with the same pedestrian families residing in their ancestral village for generations. Another striking difference was that Europe did not have a vast unpopulated wilderness which encouraged people to roam. Finally, Europe was never as horse rich as the Americas. As a result, while horse theft was not unknown in Europe, it was an uncommon crime. Not so in the sparsely-populated wilderness of the United States. Once European colonists migrated west across the prairies, they left behind the benefits of law enforcement. In a vast alien landscape filled with a variety of dangers, the horse represented the difference between life and death. Stealing a horse in such a harsh environment was more than a malicious economic crime. To deprive an American on the frontier of his horse could place the victim in immense peril or cause his death. As a result, pioneer communities often exterminated a horse thief as quickly as they would a rabid dog.

**Riding at Risk.** Few countries have been as closely associated with horses as Mongolia. In a nation that revered the horse, it may not surprise you to learn that Genghis Khan hated horse thieves. His legal code, the Great Yasa, was the collected laws, rules, and words of wisdom created by Genghis and handed down to his heirs. One well-known decree made it a crime for a rider to hit a horse with the whip anywhere forward of the stirrups. The Great Yasa took an exceptionally dim view of horse thieves. It stated, "The man in whose possession a stolen horse is found must return it to its owner and add nine horses of the same kind: if he is unable to pay this fine, his children must be taken instead of the horses, and if he have no children, he himself shall be slaughtered like a sheep." Unfortunately Genghis Khan's efforts to suppress horse theft have not lasted. Modern Mongolia is again lawless and modern Long Riders have learned to their dismay that stealing horses in Mongolia is now a national addiction. Horse thieves lurk everywhere. They are very brazen and will boldly check your stock. It is not a matter of if they try to steal your horses. It is a matter of when.

**Prove he's yours.** One of the easiest ways to steal a horse is to catch the owner legally unawares. Several Long Riders have been confronted with an unexpected ownership dispute when persons in authority or disgruntled ex-owners have used this tactic to gain control of a horse. When government authority figures, suspicious police, sceptical border guards or disbelieving locals demand proof that the horse is yours, you must be able to produce conclusive documentary evidence which leaves no doubt as to who the legal owner is. Even if someone gives you a horse as a gift, you should ask the previous owner to accept a small financial reward as evidence that a monetary exchange took place. This exchange of money will provide you with a reason to create a receipt. This vital document should be signed by all parties involved in the exchange of the horse's ownership, and if possible witnessed and signed by a neutral third party. The government of Guatemala now demands a 'certificate of origin' from Long Riders who wish to enter that country from Mexico. This is a new type of bureaucratic obstacle which has decreased the chances of riding south into Central America from adjacent Mexico. Consequently, knowing that such obstacles await you on the road, prior to your departure you should have obtained any paperwork which helps ease the fears of government authorities who are concerned about your horse's birth, breed, health and appearance.

**Positive Identification.** It's not enough to have a dream. You must travel wisely. One aspect of this is the decision to provide your horse with positive identification. The police in many countries will react to your appearance by demanding proof of ownership on the spot. It pays to

163

remember that most officers won't know the difference between a Honda and a Haflinger. Speciality terms connected to breeds and colours only confuse such a person. You must be able to produce visual and written documentation which is not only easily understood; it must instantly assert and confirm your legal rights. Positive identification is also your first line of defence if your horse is stolen. In addition to his health certificates and proof of ownership, your horse should have a document which provides his concise description. This should include photos showing the horse from both sides as well as front and rear. Remember that the colour of the horse's coat may change due to exposure to sunlight while travelling, so make sure the photographs match his current colour. You should also have close up photos that show any specific whorls, scars, brands or a identification number tattooed inside the lip. Papers, photos and identifying marks are all ways to help recover your horse. But your first line of defence is to discourage the thief from stealing.

**Think like a Thief.** A travelling horse is at continual risk. He is far from home. His owner is among strangers. There may be a language barrier complicating any rescue attempts. Bribery and corruption may be hidden factors assisting the thief. Because of these factors, the Long Rider must understand his opponent. Everything you can do to reduce the thief's chances of success increases the possibility that he will choose an easier target instead. Gangs of horse thieves are rare. It is usually a solitary man, working alone, operating under cover of darkness, who is looking for an easy target. Heavy rain or severe cold will discourage him. But you cannot rely on the weather for protection. You must instead do everything possible to reduce the chances of a thief's success. Most thefts occur at night. Do not provide unwitting assistance by placing your animals in a pasture close to a road. This will encourage a thief to make a snatch and grab raid. To discourage the thief, place your camp between the horses and the road. Don't put your horses into a paddock and then ignore them till morning. Depending on how serious the situation is, check on them at regular intervals.

**Ever Alert.** No matter how careful you've been, pay attention to that vigilant guard – your horse. Veteran Long Riders learn to rely upon their horse's superior sight, smell and hearing in dark nights and times of peril. Because the sagacious animal sees and smells all round him, no one approaches a camp without attracting the notice of the horses. The reaction of an equine sentinel will not only provide an alarm, his movements will indicate the direction from whence the threat approaches. As the journey progresses and the time spent with the horse increases, this sense of fraternal support between horse and human deepens. Any time you are concerned about theft, it pays to keep your horses close to camp. Hobbles reduce a thief's chances of a quick escape. The sound of bells attached to halters is another strong deterrent. Far better to be tired the next day after a sleepless night than to wake up to find your horses have disappeared.

**Homesick Horses.** Should you discover the horse is gone, don't automatically assume he's been stolen. Before you attribute the disappearance to thieves, some horses run home. The Argentine gauchos call the region where a horse is born his querencia. Querer means 'to like' or 'to love,' and querencia is the noun. It was a well-known fact among horse humans of old that any horse will attempt to return to its querencia if it can escape and if there are no fences to prevent it from so doing. Gauchos reported on horses who travelled fabulous distances, crossing mountains, rivers and deserts to appear finally back in their querencia. Your horses may have disappeared for another perfectly plausible reason; fear.

**The Horses Have Vanished.** It may well happen that despite your best efforts your morning is shattered when you discover the horses are missing. The first thing to do is to control any sense of panic. The situation requires clear thinking and sharp eyes, not wild emotions and rash behaviour. Your immediate concern is to prioritize the situation and inspect the scene. If you are travelling with a friend, contain the urge to set off in hot pursuit. What you need are facts, not haste. First, try to determine when the horses were last seen or heard. This will give you some idea how long the horses have been missing and how far they may have travelled. Next, carefully inspect the area where the horses spent the night. What does the evidence on the ground tell you? Can you determine in what direction the horses fled? Has a rope, hobble or fence been cut? Are there any human tracks indicating the presence of a thief? Based upon the evidence at hand, decide if you think the horses have run away or been stolen. Tracking runaways is a depressing chore. Chasing horse thieves may put your life at risk. So think carefully before you decide to leave camp and begin your search. Do not rush off in different directions. Take the time to discuss and plan the search effort. It is vitally important that you determine what each person will do, in what direction they will travel, and how long the search will be maintained before you regroup at camp.

**Setting a Guard.** There is a lot more to your expedition than just your horse. There is also your expensive saddle and all your gear to consider. Long Riders have been robbed on several occasions while they were briefly away from camp looking for fodder; so leaving your saddles and equipment unguarded for hours on end, while you wander across the countryside in search of fleet-footed horses, can add to your distress. If your horses are missing, your life is complicated enough. Don't add to your grief by losing the rest of your equipment too. Designate one person to guard the camp and gear, while the other sets off to search for the horses. If you are travelling alone, then hide your equipment, being sure to take your vital documents and most vital possessions with you.

**Tracking.** While the Long Rider makes the saddle his home, it would be an error to suppose him unobservant. Progressing at the speed of a horse's pace gives the equestrian traveller plenty of time to practise observing the ground and learning how to decipher clues. That practice will be called upon when you go looking for the missing horses. Let us suppose that you believe the horses have broken free and are loose. If that is the case, the task before you is to find them with as little delay as possible. Hopefully you will have placed bells on their halters. This may provide more clues than you think. Perhaps the sound of the bells in the night will have given you a strong indication as to which direction they fled? If not, bells still help after the sun rises. If the area is thick with mosquitoes or biting flies, the horses may have sought shelter under trees. If a horse is standing motionless in the shadows, he may be hard to detect. The tinkling of a bell is always a reassuring sound in such a situation. The second sound which lightens the heart is the whinny of a horse calling to his missing comrades. If you have managed to keep one horse under your control, and you are riding him during your search, he will express his emotional anxiety by calling out to his friends. An answering whinny gives you hope and a direction to travel towards. If you're afoot, then you will have to search the ground for tracks that betray the path of the fugitives.

If your horse is herd bound, he may have run home to his mates. If he is hungry or thirsty, his memory will urge him to return to the last known place where he was fed and watered. This may be a barn, pasture or stream. Regardless of how far back it is, the reward of slaking his thirst or comforting his stomach may have provided the lure. It also gives you a possible direction in which to begin your search. Horses are like humans in that they too are prone to follow the trail they know rather than travel blindly in a new direction. Begin your search by carefully retracing your steps along your previous day's travel. If you do not find tracks fairly quickly, return to camp and scout in a circle looking for tracks or clues. What you are looking for is any evidence of the horse's passage. Every track provides information, if you know how to decipher it. Unlike a Hollywood movie, you don't have to restrict yourself by looking for a crystal-clear horse track. Far more subtle clues may also be of help. These signs may include a slight disturbance in the grass or a change in the colouring of the ground. What you are seeking is signs of something which does not match the surrounding landscape. Because it is difficult to locate such faint clues, you should begin by travelling parallel to the trail. If you are on foot, then the area under inspection should be between you and the sun. This will allow the light to help reveal confirmation of passage. If you are tracking on horseback, you may need to dismount and study the evidence from a closer perspective. If you find horse tracks, they can reveal a great deal of information. The sharper the track the less time since the horse has passed. Rain will dimple the interior of the print. Wind will dull the edges.

With luck, you may find your horses grazing or moving down the trail. If you locate them, take care how you approach. Should you move up from behind, they may take fright and stampede further down the trail. You would be wise to circle around them quietly, coming out ahead on the trail. In this way, should they flee, they may run back towards camp.

**Calling the Police.** Where you ride will influence the reliability and participation of the local law. Not all countries believe in calling the police. Even if the identity of the thief is known, local citizens may be reluctant to involve the police because of lingering fears that the authorities are corrupt, indifferent or incompetent. Involving the police is a serious step, so consider the situation carefully.

**Public Assistance.** The local media can help. After you've discussed the case with the police, inform them you plan on appealing to the public via the press. If there is an officer in charge of the investigation, obtain his permission to share his name and contact details. Then alert the media and ask for their assistance. While most people are happy to help, it certainly isn't a bad idea to offer a reward.

**Animal Activists.** Modern Long Riders face a new type of menace, seizure of their horses by animal activists. Some people believe that asking a horse to carry a Long Rider constitutes an act of cruelty. These people seldom understand that horses enjoy travelling, and that if fed properly and ridden carefully, they conclude the journey in better condition than when they started. To offset a charge of animal cruelty, you should document the health of your animal during the course of the journey. Have your original veterinarian provide you with a signed and dated document which clearly states that the horse is in excellent condition at the time of departure. Make sure the document also states that the veterinarian has no medical objections to the horse making the journey. Once you have created this original layer of medical defence, add to it during your journey. As and when you meet other veterinarians, farriers or knowledgeable equestrians, ask them to augment your collection of medical or eyewitness accounts, all of which provide concrete evidence of your devotion to the horse's well being. Chances are that if a local policeman or sheriff has been asked to arrest you on a charge of animal cruelty or neglect, he may not be a qualified equestrian expert. Pleading that he is just following orders, he may reluctantly take you into custody or impound your horse. Being able to provide on-the-spot evidence not only undermines such a false accusation, it provides the policeman with enough evidence to decline to arrest you or impound your horse.

# Chapter 67 - Animal Attacks

Because of the emotional relationship shared with their horse, Long Riders are by practice and necessity friends of animals. Yet travel demands an adherence to caution as well. Respecting animals, and watching them with admiration, is fine. What must not be forgotten is that they can cause harm, grief or death to horse and human.

**The Dangers of Mother Nature.** Man's attitude towards animals is a fluid thing. It changes with the times. For the first time in history large numbers of humanity have no meaningful daily experience with the animal world. They have never fed or nurtured a farm animal. They have never ridden or worked a horse. They have never hunted or dressed a game animal. They have never had to protect themselves from imminent death from a predator. In the space of a few generations the majority of mankind's collective knowledge about such matters has disappeared. The result is that the average human being's daily knowledge of animal nature has diminished to an alarming extent. It has been replaced by a Disney-esque version of events where there is no dark side to nature.

Long Riders can't afford to take such a misguided view of Nature. Because the horse brings you into intimate contact with animals, a Long Rider must realize that wild beasts are neither insentient beings nor cuddly playthings. They are often hungry, and that makes them dangerous. As a result Long Riders and their horses have been the victims of deliberate animal attacks. Thus, while interacting with the animal world is commendable, protecting yourself from it is a necessity.

**Lions.** Some animals are routinely misunderstood, others under-estimated. The lion is a predatory carnivore who has earned his reputation. Mounted man has narrowly avoided becoming a lion's dinner on a number of occasions. During his exploration of Africa in 1795, the Scottish Long Rider Mungo Park nearly became the first mounted casualty. Gordon Naysmith and Ria Bosman set off in 1970 to cross Africa by horseback. Though more than a hundred years had passed since Parker's journey, they too had to avoid hungry lions. Lions still kill and consume more than 100 people a year in Tanzania alone. But the problem is not restricted to one country. Across Africa urbanized humans are pushing out city boundaries, decimating traditional game animal migration routes and increasingly encroaching on the lion's traditional hunting grounds.

New studies show that lion attacks are connected to the size of the moon and the availability of light. Bright moonlight not only decreases the lion's chances of enacting a successful nocturnal ambush, it often results in the predator going hungry. Lions hunt most effectively when the diminished light of a waning moon allows them to catch their prey unawares. Thus the size of the moon affects a human's chances of survival. This was confirmed when scientists studied evidence gathered between 1988 and 2009. They found a common factor in the nearly 500 lion attacks suffered by villagers in Tanzania. A comparison between moon phrases and attack rates confirmed that attacks were a third more frequent during the second half of the cycle, when there was little or no moonlight. Lions usually attacked humans between dusk and 10 p.m. on nights when the moon was waning. Furthermore, the majority of humans were eaten just after a full moon. Peak danger times for humans are therefore the active hours after sunset, especially the day after a full moon.

**Big Cats.** Whether it be a Siberian tiger, African lion, Canadian cougar or Peruvian jaguar, horses retain a deeply-implanted fear of large predatory cats. These big cats have taught the horse the art of self-defence. These felines use available cover to stalk unwary horses. Having stayed close to the ground, the cat makes a sudden rush at his prey. If he is fast enough, the feline will try to jump up and puncture the horse's jugular. The problem is that big cats are extremely short winded. They can only maintain a maximum high speed for a few hundred yards. This allows a horse to rapidly outrun his pursuer. Another common option is for the hungry cat to launch himself onto the horse's unprotected back. The deadly feline approaches as silently and closely as possible. It then tries to spring onto the horse's back to deliver the killing blow. After sinking his talons into the horse's withers, the cat then attempts to bite through the horse's thick protective mane, into the spine beneath.

**Hyenas.** Though they have biological similarities to felines, hyenas catch prey with their teeth as canines do. People traditionally believed the spotted hyena to be a skulking scavenger. In fact the nocturnal animal is one of Africa's most efficient pack hunting predators. The hearing of spotted hyenas is so acute they can detect the sound of predators killing and feeding on carcasses ten kilometres (six miles) away. But they don't need to feed on scraps, as 95% of a spotted hyena's diet is composed of prey, such as antelope, zebra, warthogs and Cape buffalo, which they routinely kill.

Hyenas are equipped with teeth strong enough to enable them to crush bones and consume humans, something they've been doing for a long time. The oldest human hair, dating back 195,000 to 257,000 years, was recently discovered embedded in fossilized hyena dung. More recently, civil wars in Ethiopia and Sudan provided an abundant supply of human corpses which the hyenas eagerly devoured. Being nocturnal, hyenas often attack humans who are sleeping outside during hot weather. Malawi has endured a number of hyena attacks, with a notorious pair being credited with killing 27 people. Equestrian travellers in Africa have noted two frightening encounters with these strong predators.

**Bears.** A glance at the map will quickly demonstrate how widespread bears are. They are found on the continents of Asia, Europe and in both Americas. Polar bears are restricted to the Arctic Sea area but other bears thrive in a wide variety of habitats. Most are forest species but some, especially the brown bear, inhabit alpine tundra. Though they are slower than big cats, bears can reach speeds of up to 40 miles per hour. They can also stand on their hind feet and rapidly climb trees. Under normal circumstances bears do not hunt and consume humans. But all types of bear are physically powerful, are armed with non-retractable claws and are capable of

167

inflicting gruesome injuries. Many bears charge when the animal is taken by surprise or a bear sow fears her cubs are being threatened. Yet some species are more aggressive than others. As a result, individual animals have killed unsuspecting humans in a variety of settings.

If you're a Long Rider heading into the back country of North America, then you need to spare a thought to encountering grizzly bears. These wide-ranging animals live in the Canadian provinces of British Columbia, Alberta, Yukon, and the Northwest Territories; and the US states of Montana, Wyoming, Idaho, Washington and Alaska. A recent study confirmed their numbers are growing and that the grizzly population in Montana has reached a thirty-year high. The seasonal movement of these bears matches the summer-time activities of humans. Anglers fishing in salmon streams have been surprised by the sudden appearance of grizzlies. Hunters have been driven off their kills by these hungry animals. When a traveller unexpectedly encounters a grizzly, the results can be deadly. Unlike smaller black bears who can escape danger by climbing a tree, adult grizzlies will react aggressively to any perceived threat. The majority of human fatalities are inflicted by mother grizzlies, which are quick to attack any human unlucky enough to have strayed too near her cubs.

Many people make the mistake of thinking that bears are nocturnal. They are in fact active during the day. It's not just grizzlies you need to be concerned about, as any type of bear may attack if he is surprised or feels cornered. To diminish this danger you must remain extra vigilant if your visibility is limited by trees or undergrowth. Should you be travelling with a dog, keep it close to your horses. Dogs have been known to stumble upon a bear, the result being that the angry animal chases the fleeing canine straight back to its startled master. Don't linger near dead animals as the smell of decomposing flesh attracts hungry bears.

Chances are your horse's keen senses will alert you to the fact that a bear is nearby. Most horses panic if they see or smell a bear, so your first challenge is to stay in the saddle and keep your horse under control. Grizzly bears can reach great speed in short bursts, so running away is a debateable option, especially as your retreat may trigger the animal's hunting instinct, whereupon it will view you as prey, not a threat. If given the chance, most bears will choose to retreat. Detour slowly away from the bear. Try to stay upwind so it picks up your scent and makes the decision to back off. If the bear charges, drop a coat, saddlebags or anything you can grasp easily in the hope of distracting the animal while you ride away.

Pitching camp in bear country can be a matter of life or death. There are terrible consequences if you break the rules in bear country. You must ensure that you have familiarized yourself with the habits of the bears you may encounter. You must carry bear-proof panniers which will seal off the smell of your food and supplies. You must have obtained and studied any local regulations relating to bears. You must never ignore posted warnings. If you fail to follow these rules you may die.

Bears are starving when they emerge from months of hibernation. This explains why they spend the warmer months gorging on a vast assortment of food including acorns, plants, insects, birds, salmon, small animals, rotting carcasses and human garbage. Camping in bear country requires you to think and act differently. What you do, what you touch, what you wear, what you eat, where you sleep, will all affect your chances of surviving.

Bears are attracted by aromas. That is why odours are your enemies. Some are obvious. The smell put off by cooking a greasy meat dinner is going to send the wrong message wafting across the countryside. Choose what you cook with care and keep the fire burning after the meal is concluded. Bears fear the flames and the smoke helps overcome any residual smell of food. What you must not overlook are the lingering smells created by cooking which may compromise your late-night safety. Never let cooking smells permeate your sleeping bag or tent. Do not go to sleep in the clothes you used for cooking. To increase your safety, set up your camp in a triangle, placing your tent, campfire cooking area and panniers well away from each other! Never bring food, cosmetics or anything which you suspect may produce an intriguing odour into your tent.

In addition to confirming that you understand basic bear safety procedures, many national parks in America require you to use bear-proof panniers. Yet having such a tamper-resistant box isn't enough to deter a hungry bear. You should place your provisions 100 metres away from your tent. Depending on the situation, you can either hang the panniers on a strong rope tied between two trees, or if this is not an option, then suspend them from a strong branch. Regardless of which option is available, the panniers must be at least ten feet off the ground and placed four feet away from the tree trunk.

If you find yourself in bear country after sunset, stay extremely vigilant. After you are ready to settle down for the night, tie your horses up tightly. Their lack of movement will encourage them to whinny loudly if they detect a bear approaching. If you are travelling with a friend, take it in turns to stand guard, all the while you keep the fire burning brightly.

Maintaining an odour-free camp can help keep you alive. The fragrance of cooking food is an obvious danger, but any personal product, such as cologne, perfume, makeup, toothpaste or deodorant, may also arouse a hungry bear's curiosity. Never wear anything whose smell might draw a bear's attention. There have also been studies made on the topic of the reactions of bears to human menstrual odours. Experts are undecided but caution is urged. Do not neglect your horse's safety in respect to tasty smells. Forego using oil on his hooves. Leave the aromatic hoof preserver at home. Limit bug spray to day-time use only while travelling through bear country.

**Wolves.** Long Riders may encounter a wide variety of potentially dangerous animals. The probability of attack depends on the species and circumstances. Caution and respect for any wild animal is essential for success and safety. Yet the tremendous geographic range and misleading public reputation of one predator, the wolf, marks it as a special threat. Wolves can be found north of the equator from China to California. Wolf advocates have successfully promoted a message that ignores global evidence of confirmed attacks. As a result wolves are mistakenly portrayed as being of little threat to travellers. Previous generations knew full well that wolves hunted humans and horses. That is why these predators inspired such mind-shattering terror through the ages. Evidence indicating wolves are lethal killers has been ignored, replaced by television programmes and numerous publications which depict the animal as a romantic symbol of freedom. The result of this inaccurate depiction is that many people no longer believe wolves pose a threat to humans or horses. The error of this belief was demonstrated in Russia in February, 2011 when a massive wolf pack numbering in the hundreds rampaged through Verkhoyansk in eastern Yakutia, killing thirty horses in four days. In 2012 Yegor Borisov, the President of Yakutia, said that wolves had attacked 314 horses. With the hunters gone, experts assume there are 45,000 wolves in Russia, making it the second largest wolf population in the world. Other parts of the former Soviet Union are also dealing with a dramatic re-emergence of this problem. Authorities in Tuva estimate that since the discontinuance of systematic hunting, the wolf population in that small country rapidly increased to 400 packs containing an estimated 3,000 wolves. Sparsely-populated Kazakhstan is believed to have the highest density of wolves in the world. There are an estimated 90,000 wolves in that country. Yet wolf concerns are not restricted to the former communist regime. Long Riders may encounter them in a variety of countries. Packs have moved into Albania from Greece and are expanding in Scandinavia, the Baltic States, Poland, Romania, France, Italy and the Iberian Peninsula. Whereas there was one German wolf pack in 2000, in 2015 there were at least twelve. After having migrated over the Italian Alps in 1992, packs have made a dramatic reappearance in France. Experts believe at least twenty packs now reside across that country. In 2015 there are an estimated 70,000 wolves roaming in North America.

Wolves hunt year around to obtain the 5 to 10 pounds of meat they need per day to survive. Their decision on what to eat is based on opportunity and hunger. On average a wolf will consume more than a ton of meat per year. Yet unlike lions and bears, wolves seldom totally consume an animal or return to a previous meal. Accordingly wolves kill more animals than they need in order to satisfy their immediate hunger. As wolves lose their fear of man, the reemergence of this ancient threat is of major concern to equestrian explorers, especially if they are riding across the former Soviet Union, the thinly populated areas of Siberia, the remote regions of Kazakhstan or the desolate Mongolian steppes. In March, 2012 a wolf in China attacked seven people in six days. Two of the victims died. Candice Berner was killed by wolves in March, 2010 while jogging near her home in Alaska. She was partially consumed. Wolves killed and ate Kenton Carnegie in Saskatchewan on Nov. 8, 2005.Wolves have also recently killed and eaten people in Iran and Afghanistan.

Wolves have a sense of smell 10,000 times greater than a human. They can detect prey up to 5 kilometres (3 miles) away. Individual wolves can run 40 mph while hunting. A pack thinks nothing of averaging 50 kilometres a day. Once the pack has joined chase after its victim, the lead wolf attempts to bite the victim. The wolf may use its momentum to hurl himself onto the prey's flanks. The wolf's teeth are designed to grab and hold an animal. After the lead wolf grips the victim, its weight helps slow the animal sufficiently for other members of the pack to begin biting, bleeding and eating the victim.

Death by wolf involves a tremendous amount of pain being inflicted upon the victim. When a wolf pack chases a fleeing horse, the fastest predator will try to leap on and began biting it in the flanks. Others will run alongside and try to get a grip on the horse's nose. The rest will try to bite through the tendons on the horse's rear legs. If the horse is brought to a halt and encircled, the wolves attempt to bite the soft tissue in the victim's perineum (genital and anus) area. Tearing off large pieces of soft tissue causes blood loss and rapidly weakens the horse. It is not uncommon for the pack to then tear open the abdominal cavity, causing the intestines to fall out on the ground, and trapping the victim in place. The pack then begins feeding inside the still-living horse. In other cases a horse is left standing alive, bleeding, with its hindquarters torn off. This type of excruciatingly painful death routinely occurs when a pack teaches young wolf pups how to hunt. Should the pack encounter an exceptionally aggressive horse, the wily predators will encircle their prey and then wait. They will keep the horse awake for days, worrying it constantly until it weakens from lack of sleep. When they sense its defences are beginning to slip, the pack attacks.

The Spanish say; ride near wolves and you must learn to survive! A wise Long Rider respects the wilderness and prepares for it. Education is your first line of defence. Don't bet your life on the Hollywood myth that wolves mean you no harm. Investigate the problem critically and be on the alert for romanticism. Begin your efforts by finding out if wolves exist where you will be travelling. Search for evidence of recent wolf activity. Contact local authorities prior to departure. Ask if humans have been attacked. After you arrive, speak to as many local people as possible. Once you are under way, learn to read the wilderness. Stay alert. Don't let your mind wander. Keep your eyes peeled for clues. Ravens, for example, often follow wolf packs in the hope of gaining an easy meal. Circling ravens could indicate a pack of wolves feeding below. Don't let warm weather lull you into being inattentive. You could be forgiven for thinking that if you avoid riding in winter, you might avoid bumping into a hungry wolf pack. You'd be wrong. Surprisingly, wolves inflict the most damage to domestic animals in late summer and early fall. This is the time of year when they are teaching hunting skills to their young. Ride during daylight hours. Stay along well-travelled roads. Avoid areas where packs are known to hunt. If you must ride through wolf country set up camp well before dark. Water and feed your horses early. Do not tie them to a highline and leave them unattended, as wolves may attack them in your absence. Maintain a clean camp to keep from attracting wolves into camp with the smell of food. Lay in a large supply of wood. Light a fire at dusk and maintain it during the night. Stay extremely vigilant. Don't wander into the darkness.

Learn to listen. When wolves howl they point their heads up because this allows the sound to travel further. Howls serve a variety of purposes. They allow members of the pack to remain in touch while on the move. They encourage the pack to assemble at a specific location. They enforce the pack's right to its territory against rivals. It also sends a spine-chilling message if you're travelling on horseback. Watch your horses for clues. Their heightened sense of smell and hearing will tell you from what direction danger is approaching. Should your horse hear wolves howling at close range, his instinct will be to break free. If he stampedes into the darkness, do not be tempted into following him! The horse is fleet enough to perhaps escape and survive. You, on the other hand, don't stand a chance if you venture into the dark on foot with wolves skulking nearby.

Nothing is more frightening than to see a pack of well-organized and intelligent wolves coming at you. Depending on how habituated they are to humans, wolves may show little fear. They have been known to circle their victim, snapping and growling as they look for a chance to attack. Resist the urge to run. This will trigger an aggressive attack. You have to stand and be prepared to fight for your life. Don't display any hint of weakness or fear. Don't stumble or retreat. Face the wolf but don't make any sudden movements. Lone wolves have attacked humans in sleeping bags. Use your forearm to protect your throat, get on your feet, start yelling, kicking and fight back. Try to strike the sensitive nose, strangle it or ram your fist down its throat.

A gun is a tool, just like your saddle. Being armed in wolf country is prudent, not paranoid. But because of draconian new laws, it is imperative that you never ride armed unless you are fully licensed to do so by the federal authorities of the host country. Even then you may not be allowed to protect yourself or your horses. The European Union forbids shooting wolves. An exception is made for Estonia, which has the largest wolf population in Europe. Russia has altered its former lenient view on wolves, and now considers the animals to be a threat to humans and livestock. In 1974 the wolf was granted protection by the United States government under the Endangered Species Act. As a result it is a federal offence to shoot a wolf. Therefore, even if you are legally armed, don't think that merely carrying a gun will guarantee your safety. In an effort to save their lives, but not break the law, Americans have repeatedly shot in the air at aggressive wolves, only to have the pack relentlessly return to the hunt. If you are riding in North America, portable air horns are inexpensive and may be used to startle wolves. Bear spray is also an effective and affordable option. However it only lasts a few seconds. A bear-banger is a non-licensed spring-loaded device that shoots a loud exploding cartridge in the direction of the assailant. Be sure to land the cartridge between you and animal, because if it lands behind the wolf is likely to run straight toward you. Should your journey take you to Mongolia or Kazakhstan, keep supplies of firecrackers to scare away any wolves lurking near your camp. If you see wolves approaching your camp and you are unarmed, bang pots together, scream and shout, in an effort to startle the wolves into retreating. If they continue to approach, use anything close at hand to defend yourself.

Use caution when entering wolf country. Don't underestimate the problem! Wolves are ruthless apex predators and enjoy government protection. Don't be the next victim. Wolves have been falsely portrayed by Hollywood as posing no threat to you and your horses. Do not anthropomorphize them. They are strong predators who do not possess the qualities of pity, kindness or sympathy. Don't think that wolves are only found in remote mountains. They hunt beside rivers, through forests, across steppes and along the edges of cities. It is up to you to minimize the danger when riding across a wolf-infested area. Should you fail, it may result in the demise of you, your horses, or both.

**Coyotes.** The coyote is smaller than a wolf, averaging from 20 to 50 pounds (9 to 22 kilos). They are opportunistic diners who will eat anything they can chew including deer, rabbits, groundhogs, rats, squirrels, birds, fruit, berries and carrion. But their diet has also changed. Coyotes fare well in human settlements, where they dine on road kill, garbage, squirrels, pigeons and pets. In 2015 an aggressive coyote pack in Minnesota killed a horse and then returned a few nights later to attack another equine on the same property. As the coyote's population density has increased, and its fear diminished, attacks on humans have increased. They may therefore pose a risk to one horse or rider if they find you on foot. Many times a coyote will retreat. If he circles, and then charges, do not be tempted to run, as this will open you up to attack. Bear spray is an excellent deterrent. Even a stout stick or a sharp knife can help you survive. Raise your arms, stand your ground and make as much noise as you can so as to startle the animal.

**Moose.** The moose is the largest member of the deer family. Males can stand nearly seven feet (2.1 meters) at the shoulder and weigh 1,500 pounds (700 kilos). The bull moose is equipped

171

with multi-spiked antlers which can weigh 80 pounds (36 kilos) and span up to 7 feet (2.2 meters). Unlike other deer species, the moose is a solitary creature that does not form herds. Moose like to feed along small lakes and in lush meadows, exactly the type of place where a tired horse would like to rest and graze after a hard day's travel. Moose are notoriously unpredictable animals. Though they are not normally aggressive towards humans, moose can be deadly if provoked. Deaths have occurred when a human has accidentally antagonized it and one of the short-sighted creatures has stomped the person to death. Bull moose react aggressively towards humans during the fall mating season. Many attacks occur at the height of the moose birthing season, a two-week period in May. Cows are very protective and will react violently if a human comes close to a calf. If you encounter a moose while riding, use extreme caution. A moose that walks towards you is warning you to withdraw. When a moose is angry the long hair on its hump is raised and it will lay its ears back in anger. This is a potentially dangerous situation. Look for a way to retreat. They charge when they feel threatened or their personal space is compromised. The distance varies depending on the animal and situation. Because moose are not territorial, or consider humans a food source, they will not usually pursue a human if it flees.

**Yaks.** The long-haired yak is related to cattle. The strong animals are used as pack animals by the tribes living in the Himalayan and the Karakorum mountains. Long Riders may encounter yaks in Pakistan, northern India, Nepal, Ladakh, Bhutan and Mongolia. Don't be tempted to think these picturesque animals pose no threat. You should ride with care when yaks are near. Though these animals are not normally aggressive, female yaks will charge if their calves are approached. Yak bulls can be even more dangerous.

**Bulls.** Never risk riding or camping in a field where there is a bull present. Whereas cows can react with fury usually only in defence of their young, no bull is ever safe.

**Camels.** Unless horses are trained, they will panic if they unexpectedly encounter a camel. Llamas produce similar reactions amidst unprepared horses. Riders have been injured when the unexpected appearance of a llama caused a horse to bolt. To prevent such meetings some American national parks, Yosemite for example, prohibits llamas to be used as pack animals along trails. The Pacific Crest Trail is a notable exception. It is open to hikers, riders and stock. Llamas are defined, along with horses, as stock.

**Equines.** Because of massive equestrian amnesia, modern man has forgotten how dangerous horses can be. Another contributing fact is that the vast majority of people who are still involved with horses primarily limit their dealings to mares and geldings. In a post-domestic world 98% of the horse-owning population never sees a stallion, except perhaps on a race-track. Thus, despite thousands of years of evidence indicating how dangerous equines can be, millions of people have become largely out of touch with the natural world of horses. They prefer to believe the fairytale perpetuated by modern horse whisperers which portrays horses as timid prey animals who need protection from mankind and carnivores. In fact history demonstrates instead that the horse is capable of murderous violence. There is ample evidence of how horses have brutally slain other animals and humans throughout history. Long Riders have encountered aggressive equines in a variety of countries. Jane Dotchen was making her way across England when a stallion attacked her horse. At first glance, one might be tempted to define the actions of these horses as being abhorrent or abnormal. They are neither. The horses were responding to their natural need to protect their herd or defend their territory. Always approach strange horses cautiously. Be prepared to encounter savage stallions or aggressive mares.

**Protection against Horse Attack.** Nevada is the home to America's largest wild horse population. American Long Rider Samantha Szesciorka endured numerous encounters with curious or aggressive equines in that state. Samantha's ingenious solution could be a life saver. "My 100% effective method to scare off wild horse attacks, no matter the size of the herd, is a plastic bag. I tied an ordinary plastic bag, like you get in a grocery store, to the end of a short English riding crop. It weighs almost nothing and takes up almost no space in the saddle bag. I carried it with me every day."

Multiple tests with varying numbers of wild horses proved the effectiveness of the device.

"Obviously my horse is desensitized to it but wild horses are not. When they charged, I pulled out the crop and gave it a few shakes. This inflates the bag and makes that distinctive crinkly sound. This can be done in the saddle or from the ground. I've used it to scare off lone bachelor stallions and against herds of 50 plus horses. It always works."

The device works equally well in the dark.

"When we were camped in wild horse areas, I hung plastic bags around the camp like a perimeter. If there was an evening breeze, the sound and movement kept the wild horses back. It was a handy trick which made me more confident to fall asleep.

**Snakes.** Snakes are found on every continent except Antarctica. They range in size from tiny wigglers only 4 inches (10 centimetres) long, up to an imposing 30 feet (9.1 metres). Some kill their prey by injecting it with poison. Others kill by constricting their victims. Before setting off on your journey, learn what type of poisonous snake might await you and then take steps to avoid them.

The rattlesnake presents the most common threat encountered by Long Riders. There are 32 different types of rattlesnake in the world, which can be found from Canada to Argentina. They dwell in a variety of habitats, including deserts, forests, swamps and prairies. One species, the Eastern Diamondback rattlesnake, is the largest venomous snake in North America. They have been known to grow in excess of 8 feet (2.4 metres). Whereas encountering a python is unlikely, finding yourself staring at an angry rattlesnake is a common occurrence. Rattlers lurk under logs, prowl through tall grass, nest under boulders, take over burrows and sun themselves on warm trails. When alarmed, the snake will shake his iconic rattles as a warning. Once coiled, he can strike with amazing speed. If you come across a rattlesnake while on foot, treat it with extreme caution. If possible, back away. Should you have little room to retreat, kick dirt or sand at the snake. Because rattlesnakes have no eyelids, they cannot close their eyes, so consequently, they will move away from flying sand. Your best bet is to stay vigilant in snake country. Travel through grass or brush carefully. Use extreme caution at night, when snakes are apt to hunt and travel. Do not flip over stones or wood which may be hiding a rattler. Never sit down on a boulder or lean against a log without first inspecting it. Do not put your hand into crevices which might harbour a rattler. Under no circumstances ever pursue a live rattler. Even picking up a dead rattlesnake can be hazardous. Reflex actions may cause bites up to one hour after a snake has died, even after decapitation. Rattlesnakes detect presence by heat and movement. The majority of times they will retreat if given the chance. However, it is legal to kill one if you are in danger. The reptile is born with fully functional fangs and can kill prey immediately after hatching. Large poison glands inject potent venom into its victim. As the poison travels through the bloodstream, it destroys tissue, causes rapid swelling, internal bleeding and intense pain. The majority of rattlesnake bites are not fatal to humans, so long as they are treated quickly. Do not use a tourniquet, nor apply ice to the wound. Cutting an incision on the bite, and sucking out the poison, though a favourite treatment in cowboy movies, is never recommended. Survival depends upon how quickly antivenin serum can be provided to the victim.

**Snakes and Horses.** Rattlesnakes pose an even greater threat to Long Rider horses, especially in the United States, which hosts 26 different types of this snake. When reptiles and horses share a common environment, equine injures and deaths are bound to occur. Snakes will usually move away from the sound and vibration of a moving horse. Yet a slumbering snake will strike a passing horse on the leg. This is a difficult wound to treat as the poison quickly moves into the blood stream.

**Crocodiles.** Simply walking near water can get you or your horse killed in crocodile country. There are two types of crocodiles. Long Riders may have the misfortune to encounter them in Africa or Australia. No matter where they find you, both species treat humans as prey and consume them on a regular basis. The most ferocious is the saltwater crocodile. Despite its name, this reptile can be found far out to sea, or residing in fresh water rivers and creeks hundreds of miles inland. Considered the world's most aggressive crocodile species, saltwater crocodiles can grow more than 23 feet (7 metres) and weigh more than a ton. The saltwater crocodile will consume any animal that wanders within its territory. Victims include monkeys, kangaroos, boar, dingoes, birds, water buffalo, cattle, sharks, tigers, horses and humans. Long Rider Steve Nott almost lost his horses to crocodiles during his 1986 journey across northern Australia. The submerged creature waited until Steve brought the horses down to the river to drink. As soon as they waded into the shallow water, the big croc attacked. It was driven off by rifle shots, which allowed Steve to rescue the horses before they came to harm. Crocodiles kill horses by a hunting technique known as the death roll. The reptile grabs the startled victim, and then rolls over, throwing the animal off balance and making it easier to drag under water. This technique was used in 1939, when a one ton Suffolk Punch stallion residing in northern Australia was caught by a crocodile. According to eyewitnesses, the horse was dead within a minute. Use extreme caution if you are travelling in crocodile country. Approach rivers and water sources with care. Do not camp near rivers, pools or water holes. To avoid crocodile attacks, dig a hole a few yards away from the source so as to locate safe water for you and your horses. If a crocodile attacks you on land, run. If he grabs you, strike him on the nose or in the eyes. Do everything possible to avoid being pulled into the water.

**Vampire Bats.** Danger lurks in the air as well. There are three types of bats which feed on horse blood. Vampire bats dwell in large colonies, sometimes numbering in the thousands. They hide in the darkness provided by caves, wells, mine shafts, hollow trees or neglected buildings. These nocturnal creatures can be found from Mexico to Argentina and thrive in a variety of climates ranging from arid to tropical. They only hunt when it is fully dark. Sensors in the bat's nose enable him to locate a victim's vein which lies near to the surface of the skin. Razor sharp incisors pierce the skin. A substance in the bat's saliva prevents the blood from clotting, allowing the bat to suck the victim's blood for fifteen minutes or more. Aimé Tschiffely was the first Long Rider to confirm that his horses had been attacked by the blood-suckers. Long Riders have protected their horses by spreading crushed garlic or sprinkling strong black pepper on the animals.

**Protection.** When you set off on an equestrian journey you venture into the animal kingdom. The chances of being injured or killed depend on a variety of factors. To reduce the risk, prior to your departure you should have learned what type of animals you may encounter and determined how you can defend yourself. Never neglect to seek local advice or input about potentially dangerous animals. Nomads, herdsmen, hikers, trail riders, park rangers, ranchers and farmers may be able to warn you about everything from a llama on the trail to a lion in the bush. Always pay attention to how your horse is reacting to the countryside around him. Horses are normally noisy travellers. They make no effort to hide their steps. They swish their tails and shake their manes. They nicker and whinny. Predators on the other hand rely on stealth. They travel silently when on the lookout for meat. When your horse goes quiet, pay strict attention. If he halts, starts breathing loudly, pricks up his ears, and stares – something of extreme interest, and possibly, peril, is close by. If he perceives a threat, he may bolt. Don't be taken by surprise. Should you be thrown or knocked off by a low-hanging tree limb, then you're in even more trouble. In addition to educating yourself about what animals may be awaiting your arrival, it pays to be properly equipped. Loud bells create enough noise to frighten away many skulking threats. A strong flashlight is also a basic requirement. Shining a powerful beam of light into the predator's eyes may be enough to deter him. A powerful pepper spray is legal in many countries. If the law allows, you may decide to ride armed. But know the law before you go.

# Chapter 68 - Insect Attacks

You have to realize that the odds are stacked against human beings when it comes to bugs. Because there are only a limited number of large, dangerous, meat-eating predators, you can take comfort in the fact that chances are slim that you will encounter a hungry polar bear, a lurking lion or a ravenous wolf during your journey. There are, for example, "only" an estimated 70,000 wolves hunting in North America. Contrast the number of wolves against the estimated quintillion insects, 10,000,000,000,000,000,000, residing on the planet today. There

174

are 900,000 different types of insects and 91,000 types reside in the United States alone. Thanks to these numbers, you can quickly realize the likelihood of you suffering from some type of negative insect-related experience while riding through the wilds. Previous generations of Long Riders left dire warnings about insects, explaining how the blood-seeking, disease-spreading, madness-inducing pests turned their lives into a skin-scratching nightmare. What's worse, these insect pests are anxiously awaiting the arrival of any delicious modern horse travellers unlucky enough to venture into their hunting grounds.

**Mosquitoes.** There are a number of lethal insects which should concern you. Heading the list is the mosquito. Scientists estimate there are 3,500 types of mosquito species, with 200 living in North America alone. As generations of Long Riders have discovered, daytime mosquitoes are often more aggressive than night-time feeders. Regardless of what time they strike, the $CO_2$ in our breath is a proven attractant. Only the female mosquito bites, as she needs the protein in human blood to produce her eggs. The anticoagulant she injects into the wound causes her victims to endure an intense itching. Because they feed on blood, repelling mosquitoes is often a matter of life and death. A mosquito bite can result in exposure to a number of diseases including yellow fever. But the number one killer is still malaria. Unlike other types of mosquitoes, the female mosquito which carries malaria does not hum or hover. She attacks her victim silently. Signs of malaria infection usually appear 9 to 14 days after the victim has been bitten. Because the symptoms include severe headache, fever and vomiting, malaria is often initially misdiagnosed as the flu. If medical treatment is not obtained, the disease can result in coma and death.

Scientists have confirmed mosquitoes carry another type of deadly infection; West Nile Virus (WNV). This deadly disease has spread from Central Africa to Europe, Central America, Mexico, Canada and the United States. A horse infected with WNV cannot spread the virus to other horses or humans. Death results in at least a third of all equine cases, but not before a series of alarming symptoms including general weakness and high fever, followed by depression and diminished appetite. Physical deterioration sets in, including drooping eyelids and lower lip, loss of co-ordination and pointless wandering. Twitching, blindness, inflammation of the brain and paralysis often result prior to death. Because you and your horse could be infected with West Nile Virus, you should determine if the disease has been found in the area where you will be riding. If so, then vaccinate your animals prior to departure. Horses initially require two doses of the vaccination. Limit the chances of exposure while travelling by not picketing your horses near any type of stagnant water. Decrease your own chance of being bitten by using a powerful insect repellent that contains DEET.

**Midges.** There are thousands of species of midges. These tiny two-winged insects are less than 1/8" (0.317 centimetres) long. They torment mankind from Alaska to Argentina. Biting midges are particularly fond of living near water, with marshes and mangrove swamps being obvious choices. They also seek shelter amidst dense vegetation, hedges and trees. Like their close relative, the mosquito, midges delight in calm weather and high humidity. When conditions are right, they can appear in swarms of Biblical proportions. These tiny hunters are especially active around dusk and dawn. Their diminutive size allows them to pass through wire screens that normally keeps larger insects at bay. Similar to mosquitoes, midges are attracted to the $CO_2$ associated with human breath. As in virtually all other families of biting flies, only the females sting. These females are ferocious predators. Each insect can feed on a human for up to five minutes, during which time she sucks blood which will be used as a source of protein for her eggs. Every bite produces a painful, burning sore far out of proportion to its minute size. These small red wounds cause intense itching and can result in water-filled blisters. If scratched, the long-lasting wounds become infected. Relentless attacks can last all night long, with midges crawling inside clothing, swarming the victim's eyes and face, and feasting on any available skin surface. Citronella-based repellents may hold the midges at bay on a temporary basis. If you find yourself in a country where it is not possible to purchase such a modern convenience, then rubbing garlic on your horse may offer some small degree of protection.

175

Creating a defence is vitally important as the biting midge is known to transmit the dreaded and deadly African Horse Sickness. If your horse is infected with African Horse Sickness (AHS), then you need to be prepared for the worst. Though mosquitoes and ticks can transmit the highly infectious disease, the biting midge is the usual culprit. The severity of an AHS outbreak is dependent upon a number of local conditions, all of which affect the midge activity in that area. Warm weather, rainfall and sandy soil encourage a heavy midge infestation. Mules, donkeys and horses can all be infected with AHS. In severe cases the animal loses its appetite, runs a fever and then has trouble breathing. It begins coughing, which is an indication of fluid building up in the lungs. Once serious lung congestion occurs, death follows in less than 24 hours. The ailment is so deadly that nearly 90 percent of all horses die after becoming infected. Originally considered endemic in Sub-Saharan Africa, the virus has now spread north of the equator. AHS has been diagnosed in Morocco, the Middle East, India and Pakistan. AHS has never been reported in the Americas, eastern Asia or Australasia but it has penetrated Europe.

**Tsetse Fly.** Unlike the mosquito, the tsetse fly won't politely buzz in your ear. This belligerent insect will deliberately hunt you down and then drill straight through your clothes in search of blood. Nor does his bite provoke a mild itch. It stings badly. And did I mention he's responsible for killing millions of head of livestock and hundreds of thousands of people every year? These flies look very similar to the normal housefly, except they are equipped with a long nose that allows them to suck the blood of vertebrates. During feeding, the fly transmits the single cell parasite, trypanosome. When this protozoa is introduced into humans it produces the deadly disease, trypanosomiases, more commonly known as sleeping sickness. The same germ creates a disease known as nagana in horses. After a tsetse fly bites a human, the protozoa moves into the victim's lymphatic system and swells the lymph glands. Next, the infection travels through the blood stream, eventually transferring itself into the neurological system. It eventually invades the victim's brain. Fever sets in and the victim often complains of severe headaches. This is a sign that the victim's brain is starting to swell. Confusion follows. Extreme lethargy sets in, followed by an abnormal need to constantly sleep. The sleep becomes deeper and the sick man lies without feeling or perception. Eventually the disease shuts down the cardiac and endocrine systems. Death soon follows. Signs that a horse is infected with nagana include a foul smell, fever, followed by loss of muscle, discharge from the eyes and nose, culminating with bodily paralysis. Should your horse become infected with nagana, you are required to immediately contact the local government health authorities.

Tests have proved that the tsetse fly is attracted to dark colours. This has led scientists to speculate that the zebra evolved his stripes, not as camouflage against lions, but as a means of reducing tsetse fly attacks. The threat of tsetse flies to humanity is so prolific that it has spread across 37 sub-Saharan African countries. As a result, the tsetse fly has turned an immense portion of Africa into what has been called "an uninhabited green desert." Tsetse flies are extremely aggressive. They are attracted by movement and are very active in the early morning and evening. Their bite is extremely painful. Riding through tsetse fly country should only be undertaken after careful consideration and planning. There is no drug suitable for preventing sleeping sickness. An insect repellent containing DEET will keep the pests at bay for a while. In an emergency the antibacterial disinfectant Dettol can be mixed with water to create a temporary repellent. The mixture should consist of a ratio of 30% Dettol and water. Any Long Rider unlucky enough to be bitten by a tsetse fly, and who develops a high fever or other manifestations of African sleeping sickness, should seek medical help without delay. If diagnosed early, treatment can halt the progress of the disease; otherwise the disease is invariably fatal.

**Horse Flies.** Horse flies don't make a quick needle-sharp injection like a mosquito. The big fly uses its razor-sharp jaws to rip a hole in the victim's flesh. Once the agonizing wound has been inflicted, the insect proceeds to gorge itself on blood. Horse flies have been known to repeatedly attack a horse, withdrawing up to 300 ml (10 ounces) of blood from the animal. Such attacks can weaken or even kill the victimized animal.

176

**Bees.** Stay alert for any signs of bees while you are riding cross country. If you see them hovering near what may be their nest, give them a wide berth. Unless you suffer from an allergic reaction, a single honeybee sting is not life-threatening. Things become more complicated if you encounter a hive of African honeybees. Dubbed "killer bees" by the press, these winged aggressors have a well-earned reputation for violence. They are descended from African bees imported into Brazil in 1956. When the bees escaped from quarantine the following year, they began to quickly multiply. Thereafter they began a steady northwards migration, extending their range at a rate of 200 miles per year. The AHB is now established in North America, where it has been known to kill horses. The sting of the African honeybee is no more lethal than its domestic cousin. What makes this type of bee so dangerous is that they attack in immense numbers, will pursue their victim a greater distance and remain disturbed, and very dangerous, for up to 24 hours. To make matters worse, unlike regular honeybees, it is not necessary to directly disturb the hive to initiate an attack by African honeybees. Noises or even vibrations have been known to initiate extreme attacks, which result in serious injuries or deaths. This may explain how a swarm of African honeybees killed two horses in Texas in the summer of 2010. A swarm estimated to contain about 30,000 bees attacked and chased the horses. According to the owner the horses were covered in so many bees "they shimmered. Both animals died after being stung hundreds of times by the vicious bees. In 2013 a Texas man was stung to death by 40,000 African bees.

**Fleas.** Even though the average flea is only 1/16 inch long (1.58 mm), the tiny dark insect is responsible for inflicting mountains of grief on humanity. These insects are patient, relentless hunters. If no victims are present, they will rest and wait, sometimes going months without feeding. The normal vibrations made by a traveller entering a room are enough to awaken the slumbering horde. Once they sense your arrival, the fleas have two goals; to feast on your fresh blood and then reproduce. Fleas can infest a human's hair in less than ten minutes. Their bites cause intense itching. Yet they are more than a mere annoyance. Fleas transmit a number of devastating diseases. Insect repellent containing DEET can help repel fleas. Calamine, hydrocortisone and other anti-itch creams can help treat the irritating symptoms caused by multiple flea bites.

**Jiggers.** Known officially as the chigoe flea, the jigger is the smallest member of the flea family, measuring only 1 mm (3/64ths of an inch) long. Despite its tiny size, it is capable of creating biological havoc in a Long Rider's body. The jigger thrives in tropical climates. Jiggers reside in the soil, until a victim appears. Various names are used to describe the tiny pests, depending on what country you ride through. Columbia calls them nigua in Spanish. Paraguayan Indians refer to them as tū in the Guarani language. But the Brazilians have the best description. They refer to the jigger as the bicho-de-pé, the foot bug. Therein lies a clue never to be forgotten if encountered. Mosquitoes and flies bite or sting their victims. A jigger burrows headfirst into the host's exposed skin. The foot is the most common area of attack. However jiggers also attack elbows and the genitals. Sitting on the ground presents an opportunity for them to infest the buttocks. No matter how they get in, they lose no time in creating what appears to be a tiny blister adorned with a central black dot. This is the female jigger's exposed abdomen. Her head is inside the victim's body, feeding on its blood. The tiny jigger remains affixed for up to two weeks, all the while its abdomen begins swelling with several dozen eggs. The pressure created by the increasingly bloated insect presses on the victim's nerves and blood vessels, causing intense irritation and pain. The jigger then dies and falls off. The eggs however are left within the host's body. When they hatch a few days later, they burst forth from the victim's skin, coming to light in a wiggly mass. Because of their tiny size, it is extremely difficult to protect yourself from jiggers. Wearing shoes and using strong insect repellent is critical for defence. If detected, it may be difficult to remove a jigger which is engorged with blood. Doctors use a curette to dig out the egg-infested nodule.

**Coloradillas.** Coloradillas are practically microscopic insects no bigger than the period seen at the end of this sentence. Because of their red colouring, they are sometimes called pinolillos, after the Aztec word for coarse flour. They infest pastures and tall grass throughout Central

America and attack horses and humans. The bite of a coloradilla resembles a blister and causes the victim to itch like mad. Though usually concentrated around the ankles, this vicious bug has been known to inflict its torment around the waist, the wrists or within any warm fold of skin, including the pubic area. The latter can result in an affliction known as "summer penile syndrome," which causes swelling of the penis, itching, and painful urination. No matter where they gnaw on you, the bites may linger for weeks. A powerful repellent containing DEET helps to keep them at bay.

**Bedbugs.** The flat, reddish-brown coloured insects, which routinely infest mattresses, bed clothes, furniture, luggage and clothing, have been known to live for a year without feeding. They are hard to detect because they lodge in cracks and crevices, waiting till nightfall to emerge in search of blood. When prey is located, they come out of hiding and send signals to alert others that it is safe to feed. Long Riders may suffer from bed bug attacks in many countries. Detecting the elusive insects before nightfall is highly recommended. Infestations are usually found close to the bed. Bedding should be inspected for signs of blood spots left by previous victims. Faecal droppings resembling brown or black pepper flakes are also evidence of the live pest. The bugs emit a characteristic smell of rotten raspberries. If you see bedbugs, do not voluntarily remain in the room. Do not open your saddlebags or lay any clothes on the ground or bed. Leave without delay, even if it means upsetting your host or losing money paid for a room. If you have no choice and must remain in the room, to avoid contamination always store your clothes and luggage far away from the bed and off the floor. As soon as possible wash your clothes in boiling water.

**Ticks.** Unlike regional terrors such as the African tsetse fly or the Central American coloradillas, ticks are not geographically restricted. Nor do they merely cause discomfort or inflict only one disease. They are prolific killers deserving of special attention. There are hundreds of different species of ticks, infesting countries around the world. Their immense range includes all of Europe, Russia, Central Asia, the Americas and Africa. With the exception of mosquitoes, ticks pose the greatest danger to humans and horses, as they transmit a number of fatal diseases. Yet health professionals in many countries remain unaware of this threat. Long Riders are likewise usually oblivious to the fact that ticks are more apt to ruin a journey than bandits. Though only measuring 1 mm (3/64ths inch), ticks are slow, patient and ruthlessly successfully predators. They are capable of selecting ambush sites based upon their ability to distinguish well-travelled trails. They take up a position on overhead branches or tall grass, then wait for dinner to arrive. Thanks to special sensory organs, which allow them to detect the carbon dioxide emitted by horses and humans, they can sense the approach of their victims from a great distance. After they drop onto their unsuspecting host, they bury their head into the body and begin feeding on its blood. Their bites often go undetected because the tick injects an anaesthetic to deaden the injury. Thus, many victims remain unaware that they have been bitten. Compounding the danger, symptoms from tick-based infections, such as fevers, aches, and fatigue, are not distinctive and mirror those of common summer viral infections. Once attached, a tick will feed for up to a week. At first it may look like a small beige-coloured pea. Eventually the tick will become so bloated with blood that it resembles a child's swollen thumb. Ticks acquire infections from one host and then pass the disease on to the next victim during a subsequent feeding. Because of the long list of diseases which ticks transmit, for which only one has a cure, they present a tremendous danger to Long Riders and their horses.

One such deadly example is Lyme Disease. Warmer climates worldwide, and a general decrease in pesticide use, are helping encourage the increase of the tick population, which in turn increases the number of cases of infection. It is the most common tick-transmitted disease in both the United States and the entire Northern Hemisphere. The infection is often transmitted between the months of May and September when the ticks are most active. Ticks transmit the Lyme bacteria via their saliva into a person's bloodstream. Soon afterwards a distinctive mark usually appears on the victim's body. It resembles a large, circular red bull's eye, darker in the middle and lighter along the edges. Should you be unlucky enough to be infected you won't be able to ignore the symptoms for long. They include fever, blinding headaches, violent vomiting, numbness, agonizing body pain and severe joint pains. As the disease progresses, victims also complain of having difficulty breathing and severe sleeplessness. They can experience extreme mood swings, including depression, delusions, and dementia. Should you see the telltale large bull's eye rash on your body, bring your journey to an abrupt halt before the onset of serious pain leaves you unable to travel. Make provisions for your horse's safety and then seek immediate medical assistance!

Ticks can harbour more than one disease-causing infection at the same time. This may compound the doctor's inability to diagnose what ailment you are suffering from. Additional infections may include Rocky Mountain spotted fever and Crimean-Congo hemorrhagic fever. The former is often called "tick typhus" and is the most deadly, and frequently reported, tick disease in the United States. Without prompt treatment it is fatal. The latter disease is found in Africa. It attacks the victim's liver and can lead to death. Another devastating tick-connected infection is encephalitis. Found in Europe, Central Asia, Siberia and Japan, this deadly disease kills thousands of people every year. A vaccination is available in Europe but not the United States. It is highly recommended if riding in a tick-infested area. While any insect-related health threat is serious, tick bites require you to maintain extreme vigilance. Because of the danger of these regional tick-connected diseases, prior to departure you should take the time to identify any tick associated threat in your area of travel.

It's not only humans that suffer from tick bites. Horses endure their bites and then die as well. After setting up shop on a tree branch, the stealthy tick drops onto the unsuspecting horse. The tiny assassins are fond of attaching themselves along the mane and on the front of the chest. Piroplasmosis is transferred via an infected tick bite. It usually takes a week or two before the symptoms are apparent. This begins with a lack of appetite and a loss of condition. If the fever becomes virulent, the horse may develop a fever and anemia. Jaundice, swelling and laboured breathing soon set in. This disease rages throughout Central and South America, affecting millions of horses. It is also found in Africa, parts of eastern Europe and the Middle East. Only Japan, Australia, Ireland, England, Canada and the United States have succeeded in keeping their horse populations clear of the infection.

This explains why any Long Rider travelling north towards the United States on Latin horses is riding straight into serious trouble. Though horses with piroplasmosis may recover enough strength to be ridden and travel, once infected they carry the parasite which might allow infection to spread to other horses. Because of this threat any horse which tests positive for piroplasmosis will never be allowed north of Mexico.

**Tick Avoidance.** The heightened risk of exposure means you should take every chance to prevent tick bites from occurring. Protect your skin and your health by wearing the proper footwear and clothing while travelling in tick country. Do not walk barefoot or in sandals. Knee-high boots reduce the tick's access to your skin. Wear long socks, long trousers and long-sleeved shirts. Keep your trousers tucked into your boots and your shirt sleeves buttoned tight at the cuff. If the tick infestation is especially bad, run tape around the top of your boots and the leg of your trousers so as to reduce their chance of entry. Wear a hat to protect your head. Once you're properly clothed, spray yourself liberally with an insecticide which contains 40 percent DEET. After you're in the saddle and on the move, try to avoid brushing alongside tree branches. If you're walking, stay in the centre of the trail, away from grass, to reduce the chances of ticks attaching themselves to your legs. Should a tick manage to enter your clothes, it will often wander along your body for a few hours before deciding where to feed. In truly bad tick country plan to halt every two hours to search for ticks. Wearing light-coloured clothes will help you detect the dark-coloured pests. Check your horse for ticks when you stop. At the conclusion of the day, you must make an intensive body search for ticks. First, inspect your clothes with great care, being especially attentive to the seams where ticks tend to hide. Next, inspect your body thoroughly. Ticks delight in concealing themselves in the warm, moist pubic area and armpits. Brush or comb your hair with great care at the end of the day. The time needed to contaminate a host varies between 24 and 36 hours. By removing the tick without delay, you greatly reduce the chances of an infection, bacteria or poison being injected into your bloodstream. Time is therefore of the essence. The faster it comes off, the lower the chances of it infecting you.

**Removing Ticks.** Tape can be used to lift ticks off clothes. But removing a tick from a horse can be tricky – and dangerous. It may be difficult to locate ticks if they hide deep in the animal's hair. They can often be found by running your fingers slowly along the horse's skin. When you locate a bump on the horse, avoid handling the tick with your uncovered fingers. Humans who pull off engorged ticks are in danger if they crush the vermin and are splashed with infected blood, so care must be taken. Wear rubber gloves and use a tick removal tool or a pair of tweezers to remove the pest. Removing ticks from your own body also requires care. The first thing to do is set aside the risky folk remedies which will increase the danger level. These tend to be ineffective and actually increase the risks of transmission or infection. The most popular, and misguided, method is passive. It calls for smearing the tick with ointment, Vaseline, alcohol, oil, soap, shampoo, gasoline or petroleum. Another popular method is to touch the tick with a hot match head or to pass a lighted cigarette over it. People mistakenly believe that by covering the tick with a distasteful liquid, or exposing it to heat, it will voluntarily retract its head from within the victim's body. What isn't commonly known is that before doing so, the tick often regurgitates the poisonous contents of its stomach into the victim's bloodstream. Thus, the folk remedy greatly increases the chances of direct infection. The best way to remove the pest is by using a tick-removal tool. This small, inexpensive, plastic tool has a two-pronged fork that slides between the skin and the tick. This little tool can be carried in a shirt pocket, so as to allow for quick access, and has an excellent record of extractions. Tick removal tools can be purchased in pet shops or in camping stores. If you're taken by surprise and don't come prepared, then you may have to resort to using a pair of tweezers to remove the tick. Great care must be taken that you do not pull the tick too hard, otherwise you may leave the head in your skin by mistake. Position the tweezers on either side of the tick's head and then pull the tick away from the skin with a slow, steady motion. You must not squeeze or crush the tick, as this causes it to empty the bacteria from its stomach into the victim's bloodstream. Also, take care not to leave the head buried in the skin, as this may result in the formation of an open wound. Regardless of what method you use, dispose of the tick carefully after it is removed. After removal, wash the bite site thoroughly with hot water and soap, then disinfect the wound with antiseptic or alcohol to reduce the chances of infection. Bites continue to itch for days after the tick is removed. However, consult a doctor at the first sign of skin rash, fever, muscle aches or fatigue.

**Assassin Bug.** Though originally restricted to Latin America, Chagas disease has migrated into North America and beyond. This malevolent illness is transmitted via a bite of the blood-sucking insect known as a triatomid. These black, wingless beetles are often referred to as the "assassin bug" or the "kissing bug." They measure 20 mm (51/64ths inch) long and are a deadly little menace. The dark-coloured beetle transmits a parasite in a particularly gruesome manner. Unlike ailments which are commonly injected into the bloodstream by a bite, the parasite which causes Chigas diseases is released in the faeces of the deadly beetle, which defecates when it is feeding on the victim's blood. When the victim scratches the irritating bite, he rubs the infected faeces into the wound, thus contaminating himself. One of the first clues that an assassin bug has attacked is the red ring which appears around the bite. After that initial sign, victims often develop a fever and feel unwell. The major indication is that one eye will become very swollen. After the parasite is in the bloodstream, the infection may subside and go into remission for years. When full-blown Chigas disease finally hits, the symptoms can't be ignored. Constipation turns into severe abdominal pain, which results in digestive ailments, all the while the parasite is making its slow steady way towards the heart, where it lives and multiplies. Many of the victims eventually develop an enlarged heart which will burst. The result is sudden and painful death.

**Leeches.** The leech is not an insect. It is a segmented hermaphrodite worm whose mission is to suck copious amounts of blood from unsuspecting victims like you. Some leeches are terrestrial, others aquatic. They are all aggressive blood-suckers who will feed on you and your horses if given the chance. When they draw near, they will aim for your ankles and then quickly crawl into your clothes. In addition to gorging themselves on your feet and lower legs, they will drop down onto your neck, seek sanctuary in your pubic hair, make their way up your nose and lodge within your throat. Once they're aboard, they'll set about locating a quiet, warm spot where they can begin feeding. Unlike ticks, leeches do not burrow into your skin. These ambush predators attach themselves when they bite. They use three razor sharp jaws to slice a Y-shaped hole though your skin. Don't worry. You won't feel it because the leech injects an anaesthetic to disguise the injury. Once he's peeled you open, the leech pumps a powerful anticoagulant into the wound. This ensures the unimpeded flow of your blood. Then he settles down and starts to enjoy his meal, which may last two hours. Don't panic if you find a leech attached to your body. A leech will not inflict significant blood loss. The thing to do is control your sense of repugnance and get on with the job of removing the bloodsuckers. You must take care how you go about this. Like ticks, you do not want to cover the leech with any type of liquid, such as vinegar, lemon juice, insect repellent or salt. Nor should you apply a hot match or a cigarette to the leech. Either option may result in the leech regurgitating its stomach's contents into your bloodstream. There is a safe and efficient way to remove leeches. Despite appearances, the mouth is actually located at the smaller, thinner end of the creature. The larger, wider end of the leech is also attached by a sucker, but that's not your immediate concern. Once you have determined which end is which, resist the temptation to grab the fat end and pull the little monster off. Instead, place your fingernail next to the leech's mouth and then slowly slide your nail under the sucker. This will break the suction, at which point the leech will detach his jaws. Once he has freed himself, flick him off immediately. Take care about trying to pick the leech off, as the unrepentant monster will attempt to reattach itself to your delicious finger.

There is an alternative. You can fill a bag, or the toe of a sock, with salt. Dip this in water and let the brine trickle down on the leech. This has a magical effect, as the leech will shrivel away, leaving only a little clot of blood which can easily be wiped off.

Leeches can affect your horse's health as well. They can get into the nose while the horse is drinking, especially out of ponds and streams, and although they are not absolutely dangerous, they cause troublesome bleeding, and make the animal cough and sneeze.

**Spiders.** An expert can quickly recite a long list of biological reasons that spiders aren't insects. But here's where the study of arachnids (spiders) ends and equestrian travel begins. There are 40,000 different types of spiders. They reside on every continent except Antarctica. If the wrong type of spider bites you, chances are the journey will come to a pain-filled conclusion. The good news is that a spider usually only bites in self-defence. The bad news is that "self-defence" to a spider often means protecting itself against a sleepy Long Rider putting his foot into a boot. Because spiders produce toxins which can injure or kill, it pays to be able to visually identify what type of spider you may encounter on your journey.

**Scorpions.** There are twenty-five varieties of scorpions whose venom can kill you. Only polar weather inhibits these prolific creatures, which otherwise thrive in a variety of climates and countries. Scorpions are nocturnal hunters. They use the needle sharp barb at the end of their tail to inject highly toxic venom into their prey – or defend themselves against any Long Rider unfortunate enough to sit down on them. The victim is usually in a great deal of pain. He may become nauseous or vomit as the toxin takes effect. Wash the wound with cold water. An ointment containing an antihistamine, a corticosteroid, and an analgesic will help offset infection. Administering a dose of Benadryl will reduce the pain. If you can locate ice, apply it to the wound, otherwise use a cold wet cloth. That's what you do if the case remains simple. Should the victim start to have muscle spasms, begin to hyperventilate, become disoriented or go into an allergic shock, it is time to seek urgent medical attention.

**Fire Ants.** Known as the red imported fire ant (RIFA), these aggressive creatures were accidentally transported into the United States via a ship in 1929. From an initial landfall in Alabama, the RIFA has spread across the entire southern portion of the nation. The fire ant injects venom into humans which creates a sensation akin to being burned alive. An estimated

20 million people are stung every year. Fire ants react aggressively when their nest is disturbed. Unlike other ants, who rush to protect their queen, fire ants swarm out from tunnels that radiate away from the visible mound and attack the intruder without delay. It is not uncommon for hundreds of fire ants to rush up the victim's leg and begin stinging simultaneously. If the victim retaliates the ants go into a frenzy. They have been known to kill children and small animals. This should be of concern to anyone who is trying to find grazing for his horse, as fire ants have been known to infest an acre with more than 200 individual nests. If you're riding through fire ant country, use extreme caution, as they settle in grassy areas and near water. Should you be stung, wash the area to try and flush out the toxin. An antihistamine, such as Benadryl, will help reduce swelling. But be prepared for the bites to itch and cause pustules to form.

**Protecting Humans.** There are several precautions which can reduce the chances of insect attacks. Study your route with care. Identify the insect threats that live there. Warm temperatures and ample rainfall encourage a heavy insect population. To offset this threat, use the seasons to your advantage. Once you've identified the type of pest which you will encounter, obtain the proper vaccinations to lower your chances of infection. Even if pre-ventative treatments are available, don't think you're risk free. Anti-malarial drugs, for example, will suppress the symptoms but won't prevent its occurrence. It only takes one bite to infect you. That's why it is vital that you remain vigilant, react aggressively towards any potential insect threat, and use a four-point plan of defence.

First, dress in a defensive manner. Avoid dark clothes. They attract insects. Opt for light-coloured clothing to reduce attacks. Wear long-sleeved shirts and long trousers. If the situation and climate are extreme, dress in anti-leech socks, gloves and a veiled hat. Don't leave your clothes open, so as to grant access to an attacker. Tuck your trousers into your boots. Button up your cuffs and shirt. Second, turn your clothing into insect armour. Protective clothes can be bought which are guaranteed to repel mosquitoes and other pests. Such items are not only expensive; they were not designed for equestrian travellers. The key ingredient to the clothes repelling powers is a chemical known as permethrin. But this liquid can be bought and applied to the clothing of your choice. This will not only save you the cost of purchasing the expensive preconditioned clothing, it will allow you to reapply the chemical to your clothes while travelling. Third, transform your body from a feast into a famine. Midges can detect the carbon dioxide emitted by your breath from a distance of 220 feet (67 metres). Don't make matters worse by wearing perfume, cologne or any body product which exudes an odour that might attract insects. Permethrin will be effective with your clothing but it cannot be applied to human skin. To protect your body, you must use a strong repellent. Unfortunately most products only succeed in making your skin taste unpleasant. They don't discourage insects from swarming around you. If you choose a commercial repellent make sure it contains a high level of DEET. Should you opt for a natural repellent, that not only prevents bites but also encourages insects to keep their distance, a repellent containing the oil of bog myrtle, or sweet gale, has proved successful. Use your repellent to create a vapour barrier between you and the insect hordes. Spray it liberally on your clothes. Take care around your eyes and lips, but apply it to your exposed skin. It evaporates, so be ready to reapply it every few hours. Because your riding clothes are carrying a combination of repellent and permethrin, don't be in a hurry to wash away all of this accumulated protection. Fourth, never miss a chance to search for undetected insects. Check your body and hair very thoroughly every night for ticks. Watch where you walk and do not go barefoot. Shake out your clothes vigorously every morning. Never put on your boots without checking them for spiders and scorpions. Even if you follow this four-step plan with care, you may still be bitten. Should this occur, identify the insect. Remove the stinger. Wash the bite with soap and hot water. Apply an ointment to curtail the itching. Watch for allergic reactions or any evidence the insect was carrying a disease. If you suspect the bite may be serious, seek medical aid immediately.

**Protecting Horses.** Of course, you're not the only one in danger. Insects will slay your horses if left unattended. Insect bites not only expose your horse to deadly bacteria, but a daytime sting might have deadly consequences if you're riding along a dangerous trail. After the sun

182

sets, rest is of vital importance to road and pack horses, but swarming flies and midges will cause the animal to spend valuable energy trying to protect itself from ceaseless attacks. There are other ways to reduce insect attacks on your horses. First, never trim your horse's tail, mane or forelock! Nature provided this long hair as a protection against insects. Horses can twitch their skin to frighten away insects. But he can't move the skin on the hind quarters and hind legs. That's why nature gave them tails, for protection. The longer the horse's hair; the better his chances of defending himself. Provide your horse with up-to-date vaccinations for rabies, tetanus, West Nile virus and equine encephalomyelitis prior to departure. To reduce any adverse reaction, be sure the inoculations are administered several weeks before your departure. Give a thought to the colour of your horse. Light reflects differently off the various colours of a horse's coat. Just as scientists have confirmed that tsetse flies are strongly attracted to the colour blue, researchers have discovered that horse flies are more attracted to darker colours. These aggressive pests prefer the flat light produced by the darker coats of black and brown horses, as opposed to the non-polarised light of a white-coated horse. If you're going to be travelling though country which encourages heavy insect swarms, then you should invest in an equine repellent which includes a strong percentage of DEET. Stinging flies and midges are especially active at sunrise and sunset. Because you're travelling, it won't be possible to place your animal inside the safety of a stable every night. Yet never miss a chance to lodge your horse indoors for the night if such accommodation is available. If you find yourself outdoors, make small smoky fires and place the horses within this protective circle. Don't let the sun set without having carried out a careful check on your horses. This examination should include a vigilant search for ticks, evidence of bites, signs of scratching and indications of skin infection. Because every hour counts, never delay removing ticks or applying medication!

# Chapter 69 - Long Rider Health

You can't expect to pick the rose of adventure without your finger coming near the thorn of danger. Learning to accept the presence of peril, and recognizing the frailty of our lives, is the first step in preparing for what lies ahead.

**Health and Hardships.** Because horse travel is a vigorous activity that encourages robust health, Long Riders are less often ill than at home. What people don't realize is that an extended equestrian journey makes serious physical demands on their bodies.

**Be Prepared.** There is a rhythm to an equestrian journey. Rise early. Ride hard. Day after day after day. It is this constant demand for physical activity, linked to a great deal of strenuous exercise, which will wear you down, not make you stronger. That is why it is important that you not fool yourself into thinking that you will get into shape on the ride. By the time the adrenalin has dissipated, your body is screaming for a rest. Would-be travellers must be in reasonable health and not be either over weight or grossly out of shape. They should also have a thorough medical and dental check-up before undertaking travels in remote countries. One other point of prevention is to document your personal medical details, including your blood group, any sensitivity to specific drugs and any allergies. Depending on where you ride, and how long you will be in the field, you should also consider carrying a spare set of spectacles and your lens prescription.

**Vaccinations.** Routine immunizations are also highly recommended. Study the vaccination requirements for the countries you will be riding though. Childhood vaccinations protect you for life, while routine immunizations last ten years.

**Where you Ride.** External factors may influence the chances of you becoming ill during a journey. One element which many people tend to overlook is the effect of climate on their health. Scratching a mosquito bite in Sweden's cool climate may not cause any harm. Yet if done in a hot and humid climate, the same reaction may cause the bite to quickly become inflamed and infected. Adjusting our cultural perceptions and daily practices to fit the climate is a basic step in preventative medical care.

**Traveller's Diarrhoea.** Traveller's diarrhoea causes more trouble than all other medical hazards put together. An estimated 10 million people per year suffer from gastro-intestinal infections, with some studies calculating that 20 to 50 percent of international travellers suffer from some form of this common affliction. Most travellers' diarrhoea is bacterial or viral in origin. It is not to be confused with the more dangerous amoebic dysentery, which is caused by a parasite that is found in contaminated food and drinks. Common symptoms of traveller's diarrhoea include abdominal cramps, bloating, dehydration, low fever, nausea, and vomiting, not to mention suffering from multiple watery bowel movements. Traveller's diarrhoea will not only make you feel miserable, it will keep you out of the saddle. The majority of cases are usually mild enough to resolve themselves within three days. Your ability to treat the affliction will depend upon what country you are in and your access to medical treatment. However, no matter where you are, certain actions are sure to encourage recovery. Face the fact that your body is infected. Rest. Drink at least a pint of sterilized water per hour to offset dehydration. A brief fast will help settle your intestinal tract. If you must eat, remember that bread and meat often triggers a violent relapse. Broth, soup or rice in small quantities will restore strength without taxing your digestion. Should you detect blood in the stools, consult a doctor without delay, as this may be an early indication of the more serious amoebic dysentery. Treatment with antibiotics is often prescribed for severe cases; however a treatment with a non-prescription antimotility drug, such as Imodium, often resolves the problem. The human body is an engine which requires a certain amount of food as fuel. Maintaining a balanced diet can be difficult when you are travelling across unknown country by horseback. One way to decrease becoming ill from traveller's diarrhoea is to only eat food which you have seen cooked; otherwise you don't know under what sanitary conditions it was prepared or how long it has been waiting to be served. What you eat may well influence the progress of your trip. What you drink may put your life at risk.

**Bad Water.** It is not in the province of this book to describe all of the various ailments which might adversely affect you. Yet no matter where you ride, one fundamental element is to be found in every country. It may ruin your dreams, wreck your health and take your life. I'm referring to untreated water. Equestrian travel is a thirsty business. Because they move so slowly across the landscape, Long Riders often think, dream and write about water.

Never trust the water! If you do, you may become ill or die. Because modern Long Riders understand the severity of this potential threat, they can enlist several methods to treat their water, including boiling, filtering, chemical treatment, and ultraviolet light. The most traditional method is to boil the water. This time-honoured method immediately kills all bacteria and viruses. It is not necessary to keep the water boiling for any length of time, as all micro-organisms are killed within seconds after the water's temperature passes 55° Celsius (131° Fahrenheit). Inexpensive filters are also effective. They eliminate many micro-organisms but not viruses. You can also treat the water with chemicals including putting 2 drops of chlorine bleach per litre or 5 drops of tincture of iodine per litre. Whatever technique you decide on, unless you personally ensured its safety, assume all water is potentially contaminated. Wise travellers know that water can make you ill, even if you don't intentionally drink it. For example, don't risk your health by brushing your teeth with water that hasn't been purified. Use care if you dine in a restaurant. A common trick is to serve unwary travellers untreated local tap water in a reputable-looking plastic water bottle. Make sure water bottles are opened in your presence. Another common trap is ice cubes that have been made with germ-laden water. If local circumstances are dire, the safest course is to drink hot tea, coffee or chocolate instead of suspect water. But here again, caution must be used with any hot beverage. If they have only been heated, not boiled, then they may carry contamination. Also, avoid green salads. If the local water is suspect, it is highly unlikely that the lettuce and vegetables will have been properly washed with non-contaminated water. Likewise, avoid eating raw fruits and vegetables unless you peeled them yourself.

**Hepatitis.** Hepatitis is a broad term for inflammation of the liver, most commonly caused by a viral infection. There are several types of hepatitis, with Hepatitis A and E viruses being the main culprits in terms of travel. Hepatitis A is an acute infectious disease of the liver. The virus, which is carried in faeces, is usually acquired from consuming infected food, drinking contaminated water, swimming near a sewage outlet or through direct contact with an infectious person. Following ingestion, the virus enters the victim's bloodstream and is transported to the liver, where it multiples. As the HAV virus incubates, the traveller often suffers from a vague and unpleasant unease for several weeks. Then the symptoms begin to appear. You feel morose. You lose your appetite. Your muscles ache. You become weak. You suffer from blinding headaches. You vomit. Your guts are destroyed by diarrhoea. Then, when the disease has you in its grip, it announces its presence to the world. Jaundice causes your skin and the whites of your eyes to take on an alarming yellow colour. In its final stages you are too weak to do anything except lie there and feel your life slipping away, one breath at a time. Serious cases result in seizures, coma and death. There are two things to remember about hepatitis; there is no specific treatment and it is found worldwide. Because the virus can survive for months in water, tens of millions of people become ill from Hepatitis A every year. It is especially prevalent in Africa, Asia and many parts of Latin America. If you fall ill with hepatitis, don't think you're going to drop by the pharmacy and pick up a convenient prescription. Victims are often very sick for a month or more. During this time they are advised to rest, avoid fatty foods, abstain from alcohol and stay hydrated. The thing to do is to not become infected with this painful and frightening disease. A basic step in preventive medicine is to use great care when it comes to what you drink and eat. Also, if you are going to be riding in a country that has a history of harbouring hepatitis, then you would be well advised to obtain a vaccination shot against the illness. The vaccine, which was introduced in 1992 and provides active immunity against infection, is so effective that some countries have reported a 90% decrease in cases since the inoculation was made available.

**Deadly Diseases.** In this age of instant communication and globalised values we tend to forget that certain ancient maladies still lurk along the trails we travel. One of the worst is malaria. Don't underestimate the savage power of this infamous killer. Although it has been eradicated in some countries, this mosquito-borne disease continues to plague large sections of the world. Symptoms include severe headaches, high fever, chills, sweats, fatigue and vomiting. No immunization currently exists against malaria. This helps explain why there were 219 million reported cases of malaria in 2010 alone, resulting in 660,000 deaths, equivalent to roughly 2,000 deaths per day. It only takes one mosquito bite for the deadly infection to take effect. Discouraging the insects with the use of proper clothing, insect repellent, and by sleeping under mosquito netting at night, are all essential steps in your protection.

Typhoid is a painful and deadly ailment that works in stages. It does not affect animals. Transmission is only from human to human, and is most commonly spread to the victim via the ingestion of food or water that has been contaminated with human faeces or urine. Poor personal hygiene and insufficient public sanitation conditions are often directly connected to an outbreak of typhoid fever. At the onset, the victim suffers malaise, headache and abdominal pain in the first week. By the second week the victim is often prostrate with a high fever of 40° Centigrade (104° Fahrenheit). Rose-coloured spots emerge on the patient's chest. The abdomen becomes painfully distended. Foul-smelling diarrhoea makes life a misery. Desperately ill, medical help is urgently needed for the patient. If the disease is not halted, intestinal haemorrhage due to bleeding often occurs during the third week. Many victims also become delirious, mutter to themselves, pick at the bedclothes and hit out at imaginary objects. As bad as it sounds, when properly treated typhoid fever is not fatal in most cases. Antibiotics are highly effective and are commonly used to treat typhoid fever. Long Riders travelling in typhoid-infected areas are encouraged to obtain an inoculation prior to departure, as the vaccine is highly effective. But prevention against typhoid is better than a cure. Care must be taken with food and water. Washing your hands on a regular basis also helps decrease the chances of infection.

**Snakebite.** Chances are most Long Riders will journey through a portion of the world which is inhabited by venomous snakes. That is because the poisonous creatures are widely distributed across all tropical, subtropical, and most temperate regions. Yet it is encouraging to know that few people actually die from snakebite. For example, more than 8,000 people are bitten by poisonous snakes in the United States each year, however on average only one person out of ten dies. In contrast, more Americans are killed by wasp and bee stings than by a poisonous snakebite. There are two things to remember when it comes to snakes; knowledge and caution. Do not set off on your trip without having taken the time to investigate what types of poisonous snakes might live along your route! Once you are in the saddle and under way, never miss a chance to seek out local knowledge about snakes and where they might be lurking. Caution is always better than a cure. Dress defensively by wearing boots if you are riding in snake country. Take care where you place your camp, being sure to avoid sleeping close to tall grass, thick brush, or large rocks that might shelter snakes. Safety is increased when you pitch your tent in a clearing. Don't take snakes for granted. Examine your sleeping bag before climbing inside. Turn your boots upside down before placing your feet inside. When walking at night, say to check on the horses, use a torch (flashlight) to help warn off snakes. Only bites from venomous serpents cause dangerous poisoning, which might lead to death. But even non-fatal bites can inflict severe pain and cause lasting tissue damage. If you are bitten, do not fall prey to the folk remedy which recommends cutting the skin over the bite and sucking out the poison. That works in a Hollywood western film but not in real life. The best course of action is to immediately seek medical aid at the closest hospital.

**Sun.** If you haven't given serious thought to protecting yourself against the sun, now is the time to do so, as the alternative is decidedly unpleasant. Arming yourself with a powerful sun block-er, and wearing a wide-brimmed hat, is obligatory. But there are other dangers besides sunburn to worry about. New arrivals to an extremely hot climate must allow time to become acclimatized. Training horses, lifting heavy saddles, spending time in the hot sun doing chores, could result in the newcomer suffering from heat exhaustion. First, take one grain of common-sense daily; do as the natives do, keep out of the noon-day sun, and make haste slowly! When working and riding in a truly hot climate, there is a need to make use of the cooler air found at dawn and dusk. When riding or working in the direct sun move slowly, make use of every bit of shade and do not overly tax yourself. Drink plenty of water and replace the salt lost via sweating. Ignoring the power of the sun may result in heat exhaustion. The sudden onset of exhaustion, followed by cramps and vomiting, are warning signs of an impending collapse. Dehydration can be detected from the victim's urine, which takes on a deep yellow-brown colour. The victim must be placed in the shade and urged to drink large amounts of fluids. Sudden cooling can be dangerous and alcohol should be avoided. Even worse is sunstroke. Excessive exposure to the sun can result in a failure in the body's ability to regulate heat. The victim's body becomes so hot that sweating ceases and the temperature rises far above normal. Without treatment, the person's temperature may rise above 41° Centigrade (106° Fahrenheit).This will induce confusion and may trigger convulsions. If the temperature continues to climb above 43° Centigrade (110° Fahrenheit) the victim may slip into a coma and die. The first step is to immediately cool the patient. Then seek medical help without delay.

**Feminine Hygiene.** There are certain elements of travel which cannot be avoided, despite a lack of written evidence. Though the Long Riders' Guild Press publishes many books written by female equestrian travellers, they did not reveal how they maintained a sense of privacy or attended to their female needs while living amongst thousands of men. In fact few lady Long Riders have addressed the problems faced by female travellers. What stories emerge are brief. For example, Swiss Long Rider Basha O'Reilly recalled how a Mongol man thought nothing of following and watching while she attempted to urinate discretely behind a bush. When she asked why he had callously invaded her privacy, he seemed surprised. No Mongol, he assured Basha, thought it unnatural to witness other people defecating or urinating. While I cannot attest to the accuracy of the Mongol's claim, what is known is that many countries do not honour a woman's sense of confidentiality. One of the greatest hardships German Long Rider Esther Stein had to endure during her ride from South Africa to Kenya was the loss of her privacy. It was common for dozens of people to follow her into the bush at a time when she was in desperate need of seclusion.

**Equestrian Accidents.** Even if you've been injected with an assortment of inoculations, you need to realize that there is a certain inherent level of risk which comes with horse travel. Horses are big, heavy, strong animals. Horses step on our feet. They swing their heavy heads into us. They take fright and dislodge us from the saddle. Even though most of these mishaps cause us unintentional harm, the list of potential mishaps is practically endless. Luckily, most equestrian journeys are completed without any type of incident.

**Remain Alert.** Survival experts have stated that awareness is 90 percent of survival and that the chance of a misfortune occurring can be diminished by remaining especially vigilant. That may be true if you're walking through the forest, camping, etc. However there is an additional element at play when you're travelling, namely the extremely long hours a Long Rider spends in the saddle. As the miles grow, our mind wanders, and the chance of encountering a potential accident increases. There is an added dimension to this problem; stress.

**The Onset of Stress.** Long Riders who set off to make an extended journey across one or more foreign countries are trying to survive alone in a new culture, attempting to cope for long periods of time with strange new practices, all the while struggling to express themselves in a foreign language. For all these reasons, the further they ride, the harder they strive to maintain their peace of mind. Riding in a foreign country is going to remove you from the emotional support system you enjoy at home. You're alone with your dreams, your horse and a long way to go. To make matters worse, dealing with unexpected situations is complicated by language barriers. Not knowing what behaviour is appropriate in a new culture comes as a shock. Discovering that other countries have vastly different views on personal hygiene and privacy can be upsetting. Being a visible minority can be intimidating. Suffering racial, ethnic or gender discrimination is deeply troubling. So there you are, trying to maintain charge of your life, all the while misunderstandings increase, suspicion grows, and your sense of self-control begins to deteriorate. Such unexpected situations intensify your stress levels and lead to unexpected trouble.

**Learning to Stand Alone.** Living an uncertain life, seeking shelter every sunset, having to deal constantly with strangers, enduring harsh climates, avoiding dangers; is it any wonder Long Riders often experience intense levels of stress. Even if you don't encounter an equine emergency, the strong dose of adrenalin which helped propel your departure will eventually begin to wane. As it ebbs away, the grinding reality of travelling slowly through an alien environment will become an increasing daily burden. Anxiety, confusion and frustration encourage the onset of isolation and a sense of insecurity. The further you travel the more likely it is that you will suffer from loneliness and sadness. The onset of homesickness isn't far behind. Depression and self-doubt are the ultimate results of this destructive cycle. The intensity of these emotional challenges will depend on your ability to remain mentally resilient. Their negative impact can be diminished if you learn how to tolerate strange new experiences, people and places. The onset of stress often reveals the ugly side of our personality. Our emotional limitations are displayed. Our actions may become unworthy. Our language may slip into profanity. Being embarrassed at a later date is one thing. Being deeply ashamed because we flew into a stress-induced rage is another.

**Taming Your Temper.** Countless Long Riders have lost their temper when they've been overtly cheated, given wrong directions, denied information or had their possessions stolen. What you need to know in advance is that losing your temper is one thing. Flying into a violent rage not only doesn't help resolve the situation, it may get you into legal trouble. Be warned that many countries will fine or imprison you if a local citizen claims you were disturbing the peace, acting aggressively or issuing threats. The last place you want to regain your composure is inside a foreign jail! You have to expect negative travel experiences. They're part of the trip. You can't avoid or outrun them. You either adapt to the new culture or it defeats you. Realize in advance that situations are going to arise which are beyond your control. Accept that other people are going to try your patience. Do not let a challenging situation escalate out of control.

Find an acceptable, non-confrontational solution to resolve the problem. Be familiar with the onset of a violent attack of temper. Warning signs include ignoring or not listening to the other person, followed by raising your voice and verbal abuse. Sweating, chest-tightening and palpitations are strong indications that you're slipping out of control. Physical violence and destruction of property result when you're overcome by a serious loss of temper. There are ways to decrease the chances of losing control once you're on the move. Don't let fatigue and lack of sleep fray your temper. Refrain from drinking alcohol if a confrontation may be in the offing. Reduce the chances of stress undermining your happiness before you leave. Prior to departure study the customs, culture and social environment of the country you'll be riding through. Learn some of the language, even if it is only a few basic words and local greetings. Overcome any shyness and learn to express your needs with confidence. Avoid involvement in potentially dangerous discussions involving politics and religion. Above all, ride with a positive attitude and act joyful.

**Time to Heal.** One of the complications involved in equestrian travel is the extensive time required to accomplish an extended journey. People normally set aside months, if not years, to ride across a nation or continent. The task is complicated when a serious injury knocks the Long Rider out of the saddle for an extended period of time.

**The Cost of Recovery.** Any injury which disables the Long Rider imperils the health and safety of his horses as well. When the Long Rider is injured, the horse's well being is placed at risk. Some threats are obvious. It only takes one bad meal to cause colic, a bad fence to let a horse escape or a moment of inattention to allow him to be stolen. You took on the job of being parent, provider and protector to a very large, hungry, thirsty, frightened, impatient, emotionally-dependent equine. Your absence disrupts the horse's sense of security.

**First Aid Kit.** Separate first aid kits for you and the horses are recommended. To aid in instant recognition in case of emergency, mark one "Long Riders" and the other "Horses." Recommended items in the Long Riders First Aid Kit include: sterile gauze pads, 1 inch (2½ cm.) wide adhesive tape, band-aids, a 4 inch (10 cm.) wide bandage, tincture of iodine and iodine-based surgical soap. Ciprofloxacin is an antibiotic that kills most strains of bacterial pathogens responsible for respiratory, urinary tract, gastrointestinal, and abdominal infections. Polysporin antibiotic ointment is effective in treating small wounds. Aspirin or Ibuprofen should be taken to relieve minor pain. Antihistamine, sun block, lip salve, insect repellent and insect sting swabs are all recommended. Visine eye wash, dental floss, toothache gel, moisturizing lotion and Vaseline are useful. A small hand towel, packets of sterile Towelettes and Kleenex should be included. A digital thermometer, scissors, tweezers and Q-tips for removing foreign objects from eyes or open wounds are all needed. Safety pins and a sewing kit are also recommended. You may be able to purchase medication at a lower cost in the country where you will be riding than in your home country. But do not put your pocket book before your health. Prior to your departure, discuss your itinerary with a doctor. Should your journey take you through extremely hazardous regions, make a note of the specific drugs, and their exact dosages, which are used as antidotes for tropical diseases. Also, obtain any vaccinations which may reduce your chances of becoming infected by a deadly disease. Part of your personal first aid kit should include copies of any special medical prescriptions you require and a secret supply of emergency money.

**Surviving an Emergency.** The will to survive is more fundamentally important than any pill, lotion or powder found in your first aid kit! This invisible force will help you to overcome obstacles that seem quite impossible at the time. Unlike taking a course in first aid, one can't be taught how to tap into this secret part of your soul. What you must comprehend is that your determination to survive is the single most important factor in any emergency. No matter how hopeless the situation might appear, you must never give up. Ever! Hope gives you pluck and comfort. This fundamental rule applies to every situation a Long Rider may encounter. Regardless if you are lying in pain or are facing an emotional disaster, sheer determination is what separates the survivors from the statistics. When accidents happen, you must learn to call upon the hidden reserves of strength and courage which lie deeply buried within your own soul.

# Chapter 70 - Horse Health

There are many accidents, diseases and dangers which might befall any Long Rider's horse. Your chances of avoiding trouble can be improved by understanding the challenges which lie ahead.

**Recognizing the Risks.** This book is not designed to replace a veterinary course or encourage a rash "do-it-yourself" approach to the serious subject of equine medical treatment. This section is aimed at providing vital information which should come into play prior to the arrival of a qualified veterinarian. It does not hope to provide detailed information regarding the dozens of diseases, ailments and injuries which may wound or kill your horse. It is limited to those examples which are most common to travelling horses. Though the chances are remote that a deadly accident will befall your road or pack horse, you must accept the fact that this possibility exists. One of your most important duties as a Long Rider is to understand the serious responsibilities which a fatal injury or equine death will require from you. If you are unwilling or unable to cope with this emotional issue, then you are not ready to set off.

**Horses and Hazards.** Long Riders and their horses face two types of hazards during the course of their outdoor pursuits; objective and subjective. Objective hazards consist of natural threats, such as bad weather and treacherous terrain, over which humans have no control. Subjective hazards are linked to the expedition's human element and might include the physical fitness, emotional judgement and technical skill of the team members.

**Learn to Turn Back.** Equestrian travellers who become fixated upon reaching a distant goal often endanger the health of their horses. When an equestrian journey is compromised, it is the horse that pays the price. The journey is a symbol of this unique interspecies teamwork. The horse's physical sacrifice grants you the miles. That is why the first lesson in healthy horse care is learning when to stop the journey. Never hesitate to halt the journey if the horse is placed at risk!

**O.A.D.A.** Protecting the horse's health is a primary duty of any Long Rider! Not only are there ethical considerations, the journey is delayed or concluded if the animal falls ill. To help ensure that the horse's health is never neglected, you should begin your day by making it a habit to enact the following steps. Observation - Analysis - Diagnosis – Action.

**Daily Health Check.** *Observation*; the first step in learning about equine health is to determine what are the normal signs in a healthy horse. Don't rush to groom, saddle and depart. Always take the time to study your horse as you approach him. *Analysis*; what does his body language tell you? Is he standing firmly on all four legs? Or does he appear to be avoiding putting his weight on one leg or hoof? *Diagnosis*; when you draw near, can you see if his skin is loose and his coat appears to be glossy? Is he sweating or breathing heavily? *Action*; horses may suffer from more than 200 illnesses, so if the animal appears to be hot, sweaty, panting or ill at ease, then you should immediately establish the basic medical facts. Start your day by making the O.A.D.A. process your first priority.

**Sore Backs.** Many people worry about protecting the horse's horny hooves but never give a thought to the sensitive back. They misplace their priorities. The hoof was designed to withstand injury while running across hard surfaces. But the back was never intended to carry weight. If Nature had intended horses to undertake such a task, equines would have been provided with some element of special protection. Instead of a protective shell or tough skin, the delicate construction of the horse's back invites trouble and lends itself to injury.

Sore backs are the plague of Long Rider horses, as once the skin is broken it is essentially impossible to combine healing and the carrying of a rider or burden. The list of injuries can range from a few hairs rubbed off because of a mild amount of pressure, to a swelling on the withers the size of child's head. The likelihood of a sore back is enormously increased when the rider exhibits ignorance, indifference and a lack of compassion. Because even a moderate amount of pressure and friction can inflame or injure the back, protecting this delicate portion of the horse's body is an everyday goal for the Long Rider. To understand the back you need to realize it has two constant enemies, friction and pressure. Every injury to the back, shoulders, ribs, withers, or other part of the body is brought about either singly or because of a combination of friction and pressure. Friction rubs off the hair and outer surface of the skin, exposing it to further injury. Pressure damages the body by partly or entirely cutting off the blood flow. Every sore, injury and abrasion on a horse's back is the result of a certain definite cause, which if removed produces no further effect. To stop injury and encourage healing, it is necessary to determine and remove the cause of the injury. Major reasons include; poor conditioning prior to departure, underfed during the journey, muscle loss while travelling, badly-fitting saddle, improper adjustment, dirty equipment, rider's incorrect posture, inappropriate gait, overwork, overloading, badly balanced loads and off-saddling too quickly. Any one of these mistakes, or a combination of the above, is liable to sore the horse.

The first stage in protecting a horse from a sore back is proper conditioning. Like any type of athletic test, the horse needs to accustom his body to the challenge of long-distance travel. A soft body is unaccustomed to the relentless pressure created by a saddle and rider. Even if the horse is in hard condition and his back well-muscled, the saddle may inflict damaging pressure in a remarkably short time. Proper saddling offsets the chances of serious injuries. To protect the sensitive withers, take care to ensure there are no wrinkles in the saddle blanket or pad. Be sure the pad has been lifted up into the forks of the saddle, off the horse's withers. Because the rider's body moves with the flow of the horse's motion, your road horse is less likely to receive saddle sores than the pack horse, who has a constant burden pressing down onto his body. But you can never take the horse's back for granted. Every time you halt, you should take the time to inspect the road and pack horse carefully. Many potential injuries are relieved simply by correcting the faulty position of the saddle, readjusting the blanket or balancing the weight of the panniers more carefully. Never ignore the signs of a potential sore back. Any hint of friction, a slight rub on the withers or the possibility of a girth gall must be checked at once and attended to on the spot. Injuries from oversized and heavy saddlebags are among some of the most severe; the part afflicted is the ridge of the spine where there is nothing covering the bone but the skin, and in a very short time an injury may be inflicted of sufficient severity to lay the horse up for weeks. No matter what is carried behind the saddle the golden rule is that it should be concave towards the spine in order that nothing may touch it.

There are many precautions which help reduce the chances of a pack saddle soring your horse. Begin by taking the time to saddle up correctly. Make sure that the animal's back, belly and under the tail are perfectly clean. Ensure that the saddle blanket or pad is dry, clean and well brushed. Place the packsaddle over the weight-bearing portion of the back. See that the girth is well back from the forearm and that the crupper, breastplate, and breeching fit properly. Make certain the front of the packsaddle is well clear of the withers. The heavier the load, the greater will be the damage inflicted. Therefore the first step to a light saddle is a light load. What must always be recalled is the importance of balancing the weight being carried in the panniers. When the difference in weight is ten or twenty pounds the risk of injury is enormously increased. Proper adjustment of the load is an achievable goal. Curing a sore back is not. Keep the load as steady as possible while travelling. Never travel for more than an hour without checking the panniers. Stop as soon as you see a crooked or slipped load. Keep the day's journey short. Transport animals should not be asked to trot.

One way to increase the chances of a sore back is to mount immediately at the beginning of the day's ride. Placing the rider's weight on the horse's cold back may lead to muscle damage. Think of your horse, not yourself! Give the soft tissue time to warm up. Set off on foot. Walk ten minutes alongside your horse. Check that the saddle and blanket are properly adjusted. Tighten the girth. Then mount and progress.

**Ride Well.** The better the rider, the less likelihood of a saddle sore. Never sit sloppily in the saddle. Lolling to and fro in the saddle creates pressure points on the back. Never let your body sway about. Slapdash riding causes the horse to be thrown off balance since the equilibrium of the horse is maintained by tight reins and a firm seat. Never ride off-centre. This irregularity will cause the saddle to chafe the near wither. Travel, don't meander. Walk briskly, sit up straight and never slouch.

A tired man on a tired horse is a recipe for a sore back! A long day's travel will result in the Long Rider becoming weary and cramped after sitting in one position for many hours. When this occurs, an inexperienced rider starts to twist and turn in the saddle. He will often lean forward or pull his feet out of the stirrups. Any of these movements may cause the saddle to shift off balance, pull the girth out of place or create a wrinkle in the blanket. The result may be the start of an injury.

It is a fundamental mistake to stay in the saddle all day! Not only does it encourage sore backs, it is also counterproductive to the rider's health. Do not view walking alongside your horse as a punishment. It is a reward. Dismount the moment you feel weary and lead the horse. Walking will allow the tired muscles used in riding to regain their tone. Even if you feel fine, plan to walk a portion of every hour. The removal of the rider's weight allows the blood to circulate freely through the horse's skin and offset sore backs.

If you are required to stop for any reason, do not remain in the saddle! Dismount immediately so as to give your horse's back a rest.

**Off Saddling.** Misplaced mercy can cause saddle sores. You might think it a kindness to immediately remove a saddle at the end of a long day's travel. Instead of helping your horse, you will be exposing him to grave injury. You should always walk the last part of the day, so as to ensure that the horse does not arrive hot and sweaty. Once you dismount for this last walk of the day, allow the horse to walk along slowly and shake if it wants. If hot backs are exposed to a chill breeze it is not uncommon for small swellings, known as bunches, to form. To offset this danger, never remove the saddle when the horse's back is hot and sweaty!

After you arrive, remove the saddle and pommel bags from your road horse, and take the panniers off your pack horse, but leave the saddles in place with their girths loose. The saddle has now taken on a new job. It is protecting the horse's hot, sweaty back from being scalded by cold air. Allow the horse to stand quietly; all the while the back has a chance to dry under the shielding saddle. Depending upon how hot the horse is, he may be required to stand quietly for one or two hours before the saddle is finally removed. This precautionary procedure allows a gradual resumption of normal blood circulation and drying of the back. To gauge the progress, place your hand under the saddle blanket every fifteen minutes to check how dry his back has become.

Sometimes it may not be possible to let the horse stand quietly and dry slowly. Should you be required to remove the saddle, without taking this precautionary step, pour a bucket of cold water over the horse's back as soon as the saddle is off. Then massage the back gently but firmly. The cold water dissipates the heat, encourages the blood to circulate and cools the muscles.

Saddle sores are one of the most serious threats faced by any equestrian traveller, past or present. Any combination of swellings, sores or tenderness can end your ride or cause long delays. But the chances of such a wound occurring can be reduced by proper care and careful daily procedure. Where the horse is concerned, nothing can take the place of the eye of the master. Learn to notice every rub, no matter how slight and then take immediate action.

Should a sore back occur, the Long Rider must act like a responsible caretaker, not a criminal, and halt the ride until the wound is healed. If you sore your horse, you stop your ride!

**Colic.** Of all the calamities which might impede a Long Rider's progress, colic is the deadly ailment which has most often slain great horses and destroyed historic journeys. According to veterinarians, colic is the number one cause of equine deaths. Not only does colic weaken, injure, and often kill the horse, it places the Long Rider under tremendous emotional pressure. To learn how to protect your horse from colic, you first need to understand what it is. It is not a disease. It is a symptom. When we speak about "colic" we are acknowledging the presence of abdominal pain in a horse. Experts estimate it killed five million horses in 2008 alone or one horse every fifteen seconds. That is why it is critically important for a Long Rider to know how to recognize the signs of colic and understand what steps must be taken to protect the horse's life.

Knowing what might cause your horse to colic is the first step in his defence. Horses with weak digestive organs are predisposed to this condition. A change in diet can upset the digestive system. If possible, you should try to introduce the horse to a new food source gradually, feeding him sparingly until his digestive system has adapted. Feeding unsuitable food instigates colic. Mouldy hay or damp fodder often ferments in the horse's intestines, causing severe colic. Ingesting too much dry food without proper watering may block the intestines and produce colic. Overfeeding can set off a colic attack. If you miss a meal, don't try to appease your sense of guilt by giving the horse twice as much next time. Feeding at irregular times may not provide the horse enough time to digest his meal properly. The result is colic. Placing grain on the ground increases the chances of the horse accidentally ingesting sand, which causes the intestines to become impacted. To prevent the ingestion of dirt or sand, always feed grain in a nosebag, not from the ground. If a nosebag is lost, or not available, then feed the grain on a canvas tarp or a blanket. Grazing horses on severely depleted pastures increases the chances of dirt being consumed. Failing to provide salt can cause the horse to lick salty tasting earth which will block the digestive tract. A greedy horse may bolt his food. Because it has not been properly chewed, the digestion is disturbed. Colic may occur if you feed a severely fatigued horse too soon. The animal should always be allowed time to cool and recover before receiving the meal. If the horse is ridden too hard immediately after receiving a meal, colic may ensue. The animal must be allowed enough time to digest the meal before being ridden. Should a gluttonous horse gain access to a large source of grain, or any other rich feed, colic may ensue, often with fatal consequences. Colic can happen if an overheated horse is permitted to drink large quantities of water. Drinking excessively cold water can also inspire a colic attack. Severe worm infestations may block the horse's intestines and trigger colic. Consumption of foreign materials, such as old straw bedding, tree bark and rope may set off an attack of colic. Unhealthy teeth may keep the horse from chewing correctly. The consumption of improperly crushed food may cause fermentation and start colic.

Yet one of the leading culprits in colic often involves a deadly snack and the horse's greedy stomach. A strong travelling horse has a healthy appetite. But that doesn't mean he is blessed with an extraordinary amount of common sense. Should you find your horse standing over the grain bin with a fat stomach and a guilty look, you're both in trouble. Whereas the digestive system of a wild horse can cope with the small quantities of soluble carbohydrates which it occasionally consumes, one of the ill-fated side effects of domesticating the horse is that an animal whose digestive tract is not suited to large amounts of grain, can accidentally gain access to corn, wheat, barley or rich mixtures of energy-rich feed. Over-eating a large amount of grain causes the horse's digestive process to go awry, as the massive influx of soluble carbohydrates overpowers the functions of the intestines. The level of danger is connected to the amount of grain consumed. Depending on the size of the horse and its normal grain intake, even ten pounds can cause harm. But evaluating how much has been consumed can be difficult. The severity of a subsequent attack will also depend on what kind of grain was consumed and if the horse was accustomed to being fed grain. Don't make the mistake of thinking the situation isn't a medical emergency. The horse may normally be seen as being big and strong. But in this incidence it is akin to finding the baby has swallowed a belly full of poison. Depending on the severity of the attack, the horse may suffer from abdominal distension, mild diarrhoea, simple indigestion, sweating and trembling. In extreme cases death may be caused by gastric rupture. One of the worst consequences of grain overload is that the flow of blood to the horse's hooves can be interrupted. This triggers the onset of laminitis, a crippling affliction which results in the hooves becoming hot and painful. Do not wait for indications of grain overload to appear, as early treatment is essential.

There is another factor which is often linked to an attack of colic; allowing your horse to be fed and watered by an inexperienced stranger. Do not trust your horse's health and safety to others! Symptoms will range from mild discomfort to life-ending agony, depending upon the severity of the pain produced by the colic attack. The onset of colic causes the horse to stop eating and drinking. He will appear depressed and stand with his head lowered. As the digestion process begins to decline, gas build-up causes the horse's body to swell. Faecal output will decrease or alter in colour and composition as the condition worsens. The faeces normally confirm that the feed has been well-chewed and thoroughly digested. Faeces coated in an excessive build-up of thick mucus are clues to the presence of colic. Blood on the faeces indicates severe inflammation. Light-coloured faeces, accompanied by an offensive odour, indicates an inactive liver. Heavy infestations of parasites are also often seen in the faeces. The onset of mild pain causes the puzzled horse to glance back at its flanks, nip at its stomach and curl its top lip. When the stomach begins to bloat the pain increases, which in turn causes the horse to act more agitated. The animal becomes restless, paws at the ground, swishes its tail and begins pacing nervously. Male horses may drop their penis. Regardless of sex, as the case progresses horses will stretch their forelegs and lean forward until their belly nearly touches the ground. The horse makes frequent attempts to urinate. When the horse tries to defecate, only gas and small dark faeces may be passed. If the condition continues to deteriorate, the intestines may become completely blocked, as fermenting fodder causes gas to build up. A startling symptom occurs when the horse sits on his haunches like a dog. This position affords some temporary relief and will be maintained for several minutes. When the pain reaches an intense level, the horse's body is bathed in a clammy sweat. He breathes rapidly as the bloating presses on his chest. The pulse becomes fast and weak. In an effort to escape from the unrelenting internal agony, he will lie down, roll around violently, groan and then get back up. Extreme cases will see the horse staggering from side to side. The animal's limbs tremble violently, before death ceases the struggle. Do not be tricked into thinking the horse is out of danger if, after having exhibited signs of such severe pain, he makes an apparent miraculous recovery. A sharp reduction in pain and a return to normal behaviour is often brought about because the intestine has ruptured. This releases the intense pressure that inflicted so much misery but it signals the approach of death.

The detection of any sign of colic demands instant action as even a mild case can quickly evolve into an emergency. Most horses suffer from tympanic colic. Because it resembles human indigestion, it is also known as flatulent colic. Do not be fooled into thinking that this type of colic cannot lead to a speedy death. While many cases yield to rapid treatment, mild attacks can become lethal in a short time. This is the most common type of colic and can be triggered by a variety of reasons, including watering the horse when it is too hot or a radical change in the animal's diet. Many cases occur when a horse has consumed certain types of food which ferment and then cause painful gas to form in the animal's digestive tract. Mouldy hay and decayed grain are prime suspects. Likewise, lawn clippings and too much fresh green alfalfa also ferment easily. The result will be a build up of gas and intestinal impact.

Spasmodic colic is more severe. When it occurs, intense internal pressure causes the horse to roll and display signs of great pain. Obstruction colic occurs when the stomach or bowels are blocked by an accumulation of partly-digested feed, by foreign bodies, parasites, paralysis or by abnormal growths. If not promptly recognized and properly treated, this condition often results in death. Although circumstances will vary, action must be taken as soon as any symptoms are recognized; otherwise you run the risk of a minor belly ache becoming a matter of life and death. Because colic can slay a horse in a few hours, early recognition of an abdominal crisis increases the chances of saving the horse's life. You can detect signs of abnormality by placing your ear on either the right or left side of the horse's flank. Under normal conditions you will hear what are known as peristaltic sounds. This noise, which is slightly louder on the right side than on the left, is created by the wormlike contraction of the horse's intestines. An absence of any peristaltic noise suggests colic has brought about a paralysis of the intestines. Disproportionate noise can be caused by the presence of excessive of gas or fluid in the intestinal canal. Seek the assistance of a veterinarian without delay! The availability of a medical professional, as well as his competence, will vary according to what country you are in. If you can establish telephone contact, provide as many details as you can and request immediate aid.

The onset of colic demands a cool head, fast action and efficient organization. Thus, time and ignorance are your immediate adversaries. If the horse suffers a colic attack while you are travelling, unsaddle him or loosen the girth as much as possible. If you must continue to travel in order to find medical assistance and safety, walk alongside. Allow the horse to proceed slowly and rest often. Prevent him from eating. Should the attack occur while the horse is stabled, withdraw all food at once. Allow the horse to retain access to water, but hay, and especially grain, must be removed until normal intestinal functions are resumed.

Try and establish the cause of the colic. Successful treatment is often linked to an accurate diagnosis, so identifying the origin of the problem is a priority, as colic is a progressively dangerous situation. Regardless of the initial cause, blockage of the digestive system results in gas build-up and fluid accumulation. This in turn creates an increasing amount of pain. The onset of flatulent colic may cause so much agony that the condition worsens into spasmodic colic. The onset of severe gut ache may cause the horse to lie down and then roll violently to try and break free of the stomach-ache. Do not leave the horse unattended. Keep him under close observation. Prevent him from lying down. Do not let him roll, as this may result in a twisted gut, which in turn can cause sudden death. Walking the horse slowly may help relieve cases of mild colic, as it improves the chances of the intestines functioning. But do not force the horse to undertake excessive exercise. Never trot or gallop a horse with colic. Massaging the lower stomach gently with straw may provide some relief. If there is any chance of chill, cover the horse to keep him from catching cold. In cases of colic there is no time to waste and chances of recovery depend on beginning treatment without delay. After the veterinarian has established the cause of the problem, and diagnosed the specific type of colic, he will begin efforts to reduce the swelling, empty the bowels and stop the cycle of pain. Oral medication is usually the first step in trying to re-start the digestive process. Certain cases may require the veterinarian to pass a tube through one of the horse's nostrils and into the stomach. This procedure permits the doctor to discover clues as to what type of blockage has taken effect and where it is located. After the tube has been inserted, the doctor can then administer a dose of mineral oil directly into the horse's stomach. This works as a laxative and can help break up the blockage and dispel the gas build-up. Never attempt to administer a stomach tube unless you are a trained professional, as the results can be fatal to a horse if done improperly. Likewise, never shoot mineral oil into the horse's mouth with a syringe! It is easy for the oil to enter the lungs accidentally, which in turn can produce a fatal case of pneumonia.

Alternatively, the doctor may decide to administer an enema to moisten the faeces, increase the natural motion of the intestines and stimulate a recovery. Impaction colic often responds to this treatment, as it loosens the faeces and encourages the restoration of normal digestive processes. If colic strikes while you are travelling in a country without adequate veterinary care, then administering the enema yourself may be the only option. Start by wrapping the horse's tail in a bandage or a disposable cloth. To reduce the risk of injury, the horse must stand quietly during the procedure. If you are alone tie the horse securely, otherwise have someone hold the lead rope. A human enema bag, which is widely available in many countries, may be used for the procedure. These bags come in various sizes. Never use a garden hose to perform an enema. If a larger bag is available, mix 1 gallon (3.78 litres) of warm water with 1 pint (.50 litre) of mineral oil. If mineral oil is not available, use soapy water. The liquid should be 90 to 100 degrees Fahrenheit (32 to 37 degrees Celsius).

This procedure calls for great caution, to ensure that the rectum is not lacerated, which can result in serious complications and death. To diminish the risk of injury, the end of the small hose, which is attached to the enema bag, should be lubricated with Vaseline or mineral oil to facilitate easy entry. Make sure the hose is straight and then carefully insert the end of the hose into the anus. Expect to encounter resistance from the rectum muscle after about 2 inches (5 centimetres). Gently push the hose in approximately 6 inches (15 centimetres). Once the hose is in place, lift the bag above the horse's flanks and let the liquid enter the bowels. It may take a few minutes for this to take effect. To reduce the chances of being kicked, do not stand directly behind the horse while you are waiting. Move to one side, keeping your body pressed lightly against the side of the horse. This will allow you to detect the horse's movements, while you keep a careful eye on the bag. After the liquid has drained, remove the hose slowly and carefully. The combination of warm liquid and mineral oil will begin to loosen the impacted faeces. It may require a second application before the horse begins to eject dark water and manure. If the colic is caused by a twisted intestine, then only a small amount of water will enter.

Once the veterinarian has confirmed the restoration of normal digestion, the horse can be permitted frequent short meals in a pasture or several small feeds of hay during the course of the day. If you are feeding hay, it helps to sprinkle it lightly with water. The amount of fodder can be gradually increased during the next few days, as the horse's digestive system returns to being fully functional. Even if there has been an abatement of colic signs, and the return of a healthy appetite, do not resume feeding grain. The microbial community which exists within the horse's hindgut must be allowed time to stabilize. Providing grain to the horse will disrupt the digestive recovery. If the colic has been serious, do not feed grain for two weeks. If the colic has been mild, then resume feeding grain, in small amounts, after a week. Mixing in a light amount of mineral oil helps encourage easy digestion. Regardless of the apparent recovery, keep the horse until close observation for 24 hours after the colic has been resolved.

There is always a large element of the unknown involved with equestrian travel. In normal circumstances, you are unable to predict where night will find you, nor what food might be on offer for your hungry horse. Despite the unpredictable nature of the trip, consistency represents safety in terms of dietary maintenance. Introduce new feed in slow stages. Try to feed the horse at the same time and provide the same size proportion if possible. Beware of green clover, which ferments easily, especially when it is wet or covered with frost. Provide the best quality hay available. Never feed musty or mouldy hay. Remember the "wild horse diet." Several small meals are preferable to one large one. Restrict the amount of grain fed to a minimum for the work the horse is doing. Great care must be used when feeding different types of grain. Wheat and rye are almost certain to cause colic unless they are fed in small quantities. They must never represent more than a fourth of the ration, be mixed with a more suitable grain, and always be ground or crushed. Corn can cause acute indigestion if not introduced slowly and the portion very gradually increased. It should be ground.

The length of time occupied by the stomach's digestion will vary according to the type of meal. Always allow the horse time to digest the meal before travelling. A common error is to feed too soon after a hard day's travel. The horse must have time to cool. A small quantity of hay may then be given. But the grain must be withheld for another hour. Water is often linked to colic. Do not let a hot horse over drink. Allow him a few swallows to slake his thirst and then walk him till he has cooled down. Too much dry feed and not enough water can cause trouble. Always provide access to fresh water. Ice-cold water can trigger a colic attack. Ensure the chill has been taken off the water. Always ensure the horse is supplied with salt on a regular basis. If possible, permit the horse to digest his meal in peace. Greedy horses are predisposed to bolt their food, which often causes colic. Do not let fear or jealousy ruin the horse's meal. Move rivals to a safe distance to reduce the chance of conflict. Never over-feed the horse. The best way to protect your horse from grain overload is by taking the time to ensure that he cannot escape during the night and accidentally gain access to this potentially lethal treat.

**Teeth.** If he can't eat, the horse can't travel. Before you leave, confirm the health of your horse's teeth. If preventative care is required, do not allow an unlicensed individual to gamble with your horse's health.

**Worms.** Proper equine nutrition plays an important part in any journey. You must ensure that your horse isn't losing vital nutrition to internal worms. Severe infestations can result in a horse losing weight, which in turn leads to a marked decrease in the animal's performance of his daily duties. Regardless of what type of worm has infected your horse, they all siphon off an important portion of the animal's daily intake of calories. This loss of energy is an inconvenience for horses that reside in comfortable stables and receive regular helpings of high-energy hay and grain. But road and pack horses work hard and need every atom of power they can derive from their meals. Combating worms becomes a standard part of the Long Rider's equine health plan. If you plan to travel and ride abroad, you would be well advised to carry several doses of worming medicine with you, as chances are high that the native horses you purchase will need to be de-wormed before you depart. This is especially true if you're heading into the tropics or a jungle environment. Never trust the seller on this matter. Horses which are heavily burdened with intestinal parasites are prone to breaking down under the unexpected strain of travel. An inexpensive dose of worming medicine is cheap insurance compared to the cost of replacing a horse.

**Dehydration.** Travelling horses are often exposed to high temperatures. Add in the strain of hard work and the result is a horse which generates an immense amount of body heat. Normally the process of sweating works to cool a horse down. It is not uncommon for some animals to sweat more than 10 litres (2 gallons) of water per hour. The combination of high body heat and loss of body fluids can result in the horse becoming dehydrated. The horse will appear depressed. The skin around his eyes may sink in. His skin will become dry and tight. As his body reacts to the loss of electrolytes, he will begin to experience muscle fatigue, which can lead to cramps and result in azoturia (tying up). If not treated, the condition may result in shock, then death. Because dehydration is a common problem in hot climates, you should know how to administer the simple skin test to check if your horse has become dehydrated. Under normal conditions when you pinch the horse's skin gently between your thumb and forefinger, it should snap back in place in less than two seconds. If the skin "tents," i.e. does not quickly return to normal, it indicates that your horse has become excessively dehydrated. Move the horse into the shade without delay and loosen his girth. Offer him water with a dash of salt. If you cannot provide any electrolytes to replace his body's lost minerals, rub sugar on the horse's gums. Wiping the horse with a cold wet cloth will help the animal cool down, but care must be taken not to pour cold water on large muscle areas.

**Skin Infections.** Twice-daily grooming ensures that you will quickly discover any abnormalities in the animal's skin. One of the most common skin afflictions is insect hypersensitivity. After midges, mosquitoes and flies bite the horse, bumps may erupt at the point of penetration. Wash the horse with mild shampoo and then spray him with an oil-based insect repellent. Another common ailment is hives. These itchy swellings are caused when clear fluid forms under the surface of the skin. Hives may appear because of a variety of reasons including an allergic reaction to food, an adverse reaction to medication applied to the skin or a seasonal reaction to air-borne pollen settling on the body. A rich meal of alfalfa may also cause hives. Alfalfa creates high levels of ammonia, which overloads the liver, then attempts to escape via the skin. Regardless of the cause, round, raised bumps usually form on the neck and shoulders. The first step in treating hives is to identify the source of the problem. This can be difficult because travelling horses routinely encounter a diverse daily environment which includes strange bedding and unusual food. Hives may last for a few hours or days, but the mild afflict-tion usually disappears spontaneously. If the condition persists, it may be necessary for a veterinarian to administer an intravenous injection of fast-acting corticosteroids.

**Rope Burns.** One of the most common injuries is also one of the most difficult to heal.
Because travelling horses are often permitted to graze while picketed, it is not uncommon for a long rope to become wrapped round an unwary animal's fetlock. If the rope tightens, it only takes it a few seconds for the line to cut through the sensitive skin. The result is a wound located in the hollow between the pastern and heel. Not only is this location exposed to constant contamination because of its proximity to the ground, it is also extremely difficult to immobilise the wound to encourage healing. If you discover your horse has become wrapped in his rope, the first thing is to calm him. Chances are he's been frightened for some time. So walk up slowly, speak softly and stroke his neck, before you carefully make your way towards the rope. Do not hesitate to cut the line if you believe it cannot be easily and instantly untangled from round the hoof. Once the horse is free and calm, your next goal is to establish how deep the injury is. Thoroughly wash the wound and remove any dirt or blood. Should you discover the rope has sliced through the skin and exposed tendons or bone, immediately seek the help of a veterinarian. If the wound is not that severe, you can proceed with treating it yourself. Stop any bleeding by immediately covering the wound with Wound Seal powder or EMT-gel. These are easily-obtainable, inexpensive, non-prescription, non-toxic, topical treatments that act as a

rapid anti-coagulant. Every Long Rider should carry it. Once the issue of bleeding has been resolved, take steps to offset the risk of infection. Clean the wound thoroughly with warm water and soap, being sure to remove any dirt or residue left by the rope. After the injured area has dried, trim away the hair from around the wound and then apply an antiseptic ointment or spray. This will not only kill germs, it will deter flies from bothering the wound. If the injury occurs in a remote location, and you have no access to medication, boil a teaspoonful of salt in a pint of water, then wash the wound with this warm solution. The depth of the wound will affect the decision to apply a bandage. If the cut is deep enough to have broken the skin, you will need to wrap it in gauze to help guard the injury from moisture and infection. But there is a fine line between protecting the wound and tying the covering too tightly. Be careful that the bandage does not restrict circulation or apply undue pressure. Because the horse is constantly in motion, the injured area will be subjected to movement. Regular checking is required.

**Lameness.** Sometimes when you start that day's ride, you may sense that the horse is not moving correctly. Every Long Rider should be so attuned to his horse that he can detect the onset of lameness. Never allow a sense of impatience to override your suspicions! Do not let your desire for urgent progress compromise the horse's safety. Stop the horse on the spot and dismount immediately. You cannot proceed in the saddle until you have resolved this mystery. Start by inspecting all four hooves for any obvious problems. A stone wedged in the frog will cause a horse to limp. The majority of the time this type of mild problem will be resolved within a few minutes, allowing the horse to proceed after a short rest. An unlucky horse may step on a nail. The best insurance against this type of injury is to avoid riding through construction sites or any place where old nails might be lying undetected on the ground. Depending upon the depth of the penetration, a sharp nail can cause a treacherous injury which is not only painful but carries a high risk of contamination. When this occurs, the horse will immediately go lame and attempt to avoid placing any pressure on the injured sole. Remove the nail slowly and carefully. Have a veterinarian administer a tetanus injection without delay.

**Tetanus.** Thanks to the increasing use of routine preventive immunizations, the number of horses who die from tetanus, commonly called lockjaw, has declined. Yet this lethal bacterium remains a deadly threat, especially to travelling horses. Be sure to have your animals inoculated prior to your departure. Two injections are administered four weeks apart. An immunization against tetanus is good for a year and can be increased by booster shots given at two-year intervals. Once you begin travelling, your horse will be exposed to an amazing variety of places which can harbour the tetanus virus. Pay careful attention to where you shelter the horse. Always ensure there are no sharp objects in the corral, stable or pasture which can cause an injury. The majority of horses which are infected with tetanus die. To reduce the chances of infection, make it a point of your O.A.D.A (Observation - Analysis - Diagnosis – Action) policy to promptly clean and treat any wound without delay.

**Poisonous Plants.** The vast majority of equine victims are not deliberately poisoned. They ingest a lethal substance because of their hunger, the owner's ignorance or a random accident. Long Rider horses are particularly susceptible to accidental domestic poisoning. In a controlled environment a horse grazes in a safe pasture which has been cleared of any potential plant pests or receives daily rations of clean hay in the stable. A travelling horse doesn't enjoy these routine safeties. He is continually making his way through an unfamiliar and potentially lethal environment. At the end of a long day, he arrives at another unknown locality. It is not uncommon for the tired horse to be tethered near the host's house while the Long Rider discusses that night's lodging. Growing close by are a number of visually attractive plants. Thanks to instinct and an unpleasant taste, the horse would not normally eat a poisonous plant back home. Yet as the sun sets the weary road horse wants two things, to rest and to eat. Being unfamiliar with that night's abode, a combination of curiosity and his hungry stomach tempts him into nibbling a strange new plant. The results can be devastating. The plant that looks beautiful to the home owner may be lethal to the visiting horse. Your first priority is education. Every Long Rider should take the time to determine the type of poisonous plants which may be encountered along their route. Next, always remain vigilant once you're on the move. Don't

197

count on a pedestrian home owner to know if his pretty garden plant is poisonous. That's your responsibility. If you are journeying through a variety of countries, seek up-to-date advice about what local plants to avoid. Should you suspect that your horse has ingested any type of poisonous plant, contact a veterinarian immediately. The slightest delay in obtaining medical treatment will increase the likelihood of death.

**Snakebite.** The majority of horses are bitten on the leg or the nose. No matter where the horse is hit, a rattlesnake bite delivers a deadly cocktail of three types of toxins. One destroys tissue. Another attacks blood vessels. A third wreaks havoc on the nervous system. Pain, paralysis, respiratory distress, blindness and death are all distinct possiblities. If circumstances allow, call a veterinarian without delay. Prompt care reduces the chances of tissue damage. If medical help cannot arrive quickly, arrange transport to a clinic which stocks antivenins. Should a rattle-snake strike your horse while you are travelling deep in-country, you will have to assess the situation and control the damage. If you must continue travelling in order to find help, be aware that walking will stimulate the horse's circulation, which in turn increases the chances of the venom spreading through the horse's body. Dismount and lead the horse slowly towards safety. Unless you happened to witness the attack, don't be surprised if you discover what has occur-red several hours later. You may find your horse in the pasture, for example, showing symp-toms of the poisoning such as swelling, muscles twitching, wobbling and convulsions. When a grazing horse unknowingly steps on a rattler, the snake will bite in retaliation. Leg bites are difficult for detect because the hair hides the fang marks. There is usually little swelling given that the limb has a minimum of soft tissue. The majority of horses survive this injury, unless secondary problems, such as bone infection or gangrene develop, in which case the animal may not recover. Treat a leg bite by washing the wound with soap and water, then seek medical treatment without delay.

If possible, keep the animal quiet so as to decrease the spread of the venom. Should you be forced to travel, dismount and walk the horse to slow poison absorption. Do not cut the wound open, apply ice or use a tourniquet.

Unlike a leg bite, a rattlesnake strike on the nose is far more serious as the resulting swelling can cause the horse to die from suffocation. Horses do not breathe through their mouths. They depend upon their large nostrils to supply them with air. The rattlesnake's venom will cause the nose to swell, which will close both nostrils, blocking the passage of air and resulting in death. You must keep the horse's airways open after a rattlesnake bite. If the horse is wearing a halter, make sure it is not tightly fitted around his nose, as immense swelling is imminent. Do not let the horse rub his nose, as this helps spread the venom and increases the chance of tissue damage. Travellers who routinely ride in rattlesnake country should always carry an emergency snakebite kit which contains two lengths of rubber tubing, petroleum jelly and tape. The tubing can be obtained by cutting off two six-inch lengths of garden hose. Make sure the sharp edges of the hose have been sanded smooth. Before the venom swells the nasal passages shut, place a light covering of petroleum jelly on half the tube, carefully slide it into a nostril, then tape it into place. As the nostril's swell, the pressure will help keep the tubes in place. The result may be unsightly but it will ensure that the horse can still breathe.

**Equine Infectious Anaemia** is most often transmitted by horse flies. The virus is transferred into the host when the fly is sucking blood from its prey. Equine infectious anaemia (EIA), also known as swamp fever, reproduces in the horse's white blood cells circulating through the body. Symptoms include depression, fever, decreased appetite, fatigue, rapid breathing and sweating. The disease destroys red blood cells, which leads to anaemia and results in damage to the liver, kidneys and heart. There is no cure for EIA and it can be fatal. EIA is detected by identifying antibodies in the horse's blood. Known as the Coggins Test, a negative result confirms there are no traces of the virus at the time of the test. A positive result means the horse is infected with the EIA virus. If that is the case, the results are catastrophic for the horse and owner. National governments demand a negative Coggins test before they will allow a horse to cross their border. Likewise, American state governments also require proof of a negative test prior to permitting a horse to travel within their jurisdiction. As a result, even if the EIA disease doesn't kill your horse, the vast majority of infected animals are destroyed without delay by government officials, regardless of the owner's wishes.

**Piroplasmosis.** This viral disease is not directly contagious from one horse to another. The infection is spread via direct blood transfer. The most common method of transmitting the disease is via an infected tick. There are more than a dozen different types of ticks which are known to host the parasite which infects the horse's blood. Though symptoms may vary, piroplasmosis can attack any horse, of any age, in any locale. Once the horse's blood stream has been infected with the parasites, the animal becomes a potential source which can help spread the infection. Thus even if a horse recovers, allowing this carrier of piroplasmosis into a disease-free area puts non-infected horses as risk. Piroplasmosis occurs in the majority of the world, with estimates ranging as high as 80 percent of all countries having infected horses within their borders. Those few nations who have managed to keep the disease at bay, such as Canada, Iceland, Ireland and Japan, maintain strict controls to protect their horses. The United States is a front-line nation, where occasional outbreaks of piroplasmosis have resulted in the imposition of severe equine importation regulations. This especially applies to any horses that have travelled overland from South and Central America, where the disease is extremely prevalent. Any Long Rider who wishes to bring his horse into the United States via the Mexican border should be prepared to lose time and spend money, while his animal is subjected to strict blood tests controlled by the USDA. The horse will be required to be kept in a strict, and costly, quarantine until the tests determine its fate.

**African Horse Sickness.** African horse sickness (AHS) is a highly infectious disease which affects all equines including horses, mules, donkeys and zebras. The virus has devastated large parts of the world's equine population. AHS is highly infectious but not contagious. This means that the virus is not directly passed from one horse to another. It is transmitted via the bite of an infected midge. The disease flourishes during warm, rainy weather when midges are abundant. Infection often happens between sunset and sunrise, when midges are extremely active. The onset of cold weather or a frost curtails the midge population and diminishes the chances of infection. The virus incubates for at least 14 days, after which symptoms start with a high fever of 40 to 46.5 degrees Centigrade (104 to105 Fahrenheit). As the infection attacks the horse's respiratory system, the animal stands with its legs apart and its head hanging down. Dilated nostrils, difficulty in breathing and spasmodic coughing occur as the lungs fill with liquid. A frothy discharge may pour from the nostrils. AHS is a highly infectious disease, capable of attacking all breeds of horses, and recovery is rare. Mortality has been known to reach as high as 90 percent. The onset of death usually occurs within a week.

**Biliary fever** is a malaria-like disease that is transmitted to horses via ticks. It is so prevalent in South Africa that many countries prohibit the importation of horses from that country. Because numerous horses born in the tick-infested region are carriers, they may develop some degree of immunity. However horses brought into regions infested with this fever are extremely vulnerable to infection. The deadly disease is spread when a tick transmits a parasite into the equine victim's blood. These parasites then reproduce in the red blood cells. The ticks which transmit the disease often go unnoticed due to their small size. Once they feed on their victim, the incubation period will vary from one to three weeks. Any Long Rider travelling across Africa should keep a careful eye on his horses for any sign of this viral infection. It won't be hard to spot. First, an infected horse will appear listless, act lethargic and lose his appetite. Then, due to failure in the liver, the disease causes anaemia. This results in the horse's gums looking light pink or yellow. Likewise the mucus membranes inside the nostrils and around the perimeter of the eyes will also take on this unhealthy colour. As the disease progresses the horse's breathing becomes rapid. He develops a high fever, usually exceeding 40° Centigrade (104° Fahrenheit). There is no preventative vaccine currently available to protect horses against biliary. The sooner the disease is detected, the less chance of damage or death to the horse. That is why it is not recommended that you wait until the animal's mucous membranes become discoloured, as the appearance of pale gums is confirmation that the infection has already taken hold. Blood tests can confirm the presence of bilary fever in the horse's blood. But because it can be fatal, catching the disease in advance is the best defence. Experienced Long Riders learn to carefully monitor their horse's temperatures, to check their membranes for any sign of discolouration, and keep a careful eye on the horse's diet and level of activity. At the first sign of bilary fever, treatment consisting of Tetracycline-group antibiotics, especially doxicylline, has proved effective.

**Vaccinations.** Even though common ailments such as colic, saddle sores and lameness cannot be prevented by means of an injection, the best defence is to vaccinate your horse in advance against the diseases he is likely to encounter while travelling. Consult your veterinarian prior to departure to determine which inoculations are required by law. Standard equine vaccines usually include West Nile virus, equine encephalitis, influenza and rhinopneumonitis. Travelling in remote areas will also expose your horse to the dangers of tetanus and rabies, so inoculate your horse for those problems as well. Horses should not be inoculated just before departure, as their bodies need time to respond to the vaccine. Animals who have been previously vaccinated should receive a booster. Horses which have never been vaccinated will require more time to adjust to the powerful vaccine.

**Social Critics.** Appeasing the government inspectors is required by law. You should also give careful thought to those critics of equestrian travel who may wish to undermine your journey by questioning the state of your horse's health. In an increasingly urbanized and mechanized society, there are those who wrongly believe that travelling on a horse is an inherently cruel practice. Adherents of this philosophy will attempt to use horse health as an excuse to cancel your journey. This misguided idea grants the horse a semi-sacred position and argues that it cannot be used for any but socially acceptable purposes. Animal rights activists don't understand that when done properly, Long Rider horses conclude a journey in robust health. By making welfare a daily priority, and ensuring that safety is a constant concern, the road and pack horses should conclude the journey in a stronger condition than when they departed.

**Documenting the Horse's Health.** You need to be able to offset any suspicions that your animal is ill or being treated cruelly. Do this by maintaining a written record of your horse's health. As and when the opportunity presents itself, ask a local veterinarian if he will provide you with a signed and dated document which states that your horse appeared to be in good health and was up to weight when you encountered the medical professional. This need not be a full scale examination. All you require is a brief statement confirming the horse's positive general appearance and condition. By collecting these dated statements during the course of your journey, you will be armed with factual evidence which can be presented to the legal authorities, should anyone attempt to confiscate your horse on the basis of medical or nutritional neglect.

**Quarantine.** Under normal circumstances a horse might be placed in quarantine in his native country if he was suffering from an infectious disease. In such cases the vigilant owner is nearby, the animal's attending physician is well-known and the horse usually resides in his familiar stable. Placing a travelling horse in quarantine, however, can produce unexpected and possibly deadly results. Instead of focusing on healing the equine victim, a travelling horse is placed in quarantine and thereafter treated as a potentially lethal carrier of undetected diseases. Meanwhile, the owner is often treated with suspicion by hostile government authorities. To diminish the chances of this type of diplomatic nightmare ever affecting your journey, be sure you have contacted the border officials in advance. Do not agree to place your horse in quarantine unless it is absolutely necessary. Before doing so, try to establish the rules governing his care and any cost.

**Pregnant Horses.** Many important equestrian journeys have been halted or delayed because of an unforeseen travel hazard – sex. Because a Long Rider is constantly on the move, every night presents a new challenge to the owner of a mare. In addition to finding adequate food and water, if you're riding a mare you have to take steps to make sure she is not accidentally bred by a randy stallion.

**Rest and Recuperation.** Mileage never takes precedence over justice! Horses who have suffered serious illness should never be rushed back into service, as they often suffer relapses after their first major effort. A standard 19<sup>th</sup> century medical practice recommended that a horse be permitted seven days rest for every degree of temperature over the normal temperature.

**Equine First Aid Kit.** Under normal circumstances, horses do not require medical care during a journey. Those accidents which befall them are usually not connected to a failure of Nature but are more often rooted in a human mistake. Nevertheless there is a need to prepare for the possibility of a mishap. It will pay to keep a couple of important things in mind before creating a Long Rider and equine first-aid kit. Because you always try to travel as lightly as possible, reducing weight, even in a medical kit, is a strong primary consideration. Given the sophisticated state of equine medical care that is easily obtainable in many countries, there is no need to create an extensive and heavy medical kit if qualified help can be quickly summoned via a call on a mobile telephone. Regardless if you are making a journey in your own country, or venturing further afield, it will pay to discuss your potential medical needs with a qualified equine veterinarian. Don't buy it and then fly it. Most countries have access to perfectly adequate equestrian medical supplies. Take the time to determine what is available in-country. Compare prices, not forgetting to factor in the cost of transportation, and then decide where you should purchase the necessary medical supplies. Research the legalities of transferring equine medical products across borders. Be sure to have written proof from your veterinarian so as to offset any border guard's suspicions connected to your desire to carry needles, syringes, suspicious-looking powders or pill bottles bearing a dubious foreign script. Consider the possibility that legal questions may be raised in your own country if you are discovered transporting equine medication which requires the approval of a veterinarian. Phenylbutazone, nicknamed "bute," is an anti-inflammatory medication that is available in an inexpensive paste and is commonly misused by laymen. If you have any doubt as to the legality of the medication, do not carry it. Also, be sure you ask the veterinarian how and when the drugs should be used.

The Horse first aid kit should also include: basic bandage material, gauze pads, waterproof bandaging tape, hydrogen peroxide, blood stopping powder, a can of antiseptic spray such as betadine or a bottle of iodine, insect repellent, sterile Towelettes, scissors, a sterile syringe. Travellers venturing further away from medical assistance often expand their medical kit by including a concentrated wormer paste, electrolytes, a prescription anti-inflammatory paste or gel, a course of antibiotics, eye ointment, ointment for rubs and sores, anaesthetic cream, anti-fungal salve, Vaseline to prevent chapping. If you will be travelling in an area thickly populated with rattlesnakes, then you would be well advised to carry two six-inch lengths of rubber hose, in case your horse suffers snakebite on his nose. Other items which have been carried include a collapsible bucket, antiseptic soap and a digital thermometer. Regardless of what you eventually decide to include, pay special attention to how you pack medication, so as to ensure it is not spilled or broken in transit.

**Hints.** Conditions will vary, depending upon which nation you ride through. It is your responsibility to determine what each country, and state, will entail in the way of medical documentation. The one thing you should never overlook is the need to remain calm during a medical crisis. Those who perform best in an emergency have usually taken the time to prepare for such a possibility. Steady nerves and good organization will always help see you through.

# Chapter 71 - Death on the Trail

No one can blame a Long Rider for not being preoccupied with mortality. Travelling along at the sedate pace of four-miles per hour would hardly seem to put horse and rider at risk. It is far more common to foresee our horses grazing peacefully during the course of an uneventful trip. What inexperienced travellers do not realize is that danger often approaches without warning. The consequences are swift. There is no right to appeal. There is no mercy. One minute everything is fine. The next minute you're shocked to find yourself left standing afoot. When humans and horses travel together, death sometimes sneaks into camp. The first thing to do is acknowledge that fatalities do occur during journeys. What happened may be your fault. It might be a pure accident. Regardless, it can occur. Thus, what you have to do before you depart is accept the existence of this possibility and prepare yourself for its unwelcome arrival.

**A Lack of Equestrian Experience.** No Long Rider wants to confront the death of a beloved horse. The problem is that no previous conclusive study has ever been made on this part of the equestrian travel experience.

**Ethical Obligations.** The first thing to realize is that there is a moral principle at the heart of this topic. Our initial decision doesn't lie in the armoury, it rests in our hearts. We shouldn't be preoccupied with what kind of syringe, gun or knife we use to carry out the deed. We must first realize that the subject of equestrian death involves serious ethical implications.

Making the decision to euthanize a beloved horse is always emotionally challenging, but the majority of horse owners will confront this issue close to the emotional security of their home and the physical comfort of the horse's stable. Long Riders will not have that luxury. A catastrophic accident may happen during the journey which necessitates that the horse be put down without delay. Should such an unfortunate incident occur, our first obligation is to ensure that the horse is provided with a swift and humane death. Yet the crisis is compounded by the Long Rider's isolation. Like other horse owners, Long Riders will be under a tremendous amount of stress. But they will find themselves facing an emotional crisis far from home. Their surroundings will be unfamiliar. They will be surrounded by strangers, not all of whom may be sympathetic. They may not speak the language or understand the local customs. Learning how to make the correct decisions in such a situation requires careful thought and advance planning.

**Never Underestimate the Horse.** Let's be clear about an important point. Sometimes horses die unexpectedly. Other times a traveller may have to make the painful decision to euthanize his horse. The former is difficult; the latter even more so as you may be required to act as judge and jury for your horse's life. That is why you should never underestimate the recuperative powers of the horse. Travel history is filled with amazing accounts of horses that tumbled off cliffs, shrugged off killer climates, survived raging rivers and escaped a host of other dangers. Euthanasia is a last resort. There is a fine line between ensuring there is no delay if the animal is in extreme pain and not rushing the decision to say adieu.

**Retaining Emotional Control.** Should you find yourself involved in a calamitous equestrian event, remember that you're not the first horse-human to grapple with this dilemma. This ancient inter-species relationship started when man began providing care and protection to horses. Just like Long Riders of the past, how you respond to a modern emergency will influence the outcome of events. An onslaught of emotional chaos may threaten to confuse the situation. You must remain firmly focused on the problem because every second is vital! The sudden onslaught of a medical emergency may threaten to throw you into a state of panic. Don't give in. You must keep a cool mind and find answers to difficult questions. The time will come when you look back upon these events. By retaining emotional control, you will know that your decisions were based upon careful analysis, not inspired by terror or founded in confusion.

**Evaluating the Crisis.** In order to arrive at an ethical decision, logic must rule fear. Grief must be delayed. Honesty takes precedence over emotion. Finding the answers to essential questions will help you to place the situation into its proper perspective and decide if you should order the horse to be euthanized for humane reasons. Has the horse suffered an injury which is causing it to struggle violently amidst heavy traffic or in a densely populated area? Is the horse in danger of further injuring itself or the Long Rider? Is the horse in intense pain due to a catastrophic injury? Will the presence of constant pain compromise its future? Does the medical situation involve incurable injuries such as evidence of severe shock, evisceration, abdominal contents exposed, rupture of the bowels, open fracture of a long bone leg bone or dismemberment? Even if the horse survives the immediate medical threat, what does its future hold? Will it be able to graze, get up unaided, move without assistance and keep up with its peers? Will euthanasia allow the horse to avoid incurable, excessive, and unnecessary suffering? Would transporting the horse perpetuate the pain or significantly aggravate the injury? If the prognosis is hopeless, and a veterinarian is not available, then an emergency act of mercy is required.

**A Lonely Decision.** In most circumstances there is adequate time to call a veterinarian, who will be able to judge your horse's chances of recovery and survival. Such an end-of-life discussion will help you understand the medical implications of the injury or accident which is responsible for taking your horse's life. But take heed: it is not the veterinarian's job to recommend that your horse be destroyed. He provides the information needed for you to make this difficult personal choice. Ultimately this distressing decision is yours alone. Should you find yourself isolated from expert medical advice the decision to euthanize will rest on you alone. In such a case you must be able to defend your actions legally.

**Elements of Euthanasia.** There is a vast difference between paying a veterinarian to put your horse to sleep and finding yourself forced to implement emergency euthanasia in a remote country. To avoid pain and distress requires that the technique which is used causes immediate loss of consciousness, followed by cardiac and respiratory arrest that immediately results in loss of brain function. The following information should be considered when choosing the appropriate method of euthanasia.

**Culture.** Where you ride will affect what you do because individual cultures will dictate which option is available and determine how the topic of death is collectively defined.

**Peer Pressure.** Many times there is a person nearby who is eager to pull the metaphorical trigger. Being a hunter or a rider does not automatically guarantee that a person knows how to successfully terminate a horse's life. Receiving well-meaning advice is one thing, being bullied into a premature or ill-advised decision is another. Do not ignore your instincts! They are an in-grained warning signal which has evolved over the centuries. Never allow someone with a dominant personality to dictate this decision. If it's your horse, it's your decision! Say "no" clearly.

**Legal Implications.** Ask yourself how you would react if your horse suffered an extreme injury and no veterinarian was able to respond to the emergency. Lacking any previous experience, not only will you have to judge the situation correctly, your decision to euthanize must stand up to legal scrutiny. Nations, states and cities now routinely demand that the horse's interests be protected. These legal requirements will influence your decision on how to enact equine euthanasia. The state of California, for example, maintains a legal code which oversees the enactment of the Emergency Euthanasia Guidelines for Equines.

Every act of euthanasia must be deemed humane! Certain methods have been found to cause the horse needless distress and have been declared cruel. These include electrocution with a 120-volt electrical cord, manually applied blunt trauma to the head (hitting the animal with a sledge hammer), cutting the throat without prior anaesthesia, stabbing the horse with a spear or an edged weapon, air embolism (injecting large amounts of air into the circulatory system) and the injection of non-anaesthetic chemical agents into the bloodstream. An owner who chooses such a method may find himself implicated as a criminal, as these methods are illegal and punishments are severe!

Even acceptable euthanasia methods have serious legal considerations. Most horses are put to sleep via an overdose. Yet unless you are a licensed veterinarian, it will be illegal for you to carry the barbiturates required to administer an intravenous lethal injection. Using a gun to enact euthanasia may also result in severe penalties. Draconian gun laws in some countries, such as Great Britain, have made this traditional option nearly impossible. Veterinarians in the UK advise their clients that because they are no longer allowed to routinely carry a firearm, an appointment must be made in advance before the horse can be put down via this method. In countries where guns are still widely available, such as the United States, local laws concerning the discharge of firearms will apply. Not only must a Long Rider comply with the laws govern-ing the possession of a firearm, it must be established that no local ordinances prohibit the emergency discharge of a weapon within the metropolitan area. There are also severe reper-cussions if the firearm is used in an irresponsible manner. If done properly a single lethal gunshot will inflict instant death to a horse without causing pain. Persons shooting a horse repeatedly can be charged with animal cruelty. Penalties in some American states include fines of up to $20,000 and imprisonment for up to three years.

**Reliability.** Three dependable methods are now generally used to euthanize horses. They are able to induce death quickly, without inflicting anxiety or pain to the animal. The most common is an overdose of barbiturates, which instigates cardiac arrest. The second option is the destruction of the brain caused by a gunshot or via a penetrating captive bolt gun. Finally exsanguination is the term used to describe the massive blood loss brought about after anaesthesia has been administered and the arteries are severed. While all three are effective, to be practical they require tools or drugs which must be locally available.

**Human Safety.** Each of these methods, while ethically and legally acceptable, involves basic requirements. The first of these is the need to protect the safety of the person carrying out the procedure. Forethought should include the uncertainty of how a falling or thrashing horse may react, as well the possibility of a ricocheting bullet.

**Horse Welfare.** The size and strength of the horse must also be taken into account. The method chosen must bring a quick and painless death, at the same time ensuring the safety of the Long Rider. Depending upon the animal's condition, each method will require a differing amount of restraint.

**Cost.** One basic consideration is the financial concerns involved with each option. In 2010 an English veterinarian service charges £92 to administer a lethal injection and £86 to shoot a horse. Sedation is an additional £20. You should also be aware that there will be a sizeable financial outlay to have the body buried, as large equipment is required to transport the corpse and dig the grave. One English company charges between £200-£300 for collection and disposal depending on distance travelled and whether or not it is out of hours. Once the decision has been made to euthanize the horse, it is time to consider the method.

**Lethal Injection.** Because it is fast and pain-free, administering a lethal injection of barbiturates is now the most popular method of ending a horse's life. The procedure calls for the veterinarian to inject a large dose of sodium pentobarbital. To accelerate the process, the barbiturate is often injected into the jugular vein. When properly administered, the powerful drug rapidly causes cardiac arrest. As a result, the horse quickly loses consciousness and succumbs peacefully. What is not commonly known is that a sedative must first be administered to the horse, as by itself an intracardiac injection of a barbiturate will cause pain to the animal! By first administering a large-animal sedative, such as detomidine, the horse relaxes and then slowly collapses when the barbiturate takes effect.

There are a number of positive considerations to this method. Intense pain is immediately relieved. The animal slips out of consciousness peacefully. It is less emotionally traumatic for the Long Rider. Yet there are drawbacks. While barbiturate overdose is less disturbing to observers, it is also more expensive than other options. More importantly, euthanasia via lethal injection can only be legally delivered by a licensed veterinarian. Should you be riding in a distant location or in an isolated country, telephoning the local surgery will not be an option. Another drawback is that the horse's injuries will affect the chances of successfully administering the drug. Locating a suitable vein may prove challenging if the animal is thrashing about in pain. Also, if the wounds are sufficiently serious. the horse may have lapsed into shock. This can weaken its pulse and reduce the circulation's ability to swiftly transmit the barbiturate to the animal's heart and brain. The inability to promptly locate a veterinarian who has access to the necessary drugs overrides all other concerns. If the horse has suffered a devastating injury, you can not allow the animal to linger on in great pain while a search is carried out for an available medical professional. In such an episode, you may have to take steps to shoot the horse rather than let it continue suffering. The problem is that few people know how to successfully carry out this grim task.

**Firearms.** The history of equestrian travel is filled with millions of accident-free miles and thousands of trouble-free trips. It is extremely rare that a travelling horse has had to be destroyed. When such an event occurred, having a firearm proved to be a blessing as there are a number of advantages to this method; it is inexpensive, widely available, invokes an instantaneous death and does not require physical contact with the horse. If carried out correctly, shooting a horse is quick and painless. If done improperly, it can cause further harm and create additional victims. First, you must confirm the legality of using a firearm to end the animal's life. The probability of gun ownership depends on where you make your ride. Certain nations, like the United States, encourage private gun ownership for citizens. Restrictions in other countries preclude this option. Even if a gun is legally available, there is a great deal more to shooting a horse successfully than most people realize.

**Bad Shots.** If done properly, using a firearm is reliable and humane. Choosing the proper ammunition and weapon is critically important. Knowing how to shoot an animal while hunting is not the same as understanding how to euthanize a horse with a firearm! In inexperienced hands a gun can be brutal and hazardous. Not all veterinarians know how this is done. Hollywood has traditionally depicted the cowboy standing above his wounded horse and then shooting down at the animal. This is a misconception which can have terrible results. Using a firearm to dispatch a horse must be done with great care, so as to minimize the danger of a ricochet.

**How to Shoot a Horse.** Being faced with the necessity of putting your horse down in an emergency permits no mistakes. Simply wanting to do the deed well, and doing so, are vastly different. There are several vital factors involved in shooting a horse; controlling the animal, choice of the proper firearm, position of the shooter, accurately aiming at the exact spot and ensuring no bystanders are wounded in the process. Horses can become overly excited even under routine circumstances. An injured animal will be prone to panic. If a veterinarian is available, administering a sedative will increase the chances of keeping the horse quiet. It is important to minimize the horse's anxiety by acting in a quiet, calm and reassuring manner. For the process to work properly the shot must be precisely targeted, otherwise a second shot will be required! This makes it essential that the horse not shift his head. A strong halter and an appropriate length lead rope must be in place so as to keep the horse from moving. But do not tie the horse up on a short rope, as this may cause him to pull back in fear. Some horses object to having anything brought too near their head and eyes. To increase the chances of keeping the horse calm, you may choose to blindfold the animal. Not only will this prevent the horse from shying at the critical moment, it may be of emotional assistance to the person wielding the firearm. Given proper placement, death by gunshot produces instantaneous results, as the bullet travels through the brain into the upper end of the spinal cord.

Employing the wrong type of firearm or ammunition is inhumane and dangerous. A handgun is preferred because there's no need for other personnel besides the person pulling the trigger. The shooter can hold the horse's lead rope in one hand and the pistol in the other. If a rifle or shotgun is the only firearm you have access to, the shooter will need to recruit someone to hold the horse on a loose lead. The assistant should stand behind the shooter. Should a handgun be chosen, be sure the ammunition is powerful enough to dispatch the horse with a single shot. The smaller .22 calibre bullet might not have sufficient velocity and mass to penetrate the skull, especially in the case of a large animal. The horse may be rendered unconscious if the shot is not lethal. In such a case, exsanguination will also be required. For euthanasia with a handgun to be assured, a larger calibre such as a 9mm, a .38 or .357 should be employed. Likewise, be sure not to use a small .22 calibre rifle. The bullet should be .223, .308 or 30 calibre to ensure certain death. Regardless if a handgun or rifle is chosen, soft-nosed hollow-point ammunition is more appropriate than full metal jacket bullets. Should a shotgun be the only option, a rifled slug .410 gauge or larger must be used.

A horse in pain is liable to move unexpectedly. The last thing you want to do is further wound the animal. To shoot a horse correctly, the individual should stand directly in front of the animal. If the horse is lying prone on the ground, then the individual must kneel close to the animal's head. If you are using a pistol, it should be positioned perpendicularly to the forehead. Do not place the muzzle directly against the horse's head! Hold the muzzle about three inches away from the horse's skull. Not only will this distance allow the bullet to gain more velocity before striking bone, the firearm might explode in your hand if the gas and gunpowder are confined within the barrel.

A scientific study was made on the trajectory of bullets used to euthanize horses. The most common mistake was aiming the weapon improperly! If the gun is held at the wrong angle the round will miss the brain. When done correctly, only one bullet is needed as the bullet passes through the brain and enters the spinal column, causing instant and painless death. However the placement of this one shot is dependent on the angular direction of the bullet. Where you aim the firearm is species-specific, so targeting a horse will differ from other animals. The horse's brain occupies a relatively small portion of the head. This helps explain why the tendency is to aim too low between the horse's eyes! Horses vary greatly in size, ranging from giant draft horses to petite ponies. Despite this variance, there is no need to guess where you point the gun.

Picture an imaginary X on the forehead. The ears and eyes mark the four corners of the X. The middle of the X is found to be a little above the twirl of hair in the centre of the forehead. Take aim at the centre of the X. Given proper placement, death by gunshot produces instantaneous results, as the bullet travels through the brain into the upper end of the spinal cord.

Regardless if the horse is in an unnatural position, such as twisted or entrapped, aim directly at the X. This will help ensure a safe knockdown and help keep the bullet from injuring a bystander. You must take into account how and where the horse will react. The animal will usually collapse where it stands. But occasionally the horse will lunge forward. To minimize the chances of being injured, be sure you have left yourself room to manoeuvre. Expect the limbs to reflex and the muscles to twitch. There will be a certain amount of bleeding from the wound and the nostrils. Cover this discharge with earth.

Emotions run high when a horse is badly injured. If you are performing emergency euthanasia to alleviate the animal's suffering, you must remain calm when using the firearm as your actions may place others at serious risk. Any time a firearm is employed, you must consider the environment around the accident site before you pull the trigger. Because a bullet may emerge and still travel a great distance, do not fire if anyone is standing behind the animal. Because a bullet may ricochet, do not fire in an area where a missed shot might bounce off a hard surface and wound someone. If possible, hiring an experienced veterinarian is recommended. In an extreme situation you may enlist the aid of a police officer. Because of the risk of injury to the horse and bystanders, do not chose the latter option unless you have confirmed that the officer knows exactly where to place the shot.

**Exsanguination.** This term is derived from the Latin "ex" (drained of) and "sanguin" (blood). It is a complicated term for a simple act wherein massive blood loss prevents the precious fluid racing from the heart to the brain. Unfortunately a great many clichés exist about this method of euthanasia. One misconception is that the animal does not feel any pain. That is true for a lethal injection but not massive blood loss. Another mistake is to think the horse dies immediately. That is correct for a fatal gunshot but not when the throat is cut. Equestrian reality is different from pedestrian romance! A horse isn't like a laptop. You don't push a button, turn it off, then walk away all neat and tidy. Things get blood-soaked and messy when you attempt to slay a horse with an edged instrument!

A large animal goes into a state of wild terror as its blood is being lost. Because it cannot comprehend what has occurred, the animal experiences great fear, remains conscious, is fully mobile and will fight madly in an attempt to escape! Nor is it quick. Even after its jugular and carotid arteries had been severed, and with an elevated heart rate brought on by panic, it usually takes the animal more than a minute to die. That seems like an eternity when you are witnessing it. So the question then is when and how can you use employ exsanguination to end a horse's life? Regardless of what method of euthanasia is chosen, minimizing stress and relieving pain to the horse is always of fundamental importance. This is especially true with exsanguination, as even a horse suffering from shock will exhibit incredible distress when hypoxia (lack of oxygen) begins to take effect. Because the process is extremely painful, exsanguination should not be attempted without prior sedation, anaesthesia or a fatal gunshot! Let me repeat that. The horse must be unconscious before the fatal cut is made! Unlike the process of using a syringe or firearm, it is vitally important for the person undertaking the exsanguination to know what to expect.

**Beware of Cultural Prejudices.** Do not mistake cultural practices with equestrian ethics! Preparing a meal is different from putting down your horse. Islamic and Jewish law forbids the adherents of those religions to consume the blood of dead animals. To avoid this religious taboo, Muslim and Jewish butchers practice halal and kosher methods, both of which mandate slaughter by exsanguination to rid the body of blood. Both religions also forbid the eating of dead animals, which are regarded as carrion. This means that pre-slaughter paralysis is not allowed. This combination of no-blood and not-dead means that Muslim and Jewish butchers cut the neck without first stunning the animals. The needs of a Long Rider should not be confused with the dietary laws of any religion!

**Be Properly Equipped.** The process of exsanguination must not be attempted without the proper equipment. Because of its extraordinary sharpness, a surgical scalpel might seem like the perfect tool. In fact the horse's tough skin and thick musculature in the neck may break a thin scalpel blade. Nor is the common three-inch blade found on a Swiss-army style pocket knife sharp or strong enough. Exsanguination requires a strong knife with a blade length of at least seven inches. Moreover, the blade must be extremely sharp. In skilled hands, a properly honed blade severs nerves and arteries instantly. A blade that is nicked or dull inflicts pain as it tears the flesh.

**Understand the Biology.** To undertake a successful exsanguination you must know a few critical facts about the horse's biology. The operation will be focused on that part of the horse's anatomy known as the jugular groove. Ideally it should be known as "grooves," as this feature is located on both sides of the horse's neck. Regardless of which side you pick, there will be an indentation just above the windpipe. Inside this portion of the horse's neck are the jugular vein and carotid artery. Do not confuse their functions. Many people mistakenly believe it is the jugular vein that spouts blood if it is severed. De-oxygenated blood flows from the horse's head back to the heart via the jugular. It is easier to halt blood flow from a vein than from an artery. The carotid artery carries the blood in the opposite direction. When you feel the pulse throbbing in the jugular groove, it is the carotid artery that is tasked with carrying oxygenated blood from the horse's heart to its brain. For exsanguination to be quick and effective, the carotid artery must be severed. Cutting the jugular vein is also recommended.

**Anticipating Resistance.** Regardless of any wounds, including broken legs, no horse willingly surrenders its life. It will fight to protect itself in a variety of ways. This may result in a struggle that can injure a person who is emotionally unprepared. Exsanguination should never be attempted unless you have taken steps to protect yourself against serious injury! A strong halter should be snugly fitted. Likewise a lengthy lead rope should be firmly attached to the halter. Location is critical, not only because of the amount of blood which the procedure will produce but to ensure that the person can avoid being hurt if the animal begins to struggle. Prior use of a gunshot, or the injection of a powerful sedative, will cause the horse to collapse to the ground, at which point the exsanguination can take place. Never attempt to use a knife to euthanize a horse if it is fully conscious and standing! If the animal is not unconscious, it will feel the blade penetrating the body. This is not only unethical and cruel; it also places the human in danger!

This method of euthanasia requires a tremendous amount of self-confidence. Having a knife with an acutely sharp point is vital. Once the horse has been incapacitated by a shot or injection, the knife is thrust in strongly at a point just behind the point of the jaw. The knife is then pulled down strongly so as to sever the carotid artery, the jugular vein and the trachea. To quicken blood loss, the procedure can be repeated on the other side of the jugular groove. How quickly, or even if, the horse dies, depends on a number of factors; what was cut, how deep, the position of the neck and body. If the procedure has been carried out efficiently, then the carotid artery and jugular vein have been severed. Cutting the carotid artery ensures that the oxygen-rich blood flowing to the brain has been interrupted. Severing the jugular vein will damage the heart's ability to pump blood. The result will be death but not without physical and emotional consequences. The carotid artery and jugular vein are large. When they are disconnected the tremendous pressure of the heart causes a large volume of blood to flood out of the body. It is not uncommon for blood to spray everywhere. Add to that the increase in blood pressure caused by fear and panic, and you have a very messy death. Moreover, if the weather is cold, the hot blood will cause steam to rise. Body posture will affect the rate of blood loss and the onset of death. If a fully-conscious horse is stuck with a knife while it is still on its feet, the animal will struggle violently while it bleeds to death. It is not uncommon for the process to take twenty seconds or more before the animal collapses. After the animal has fallen, it will kick violently, especially the back legs, attempt to run, try to rise, roll from side to side, all the while blood continues to be released. It often takes more than a minute for the blood loss to become lethal. Even after the animal has died, it is not uncommon for the muscles to twitch and the legs to kick.

Thankfully, the mathematical probabilities of a Long Rider being required to euthanize a horse via exsanguination are extremely small. Yet if such a rare incident should ever arise, you must take steps to ensure that you are in control of the situation before permitting your animal to be slain in this manner. Do not allow panic to frighten you into a decision! Do not be rushed into a decision by a well-meaning but uneducated onlooker. Do not agree to enact exsanguination if a lethal injection or a fatal gunshot is available instead. Do not attempt the procedure unless the horse has first been shot or heavily sedated. Do not attempt it unless you are emotionally confident, properly equipped, have the horse under control and are in a place which can handle the disarray!

**Other Considerations.** Unfortunately, deciding to put your horse down and enduring the process is not the end of it. Regardless if the incident involves an accidental death or euthanasia, there will be medical, legal, financial, environmental and emotional concerns to contend with. Verification of death is essential, either by you or the veterinarian. Strict legislation regarding equine burial is increasing. If the horse has died of natural causes or been shot, things are relatively simple in terms of environmental concerns, the main one being that the burial spot must not result in contamination of ground water, such as a stream or well. If the horse has been euthanized via lethal injection it may not be possible to bury the animal because of biosecurity concerns. Whether the horse has been euthanized or died from an accident, do not delay the burial. Rigor mortis causes the body to become stiff an hour after death. This makes it very difficult to move the deceased animal. If your horse is insured, protect your rights by making a timely notice to the insurance company. Ensure that you document your efforts. Keep a written record of who you spoke to, what was said, what time you contacted the company, etc. Obtain the names and contact details of witnesses, especially the attending veterinarian, who can verify your attempts to involve the insurance company's representative without delay.

**Hints.** Every horse has the right to receive justice and protection from the hands of the human who rode it! As far as possible, the horse should be protected from pain. Should the situation require the animal to be put down, you must ensure that euthanasia is carried out professionally, that it is done without cruelty and every effort has been made to reduce fear. Travel has always involved a certain degree of peril. Illness, injury and death may unexpectedly strike our horses. Taking the time to deal with death isn't paranoia. It's a sign of responsibility and maturity. Regardless of what country you ride through, you should have given careful thought to how you might deal with a life or death situation. Having answers in advance, knowing how to enact humane euthanasia in that country and being emotionally prepared, will save you and your horse from additional heartache and pain.

# Section Five – The Journey

## Chapter 72 - A Day in the Saddle

When do I wake up? How much time should I allow to to feed the horses, pack up camp, load the gear and tack up in the morning? How should I start each day's journey? How fast should I ride? Do I walk, trot or canter? Do I always stay in the saddle or should I walk sometimes? How do I handle the pack horse? What about lunch for me and the horses? When do I water them? How often do I rest the horses during a day's travel? How many miles should I hope to travel every day? What kind of obstacles and delays may await me? When do I start to think about stopping for the day? What kind of place should I look for? How do I conclude the day's ride? What must I never do when unsaddling at the end of the day? Do I picket, hobble, highline, free range or stable my horse? What should I check for before leaving my horse in a strange stable? What do I feed the horse? What if there is absolutely nothing to feed the horse? Where will I sleep at night?

These aren't the kind of questions you answer from the comfort of your chair while sitting beside the fireplace at home. The answers to these mysteries can only be found in one place; the saddle!

**Standing on the Threshold.** Without realizing it, you've already begun your journey, for you stand on the threshold of a new way of life. Yet an equestrian journey is more than the outcry of our elemental passions and a gallop towards our longed-for freedom. The way we organize our daily affairs is of critical importance, as there is much to do and few enough hours in which to do them. To set off cloaked in enthusiasm is one thing. To arrive much later at our distant destination, wise and travel-stained, is a far different proposition. Clues to how to maintain a daily and weekly routine can be found by studying the practices of the great Long Riders of the past, as they left records which demonstrate how to successfully accomplish each day's journey, one step at a time.

**Long Rider Lessons.** By doing things carefully, in order, throughout the day, miles are gained, all the while decreasing the chances of inflicting hardship on the traveller or the animals.

At the conclusion of her 1939 ride from Cornwall to Scotland, Margaret Leigh left a warning for would-be Long Riders. "In our kind of travel you have roads and maps and farms and a good climate; but you have also to do all your own animal management, packing, camping, cooking, photography, writing and surveying, as well as the mere physical activity of getting from one point to another. It is all great fun, but it takes time and effort, and the first few days will always be a trying period of experiment, delay, fatigue, and minor annoyance, in which a lively sense of humour is more valuable than the most foolproof equipment. Trial will show that on this kind of travel you will spend nearly as much time and effort on camp work and packing as on the march itself."

Regardless of where other Long Riders have journeyed, they have all left similar messages. A German said, "One to one and a half hours should be allowed for getting ready to travel." An American wrote, "I always set aside two hours every morning to feed, groom properly, pick out hooves, pack my gear and saddle up correctly." A New Zealander advised, "No matter how far you ride, the two-hour morning routine won't get any shorter or easier."

**Rise and Shine – and Work.** The exact time you rise will alter, depending upon the time of year. Regardless, plan on your day beginning early for two consistent reasons. Because they go to sleep early, horses are early risers who have a demanding appetite. Also, the horse should be allowed enough time to have comfortably finished his morning feed well before starting that day's travel. Attending to the horse's needs is your immediate daily task. Avoiding any haste and excitement while doing so is the first order of the day.

**Dawn Inspection.** If there are two or more of you travelling, then the first one with his boots on checks on the horses. Even if you're riding alone, this part of your routine never varies. Your brain may still be sleepy but your eyes need to automatically register the facts. Does your horse stand alert and expectant when you approach? Is his head raised? Does he neigh when he sees you? As you approach closer, is his head up and are his eyes bright? Is there any irregularity in the way he moves? Can you see if his legs are free of wounds or swelling? Does he act eager for his morning feed or is he lethargic, inattentive and anxious? Before you begin to prepare his morning feed, look for evidence that he finished all of his feed from last night's feeding? Is his manure well-formed or does he show signs of diarrhoea? Can you tell if he has drunk during the night?

**Morning Feed.** The morning routine depends on how many are travelling in your party. If there are at least two of you, then one person can attend to the horse's morning needs while the other Long Rider begins to prepare breakfast. Regardless of how many are travelling, the first chore is to water the horses. They may react indifferently to being offered a drink, especially in cold weather, preferring to take only a few sips. Nevertheless, it is always water before grain, never in the opposite order!

Because Long Riders are constantly on the move, there will be mornings when the horses will have to be brought in from a nearby field. Chasing frisky horses before you've rubbed the sleep out of your eyes is never a pleasant way to start the day. A smart Long Rider foresees this problem. Prior to departure, he trains the horse to associate coming up in the morning with a quick reward of tasty grain. This is an easy task, which begins by approaching the horse in a field while carrying grain in your hat. It won't take long for a clever horse to associate the sound of the delicious grain being shaken in the hat with your approach. After you begin travelling, you can rely on the horse's memory of this grain trick to make catching him easier in the morning. It can even be used if he unexpectedly runs away, as by shaking pebbles in your hat you can imitate the sound of grain being offered.

Feeding grain to travelling horses will depend upon availability, finances and culture. Equestrian nations such as Mongolia do not grain their horses. Sometimes you may not be able to obtain it, even in a country where such practices are routine. Perhaps your pocketbook won't allow the extra expenditure. However, if you do grain your horses then plan on splitting each day's ration into three parts; a quarter in the morning, a quarter at midday and 2 quarters given when the day's work is over. As soon as the horses have drunk, place one third of their daily grain ration in their feed bags and then allow them to quietly enjoy their morning meal. If time allows, after the horses have finished their grain you may allow them to graze nearby while you begin clearing up camp.

**Tacking up.** Your work begins as soon as the horse starts eating his grain. Time is of the essence in the morning. What you eat for breakfast, and how long you spend preparing it, will affect your departure time. Better to have a light meal that is easy to arrange and then get on the road without delay. Be careful about beginning the day's activities before sunrise. Even if the idea is to avoid the onset of the sun's heat, feeding is more difficult in the dark, saddles may not be accurately adjusted and articles are often left unseen in camp. Prior to cleaning the horses, make sure the saddles and tack are in order. Eleventh-hour repairs should only be made if they are absolutely unavoidable. Unless the problem will cause injury, it is better left alone at this moment and the repair done at the end of the day. After the horses have had time to eat and digest their morning meal, they should be carefully groomed. Pay close attention to their hooves. If they are shod, make sure that all the nails are properly set and the shoe is sitting tightly against the hoof. Bunched hair under the saddle can cause pain and lead to a sore back. That is why, according to ancient custom, Mongols always made sure to face their horses into the wind when saddling, so as to decrease the chance that the hair on the horse's back be blown the wrong way. Many horses learn to inflate their belly while the girth is being tightened. This causes inexperienced riders to routinely over-tighten the girth before mounting. Do not secure the girth too forcefully! It should only be snug enough to keep the saddle from moving, not so tight as to cause the horse discomfort. If properly secured, you should be able to slide two fingers between the girth and the horse's stomach. This is especially important in the morning, as you won't be mounting up and riding out of camp. You want the saddle to be in place, not screwed down tight. Trust this task to no one. You must be absolutely certain in your own mind that the work has been done correctly.

**Setting Off.** Do not water your horse immediately before you begin the day's journey. Travel only when it's light. Do not mount up and begin riding immediately! Start the day's march by walking alongside the horse for fifteen minutes. This allows his muscles to limber up, stimulates the circulation of blood to his hooves, and allows the horse's back muscles to become used to your weight. Use this time to check the action of the horse's movements. After a quarter of an hour, halt, check the adjustment of the saddle, tighten the girth and prepare to mount.

**Mounting Up.** After walking alongside the horse for fifteen minutes, find a safe place to stop. Then check to make sure the saddle and tack are all in accord, as any maladjustment will usually show up during the first walk of the morning. This is especially true if you started at dawn, when the light is poor and some minor detail in saddling may have escaped your notice. Take this opportunity to tighten the girth, leaving enough room for the horse to breathe easily and being sure not to wrinkle the skin.

**In the Saddle.** Never set off until everyone is mounted and ready to depart! Once you are under way, lead out in the prearranged direction. Always keep one horse length away from the horse in front of you. Few riders realize the potential trouble they inflict upon their horse by riding in a sloppy manner. If you ride the horse badly, the distance won't become shorter. Careful handling ensures a longer-lasting horse. Rough handling is a sure sign of incompetence on behalf of the rider. Don't fret with the reins. Ride with quiet hands and never pull back and forth on the bit. It's made of iron and a horse's mouth isn't made of steel. Always keep your eyes on the move, watching far ahead for trouble, glancing down to check on your horse, throwing a swift look back at the pack horse, then sweeping round in all directions. No matter how tired you may become, never slouch in the saddle. If you feel yourself starting to slump, then the time has come to dismount.

**Dismounting.** Too many modern Long Riders swing aboard and then mistakenly stay in the saddle during the course of a long day's travel. This is a fundamental equestrian error! Dismounting helps the horse. Every Long Rider should dismount and walk beside the horse for a portion of every hour, as this practice produces benefits for both horse and human. Walking is good for the Long Rider as it offsets cramp. It prevents the traveller from getting lazy and rolling in the saddle. It has the further advantage of bringing into play other muscles besides those exerted in riding. Always remain flexible in terms of when you dismount and walk alongside the horse, as every bit of assistance you provide favours him in the long term. Even a few minutes walking provides significant relief to the horse as it relieves the weight on his back, allows his muscles to relax and restores vital blood circulation to his skin. Steep hills are particularly suitable places to relieve horses by dismounting and walking. It is equally important that you do not sit on your horse when halted. Dismount at every stop, however short! The relief to the horse is immense. When you halt for a rest, don't forget to loosen the horse's girth. He, too, is entitled to be comfortable and to breathe freely.

The welfare of your horse is a never-ending priority. Compromising your comfort is part of travelling in an ethical manner. Mixing walking with riding should be part of your hourly routine.

**Rest Halts.** It is a mistake to climb into the saddle and stay perched there like an obstinate tyrant. Your horse's health, especially the sensitive nature of his back, must be of constant consideration. To help reduce the strain placed on the road horse's back, each day's journey should include hourly halts. The first halt should be made after travelling 45 minutes or about two miles. This rest stop is important as it will allow the horse time to stale (urinate). Allow fifteen minutes for the horse to stale, rest, shake and grab a few mouthfuls of grass before proceeding. After the first halt you should travel for 50 minutes and then allow the horse a ten-minute rest every hour. After three to four hours travel, you should allow the horses a longer rest. Time and circumstances may not allow you to off-saddle. However you should loosen the girth so as to relieve pressure on the back and to encourage circulation of the skin to be restored.

212

These halts are primarily made to protect the health of the horses. But discipline and common sense dictate how, when and where you rest. Horses must never rest along the edge of the road. Always move them well away from the traffic. Never halt on a curve, close to a railroad crossing or near the crest of a hill. Always look for shade in summer or protection from the wind in winter. Particular care should be taken in choosing where you take the first halt of the day, as Long Riders may wish to attend to personal matters or relieve themselves. Once the spot has been chosen, always dismount at once.

Before departing after an hourly halt, sufficient time should be allowed to allow you to carefully inspect and when necessary adjust the saddles and equipment. The time spent on this minor chore is well spent, since this precaution helps prevent trouble later in the day. The rest period made in the middle of a long day's journey is termed the noon halt. How much time you spend on this important halt depends upon local conditions, weather and the length of that day's travel. If you are going to be in the saddle longer than six hours, then you should plan on giving the horses an extended noon halt. Allow the horses at least an hour to eat and digest their afternoon ration of grain. If the rest is a long one, the horse will be eager to graze or may even doze after finishing his grain.

Hot weather will also influence the decision about a noon halt and how long it should be. Don't be tempted to take a relaxing afternoon siesta, as unnecessarily-long halts on the road should be avoided. It is always best to arrive at that night's destination as early as possible, as this will provide the horse with a far better rest.

Be careful not to automatically pull either the riding or pack saddles off the horses, as what you perceive to be an act of charity may in fact cause immediate harm to their hot and sweaty backs. Loosen the cinches on the riding and pack saddle. Remove the panniers from the pack horse.

**Watering.** It is of the utmost importance that your horses be frequently watered while travelling. The usual practice of watering before his morning feed should of course be adhered to. But horses may be reluctant to drink in the morning, especially if the weather is cold. They are however often anxious to drink after they have set off. No matter what the weather, travelling is a hard business. Too-infrequent watering will have a serious effect on the horse's condition. Never pass up an opportunity to offer your horse a refreshing drink from any clean source of water you encounter. A small quantity is far better than a copious draught and far less dangerous. Offer the horse his first drink after you have been travelling for at least 30 minutes and it has been at least an hour since he was grained. After that, if circumstance permit, plan on watering them on average once every two hours. If you find a water source during the day's ride, you can permit the horse to drink with the bit in his mouth, as this does not interfere with his drinking. Then move on promptly so as to prevent chilling and possible foundering. During a short ten-minute halt water can be given at once. If the halt is to be longer the horses must be allowed to cool off before watering. At the end of the day, remove the bit and lead the horse to drink in his halter, as if he is very thirsty he may drag you into the water. No horse should be permitted to leave until every horse is finished drinking.

**Feeding during the Day.** When you come across clean grass, dismount and permit the horse time to graze. If this happens to coincide with the ten minute halt you and the horse enjoy at the end of every hour's ride, fine. But do not restrict the practice only to rest halts. While permitting your horse to stop and graze is recommended, allowing him to snatch at grass while you are travelling together puts your safety at risk. A horse whose mind is occupied on grabbing a few mouthfuls may well lose his balance, trip over something, or be startled by an unexpected noise. Do not let the horse's hunger put your combined safety at risk. If you want to let him eat, then stop, dismount and allow him to graze. The other exception to always seeking food is to never allow your horse to feed on grass cuttings from a mown lawn. This grass, which is often moist and hot, can quickly cause severe colic.

**Concluding the Day's Ride.** You always walk the first mile to supple the horse. Likewise, you should also walk the last mile to cool him. When your day is coming to an end, dismount and loosen the girth.

**Nightly Routine.** Your work starts when the horse stops! It is an inflexible rule of the road that you must always see to your horse's welfare before your own. Though it requires diligence and discipline to begin the ride soon after daybreak, this will ensure that you will have completed the journey by early afternoon. An early conclusion provides your horse with vital time to feed and rest. You should start looking for a suitable camp in mid-afternoon, to ensure that you will have enough light to do chores, which will include negotiating with the locals, tending to your horses, feeding yourself, and if time allows maintaining your diary or updating your internet presence.

**Off Saddling.** While the majority of modern equestrian travellers would not knowingly subject their horses to any sort of unkindness, they inadvertently place the animal at grave risk when they off saddle incorrectly. There is a danger when the day's march is completed. By removing the saddle in haste you expose the horse's hot and sweaty back to cool air, which increases the risk of swelling and saddle sores. Therefore it is critically important that you take steps to protect the horse's back at all costs or risk inflicting a harmful saddle sore. Instead of instantly removing the saddle, loosen the girth and leave the saddle in place until there is no sign of sweat or heat under the saddle blanket. This practice allows the horse's back to cool, all the while blood flow is restored and the fluid gradually dissipates. Always lighten the road horse's load before you begin off saddling by removing the cantle roll and saddle bags. When travelling with a pack horse, loosen the girth after arriving at camp and remove the panniers.

**Grooming.** It might seem obvious, but your horse's welfare is always the number one priority. After carrying you all day, he is tired and hungry. Take care of him without delay, unless you want to continue the rest of your journey on foot. After off saddling, always run your hand down his withers, spine and sides looking for sore spots, lumps, bruises, blisters, chafing or rubs. Pay special attention to the girth area, which might have been galled. Examine the state of the shoes at the termination of each day. Pick out his feet with care, removing any gravel and rectifying any problems without delay.

**Feeding at Night.** It is a mistake to feed and water the horse too soon after you arrive. Watering is as important as feeding, as thirst very quickly reduces the horse's ability to travel and work. But care must be taken that the horse is not watered until he has cooled off. Loosen the girth and allow him to rest in the shade. This will not only allow his back to cool, it will encourage the blood needed to replenish his digestive system to circulate, as too many demands on his system might cause an attack of colic. If you have been riding in extremely cold weather, take care not to water a horse immediately upon concluding the ride. He must have time to rest; otherwise the cold water encountering his heated organs will induce colic.

Water should always precede feeding. After the horse has cooled, he should be allowed to drink his fill. If this requires you to take the horse to a muddy stream, dry his legs and heels afterwards. This is especially important in cold weather. Then allow him to feed on a small an amount of hay while you are grooming him. Once he is cleaned, feed the horse his nightly grain ration. Be sure to check the adjustment and fit of the nose bag when the grain is given. Give him his largest feeding at night, rather than in the morning just before a day's work. Hay or other roughage helps digestion of the concentrated grain ration. Before going to bed, give the horse a generous amount of hay. This will keep him quiet and busy during the first part of the night. Giving him a hearty meal at night is also better for his digestion than allowing him to feed to heavily prior to setting off on that day's journey.

**End of the Evening.** Always check on the horses before you slide into your sleeping bag. Don't spend too much time around him after the end of the day's ride. Weighed down by his evening meal, and tired from carrying you all day, the horse will appreciate a rest more than anything else.

**Hints.** Here is a quick summary of the day's feeding and watering. Water the horse after morning inspection. Feed 1/4 of the daily grain ration after watering. If time permits, allow grazing while camp is cleared. After at least an hour has passed since he was grained, and the horse has been travelling for at least 30 minutes, offer to let him drink. Thereafter allow him to drink as circumstances permit, trying to ensure that he drinks at least once every two hours.

214

Never pass an opportunity to allow the horse to stop and graze on clean grass. Feed 1/4 of the grain ration at the noon halt, after he has first been watered. Never feed and water the horse too soon after you arrive. Water him after he has cooled. Feed him a small amount of hay while he is being groomed. Feed 2/4 of his grain ration. Feed him the majority of his hay ration at the conclusion of his day.

# Chapter 73 - Daily Distance

There are guidelines that have been used by generations of experienced equestrian travellers. These principles still hold true and can help modern Long Riders estimate how far they can travel in a day.

**Recognizing Reality.** Our Long Rider forefathers understood that there are no guarantees in horse travel and that miles are won by great effort. Daily mileage will always vary because of the inherent difficulties associated with horse travel.

**Time not Miles.** Distance on horseback is measured in time! This is one of the oldest rules of equestrian travel and was first recorded by the English Long Rider Fynes Moryson who explored Europe extensively in 1592. He wrote, "The miles of Switzerland are so long that they reckon the journey on horseback by the hours not by the miles."

**Understanding the Challenge.** The distance a Long Rider may travel in the course of the day will depend on a number of factors, the most basic of which is the size, age and condition of the horse. Another critical aspect is how much the rider weighs and how talented a rider he is. How much gear, including saddle, bridle, saddle bags, etc., is the riding horse carrying in addition to the rider? The time of year matters too, as do the length of the days. Weather, the climate and the amount of available daylight affect daily progress, which will vary depending upon the type of terrain that is encountered. The gradient of a steep road will always delay horses. An increase in the number of horses will invariably reduce the overall progress, especially if pack horses are involved. The larger the force, the slower the progress. How much the pack saddle weighs will influence the equation. If the road horse and pack animal work well together, this can have an effect on daily events. The availability of water and grazing will add to, or hamper, speedy progress. All of these points alter the daily distance

**Rate of March.** Each of these reasons might influence daily events. However there is one aspect that is always present; the speed of the horse. Though horses differed in size, cavalry officers were able to establish that the average pace was about 78 centimetres (31 inches). Using the pace as a basic measure, riders were taught to calculate distance by determining how many paces the horse took at any of the four gaits; walk, trot, canter and gallop. Experts agreed that the speeds at which the average horse travelled were:

4 miles an hour is 1 mile in 15 minutes
5 miles an hour is 1 mile in 12 minutes
6 miles an hour is 1 mile in 10 minutes
7 miles an hour is 1 mile in 8 ½ minutes
8 miles an hour is 1 mile in 7 ½ minutes
9 miles an hour is 1 mile in 6 ½ minutes
10 miles an hour is 1 mile in 6 minutes

The fundamental gait for all cavalries was the walk. Knowing that even a slow-moving pack horse walks a minimum of three miles an hour, a cavalry officer could count on covering a minimum of 21 miles during a seven-hour day.

**Setting the Pace.** Too many modern travellers swing into the saddle and then proceed to amble down the road at a leisurely walk. Such a slovenly style is bad for the horse. These riders fail to understand a vital fact. The weight being carried by the horses is guaranteed to produce fatigue irrespective of the distance travelled. Thus, you are harming your horse, not doing him any favours, by travelling along at a dawdling amble, not a brisk walk! It is the lazy gait which causes the most weariness. That is why it is a priority to bring the horse through each day's travel by subjecting it to the least number of hours under saddle, as the quicker a journey is completed the less strenuous is it to both horse and rider. Of all the gaits, the walk is the most important for equestrian travellers, followed by the trot. Canters seldom figure into travel and galloping should be avoided.

**New Century, New Problems.** Historical facts demonstrate that until the mid-twentieth century a person could make an accurate estimate based on level, trouble free travel. Twenty miles was in fact an average daily distance. That number was based upon there being no geographic challenges, no extremes of temperature, the roads being good, forage and shelter being routinely available, and the riders and horses both being properly conditioned. The question then becomes, what can a modern Long Rider estimate as the average modern day's distance? Popular belief is that under favourable conditions you can still aim for 20 miles per day as an average. In actuality the dawning of the internet age brought an end to mankind's rapid equestrian progress. The daily average has decreased by nearly half in the 21$^{st}$ century, with today's equestrian travellers averaging between 11 and 15 miles per day. What caused this sharp decrease in mileage?

Previous generations were most often delayed by harsh weather and bad roads. From a purely technical point of view, ghastly trails, cruel weather and challenging terrain will still delay any Long Rider's progress. The Gobi hasn't become any cooler or the Himalayas any smaller. But in the past Long Riders travelled through a world largely devoted to the pursuit of agriculture. This meant suitable food and adequate shelter was often available and costs were minimal. Things are different for the modern Long Rider. He has become an anomaly, an equine oddity looking for grain and hay in a motorized age. As a result Long Riders around the world increasingly devote a large part of the afternoon searching for food and shelter. This in turn decreases the daily mileage. Other new types of delays abound. An ever-increasing number of cities are banning horses entirely. Police regularly harass mounted travellers. Motorized traffic is a murderous menace. And there is another reason daily progress has decreased; a radical change in the social climate. In the past people routinely saw horses during the course of the day, as major cities were the homes of vast urban herds of equines that worked in a wide variety of occupations. Seeing a horse did not elicit surprise or draw large crowds of astonished on-lookers. Times have changed. The sudden appearance of a Long Rider reveals a travelling remnant from another age. Suddenly an immensely large, beautiful and mythical animal has entered into a mundane world addicted to chrome-covered machines. Modern Long Riders have learned that their travel plans are increasingly delayed by people seeking to touch the horse, to ask questions, to take photos and to share the magic of the journey. Such interactions take time and delay progress.

**Delays and detours.** There are a number of consistencies in the history of equestrian travel. One of them is how Long Riders throughout the ages have struggled to move forward. Never under estimate the day's challenges. Expect them. They're unaccountable, unavoidable and will test your resolve. Bad weather, difficult terrain, natural obstacles, poor roads, inaccurate direct-ions and curious people will all cause delays.

**Decreasing Delays.** To reduce delays, you should ask yourself these questions every morning. Are the horses fit? Have all the shoes been checked? Are the riding and pack saddle in proper order? What is the designated start time? How many miles will be travelled? Has sufficient time been allotted? Is the state of the road known? Are there any rivers or bridges to cross? What are the weather conditions? Is there sufficient water on the route? Are the locations for the first, hourly, and noon halts known?

**Travelling at Night.** Modern Long Riders who are forced to ride across a harsh landscape, where scanty amounts of shade may result in lethal exposure to the hot sun, might be tempted to think that riding in the cool night air will provide an acceptable solution. Such inexperienced travellers fail to realize that riding at night presents an alarming number of potential dangers to the horse and tactical problems to the rider. There are many reasons not to be tempted to ride after dark. One of the primary ones is that a life under bright lights has weakened your night vision and made you forget how truly dark it can become. But there are other equally alarming reasons to consider. Breaking camp is difficult and time consuming. Valuable objects are easily overlooked and often left behind. Special care must be taken when saddling. Darkness increases the difficulties of finding and following unknown roads, which in turn slows the journey. Unless the road is well known the journey may be lengthened by an error in direction. Because you are riding more slowly, you spend a longer time on the horse's back, which in turn makes night travel more fatiguing than in the day.

If you absolutely must travel after dark, never ride on a moonless night. Plan to take advantage of every minute of moonlight. Whenever possible use a local guide who has knowledge of the road ahead. Only travel over good roads. If travelling near motor traffic, affix a light on your pack saddle or around your leg, so as to warn drivers. Wear bright, reflective clothing. Allow extra time to complete the journey.

**No Cruelty.** No discussion on daily distance would be complete without acknowledging how mankind has on occasion treated the horse with incredible cruelty. Animals, like humans, differ greatly. The horse, for example, is unlike the dog. The dog, the faithful companion who never forsakes his master, when over fatigued will lie down on the wayside, leaving his friend to proceed alone; no entreaty can urge the canine to exert himself unto death. Not so the faithful horse. No matter how fatigued or ill he may be, the devoted horse plods on his weary way till death kindly relieves him. What other animal does this? Constant hard days on the road will push the horse too hard. If high mileage is demanded for several days it will adversely affect the health of the horse. Have a care! Exhausted horses can be a danger to themselves and the rider. A horse ridden too hard is more prone to stumble, step off the trail or make mental mistakes. If abused, a horse can be ridden to death. No journey may be counted a success unless you have taken more care of the horse than yourself.

**Hints.** The length of each day's journey and pace must be adapted to the condition of the horse, the state of the road and the season of the year. Count no mile until it is ridden. Every mile travelled is a mile survived. One day done; many more to come. He who goes gently goes safely; he who goes safely goes far!

# Chapter 74 - Hospitality or Hostility

Equestrian travel history demonstrates that the success of any Long Ride depends upon the traveller's ability to pass through the countryside peacefully. Unfortunately, while that is an admirable goal, Long Riders have often found themselves forced to cope with hostility, suspicion and danger. There are certain fundamental rules connected to the practice of equestrian travel which apply in any age and in every country. One of these principles states that if hospitality is withheld the traveller and his horse will surely suffer and perhaps die. Long Riders quickly learn that you never take hospitality for granted.

**Different Views on Hospitality.** The concept of hospitality differs greatly among nations and the citizens of every country. Some nations enjoy a reputation for kindness. Others will let you die on the doorstep. Primal hospitality is not the readiness to receive into your house a gentleman who has made a favourable impression on you at a social gathering. It is the willingness to host the passing stranger, in need of assistance, whom you never saw before, and never expect to see again. This is the test that is applicable to a country where distances are great and the traveller liable to find himself fatigued or benighted where public accommodation is not to be found.

**A Sacred Trust.** Though Long Riders are required to spend a great deal of time alone in the saddle, theirs is not a lonely endeavour. Circumstances demand they become socially involved with the people whose country they are riding through. The weary Long Rider appears in search of the legendary requirements of all equestrian travellers: food, fire, shelter, grass and water. In exchange for providing these necessities the host receives an emotional return from the traveller. For at night his home is enlivened with stories from afar. Thus is established the sacred bond of trust between a Long Rider and his hosts. But seeking hospitality makes us emotionally vulnerable. We must summon the courage to approach a stranger and ask for help. The host in turn is suddenly asked to unlock his door and tend to the needs of a stranger. The concept of hospitality is a two-edged sword. It is vitally important to the success of your journey but receiving it depends upon the acceptance, trust, tolerance, assistance, patience and generosity of strangers.

**Expect Rejection.** It seems obvious, but most fledgling Long Riders do not allow enough time to find nightly accommodations. So long as the sun is shining they push their luck and diminish their chances of locating a safe spot for the night. Starting as early as possible in the morning allows you to make good mileage, permits your horse to rest at mid-day and then have time to locate a good night's lodging. If all goes well, you should try to be off the road by 3 p.m., as this will provide your horse time to relax, eat and rest. But finding such a rarity as a nightly host is not an easy task. Straight away you should not always expect to find anyone at home in every house you see. If they are home, you have to expect opposition and be ready for rejection. One Long Rider accurately summed up the search for a host when he wrote, "Some couldn't. Some wouldn't." Finding food and shelter is a time-consuming daily task. You don't start looking and asking at sundown. You have to expect rejection. You have to allow enough time to move on.

**Your Appearance.** You may be tempted to think that when you are travelling no one worries about the look of your clothes or the dirt under your fingernails. Appearances can be deceiving. Your travel-stained face and unclean garments may work against you. It is well known that the horse is exceedingly strong in odour. The overpowering smell of his sweat clings to your hands, soaks your clothes and makes the hot saddle blankets a stinking offence. You increase your chances of success by giving a thought to how you look.

**Riding to the Door Protocol.** No matter where you ride the tradition in most countries is that a stranger never gets off his horse until he is invited to do so. How and when you dismount depends upon several factors.

**Safety in the Saddle.** Travelling with horses places us in close physical proximity to strangers. Thus there are issues of personal safety involved every time you dismount. A keen-eyed Long Rider always looks the scene over carefully as he approaches a potential night's shelter. He knows that more than just social custom require him to stay in the saddle until he is certain all is well. As the day reaches its climax many Long Riders are inclined to look for a potential host among people who happen to be outside their homes already. The watering of a horse affords an excuse for entering a village or starting a conversation with a stranger. That initial question may in turn lead to a discussion about the availability of grazing, the possibility of obtaining grain or the advisability of the next day's route. All the while these questions are under way it is the Long Rider who is making his own careful judgment of the prospective host and the safety of the physical surroundings.

During his journey from Mongolia to Hungary Australian Long Rider Tim Cope developed a careful strategy which he used before dismounting. "This was part of my plan to drop my guard cautiously, layer by layer, in case I could not trust my hosts. It became a protocol that I would adhere to religiously. The first step was to trust the stranger enough to get out of the saddle. If I felt comfortable after getting out of the saddle I would risk unloading the animals and enter the home. Only over a cup of tea would I explain who I was and where I was headed. The ultimate shedding of defence was unsaddling the horses."

**Explain Your Needs.** Once you have decided it is safe to dismount, articulate your needs. If you are carrying a firman (official letter of introduction) this is the time to show it. Newspaper stories also help establish your credibility. Always explain how briefly you plan to stay and that you will be sure to clean up any manure left by your horse. Articulate your basic requirements; grass and water for your horse, a corner where you might sleep. Of course modern amenities like a meal and a shower wouldn't go amiss. Be quick to offer to pay for anything you need.

**Repaying Hospitality.** One of the consistent threads that runs through the history of equestrian travel is how kind-hearted hosts refuse to accept offers of payment. Repaying hospitality and spontaneous generosity is always difficult, especially in a country where both are regarded as obligatory and money, apart from payment for grain and hay, would be an insult. Knowing in advance that this problem will arise, many Long Riders dispense small gifts which they bring along for this specific purpose.

# Chapter 75 - Surviving Local Accommodations

**Adjusting your Expectations.** A common thread weaves its way through Long Rider history. Where you spend the night is as varied as the geography across which you pass. You have to expect to rough it! Long Riders have slept in jail cells, school rooms, grain silos, airplane hangars, hospitals, abandoned buildings and barns. They have pitched their tents in cemeteries, behind gas stations, atop baseball fields and on golf courses. They have gone to rest amidst the crops, beneath the trees and under the stars. No matter where they manage to find a few hours' rest, they have learned that sooner or later they are going to be required to endure hard times, rough circumstances and the company of uncouth company.

**Respecting the Locals.** It might be seem obvious but be courteous. Don't impose. Shake hands with everyone and smile a lot. Shaking hands is a useful gesture of goodwill. It can take away tension and makes people well disposed toward you. With the demise of the stables and inns which routinely catered to equestrian travellers, finding accommodation for one traveller and a horse will present a tactical problem in an urbanized setting. Most potential hosts are not equipped to offer shelter to more than two travellers.

**Mongolian Manners.** In the West the round felt residence is commonly known as a yurt. But the Mongols correctly refer to this mobile house as a ger. No matter what you call it, there are strict rules in how you act inside and around it. If you step on the threshold of a ger you will insult the owner. If you trip at the threshold it will drive away happiness. If you enter with a sigh, it is disrespectful. You must move inside the ger in a clockwise direction. Do not cross the path of an elderly person as this is considered disrespectful. Do not whistle in a ger as it will bring bad luck. If you step on a hat it will insult the owner. If you step on a lasso it will bring bad luck to the owner. Touching the rim of a cup with your fingers is considered a bad omen. Make sure your sleeves are rolled down. It is disrespectful to turn your back to the altar or to sit in front of it. Do not put anything into the fire. Most importantly, do not lie with your feet pointing toward the fire as this will drive out the household gods. When you are outdoors near the ger, do not use an axe near fire as it threatens the god of fire. Never stamp out the fire with your feet. It is sacred. If you step on ashes, it will bring the spirit of the dead into the ashes.

# Chapter 76 - Adapting to New Cultures

The way our brains operate is affected by our geographic and cultural background. Such divisions in thought have been detected between nomadic people and subsistence farmers, as well as Eastern and Western nations. Research suggests that the mind's capacity to adapt itself to cultural and environmental settings is far greater than had been assumed. This isn't to say that everyone is going to welcome you with open arms. In fact chances are that you're going to be treated rudely, be asked to consume some gut-wrenching meals and have your sense of privacy routinely violated.

**Practising Tolerance.** No thin slice of humanity has all the answers or represents a monopoly on the truth! The rest of the world doesn't doff its cap in respect to your ingrained sense of cultural superiority, isn't willing to accommodate your desires, accede to your demands, agree with your religious views, tolerate your dietary preferences or even treat you with anything but cool disdain! Who you were, what you drove, how much you made at home, means nothing once you are in the saddle and far from home. The rules have changed and it is you who had better learn quickly or perish. Knowing that your own beliefs and practices are not sacrosanct is the first step in realizing how much you still have to learn about other people and cultures. A Long Rider must throw down the walls erected by years of enforced cultural practice. He must make a conscious effort to view things from the perspective of his host nation. He must be seen to respect local customs.

**Humour.** Many invisible traits make up a successful Long Rider. Having a sense of humour is one of them. Don't take yourself too seriously. A smile has opened more doors than money. Never underestimate how important humour is.

**Lack of Privacy.** First-time travellers from Occidental countries are often deeply disturbed by how other cultures have an utter disregard for the concept of privacy. Being gawked at, the very moment they are most in need of seclusion, has caused many a Long Rider of both sexes to snap under the stress of finding themselves in this situation. Shouting at the curious locals to leave you in peace at this delicate moment generally elicits peals of laughter from the crowd and a general wonder why the stranger is so shy about such a natural function.

**Learning to do Without.** Not all the world is a "land of plenty." Food is often scarce. Clean water is a luxury. Food takes on a special meaning to a Long Rider. Brushing big horses, breaking camp, loading up equipment, lifting heavy saddles, riding all day and enduring harsh weather gives you the appetite of a ravenous lion. The problem is that your stomach is a rascal. It doesn't remember how well you treated it yesterday. It will cry out for more tomorrow. After a few weeks on the trail, most Long Riders judge food by its quantity rather than by any standard of taste.

**The Commissary.** Even if you're planning to take along a pack animal, your ability to carry food and supplies is going to be severely limited. That is why careful planning for this part of your trip is of great importance. There are a variety of factors which will affect your diet. The state of your finances first has to be considered. How many mouths will you have to feed? How far will you travel? Is the land bleak or plentiful in terms of availability of food? Will you be able to replenish supplies along the way?

**Dietary Customs.** Few things separate us like food. Culinary preferences and dietary customs have a way of influencing daily events. Many nomadic cultures consider bread and salt sacred. Not eating or trying the bread shows a grave disrespect for the host. It is often customary in Islamic countries to forego the use of cutlery, with the diners using their right hands to eat from a common bowl or platter. Another tradition is that all talk ceases lest it insult the quality of the food.

**Hippophagy.** Adjusting your expectations includes realizing that what other cultures consider a delicacy may not match your expectations. One of the most challenging taboos which Long Riders from the Occident will encounter is the way other cultures enjoy eating horse meat! This practice, known as hippophagy, is connected to cultural and religious practices. Countries such as the USA, UK and Australia largely view horses as companion animals that should not be consumed. Other European nations view horse meat as a tasty national tradition. Austria, Belgium, France, Germany, Hungary, Italy, Netherlands, Serbia and Switzerland are just some of the countries which partake of this particular type of protein. In other parts of the world, where you go will determine if you are faced with the possibility of being served this type of meat. It is considered taboo to consume horse meat in Argentina but next door in Chile horse meat is often eaten. Mexico is the second largest producer of horse meat in the world but you can't buy it in Venezuela. Values even differ within countries. You can buy horse steak in French-speaking Quebec but not out west in Victoria. Some cultures, such as the Mongols, eat horses only in the winter. Other cultures, such as the Kazakhs, eat them all year. Many Long Riders who have journeyed across these two countries have been confronted with a meal of horse meat. Consuming it is as normal to the inhabitants of those nations as enjoying a hamburger is to an American. There are many personal, religious, cultural and dietary factors which will influence your individual decision to avoid or eat this type of meat. What you should be aware of is that the majority of the world does not adhere to the Anglo prohibition of not consuming horses. So having researched the dietary practices of the country where you plan to travel, you should not be taken unaware if the choice is presented to you.

**The Dangers of Drinking.** Drinking and long riding often bring about dangerous or unfortunate events. Consumption of vodka in Russia is still a major social problem, where the average Russian consumes nearly 16 litres of vodka per year, twice the average intake of most countries. The high prevalence of alcohol consumption means that an equestrian traveller is likely to encounter intoxicated and aggressive men who have participated in binge drinking. Alcohol can also turn a friendly encounter with a local into an episode linked to theft and robbery. Another problem connected to alcohol is the theft of horses and equipment. Mongolia has a reputation for aggressive alcohol abuse. Travellers have had their horses and equipment stolen by locals drunk on kumis and vodka. Physical attacks and thefts are heightened during the summer months, which coincide with the peak production of mare's milk and the fermenting of kumis. One other problem associated with alcohol is the possibility that you might be arrested for riding your horse while intoxicated. Various American states enforce statutes which make it a crime to ride if you are under the influence of alcohol.

**Taboos.** No society is immune from adhering to some level of taboo. They touch on the topics which challenge a society's comfortable values. Death, sex, family, food and religion; these are just some of the issues which expose our collective beliefs. There are various reasons why people adhere to these prohibitions. Many are religious. Some are regional. Most are cultural. They can be of recent origin, though most have been passed down for generations. Some are out of date. All of them are dangerous! Taboos vary widely from one country to the next. They are psychologically powerful and can be extremely hazardous. It's not your job to diagnose or comment on taboos but to avoid breaking them! Many of the cultural taboos which held sway for thousands of years, especially those connected to sexuality and bigotry, have undergone recent changes. But adherents of traditional beliefs are left feeling angry and bewildered when their beliefs are undermined.

**Films and Photographs.** Bringing out a camera changes the chemistry of a social situation. Unless it is done with care, filming and photography make many people uncomfortable, nervous and even dangerous.

# Chapter 77 - Stables and Shelter

A Russian proverb states, "The wagon rests in winter, the sleigh in summer, the horse never." Nothing wears out a horse faster on a journey more than the want of sleep. It is vitally important that every effort be made to provide the horse with the best quarters circumstances permit and to then allow him every opportunity to enjoy a night's sleep.

**To Sleep, Perchance to Dream.** Wild horses spend their time travelling across the land looking for grazing and water. Their need to protect their lives at a moment's notice means that, no matter how weary, they must be ready to instantly run away. Wild horses normally never lie down, as cows and camels do to rest, unless they are confident as to their safety. They sleep while standing, with three and a half hours often being sufficient to refresh a horse. Midnight is when a horse usually sleeps soundly, if undisturbed. But it is generally believed, that a horse sleeps best, generally, early in the morning. Another important observation is that road horses will use the afternoon lunch break to doze, rest and recover. No matter if your horse is dozing in the sun during a lunch break or sleeping deeply in a safe stall for the night, your challenge is to find a place where you tired companion can rest.

**Changing Times.** The world has changed, meaning that all of the traditional services connected to horses and equestrian travel have becoming increasingly difficult to find. This isn't to say that people's hearts have hardened; only that towns no longer employ people who understand horses and can offer them basic services. In their place a new type of urban human has come upon the scene. Though they are generous, they are unaware of a Long Rider's needs. That is why it is important to know what to look for when it comes time to stable or shelter your horse for the night.

**Sheltering the Horses.** In bad weather, even the worst shelter is preferable to having the horses standing exposed to the elements. But circumstances often dictate that a traveller must make a decision as to where he can safely place his horse outside for the night. That is why the provision of a good place for your horse to bed down is an important detail in keeping your animal happy and healthy. The selection of where the horses will be placed depends upon the length of stay and the time of year. Regardless of the country, pure air, good light, dry ground and good water are the essentials sought at day's end when a suitable spot is needed to picket horses. That is why the prospective night's lodging must be considered carefully. First, assess the potential site in regard to access to a good water supply, availability of fodder and protection against wet and cold. Be sure the area is large enough to provide adequate space for each horse to move comfortably. The state of the ground is of great importance. Avoid placing your horse on a steep hillside. Try to choose flat level ground for the horses to stand on. Horses can obtain a considerable amount of rest standing, and in fact there are some which rarely lie down; but the more rest they can be induced to take, the longer their legs will last, and the more likely are they to keep in good condition. That is why it is important that the site should be cleared of stones and any other objects which might interfere with the horses lying down comfortably. Ideally the ground should have good drainage to carry away storm water. Marshy ground should always be avoided as dampness causes hoof rot. Avoid river bottoms which may flood.

When travelling in hot climates, providing protection from the sun is essential and in this case any light structure or trees may be employed as shelter during the day. Horses are almost indifferent to the greatest extremes of dry cold; yet, if exposed to wind they lose weight rapidly, and are intensely susceptible to draughts. Always try to choose a spot which acts as a wind break and offers some degree of natural protection from the prevailing wind. Choose an area free from briars and poisonous plants. Whenever possible, always chose a spot as close as possible to where you will be camping.

**Safe Stables.** Stables used to be a standard feature across the landscape of many nations. Nowadays they are increasingly rare. Travelling horses soon learn to associate the setting sun with journey's end and food. Should the chance present itself, and you are invited to let your horse spend the night in a strange stable, be quick to express your thanks and then inspect the premises in as diplomatic manner as possible. If the horse is to be placed within a stall, spend the time to look for unknown dangers in advance. Be sure to run your hand along the edges of the manger to make sure there are no sharp edges. Pay careful attention to examining the walls for sharp objects that can cause injury, otherwise your mount will suffer the moment you turn your back. Exposed nails in stalls are especially dangerous as they can be a source of the deadly tetanus virus. Before you ever enter into the stall, be absolutely certain that the door operates properly and can be opened quickly in case of an emergency. The stable should be a refuge not a prison cell. The stall should ideally be well-ventilated and allow plenty of light. Because you will be a guest for the night, you must use your wits and exercise your diplomatic talents if your host offers to place your horse into a stall covered in old straw or thick dung, as both can harbour bacteria. Your horse doesn't need a soft bed as much as he needs a dry, level, clean surface where he can rest quietly. There are other practical preparations involved in safe stabling, including determining a safe place to tie or secure your horse. Never rope your horse to dangerous and moveable objects such as doors, heavy equipment or wagon wheels. Once you have established that the stall is safe, lead the horse in and remove the halter. Leaving a halter on overnight might result in the animal getting caught and then going into a panic.

**The Danger of Fire.** There is another element connected with placing your horse in a strange stable for the night; safety. From a practical point of view, you should try to sleep as close as possible to the stable. This helps deters the theft of your horse, saddle and equipment. Yet the worst possible safety scenario involves a stable fire. Should you awake to find the barn or stable is on fire, do not enter the building if it is already engulfed in flames! In their desire to save their horses, many people have perished by becoming trapped inside a burning barn that collapsed on them. If you believe you can enter the building with some degree of safety, concentrate on evacuating the horses closest to the doors. Do not think that you can simply open the stall door and drive the horse outside towards safety. Horses are particularly terrified by fire and if freed from their stall have been known to rush into the burning building, not away from it. Immediately place a halter or bridle on the horse. Then blindfold the horse with any convenient cloth that is close to hand. When horses see or smell fire, they often obstinately refuse to walk towards safety. If he declines to move forward, back him out of the burning stable. Once the horse is outside, do not let him run loose as he may return to the burning building. Tie him or place him within a secure fenced area away from the flames.

**Pastures.** Long Riders are often forced by circumstances to accept whatever accommodations are on offer for their horses. This frequently means that they will be required to place their animals in a strange pasture for the night. Placing a horse in a pasture or a field for the night does not automatically guarantee that the animal will receive a full night's rest. Horses are gregarious and mischievous. If left to their own devices, they will spend part of the night grazing. Once their initial hunger pangs are salved, they may begin to misbehave. They will chase each other, bully smaller animals, and expend valuable energy which will be needed for the next day's work or travel. If you have been travelling with your own horses for a long time or across a great distance, then placing them alone in a pasture for the night may not result in any loss of rest or energy, as most road and pack horses are wise enough to recognize the need to eat as much as possible and rest for as long as they can. But placing your horses in a pasture populated by strange horses exposes them to the danger of being chased, bitten and kicked. So have a care before you put your valuable equine friends inside a pasture and walk away thinking that all is well. Inspect the field before you put your horse in it. It is not just stray pieces of barbed wire you have to be worried about, but be on the lookout for broken glass or any sharp objects which might also cause an injury in your absence.

**Protect Your Horse.** At the end of a long day in the saddle, you will want nothing more than to sit and rest. But always put your horse's safety before your own comfort! The temptation is that, upon reaching what appears to be a point of physical and emotional safety, you may relinquish your responsibility to a stranger. If you remember one single thing from this book, remember this. Trust no one with the welfare of your horse. Ever! The moment you take your eye off your horse he is in peril of damage or death. Don't trust his welfare to strangers, no matter how well meaning they appear. Don't drop your guard when it looks like the coast is clear. As equestrian travel history proves, it's when things look safe that your horses will be killed by strangers or misguided kindness.

**Rest and Relaxation.** Rest makes a new horse. Some Long Riders ride for five days, then allow their horses two days off to rest and recover. Others never go more than four days without giving the horses a full day's rest. If you are travelling on an extremely long journey, which may last a year or more, then you should plan to stop after two or three months on the road, depending upon the climate, terrain, and conditions you have encountered, and allow the horses at least a week to rest in absolute peace and quiet.

# Chapter 78 - Finding Fodder

Food becomes very important to a travelling horse. First, it provides the raw power that allows the journey to continue. But on a deeper level it affords a potent emotional reward, which, because it always comes from the loving hand of the Long Rider, becomes a source of constant daily happiness. Food is therefore more than mere fuel. It is a reassuring comfort in a world full of strange terrors. Because of this it does more than just nourish the horse's body. It strengthens his soul.

As the sun begins to dip down towards the horizon, the horse often starts to show subtle signs of emotional agitation. He has carried you all day, and now he wants his reward. But finding anything to feed your horse in a bleak landscape is a stressful challenge. It will require you to be part diplomat and part wily trader in order to obtain the food your horse needs. This is why you must always start your ride early, so as to allow sufficient time towards the end of the day to undertake this vital part of your work.

**Do the Maths.** The heavier the weight he carries, the more nutrients the horse will require to replace the energy expended during travel. 26 per cent more net nutrients are required when the horse walks a mile at the speed of 3.5 mph than 2.5 mph. When his gait is hastened to a trot, nearly twice as much food is required per mile of travel than at the slower walk. In climbing a hill the horse does much more work than when going on a level course, for besides propelling his body, he must raise it against the force of gravity. In ascending a grade at 3 mph (5 kph), a horse will expend more than 3 times the energy as in walking the same distance on the level. In raising his body 200 feet (60 metres) in going up a grade, he would use almost as much feed as in travelling a mile horizontally!

**A Daily Obsession.** A Long Rider must learn to keep a sharp eye out for every chance to find grazing, locate grain and do everything possible to add to the overall strength of the horse. The search for horse food becomes an unexpected dominant factor in your daily life.

**Never Pass Grazing.** Grass is a precious commodity that translates calories into miles. But relying on finding a lush pasture owned by a kindly farmer as the sun sets is a fairytale believed by children. Even if he's not working or travelling, to maintain his strength without grain a horse needs at least eight hours of good foraging a day. Never pass up a chance to let your horse graze during the day's travel. Giving him every occasion to graze helps maintain his physical strength. Also, the horse will walk forward with eagerness if he thinks he is moving in search of the next patch of succulent forage. If you see grass, stop and let your animals enjoy it. It must become second nature to let your horses stop and graze when the opportunity occurs!

**Refused Hospitality.** Long Riders have heard many excuses why they can't be permitted to spend the night and graze their horses. One of the most common claims is that permission can't be granted because the person in authority is absent. Time after time, night after night, you are going to be faced with the difficult task of negotiating for permission to stay on someone else's land. Determining who is capable of making the decision to let you stay often takes a bit of nerve. Never leave this vital negotiation until the end of the day! You need the best pasture you can find and locating the person who can grant you permission takes time and patience.

**Hay - A Precious Commodity.** Many first-time travellers make the error of thinking their horses can survive only on a diet of grass or hay. The average horse needs from 10 to 12 pounds (5 kg) of good hay a day. There are a variety of reasons why locating hay for your horses may prove to be challenging. First there is the logistical problem of what to do with the horses during your absence. As one Long Rider wrote, "I needed hay and food for myself but have you ever tried going shopping with two horses in tow?" Also, time after time an equestrian traveller has arrived at an isolated village only to be told there is no hay or grass to spare. The idea of selling hay for a profit is either not considered or not appealing. Therefore instead of being viewed as an unexpected source of potential profit, the sudden appearance of mounted strangers is often viewed as a nuisance. A common ploy is to urge the Long Rider to travel on to the next village, which is falsely described as being rich in fodder and a legendary centre of hospitality.

**Finding Grain.** If the horse's diet does not include a grain ration, the animal will become potbellied, fall in flesh and lose vitality. If you are riding in countries like the United States, Canada, Western Europe, Australia or New Zealand, then chances are that local tack or feed stores will be able to offer you a wide variety of premixed, commercially created and highly nutritious grain-based supplements to help augment your horses' diet. As you are travelling you will also find that local riding clubs, horse-breeders, farmers and ranchers may be able to help you in terms of finding grain. No matter where you ride, remember the old British cavalry adage which stated, "Nosebags should be kept full, no matter what the contents, so long as they are eatable."

# Chapter 79 - Camping

**Reconnecting with Nature.** Riding a horse across the landscape creates an astonishing link between you and Nature. On horseback we experience the world in the unprotected raw. We cross countries on tiny tracks, ride across mountains, ford rivers and are not bound by any path.

**The Limits of Advice.** The world of equestrian travel is so vast, the countries which may be visited so numerous, the type of topography so diverse, the climatic conditions so extremely variable that it would be impossible to create a "one size fits all" study on the topic of how camping influences the outcome of every equestrian journey.

Some Long Riders may never spend a night under canvas, preferring to sleep in the relative comfort of the horse box/trailer that accompanies them. Many move along a stream of hospitality which includes family homes, riding schools, and accommodating barns. The majority find themselves face to face with the elements. Like their mounted ancestors, they must contend with rain, cold, wind, sun and every other nuisance or menace which Mother Nature can throw at mounted man. Camping, like equine health, requires careful study. Testing your camping skills is a vital part of your preparation.

**The Tent.** There are many reasons to take a tent. The most obvious is that it provides a source of protection from the elements, a vital point which we shall consider. But the tent provides other important services as well. It grants you a great degree of independence, because it permits you to sleep where you like. It makes economic sense, because it frees you from paying for a night's lodging. It provides you with a degree of privacy from the prying eyes of strangers. Lastly, it offers a sense of safety in a world swirling with insecurity.

Out of 100 expeditions, 90 per cent of all first-timers fail to reach their goal. Half of them don't make it more than three months. The main reasons are these. The two most important things on an expedition are to sleep and eat well. Therefore, before leaving on an expedition, adventure, or travel, you need to spend a lot of time learning to live outdoors in a tent. This is your home. Your life goes on inside these walls. When you are tired, your tent is where you recuperate. When things go wrong, it is your fortress against worries and the place of peace. Before you leave home, make it comfortable. Then spend lots of time sleeping outdoors, until the day arrives when you sleep well and feel secure.

Even if you have a tent, you're under no obligation to always use it. You may find that awakening with a little dew on your sleeping bag is a small price to pay for having had the chance to watch the stars dance over your head all night. Should bad weather force you to sleep outdoors without the aid of a tent, then much depends upon where you choose to sleep. Staying warm relies upon avoiding being exposed to a cold wind. Amateur travellers often choose a tree to camp under. But even though the tree spreads out into the sky above, the only shelter it offers the traveller is that of the trunk below. Thus the tree is a roof but not a wall. A Long Rider lying on the ground is so small that a low screen will guard him from the wind more effectively than a tree. A thick hedge protects from the wind on the leeward side a distance of up to ten to fifteen times the height of the hedge. If a hedge can't be found, then a pile consisting of the saddle and any other equipment can be constructed as a screen against the wind. Such a screen need not be much higher than 18 inches to guard the traveller against the wind.

**The Sleeping Bag.** There are several items whose importance cannot be stressed enough. The sleeping bag is high on that list. Equestrian travel is hard work and many a Long Rider has crawled into his sleeping bag after an exhausting day and longed to rest – only to discover that the cheap bag he purchased is leaving him shivering on the cold ground. A good night's sleep will ensure that you feel emotionally rested in the morning. During the course of your journey, you will spend many hours in your sleeping bag, resting, reading, writing and sleeping. That is why you should exercise great care when you purchase your sleeping bag. A cheap sleeping bag will make you miserable. Yet a well-constructed one will keep you warm even if arctic weather is howling outside your tent.

**Equipment.** Cheap equipment is utterly useless, as horse travel knocks everything about in a fearful manner. Invest in the best equipment you can afford! Don't be tempted to rely on a GPS. If you want to take one along, fine. But this is a high tech solution to a low tech problem. GPS technology relies on batteries. If they run out, you may find yourself far from any source which can replace them. Always carry a reliable, small, light-weight compass which you keep in your pocket.

**Knives.** Knives are like religions. Opinions differ. Everyone has a story. Most people think what works for them is best. It's your task to keep an open mind and make your own decision. The majority of Long Riders find that nearly all chores can be handled by a folding knife equipped with a 4 to 6 inch (12 cm) long blade. It should be strongly made, keep a good edge, and, most importantly, the blade should lock into place.

**Rope.** If you've been raised in North America, Australia, Europe, or other parts of the world with easy access to plentiful supplies, then you probably just take high-quality rope for granted. In industrialized nations rope is always available at a nearby building supply store. Moreover, it's not only plentiful, it's cheap. Not so when you ride in distant parts. There it is a precious commodity, seldom seen, always useful and forever being stolen. Some countries, especially Mongolia, have a reputation for stealing this valuable tool, which is of such practical daily use to people who own large herds of horses and other animals. Other nations may have rope available, but you will find to your dismay that it is of inferior quality. This not only renders it inflexible but makes it very difficult to tie knots. Before travelling to foreign parts, wise Long Riders purchase high quality alpinist rope.

**The Axe and the Saw.** There are two points to consider when the topic turns to carrying an axe. The first is what a practical tool it is if you are going to build a fire or remove a tree that may have fallen across the trail and prevented your progress. The second is that in certain parts of the United States you are required by law to carry an axe if you travel through the wooded mountains with horses. Another piece of equipment which is often required is a small saw. While hikers can walk around or climb over a fallen tree, Long Riders have found they often need to cut through a fallen tree or clear timber off the trail. A small folding saw with a 14.5" (35 cm) blade is capable of cutting through at least a 15" tree.

**The Camp Fire.** A campfire is a complex thing which serves a number of purposes. First, it protects you against the cold. A deep emotional comfort radiates from a campfire. And of course, one can cook over an open fire. There are drawbacks; some of which you might not expect. Some countries do not have an abundance of firewood. Because of the threat of forest fires countries like the United States have passed an increasing number of restrictions making it illegal to have an open campfire except in established campsites.

**The Stove.** The majority of Long Riders carry some sort of portable cooking stove. There are two major factors to consider before making this purchase: where you are going to be travelling and how many people you will be cooking for. Portable stoves operate on different fuels, including white gas, kerosene, propane, butane, alcohol, paraffin, diesel and petrol. It is very important that you determine what fuel is most easily obtainable in the country where you will be riding, as replenishing your fuel will be of strategic importance. So the more versatile and adaptable your stove the better your chances will be of having a warm meal.

**Food.** Most Long Riders always try to carry enough food for at least two days' meals on the road. Yet supplies disappear at an alarming rate. Replenishing them will be influenced by the country where you are riding. Prior to your departure you should stock up on dried foods that can be carried and cooked with ease. Non-perishable options such as rice, pasta, instant noodles and dried potatoes can be served in a variety of ways. Instant oatmeal, along with a hot cup of coffee or tea, has served many a Long Rider as an easy breakfast. What you need is food that is simple to prepare, provides a warm and comforting meal, and is easy to clean up afterwards. Many products come in cardboard boxes which are filled with air. Repack such food into strong Ziploc bags, being sure to cut off any cooking directions from alongside the box and place it into the bag. Avoid carrying glass bottles. Not only can they break during travel, and thereby ruin everything in your pannier, broken glass is a hazard. One final word about food; always keep your food and fuel packed in separate panniers!

**Cooking.** Opinions vary as to what type of minimum cooking equipment to carry. Common items include a frying pan, coffee pot or tea kettle, a four or six quart pot, cutlery, plates, bowls, cups, can-opener and corkscrew. Camping stores offer cooking pots that nest inside themselves. Aluminium is the most common and inexpensive, but it can be hard to clean and dents easily. Another consideration is the choice of your dinner ware. Metal plates are hot to hold and metal cups may burn your lips. Hard plastic plates, bowls and cups work well. You should practise cooking your meals using your stove and cooking gear before setting off, as keeping your strength up with the help of tasty, nutritious meals is vital to your success.

**The Bucket.** Having a heavy-duty folding bucket is a necessity. The bucket can be used to supply a thirsty horse with a drink. But in addition, it can be used to wash and prepare food prior to a meal. Afterwards it serves as a sink to wash the dishes in. On rest days it can be turned into a tub to wash clothes in or it can be used to collect water from a river for a bucket shower.

**Selecting the Camp Site.** Because you are travelling with horses, you should always begin looking for a suitable camp site well before dark. Even before you arrive, you should have decided if you're looking for a one-night stopover just to sleep before moving on in the morning. Or are you planning to spend a few days resting? The amount of time you plan on spending at the site will influence your decision to stay or ride on. When you arrive at a place which you believe may be suitable, do not ride directly into what you think may be the actual campsite. Halt your horse, sit in the saddle and study the site from a distance. This allows your road and pack horse to relieve themselves at a distance from what will soon be your living and cooking areas. There are requisites and criteria which will make a campsite happy or hellish. Does the campsite have abundant grass and clean water for the horses? What about your own requirements? Is firewood available? Can you purchase grain, food and supplies close by? Your safety and that of the horses comes after that. Are you far enough away from any busy roads? What about the local weather and the next day's travel? It is always preferable to set up camp on the far side of a stream or river, as a flood during the night may delay your next day's travel. Avoid camping in tall, dry grass, which may be a fire hazard and can harbour snakes. Insects will torment your horses if given the chance. Avoid swampy ground, which is a natural breeding ground for mosquitoes, gnats and flies.

**Where to Place the Horses.** One of the most important decisions connected to choosing a campsite, is where to picket, tether, tie or pasture the horses. Once you have scouted your camp, take your horses directly to the area where they will spend the night. Make sure it is far enough away from your tent and cooking area so that manure will not attract flies. Attention should be given to the weather and the prevailing winds. In dry, sultry weather horses should face the direction of the prevailing wind. In stormy weather their tails should be turned to the gale. If camped near water, place horses away from any river timber, which is likely to be full of mosquitoes.

Horses can inflict severe harm to trees and the environment in the space of one night. This is why you must make an effort to protect the integrity of your surroundings. In the past it was common practice for people to tie a horse to a tree. But bored horses tend to paw the trees roots, which causes serious damage. They may also strip off the bark, which will kill the tree. If you decide to place your horses on a picket line, choose a place with little or no vegetation, use a tree saver to protect the tree's surface, keep the horses at least six feet away from the trees, place the animals well apart from each other and at the first sign of any damage, move them to a new location. Be sure that your picket line is at least chest high, so as to discourage the horses from stepping over it. Should you tether your horse, move him as soon as you can see the circle where he has been feeding, so as to reduce trampling and prevent over-grazing. Never place your horses too near the tent, otherwise they run the risk of becoming entangled in the tent ropes during the night.

**Watering.** One of the decisions about where to pitch your camp will be connected to the avail-ability of water. Remote pools often provide the worst water. Unless very inaccessible under boulders or in fissures of rock, they are nearly always foul with excrement of wild and domes-tic animals. If chance forces you to camp near running water, camp above a village, not below it. But there may be another village higher up river and out of sight. Always scout the creek, stream or river not just for dead animals but for signs of industrial or agricultural pollution. Long Riders travelling alongside the Gila River in the United States, for example, were warned not to trust it because of the chemical pollutants which poured into the water from nearby ranches and farms. Use a filter. Boil your water. Use sterilizing tablets. Treat it chemically with drops of iodine to purify it. No matter what method you choose, always use caution when drinking suspect water. While most people remember to purify their drinking water, they over-look the importance of using clean water for cooking and washing. This often results in travellers becoming ill from the Giardia bacteria, which lurks in rivers, lakes and streams. If chance offers you to camp alongside a river or stream, then you should look upon the water source as having different sections for various purposes. Your drinking and cooking water come from upstream. The horses' watering place is next along. Still further downstream is where you wash dishes and bathe, being careful to keep any soap away from the animals.

**Sanitation.** Living outdoors means taking care of human waste and toilet paper. Set up your privy at least 100 feet away from camp. If you are going to be staying in camp for a rest, fastening a tarp to an adjacent tree can provide a degree of privacy. Unscented, biodegradable white toilet paper is recommended. Bury it, and human waste, in a hole under about six inches of soil. Some Long Riders have carried small, folding military spades for this purpose, but more recently Long Riders have reported that a metal garden trowel equipped with a 4 inch wide blade works well.

**The Chores.** Certain things are consistent. Sharing the duties around camp is one of them.
If you're riding solo, then all the work falls on your shoulders but if there are two are more of you, then you will find that democracy is the only fair way to allocate the chores.

**Nightly Check.** Just because you've halted for the day doesn't mean that you can stop making decisions. After dinner, decide if you are going to stay or move on tomorrow. If you're going to be riding, then discuss your next day's travel plans. Make sure everyone knows the route. Decide in advance if a midday halt is going to be made. To reduce the chances of a misunderstanding, use 24 hour military time to avoid mistakes between a.m. and p.m. Don't turn in without looking at your supplies, checking the safety of your equipment and carefully inspecting the horses to make sure they are tethered or picketed securely.

**Camping in Hostile Country.** Setting up a campsite places you and the horses in a vulnerable position; strategically, emotionally and legally. If you are planning on travelling through American state or national parks, then be sure you know the grazing regulations in advance and abide by them. If permits are required, obtain them in advance. In hostile country, it is better to stay overnight in a village. The same people who would rob you in the bush are honour-bound to protect you and your possessions if you stay in their village.

**Curiosity and Common Courtesy.** If someone visits your campsite on horseback, do not let them ride directly into the area reserved for your tent, campfire or living area. Suggest courteously that they secure their horse well away from your camp.

**Standing Guard.** Should you feel uneasy about your location, there are traditional safeguards which Long Riders have been practising for centuries which still hold true. First, choose your campsite with care. In hostile country avoid camping on ground which can be overlooked or where one can be seen against the skyline. If you don't want to be seen, avoid making a fire, remembering that a lighted match or the glow of a flashlight can be seen for a mile off. Next, forsake the tent, as it betrays your exact location to marauders or enemies, whereas a Long Rider sleeping on the ground is difficult to locate. Sleeping outside also heightens the chances of hearing any suspicious noises. If the camp is likely to be attacked, leave a small fire burning bright, but bed down at a safe distance away on defensible ground. Double-check that your horses are tied safely. If they have bells, be sure they are worn on such a dangerous night. Patrol the perimeter of the camp with a light, so that it is obvious you are aware and on guard. Make a strong mental note about the layout of the camp before you close your eyes. If you decide to have a campfire, have wood stacked up ready to keep it going during the length of the entire night. Before retiring, point your saddle in the direction of where you will be travelling next morning. Give a thought about where you lie down, as a startled man always jumps up in the direction his feet are pointing. Keep your torch/flashlight/headlamp and/or your weapons close by your head. Do not take off your boots or zip up your sleeping bag. If there is more than one of you travelling, take turns standing guard, paying especial attention to the horses.

**Avoiding Horse Thieves.** Mounted foreigners are often seen as rich and easy pickings. Mongolia currently has a reputation where more Long Riders have their horses stolen than in any other country. Once your camp has been spotted, it is not unusual for a group of Mongols to ride to your camp, dismount and attempt to intimidate you. They usually ride away after having carefully studied the layout of your camp and the location of your horses. Then they return after dark to steal your horses. Under normal circumstances always bell your horses so you can monitor their movements by the pleasant jingling that occurs during the night. If you suspect horse thieves may hit your camp, it is a safe precaution to keep the dominant leader of your horses saddled and picketed in camp. This will ensure that you are not left afoot. Plus, the other horses will be emotionally reluctant to leave their companion. And should you need to set off in search of your stolen horses, you can do so quickly. One thing to keep in mind is the danger of a stampede. If horse thieves intentionally charge your horses through your camp you run the risk of being trampled to death.

**Breaking Camp.** Dismantle your camp with care. Have the horses been properly fed, watered, groomed and tacked up? Have you remembered to cover your latrine? Have you cleaned up the area where the horses were picketed, kicking apart any piles of manure? Did you pour water on your campfire to make sure it was out cold? Have you packed away any trash, ready to carry it away and leave the campsite clean for the next traveller? Did you remember to walk through the campsite one last time to make sure small articles may not have been mislaid or trampled into the dirt?

## Chapter 80 - Life on the Road

**Reality versus Fantasy.** We all paint idyllic pictures on a canvas of dreams. But ask any seasoned equestrian traveller about what it's really like out there on the long grey road and you'll quickly get more than you bargained for. Long Riders learn that life changes when the horse's back becomes your only residence. What sounded like an alluring dream is often revealed to be a serious trial. After the initial excitement has died down, you come face to face with the reality of making your slow, plodding way across a vast landscape. When that moment arrives, what had sounded so thrilling in prospect in fact becomes immensely wearisome and monotonous. This is just one of the reasons why few set off, and even fewer make it to their distant geographic goal, because there are unforeseen pitfalls waiting to demoralize an unwary Long Rider. Knowing what lies ahead, being prepared in advance, heightens your chances of success.

**What Does It Take?** As the miles begin to fall behind you realize that you don't "conquer" the road. It merely relents and allows you to pass, sometimes with relative ease, sometimes after demanding a terrible toll. This is a hard task we are discussing, this equestrian travel, and it makes tremendous emotional and physical demands upon a person.

What does it take to become a Long Rider? If you are a person who loves comfort, conformity, routine and an active social life then you better find another way to travel, because the traditional pleasures of home must be dispensed with. Plain food becomes standard fare. There are periods of intense isolation. Exposure to hardship, suffering and various types of dangers become routine. The ability to adapt and endure is of paramount importance. A person who undertakes an equestrian journey must be willing to forfeit the luxuries in exchange for personal liberty, outdoor excitement and the pleasure of roaming the world at will. History demonstrates that the traveller's life is neither wildly exciting every day nor is it always monotonous, as something of interest happens every time the sun rises and sets. With experience comes the realisation that there is a balance between insecurity and tranquillity, that fear and spirituality are both found on the same journey, and that the long-term emotional compensations outweigh the immediate physical hardships.

**The Benefits.** There are many incredible benefits which result from undertaking an equestrian journey.

**Freed from Time.** Time passes at a different pace during the course of a long horse trip. First it seems to slow, as you find yourself sliding back into an ancient rhythm which, having been buried deep within your DNA, has been awakened from its slumber. The pace of life on the horse proceeds so leisurely that the notion of time begins to become an abstraction. You are no longer chained to your watch. You're too busy observing the seasons. You are not anxiously awaiting the arrival of a text message. You've rediscovered the stars. You are not confined within four walls. You've become aware of the four directions.

**Personal Liberty.** Your freedom extends beyond the release of any obligation to the clock. Travelling on horseback grants you the liberty to explore the country as and where you wish. You are not restricted to the road. You are can detour and linger. You don't speed across the countryside encased in a metal cocoon. You are a moving part of a living landscape. You are not disconnected from humanity. Your need for grass, water and shelter brings you into constant contact with the lives of common people. You are not an interloper. You are free.

**Reducing Your Needs.** One of the earliest lessons any Long Rider learns is, "The more you know, the less you need." Long Riders learn to be content with very little. They have broken the chains which linked them to objects that previously dominated their existence. They have replaced consumerism with simplicity. They have realized the pointlessness of filling our outer existence with things, if our inner lives are empty.

**Disconnecting from the World.** Previous generations of Long Riders realized that the further they travelled, the stronger grew the feeling that they were becoming increasingly disentangled from the activities of the rest of the world. For some, there was a gradual inkling that the journey had taken them to an unexpected emotional place in their lives. The further one rides, the more often one finds that links to the outside world have been severed.

**Health Benefits.** Others will not only envy your freedom but your health. Not only will you become physically hardened; as your health improves your spirits will soar. One of the results of feeling stronger, inside and out, is an increased sense of self-respect.

**In Touch with Nature.** The Long Rider does not dominate his environment; he belongs to it. He greets Nature as a communion not a conqueror. He blends with the countryside. He feels his surroundings intensely. One of the benefits of being a Long Rider is the ability to re-establish relationships with earth, wind, fire and water.

**Twin Souls.** There is one other remarkable benefit which I would be remiss not to mention; the astonishing emotional bond which springs up between horse and human. The journey forces the horse and human to become immersed in the same world. They suffer the pangs of hunger together and then rejoice over a meal. They face the same perils with the same chances of escape or annihilation. They endure the same dreadful weather. They wander towards the same distant goal.

**Emotional Readjustment.** Departing on a long equestrian journey requires the traveller to learn new lessons and to readjust emotionally. The first such requirement is to move forward with eagerness, instead of looking back with homesickness. Unless a traveller makes himself at home and comfortable in the bush, he will never be contented with his lot; but will fall into the bad habit of looking forwards to the end of his journey and to his return to civilization, instead of interesting himself in its continuance. This is a frame of mind in which few great journeys have been successfully accomplished; and an explorer who cannot divest himself of it, may suspect that he has mistaken his vocation. Make the bush your home. Interest yourself chiefly in the progress of your journey, and do not look forward to its end with eagerness. It is better to think of a return to civilization, not as an end to hardship and a haven from ill, but as a close to an adventurous and pleasant life.

No matter where you plan to ride, it is impossible to predict life. Because things never proceed exactly as predicted, a Long Rider must learn to keep worries in perspective.

**Daily Schedule.** Life on the road with horses requires one to adjust to a new set of circumstances and to learn to divide the day into four sections. The routine of daily life is a little trying at first, but easily learned; each twenty-four hours is divided into four parts, the period of hurry and activity in the early morning, a longer one of comparative tranquillity on the march, the brief hour of bustle on arriving at our destination, and then, nirvana, the dreaminess of sleep of the night. To rise early is essential. As soon as the horses are watered and enjoying their morning feed, the traveller grabs a quick bite himself. If the tent has been used, then it must be packed away and the equipment prepared for departure. The horses are groomed, tacked up and standing ready. A last walk round the camp is made for lost or forgotten articles. Then it's time to march. Chances to graze during the day are never forsaken. A mid-day meal allows horses and humans both a chance to rest and refresh themselves. Then the trip continues until the early afternoon, at which time the necessity of choosing a camp site or finding shelter takes precedence. It is a life that requires physical strength and emotional effort, so most Long Riders retire early and sleep deeply.

**Rest Days.** Travel is hard work, both physically and emotionally. That is why it is vitally important that every opportunity be taken to conserve the energy of the horses and riders. Horses and humans must both rest. You must always give the horses an appropriate number of rest days to recuperate emotionally and physically! Nor will you regret stopping yourself, as it won't take long before you become overworked by the demands of travel, the physical labour of horse care and the emotional stress which comes from dealing with a constant stream of strangers.

Most Long Riders agree that one day off is not enough for either the horse or the rider. The horse does not have time for sufficient rest and feed, while the rider rushes about on his "day off", going shopping and doing laundry etc. The first day the horse eats as much as he can, the second day he rests. The first day the Long Rider attends to overdue chores, the second day is when he too rests. Chose your rest days carefully. Many Long Riders travel for five days and then stop during the weekend. This allows them to avoid the heavy weekend traffic. But do not think that this is a rule carved in stone. Horses are not motorized transport. You have to keep a careful eye on them. Time is not measured by days, weeks or hours but the fall of the seasons and condition of the animals. If you are travelling at high altitudes, in great heat or where the terrain is very challenging, then you may wish to consider riding for only four days, and then let your horses rest. The point is to be flexible, adapt to local conditions, but to always give your horses the chance to rest and relax as and when they need to. Modern Long Riders should also pay special heed to the need to allow their horses to have quiet time – away from noisy humans. As fewer and fewer equestrian travellers are seen on the road, it is not uncommon for large crowds to gather round them upon their arrival. What seems like a warm welcome to the Long Rider can become an emotional burden to a horse who is tired after a long day's travel.

**Chores.** Horse travel demands daily labour on the part of the Long Rider. Use your rest days wisely, concentrating on accomplishing one set of tasks at each stop. If you are travelling in a foreign country, then consider the extra time required to communicate in a different language and the patience needed to negotiate with an alien culture. Under such conditions, accomplishing one major task or objective a day is a reasonable expectation. The romance rapidly fades when equipment breaks, your clothes tear, the tent needs patching and items need mending. There are always a never-ending number of routine tasks which must be done on a regular basis. They include repacking or reducing the equipment, checking saddles for wear, saddle-soaping all the leather, cleaning the bit and exposing the saddle pads to the sun.

**Your Diary.** Don't rely on the treacherous notebook of your memory! Never stir without paper and pen. Commit to paper whatever you see, hear or read that is remarkable, with your observations on observing it. Do this on the spot, if possible, at the moment it first strikes, at all events do not delay it beyond the first convenient opportunity, for circumstances which often appear trifling to the traveller are very interesting to friends and readers. Long Riders have found that after returning home, because they omitted to write down the details at the time, their memory later almost entirely fails them and they have only a vague recollection of places they rode through. Writing up your observations every evening is an important task. If you're maintaining a diary/journal then you should update it while the day's events are fresh in your mind. Avoid abbreviations. Write clearly, making sure to note the date and time of events. Record the name of the town, no matter how small or apparently insignificant. Ask for people's names and be sure to spell them correctly. Make notes about the availability of feed and water, for the possible use of other Long Riders.

**Anticipating Delays.** The length of the journey will influence how often you will be unexpectedly delayed. The reasons vary enormously. The point is that keeping to a strict schedule is neither realistic nor advisable. Flexibility in the face of adversity should be your rule! Living an open-air life, you learn to readjust, to settle down to hard work, to expect discomforts, to focus on the future and not let the problems of today derail your dreams.

**Time Bandits.** Some problems can be foreseen. One such challenge will be the invasion of strangers into your personal space. An early lesson will be learning how to balance your need for solitude against the curiosity of others. Stories abound about Long Riders who become the unwilling focus of other people. The intensity of the exchange depends upon the country. What must be remembered is that meeting a Long Rider is often a singular experience for most people. They are excited at seeing you, are curious about your journey and perhaps want to offer help or a night's accommodation. Many are also lonesome, and the idea of talking to a far-roaming Long Rider gives them a chance to express thoughts they are often reluctant to discuss with others. There are two problems with spending time with strangers, either in the saddle or on the ground. First, you're a traveller. If you spend your time stopped along the side of the road, gossiping with visitors, you're not going to cover that day's necessary mileage, find the campsite you need, care for your horse properly or have the time required to attend to daily tasks. Next, even if you speak the local language, repeating your story over and over again becomes emotionally draining. This is why it saves time to have a small flyer or postcard, printed in the local language, ready to pass out to interested people. With a smile on your face, you can explain that all the information is provided on the flyer. This brings up another aspect about stopping to talking to strangers. You need to courteously explain to curious pedestrians that taking care of your horse is your primary need. If circumstances require you to stop and talk, then dismount out of courtesy to your mount. If you feel inclined, you can invite the friendly stranger to meet you later that day at your next stop, where you can talk after you have off-saddled.

**Small Goals.** There are a number of ways of maintaining your spirits during a long journey. The first is to remember to relish the moment. You're not just rushing across the landscape, you're a part of the world, you're aware of the weather, and you come across secret places as if magically revealed. Take the time to recall how good it is to be on the journey. While it is important always to keep the final destination in view, the journey is made emotionally easier if you have short-term goals. By breaking the trip up into limited objectives, the completion of each smaller stage becomes a reward unto itself. Reaching these places, which were once nothing more than exotic names on a map, creates a sense of intense emotional importance to a Long Rider. The reaching of such a goal is more than a means to interrupt the monotony of travel. It is a cause for celebration. Reward yourself. If you are in a city, then try to arrange for comfortable lodgings where you can bathe and sleep deeply. After having endured such grim fare on the road, enjoy a good feast. If the opportunity arises, observe local holidays and participate in festivities. Don't forget to reward the horses too. After every 500 miles allow the horses the chance to spend between four and ten days to rest, depending on how difficult the previous stage of the journey had been. These scheduled rest stops give you something to look forward to. But don't forget to be flexible. You're a Long Rider, not an endurance racer. If the weather looks bad, and you're in a safe, dry spot, sit out the bad weather, let your horse rest and enjoy yourself for the day.

**Physical Fatigue.** The journey may indeed take you to a better place – but not without a tremendous effort. Perhaps if you are only travelling for a brief time, over easy ground, in good weather, then your journey may be relaxing; but the longer the distance the greater the amount of physical fatigue. There are no exceptions to this rule. No one is immune from the physical payment demanded by the miles.

**Emotional Exhaustion.** An equestrian journey is exciting to plan, and wonderful to recall years later, but it can be hell to endure it at the time. Intense physical fatigue usually results in emotional exhaustion! Weariness overcomes not just your body but your heart. Some small stressful incident becomes the cause of your temper shattering. Disillusionment appears without warning. Curses rain down on yourself, your comrades, your horse, the whole bloody journey. Dealing with emotional stress is part of a Long Rider's life. Unlike hikers and bicyclists who travel in a relatively carefree manner, equestrian travel involves a large daily dose of anxiety.

Where will you find food and shelter for your horse? Will the next town be friendly? Can you cross that tricky border looming up ahead? Worries vary from the minimum to the profound.

**Dealing with Disappointment.** Just as you should reward yourself after you've reached a certain spot along your route, so as to celebrate your physical progress, you should also protect yourself against the possible emotional disappointment which may arise when you finally arrive at a longed-for goal. It's when you're tired, body and soul, that your spirit begins to deceive you.

**The Lure of Home.** As troubles increase, the rigours of travel will reach a point when they erode a Long Rider's original enthusiasm. The onset of physical and emotional exhaustion makes him long to return home, to see his loved ones, to enjoy a home-cooked meal, to sleep without worrying about tomorrow.

**Sisu.** Sisu is a Finnish term which means the ability to summon up strength of will, determination and perseverance in the face of adversity. Sisu is not the same thing as momentary courage. It denotes the decision to sustain an action against all the odds, regardless of the hardships, despite previous failures, in spite of how grim things may appear at the moment.

**The Ballereau Barrier.** No matter how determined you are; no matter how skilled you are; regardless of how many hard-won miles are under your saddle; despite the validity of your cause; your journey may be destroyed by unexpected circumstances which are beyond your control. Like a sailor encountering a tsunami at sea, one moment you're on course, the next you're struggling to stay alive. It happened to others. It stopped the best. It could strike you. Accept the possibility intellectually and prepare yourself emotionally.

**Hint.** Remember it's about the journey, not the finish line!

# Chapter 81 - Long Rider Ethics

One of The Guild's primary purposes is to ensure that the travelling horse is never deliberately abused. Unfortunately there are individuals who would sacrifice the horse to satisfy their ego. No one who mistreats a horse is fit to own one!

Man has a moral responsibility to treat animals with kindness, dignity and charity. Some people have a lust for recognition. When such men and women take to the saddle, their craving for public attention makes them blind to the pain they are inflicting on their horses. As their addiction to adoration grows, they choose to ignore the extended agony of the animal and subject it instead to torment. Having no hint of dishonour, these individuals reveal the egotistical monstrousness which lurks in mankind. There is more to equestrian travel than tying knots and picketing horses. Discovering your ethical responsibilities is a vital part of reaching your ultimate emotional goal!

Sadly, just like any human effort, there are occasional outlaws who appear in the world of equestrian travel. When these villains appear, they abuse their horses, ride them too hard, do not feed them properly, and continue the journey even if the horse becomes wounded. Such actions are embodied in the Hungarian word *lóháldl*, which states that the horse is expendable.

**No World Records.** There have been occasions when a journey was reduced to a cruel spectacle in an ill-advised attempt to set a world record. Not all travellers are pure-hearted. Once a conman realizes the attraction of the horse, he can misuse the public's trust so as to obtain gifts and money in a fraudulent manner. It is not uncommon for such individuals to invoke God as the justification for their journey, thereby tapping into the religious piety of those they meet.

**Tradition Doesn't Excuse Cruelty.** Many Long Riders are motivated to undertake journeys because of heroes of the past. This inspiration takes various forms. Costumes cannot conceal cruelty.

**Equestrian Narcissistic Disorder.** During my years researching equestrian travel I have collected evidence of what I term "Equestrian Narcissistic Disorder" (END). Narcissism is often associated with egoism, vanity, conceit, selfishness and an indifference to the plight of others. The "others" in this case refers to the horses which are exploited, abused, starved or killed by merciless travellers or mounted criminals. There are many common traits found in the actions of individuals who exhibit the presence of Equestrian Narcissistic Disorder. These include an excessive need for admiration, a preference for showy clothes or historical costumes and a tendency to be an exhibitionist. They commonly overestimate their abilities, exaggerate their achievements, brag persistently and emphasise any trace of danger or hardship. Because their personal goals take precedence over the horse's well-being, they proceed recklessly. If a horse is injured, they are reluctant to halt the journey. They are often in a state of denial about the seriousness of setbacks, injuries or defeats. Even if the horse is killed or injured, they commonly refuse to express remorse or accept responsibility. Having learned how to use the horse to secure the public's trust or to attract an audience, they use cunning to exploit others without regard for their feelings or interests. Their manipulative efforts thrive by continually enlisting the help of unsuspecting victims whom they meet as they ride across the country. They tend to avoid Nature, targeting urban areas which in turns mean they are inclined to follow main roads. Most prefer couch camping in a host's house to sleeping in a tent. Since they are searching for fans, not equals, they avoid contact with genuine Long Riders but take every opportunity to attract the attention of the press and social media. Their desire for attention becomes addictive. Desperate to be labelled the first, the fastest, bravest, sexiest, etc, they never volunteer information about other equestrian travellers to the media, as they are averse to being held in comparison. Most are anxious to deny, ignore or belittle any spiritual aspects of the journey or cannot identify with such an experience. After the trip is completed, they are disinclined to share critical or even life-saving information with others, as this knowledge may benefit Long Riders whom they define as competition. Having essentially ridden alone, they are unable to have friendship with their peers within the equestrian travel world. In his or her eyes, the completion of their journey reinforces a view of himself as being historically special.

**Animal Ethics.** From a purely practical point of view any traveller who fails to protect the welfare of his horses not only exploits the animals' health, he also jeopardises the success of the journey. Additionally, each Long Rider must also listen to his conscience and acknowledge his ethical responsibilities to the animals participating in the expedition. To treat these sentient beings as nothing more than a disposable source of raw power is to disregard the creatures' capacity for suffering. Thus every Long Rider has a moral duty to practise compassion with his equine travelling companions.

**Protecting Horses and the Public.** The Long Riders' Guild was formed to advance the ancient art of equestrian travel and to educate people on how to make a successful equestrian journey. Another important part of our work is to alert the public to the need to exercise emotional and financial caution. The presence of a horse does not automatically denote a trustworthy rider. The Guild is not an international police force. It is a brotherhood of equestrian explorers. Unlike the majority of the modern equestrian world, the Long Riders' Guild does not endorse competition, commercialism or nationalism. Being a Long Rider is not about how fast you can ride across a continent. It is about how the horse encourages personal and spiritual growth during a journey. We collectively realize that accidents occur to horse and rider without premeditation or warning. In such a case the Guild requires that the journey be halted so as to allow the horse the time it needs to heal. There are many examples of ethical Long Riders who have stopped their journeys prematurely because they understood that the physical welfare of the horse takes precedence over their ego.

**Validating Your Journey.** There is another element to ethical equestrian travel. You may be called upon to provide proof that the journey was authentic and that your claim to have reached a distant goal can be confirmed by reliable evidence. Long Riders have recognized the need to document the accuracy of their journeys. These travellers did not keep military style records or collect letters from governors. They carried a special book which contained the names of the people they met, along with that person's signature, date and a personal comment. Friendship Books provide vital evidence which proves the accuracy of your journey.

**The Media.** Dealing with the media has benefits and disadvantages. One of the major inconveniences is that granting an interview is time consuming. You can't afford to be disrespectful; however you also can't sit up on your horse answering questions while valuable travel time slips by. Plus, a Long Rider and his horses attract attention and can distract passing motorists. At least one major automobile accident occurred when an American Long Rider stopped alongside a busy road to answer questions, thereby diverting the attention of nearby drivers, who crashed into each other. It is always better for the horses, and safer for you, to arrange to meet the reporter at day's end, at some secure prearranged spot. Reporters recognize an interesting human interest story when they see a Long Rider. That is why they are usually willing to comply with this simple request.

In addition to the inconvenience, there is the problem of personal intrusion. With the onset of the internet age, Long Riders need to be careful who they speak to. There is a vast difference between a legitimate reporter and a nosy private citizen. A genuine journalist will be able to provide evidence of who they work for. A vindictive cyberstalker pretending to be a reporter will lack such credentials. If you feel any suspicion about the person's authenticity, don't hesitate to politely decline to engage in any type of conversation, telephone call or email exchange. Even if the reporter is authentic, you are within your rights to decline an interview if it conflicts with your travel plans. You are under no obligation to answer questions about your private life! If you feel the interview is going badly, don't hesitate to politely conclude it. Unless you deliberately sought out notoriety, you are not by definition a public figure simply because you chose to travel on horseback.

## Chapter 82 - The Long Quiet

**Turning Away from the World.** There is more to the journey than mere mileage! All brave souls who venture deep into the unknown sooner or later make this discovery: there are two worlds; the physical world which can be mapped and that other world which lies just beyond the edge of everyday events. The value of halting the normal routines of life and learning to reflect inwardly may seem out of step with a world where everything seems gauged towards immediacy. You have to realize that the horse isn't merely taking you towards a distant geographic goal. He is moving you at the same time away from the daily drama of world events. The journey allows you to leave behind the distracting chatter of others and turn off the noise of modern life. The further you ride, the more intense becomes this experience.

**The Onset of Silence.** Few equestrian travellers have realized that their journeys will expose them to such prolonged periods of silence and introspection. Prior to their departure, they are busy trying to learn the skills needed for their journey; how to overcome detractors, how to choose the right horse, how to use a pack saddle, how to summon up the courage to depart. Once they are on the road things settle down into a peaceful pattern. That is when they notice that there are elements to the journey which they had not anticipated. Day after day the gentle rhythmic motions of the horse induce a calming effect upon the traveller. The soothing progress brings on a peace of mind. Silent, alone in his own thoughts, the traveller learns to ride, react and receive. Without distractions, there is time to nurture ideas and to turn inwards with reverence.

Released from the press of the present, their journeys intensify their emotions and enhance their sense of clarity. Thus these long periods of inner silence found on horseback bring many surprises, all of which are more profound that the passing attainment of reaching a distant ocean shore or riding into a foreign city. What is seldom understood is that during the course of an extensive equestrian journey many Long Riders experience epiphanies. Thus the secret of a successful equestrian journey is that you don't find what you thought you were looking for. It's what happens during the "getting there" that reveals the ancient mystery of equestrian travel.

**The Long Quiet.** The Holy Grail is not an object. The Holy Grail is a state of mind. The Long Quiet arrives when the Long Rider least expects it. And the invisible bond that Long Riders share makes for a brotherhood of people who do not ever need to know or speak or write to one another to understand that they share a mystical link. The Long Quiet is why Long Riders never want to come home. To reach the Long Quiet is to touch on a metaphysical link to the wonders of the natural world - to the meaning of the natural universe. Achieving that feeling described as the Long Quiet inspires creativity. It nurtures original ideas. It allows questions to arise unbidden. It encourages creative problem-solving. It enhances deeper understanding.

**Taking your troubles with you.** Equestrian travellers are increasingly expressing concerns about the effects of technology on their journeys. You can't look inwards for the Long Quiet if you're looking downwards at your mobile phone! With the onset of clamorous dissonance, the contemplative mind is overwhelmed and the inward eye is closed. That sense of contented calm is threatened or destroyed when the traveller is unable to disconnect themselves from the social networking scene. Electronic intrusion plays a sort of Russian roulette with the Long Rider's emotions, as the arrival of every email might bring disturbing news. Instead of leaving their troubles behind, they lug them along and check them compulsively via Facebook, Twitter, etc.

**Setting Limits.** The journey should allow you to draw a deep breath, to ponder ideas, to search internally, without being constantly distracted by external stimuli. In order to do this, Long Riders should regulate technology rather than be consumed by it. Just as we are expected to be sensible about not overeating or drinking too much alcohol, we also need to learn to use technology judiciously. Set limits. Evade the constant assault of information. Turn off the noise. Unplug the technology. Seek the Long Quiet. To find the Long Quiet one must swing into the saddle, disconnect from distractions, venture into Nature and explore one's own soul.

# Section Six – The Aftermath

## Chapter 83 - The End of the Journey

**Lessons of the Road.** Many parts of an equestrian journey are predictable and some things you expect. Everyone will have to contend with the caprices of nature. Long Riders past and present have had to overcome a host of hardships. When trouble comes it seems as if the journey has become a relentless emotional and physical trial, specifically designed to break your spirit and destroy your dreams. Then, after the immediate disaster or danger has been overcome, how easy it is to forgive and forget. The scorching sun and the torturing wind of the day are replaced by the comfort of a campfire and the shine of starlight. Curiously enough, despite knowing that more hardships lie ahead, after a night's sleep a fever of restlessness takes hold of the Long Rider. He longs to resume the trek. He sighs with contentment when he is back in the saddle. He ignores the fact that privation may be awaiting him further down the road. The elation of travel has awakened in his blood.

**Life in the Saddle.** Equestrian exploration is a very specific discipline. In order to be successful certain skills must be mastered. Objects such as the saddle, the axe and the tent, which at first seemed exotic, become trusted tools that link the Long Rider in an unbroken line to the past. Wisdom isn't marked on the map. Such understanding occurs incrementally. As fears fade, they are replaced by a desire to press on. The longer the journey, the deeper the mark it leaves. Often a Long Rider passes some invisible point on the earth's surface. When this happens the saddle is transformed from being a symbol of an exotic escape into an altogether unexpected icon.

"Home?" American Long Rider Frank Heath wrote in his diary in 1927. "I have no home except my saddle for a pillow and the blue sky for a roof. I feel free that way, as though I have more room in which to grow."

No one understood this more clearly than English Long Rider Mary Bosanquet. Having set off from Vancouver in 1939, she had ridden solo across Canada. As she neared her final destination of New York City, she lamented the conclusion of a journey that had become a quest that transformed her.

"In ordinary life the houses in which we live are our geographical centres. We go out of them, but only to return. We are like ships at anchor, riding to the length of the anchor chain, but not leaving the harbour. And so we come to belong to the places in which we live. No matter how much we travel from place to place, we are still only scudding from harbour to harbour, only changing our position from one stationary point to another. But in these months with the horses, only the journey has been constant. For I no longer travel to arrive. I no longer belong to lights and fires, to pleasant meal times, to books and pictures and windows curtained at night, but to roads and rivers, to fields and forests, to weather and sky," she wrote. Mary had, she realized, become comfortable with swinging onto her horse and riding, "Out of the unknown, into the unknown again."

**Proceeding Slowly.** Mary and Frank both learned to make the road their home. They never rushed forward thoughtlessly. They never put their horses at risk. They became acclimatised and rode with thoughtful dignity. They did not dwell on the hardships. They took an interest in their progress and enjoyed every moment of the journey. They did not look forward to the end with eagerness. Nor did they think of a return to civilisation as an end to hardship but as the closure of an adventurous and pleasant life. By travelling in this manner, unrushed, at the speed of the horse, they still managed to cross the North American continent with what later seemed to be surprising speed.

Time moves on but enduring truths remain.

In 2014 Brazilian Long Rider Filipe Leite neared the end of his 10,000 mile journey from Canada to Brazil. Filipe wrote in wonder, "As I look at the map, it is hard to understand just how I got here on horseback. It seems impossible! But when you focus on one day at a time and when you put all of your energy in the moment, it is amazing how far you can get."

**Never Ending.** Mary, Frank and Filpe all reached a point in their travels where the rhythm of the journey had become so strong that they didn't want it to end. They had learned the value of simplicity, had experienced the wealth of human kindness, had learned to sleep in a different place every night, that the perfect journey is never finished, that there is always one more track to explore, one more mirage to follow. The trip, which had at first represented such an incredible challenge, had become part of their lives. Instead of hardship they had discovered solitude and peace. These Long Riders and many more reached a point in their journey where only an ocean could have stopped them. They longed to ride on forever. Then sorrow caught up with them.

**The Realisation.** Suddenly it is over. You spend your last day in the saddle looking at the faithful horse that has carried you so far. You hold the reins in your fingers and marvel at the simple beauty of these strings of freedom. Everything looks fresh, alive, and you know you're going to miss it – for the rest of your life! Long Riders often experience a sense of shock at the end of their ride. Looking back on the journey, the days seem to have gone by so fast. The distant goal has been reached. But instead of a sense of triumph, there is often a feeling of regret. You realize that there will never be another day like this. Tonight you will not fall asleep under a wild moon. Tomorrow you will not sit astride your proud steed. The victory is bittersweet.

**Preparing to Return.** The beginning and the conclusion of a journey are both important events. However they arouse different emotions. Whereas you set off with a tinge of excitement, it is often common to feel a bit of fear when you receive your marching orders out of paradise. People feel uncertain, apprehensive, unresolved, bewildered, sad and exhausted when their journey ends. They are going to be required to go from a life of freedom back into the cramped and conventional world. Instead of looking for grazing, they will be looking for a job. Instead of worrying about the weather, they will be worried about money. To return again to all the cares of life called civilised, with all its listlessness, its newspapers all full of nothing, its sordid aims disguised under high-sounding nicknames, its hideous riches and its sordid poverty, its want of human sympathy, and, above all, its barbarous wars brought on by the folly of its rulers, is not an alluring thought. Before the final day arrives, you should give serious thought to how you want your journey to end, because many years later your memories of that special day will be as vivid as if they were yesterday.

**The Quiet Arrival.** Most people never depart on a life-changing journey, preferring to stay huddled at home. For those who do set out, the arrival at a distant destination may represent a variety of internal meanings including personal redemption, the renewal of hope or the solution to a spiritual dilemma. For some it may be an intensely private moment whose origins stretch back many years. There are no odometers on a saddle. There is no magic mark in the dust. Often there may be no obvious landmark to mark the conclusion of the trip.

**The Big Finish.** For some the conclusion has been a moment of public celebration. When Aimé Tschiffely completed his legendary ride from Argentina to the United States in 1927, he was greeted as a hero by the American President and received a ticker tape parade as he rode through New York City. But sometime things don't fall into place when you reach the end of the rainbow.

**Disappointment.** Long Rider dreams don't always come true because things don't always turn out the way you expect. You underestimate the budget. Borders refuse to open. Horses become ill, are stolen or die. A companion deserts. Illness knocks you flat. At some point you realize you're not having fun any more. You're riding out of duty. That's when you know it's time to stop. The line of travel you had drawn with such confidence on the map back at home will never be completed. Or if it does you may not be happy with what you find when the journey ends. There is another element which comes into play at the conclusion of an equestrian journey; fate.

**Broken Dreams.** Not everyone returns to happiness. Sometimes you become vulnerable to bitter disappointment.

**Judging the Rewards of Failure.** The topic of "failure" is of vital importance to those of us who participate in and study the ancient art of equestrian exploration. And whereas the public is always eager to hear a tale about a bold victory, those of us who have journeyed know that success often hangs by a slender thread. After surviving a ride across the Libyan Desert in 1923, Egyptian Long Rider Sir Ahmed Mohammed Hassanein wrote, "To the outside world the work of an explorer is either failure or success with a distinct line between them. To the explorer himself that line is very hazy. He may have won his way through, amassed all the information that he sought, be within a score of miles of his journey's end; then suddenly, his camels give out. He must abandon the best part of his luggage. Water and food take precedence; the boxes containing his scientific instruments, his records, have to be left behind. Maybe his plight is still worse, and he must sacrifice everything, even his own life. To the outside world he would be a failure; generous critics might even call him a glorious failure, but in any case he has failed. Yet how much is that failure akin to success! Sometimes on those long treks the man who fails has done more, has endured more hardships, than the man who succeeds. An explorer's sympathy is rather with the man who has struggled and failed than with the man who succeeds, for only the explorer knows how the man who failed fought to preserve the fruits of his work."

**Defining Success.** In this day when it is all too often argued that there are no "white spots" left on the map, critics falsely claim there is no longer any purpose to explore. Why go there, they say, when you can gaze at a faraway spot thanks to Google? For those of us who have responded, and gone, we know that the mere act of setting off is in itself a victory. As for "failure," that is a term all too often misunderstood, and frequently used, by those who stayed behind in the comfort and safety of their homes. Many Long Riders have felt the past calling to the present. They have longed to venture into unknown lands and satisfy their desire to see things first hand. Not all their dreams and journeys were realized.

**A Safe Conclusion.** As this chapter demonstrates, there is a need to consider how you conclude your journey. Will your ride end alone in a quiet place? This is often what happens when people ride "ocean to ocean" across the United States. Do your plans require you to finish your ride at a symbolic spot, a historical monument or a public building? If so then you should have allowed plenty of time to arrange for the conclusion of your ride to be planned well in advance. Government representatives are always busy, so if you wish to invite them to attend in an official capacity then you should give them plenty of advance notice. One traveller who made a dramatic journey across the United States failed to understand this. Consequently when he arrived at the state capital, there was no one there to meet him. Don't forget the press. On the last day of an extensive journey Long Riders experience a range of emotions including euphoria and exhaustion. Care should be used if you are interviewed by the media. Finally, there is always the practical side of things. With cameras rolling, photos being taken and newspaper reporters asking questions, your attention will undoubtedly be diverted. This is an excellent opportunity for thieves to loot your gear while you are distracted.

When you step down from the saddle on that last day, remember this Navajo prayer.

"May it be beautiful before me. May it be beautiful behind me. May it be beautiful above me. May it be beautiful all around me. In beauty it is finished."

# Chapter 84 - Saying Goodbye to your Horse

On a journey like this a traveller does not possess his horses; they possess him, body and soul. Equestrian travel has never been about riding in circles, winning blue ribbons or garnering the acclaim of the mob. A journey marks the soul's solitary progress across the physical plain of our temporary existence. This passage on horseback becomes a metaphor for life.

Early on, our desire is threatened when people try to talk us into not setting off. Being consumed with fear themselves; they envy our determination to undertake what they know they lack the courage to try. So they fill our ears with tales of certain death, appeal to our sense of responsibility, attempt to burden us with guilt. Not knowing if we will live, die or succeed, we suppress our concerns and set off into the unknown anyway. Along the way we encounter unexpected dangers, endure hardships, suffer loss, overcome superstitions, conquer dragons, face our fears, find ourselves – or not. All too often we are betrayed, disappointed and deceived along the way by those we trusted, loved and respected. Sometimes we fail. Occasionally we die.

But the journey, like life, has unexpected turns. If we succeed, we are blessed, enlightened, changed from what we were into someone we only suspected dwelled within. During the ride the horse has been an inspired leader, strong servant, trusted guide, brave companion, fleet messenger and faithful friend. He has done more than merely carry us. He has enchanted our heart.

Hidden behind the veil of nature, however, is a touch of sorrow. We have kept him from harm's eye. Now, with our journey ended, our greatest desire is to provide him with the two things he most rightly deserves, protection and freedom. Instead we watch as he is led away by a stranger into the unknown. After he is gone we are like a tree with only one branch. We are left with an affliction of love. Events link the two of you like the shores of an immense sea. Though you may never meet again; all roads lead back to his memory. Perhaps he will talk to you in your dreams.

**The Bond.** One thing remains consistent. Time after time, in journey after journey, hardship, fatigue, and hunger have brought horse and human closer and closer together. The two travellers may be from different species but they shiver together in wind and rain. They jointly endure bitter cold and blazing heat. Together they starve and then rejoice over a meal. They face the same perils with the same chances of escape or annihilation. Theirs is a community centred upon cooperation, sharing, sacrifice and support for one another.

**The Guide.** But there is more to this relationship than just loyalty. A mounted brute calculates the animal's value in terms of its efficiency. For him the horse is merely there to provide the physical means of locomotion. To many the horse is a source of friendship and camaraderie. A few Long Riders learn that the horse sometime serves as a vista into another world. Though speechless, he becomes the spiritual kernel of the journey. The horse has often changed the fundamental identity of the Long Rider. In such cases there is a mixing of horse and human; a merger of instinct and reason. The two halves induce a third, a rare and perfect whole.

**How they view the journey.** According to the laws of Nature the horse relies on senses which humans have either lost or never attained. On the surface he appears to be emotionally self-contained, inhabiting a world which lacks deception. Thus we can only guess what he feels in his heart. But you don't need much imagination to realize that horses love to travel. In return for some hay, a measure of grain, a drink of pure water and a kind word, they exhibit a source of perennial optimism. They exalt in their freedom, as is evidenced when other horses, trapped like convicts behind fences, run up and stare enviously at the road horse that is passing by on an adventure.

**The Nomadic Horse.** Nature didn't design large horses to spend their lives cooped up in cramped stables like rats in a lab cage! They were bred to live beneath the sky and run in the sunlight. A road horse is a return to that earlier time. Circumstances may cause the road horse to endure driving rain, biting flies and small meals. But in return it has been blessed with a dazzling dose of freedom. The constant walking makes it incredibly fit. The animal has a robust appetite; develops the ability to sleep anywhere, becomes hard, lean, resilient and resourceful. In addition, the constant motion awakens the wanderlust in horses. Like their riders, they acquire a love of travel and are always anxious to start a new day full of adventures.

But with the journey concluded, a question arises. What will these unique, brave and curious horses do next? Like their human companions, the answer depends upon the individual. Some settle down contentedly. After travelling for thousands of miles under the wandering moon, road horses often have a problem adapting to life in a stable. In cases such as these the horse has reached the point where it believes that tomorrow will be just like today. It thinks it will spend tonight in a different field and then move on with the sun. It never suspects that the journey has an ending. When told, if the horse could speak, it would undoubtedly say, "I've

240

served you well and loyally. And I am eager to continue. My only regret is that I am no longer needed and we cannot travel on together."

Now comes the moment in the journey when the future of the horse must be decided with dignity and justice.

**Three Emotions.** No matter what century or country, all Long Riders share certain things in common. Through everything the horse has provided unchanging companionship and unbroken trust. He has been tireless and kind. He has suffered and helped you. As a result the two of you are bound by feelings of friendship and the memory of dangers shared. Yet all the while you've been riding, anguish has been stalking silently behind you. Like two sides of a river, you have never met. Now, after having survived it all, Fate saves her harshest trick until last. Destiny has pronounced a decision from which there is no appeal. The time has come for the Long Rider to learn that the journey is a trip through three emotions; Hope, Trust and Remorse. There is sorrow in the final discovery that for many Long Riders this incredible companionship must now end.

**A Long Rider's Obligation.** A moral fault line runs through our journey; sentiment versus necessity.

How do we balance our personal needs against theirs? Are horses partners or victims? Powerful or powerless? Though religion and science can conflict, both offer similar evidence about the need to provide justice for your horse. The Sufis speak of zikr, a spiritual state of mind and heart wherein devotees seek to realize the presence of God. Such striving of oneself in God's way, via an ordinary daily activity, can be seen in the Long Riders love and devotion to his horse. Goodness, kindness, generosity, courage, devotion to duty, as opposed to vanity, cruelty and unworthy motives. Even if he is not religious, a Long Rider shows that though the horse may be devoid of civil rights, he is nevertheless a divine gift and deserving of our sympathy and practical service. Disregard religion and ignore science; you'll still realize that adventure and adversity equals duty. After such shared suffering, there can be no victorious end if you treat your horse with shame! Every Long Rider must discharge this ethical obligation conscientiously. By ensuring the horse's welfare you guarantee that the journey concludes with integrity. For any member of the Long Rider's Guild, this is the sacrosanct principle. It underpins any expedition on horseback. In all that is written in the hundreds of books that the Guild publishes and the thousands of pages which its web site provides, this conviction remains unassailable. The well-being of the horse is paramount!

**Weighing Your Options.** Many famous tales have been told about friends who depart together on a journey. Over the months they survive many challenges and forge an unforgettable relationship. But there is a difference among travellers. When Jason returned with the Golden Fleece, he said goodbye to his fellow Argonauts. He didn't sell them. To part with a horse who will not miss one is bad, but to part with a horse who will miss one is as bad as anything I know. The question then becomes, what do you do with the horses? According to Mongol custom, a horse that had survived combat was retired to a life at grass. You may not have that option. Depending upon what country you are in, the choices confronting you can range from acceptable to horrific.

**Separating the Horses.** The first challenge depends upon how many horses you have. Do you keep them together or separate the group? Horses may not have the capability of expressing speech but science has proved that they have excellent memories which enable them to learn and memorize human words. They are also skilled communicators among their own kind. They whinny if one of their fellows wanders too far away. They form tremendous bonds of loyalty to one another during the course of an extended journey. Most importantly, they display signs of extreme emotional distress if separated from their travelling companions. Many Long Riders have witnessed their horses suffering intense separation anxiety.

**Friends for Life.** Various Long Riders have confirmed that the bond which is formed among their horses is so powerful that when the journey is over, road horses tend not to mingle with non-travelling horses. Years after her journey, Basha O'Reilly's stallion, Count Pompeii, still routinely ignored other horses. After riding 13,000 kilometres (8,000 miles) across the United

241

States, Lucy Leaf's gelding, Igor, also preferred to live alone. An intense emotional bond is created among travelling horses and separating them presents a serious problem. Keeping them together depends upon the options available in the country where the journey is concluded.

**Running Free.** Straight away, you can forget the Hollywood mythology of just setting the horse free in a sea of green grass where it will run and play among other horses. That might work as a fairy tale ending to a movie like *Hidalgo*, but not in the harsh reality of the modern horse world. Wild horses are rounded up every year by American government authorities. Cruel methods are often used. The captured horses are held in pens for years and are then auctioned off to an uncertain future, which might include being shipped to a meat factory. Because of this American Long Riders have opted to keep their horse rather than grant it a freedom that might cost the animal its life.

**A Home for Life.** Many Long Riders are blessed with the option of providing a permanent home for their horses. The question then becomes, how to get the horse home?

**Bringing Them Home.** One thing to keep in mind is that it has never been easy to bring horses home. The cost of shipping horses overseas has always been expensive and remains so today. After buying horses in Australia in 2004, Edouard Chautard and Carine Thomas rode 5,000 kilometres (3,000 miles) along the Bicentennial National Trail. They then decided to ship their three horses home to New Caledonia. The price was US$5,000 per horse. A bank loaned them the money, after they agreed to a three-year repayment plan.

**Gifting the Horse.** At the end of a long and dangerous ride, many Long Riders find themselves in a strange country. They are physically and emotionally exhausted. They are almost always financially impoverished. In such cases some equestrian travellers decided to give their horses to friends. Some Long Riders presented their horses to a person who was full of respect for the journey that had been made. After Baron Fukushima completed his journey from Berlin to Tokyo, the Emperor of Japan expressed admiration for the Long Rider's hardy native horses and then guaranteed their safety for life. Other Long Riders have discovered places which could provide safe havens for their horses. Tim Cope donated his three horses to a Hungarian orphanage, where they were ridden and cared for by loving children. Other Long Riders have given their horses to someone who can use them for work in exchange for feeding them.

The conclusion of a journey places a Long Rider at a tactical disadvantage if he is overseas. Time and money may be short. The desire to return home may be pressing. In such circumstances it is easy for a smart stranger to take emotional advantage of a tired traveller. Do not be deceived by appearances. Question the possible new owner thoroughly. Inspect the property carefully. If possible, ask for a written agreement which states that the horses are being donated provided certain conditions are met. This might include not separating or selling the animals without first notifying the Long Rider. Updates on how the horses are doing may also be a term of the agreement.

**Harsh Realities.** Finding a kind-hearted person who is willing to give horses a home for life is rare. All too often the traveller cannot foresee the unpleasant circumstances which await him. Sometimes injuries occur during the course of the journey which prohibit the horse from continuing. Such an accident forced Tim Cope to find a home for his first pack horse.

Government interference is another cause of concern. After English Long Rider Donald Brown completed his ride from the Arctic Circle to Copenhagen in 1953, he encountered such bureaucratic obstructions. He was particularly distressed at the loss of his remarkable mare, Pilkis, who could not be shipped to England because of legalities.

A lack of money has forced many a Long Rider to realize he cannot afford to keep his horse. After completing a gruelling ride in 2013 across the deserts and mountains of the American West, Clay Marshall realized he had could not keep his horses. "Sadly my life in the civilized world couldn't support the needs of an equine family. My wife and I lived in the city. We didn't own a barn, pasture, or even land and we didn't have the time and money to give the horses the attention they need. Even if I could have afforded it, I wouldn't pay for my horses to waste away in a stall the remainder of their days."

The goal is to end the journey with an upright heart and a happy horse. In each of these cases, the Long Rider found a suitable home for the animals. Because they were forced to sell their horses, the decision left scars on the travellers' souls. Other individuals have had no qualms in sending their horses off to a cruel future.

**Easy Come Easy Go.** There are all types of sins. The Bible warns against seven notorious examples; anger, greed, laziness, pride, lust, envy and gluttony. It forgot to include the misdeed of deliberately delivering your horse to a pitiless fate or an unkind master. Sometimes fate forces a Long Rider to sell a horse. It can't be helped. But that doesn't excuse those individuals who purloined their honour by selling their horses without a thought to their future welfare. Some things are so fundamental that they should be obvious. Yet none of these individuals understood that the need to protect the integrity of the horse doesn't stop when you step down from the saddle. In each of these cases the traveller turned the journey into a publicized stunt wherein ego and public acclaim become more important than the horse-human relationship. One cannot reduce equestrian travel to that of a product! It is never a jar of jam or a dossier of dust-covered facts ready to be presented for scientific inspection. At the heart of the matter is the mutual journey carried out by two sympathetic beings, a Long Rider and a Road Horse. I speak with great conviction because I have been forced to part from a horse I loved. I learned from painful experience that it is never the mileage that matters. The miles never blind us to the heart ache of leaving an equine friend. And if, like me, you set out on the long grey road then you too may be forced to leave behind your treasured horse.

**The Emotional Cost.** No Long Rider can come to this tragic parting without learning the meaning of real sorrow. Other Long Riders have written about the depth of their emotional attachment to their horses. The toughest equestrian explorers, who have ignored hardship and sneered at danger during their journeys, have experienced incredible remorse when they are forced by necessity to leave their gallant horse behind.

**Selling.** There is an old Long Rider saying, "Horses are our life. They are not our livelihood." This concept is based upon the fact that your horse has carried you further than you thought possible. He has been your trusted ally in unknown territory. You have built a life together. You have felt his soft breath across your face. How can you leave such an animal? But harsh reality sometimes forces us to do so.

**The Practicalities.** Like all aspects of equestrian travel, if circumstances dictate that a horse must be sold then there are realities which cannot be ignored. Normally, a horse owner living in his own country has the luxury of making sure the animal looks its best. The horse is advertised in such a way as to highlight its beauty, training and performance. Time is often on the side of such a seller. Those are not the type of circumstances which Long Riders normally encounter. If you are in a foreign land the potential buyers know you are cornered and under pressure. That is why you can count on them to exploit you financially and emotionally.

First, do not think that your horses will be accorded any degree of fame because they have just completed a remarkable journey. On the contrary, crafty buyers routinely ignore the animal's obvious robust health. They tell the Long Rider that the journey has rendered the horse "weak." Never expect to sell the horse for the same price that you originally paid. Throughout history equestrian explorers have learned that profiteering is a highly-developed skill among horse dealers. The majority of Long Riders have been forced to accept a financial loss rather than run the risk of keeping the horse in the hope of a better price at a later date. The expense and uncertainty of this practice are too great. It doesn't help your chances if there is a glut of horses already on the market.

Another problem Long Riders encounter in foreign countries is that potential buyers have no actual currency. The first part of Tim Cope's journey took him across Mongolia. But he was not permitted to take his horses out of the country. To Tim's surprise, his idea of selling the horses to local nomadic herders was complicated for an unexpected reason. "The problem with selling is that you usually need to sell quickly. But nomads make such decisions very carefully and very few of them need any more horses. Worst of all I found it very hard to find any herders who had any cash. Most were willing to swap in exchange for another horse, a sheep, a yak or maybe a saddle with stirrups."As a result, Tim lost "at least 50 per cent of the value" of his horses when he finally sold them.

When the time comes, always write up a dated "Bill of Sale" for each horse being sold. Include the physical details of the horse, including age, sex, colour, markings and the condition of its health. This is to protect you against a case of "buyer's remorse," if the horse is returned and the money demanded back. Note the price being paid and state if the purchase price is being made by cash, cheque or in trade. Be sure the buyer, seller and a witness all sign this dated document. The "Long Rider International Equine Bill of Sale" provided in this book will serve this purpose.

**Deadly Deception.** The ancient Latin phrase "Caveat Emptor" translates as "Let the buyer beware." It is usually used to emphasise the point that the buyer is often not in full possession of all the facts.

Long Riders should instead memorize the phrase "Caveat Auctor," which means let the seller be on his guard. Should circumstances force you to sell your horse, your legal rights and the horse's life may both be forfeit.

**Slaughter.** Before making an equestrian journey, it pays to learn if the inhabitants of that country eat horses or export them to other nations to be used as meat. These practices make selling horses a dangerous proposition if you are trying to ensure its long-term safety. Mongolia and Kazakhstan both have a strong reputation for consuming horse meat. Whereas the Mongols normally eat horses in winter, the Kazakhs consume them all year round. Tim Cope was terribly aware of these cultural and dietary practices. Whereas in the past nomads valued a horse for its abilities, Tim learned that times had changed. Instead of caring how strong or beautiful the horse was, modern Kazakhs were interested in how much fat and meat was on the animal. That is why, after buying his horses in Kazakhstan, he had no illusion about what fate awaited the animals if they were left behind. He advised other Long Riders riding in Kazakhstan to try to avoid selling a horse in a town or city because "the horses will most likely end up as meat." He also warned that the province of Bayan Olgiy has a strong reputation for horse-meat consumption. His advice is to try and find a nomadic herder to sell the horses to.

Bonnie Folkins, who has also ridden in Kazakhstan, offered another valuable insight. Although the idea of donating the horses might appear to be noble, she strongly advises against trying to give the horses away as gifts. "The mentality is completely different there," she warned. "People in Kazakhstan will not understand that sort of philanthropy. They will think you are foolish for giving away expensive horses and in turn will not treat you with respect. In fact, they may even be somewhat suspect if you do this. If they are given away as gifts, whoever ends up with the horses will simply try to sell them for profit and may not treat them well." Bonnie advised, "If you have good horses, they will command a reasonable fee. If they are purchased by respectable dealers, farmers or trades people, they will be treated kindly and such people will take the animal's best interests to heart. Anyone making such an investment will be prepared to make a sacrifice and be committed to keeping the horses in good health and sound condition."

**A Life of Cruelty.** There is no point in pretending that other countries share the same values. Many Long Riders have noted the cruelty inflicted upon horses by people with varying views on animal kindness. Long Riders must recognize the fact that there are savage countries which tolerate brutal customs.

**The Last Resort.** Previous generations of Long Riders were perfectly aware that many countries treated horses with unspeakable cruelty. When the journey ended they opted to protect their horses from a lifetime of pain by mercifully putting them down.

The idea of putting your horse down may seem shocking and abhorrent to modern readers.

But if you absolutely cannot assure yourself that you can find safe, decent, homes for your horses then put them down rather than permit them to be abused. Allow your horse to retain its dignity. A bullet is kinder than years of starvation and torture. A lethal injunction is preferable to a delayed life of misery. Euthanasia is better than a cooking pot.

The ultimate outcome of your horse's future depends upon actions. Don't believe honeyed words and false promises. If in your soul you have doubts about the other person's sincerity, listen to your instincts. Never let your horse fall into cruel and unholy hands.

**Saying Goodbye.** How the world gives and takes away. You remember what you have both gone through. But the last day has dawned. The friend who has changed your life is leaving. You can't believe this moment has arrived. Life won't be the same. Many a brave Long Rider has struggled to sum up what won't go into words. Many a Long Rider has found him or herself standing there, alone in the road, feeling forlorn, lonely and unsure of what to do next.

**Grief.** How do you say farewell to the companion of your finest days? What do you do when you find yourself caught in a whorl of anguish and grief? It's hard to comprehend the dimensions of the heartache a Long Rider often experiences. Many travellers report feelings of loss and recrimination.

Nothing in truth can replace a Long Rider's equine companions. You are bound forever to your horses by a treasure of common memories. Theirs was a friendship which neither time nor distance can mar. The feeling of brotherhood lasts longer than the journey which produced it. This is something which no Long Rider can explain but every Long Rider has felt.

# Chapter 85 - Who You Have Become

When the trip is over, the land remains the same. Not so the Long Rider. You set off like a shy child. But now the seasons of the journey have altered you in an invisible manner. You sit at the table amongst those who knew you prior to your departure. Though you returned physically, you are no longer one of them. There is a distance in your eyes. You hear them speaking to you, using the same name as when you left. But they no longer know you. The journey challenged you, broke you, rewarded you, liberated you, renewed you and erased you.

Later, when you look in the mirror, thoughts come unbidden. What marks a man, you ask yourself? What scores his soul? I am not me any more, you conclude. I am not who I was. A stranger has returned bearing my name.

Equestrian travel is, on the one hand, simply a manner of transportation. Yet as history has repeatedly demonstrated, Long Riders are far more complex than that. They consistently refuse to join the mainstream. Instead they set their own standards and maintain their own individual ideals. Over and over they demonstrate that it's not about settling for who you are. It's about believing in who you can become.

What the Long Riders in this book represent is hope; hope that all of us can do something special with our lives, hope that we can make a difference, hope that we too can find excitement in an all-too-predictable world. Eventually the waves of time will wash away all these lives and the memory of many of these journeys. But for the Long Riders who made these trips that will not matter because they will have sanctified their existence by their mighty efforts. Mary Bosanquet understood that. She spoke for all the Long Riders when she wrote, "Whatever comes, I shall have done one thing for which I thank God. An urgent, vital day. A day that says, live while you can, and die when you must; take all that comes and give everything you've got; only don't fear, don't waste; be alive while you can."

**The Journey.** Even though Long Riders travel in a straight line towards a distant goal, the journey marks a turning point in their lives, the sharpest turn many of them will ever encounter. The journey has two levels, the outer and the inner. The former is a transitory geographic goal. The latter is a link to the eternal. Travel is an art, not only of fastening the buckles and keeping things together, but relating to what you see. Wise Long Riders understand that the journey can be experienced by the senses but never fully explained by words. It becomes a symbol of the unity of worlds visible and invisible. Long periods of time spent in the saddle envelop the traveller in silence, listening, remembering and, hopefully, understanding. Though the traveller rides alone, he realizes that he is linked with those who rode in previous centuries. Exploration is no longer about planting flags and staking claims: it's a right and a duty for every generation to satisfy its longing for meaning and purpose. Yes, a potential flame can burn in every heart but it cannot shine amidst confusion. The joy of riding in freedom has different effects. Self realisation comes to some.

**Choices.** Few Long Riders realize there may be emotional implications associated with their return. Prior to their departure they were too busy protecting their dreams from the critics who stay behind to give any thought to a distant homecoming. It is never easy to ride away from the mentality of the herd. The poet e e cummings warned, "To be nobody but yourself in a world which is doing its best, night and day, to make you everybody else means to fight the hardest battles which any human being can fight, and never stop fighting.

But the act of departure signals more than the start of a long march towards a distant geographic goal. It is a declaration that the Long Rider is responding to a desire to live in a way different from that which was dictated to him at birth, by parents, culture, religion, sex, politics and economics. Even before he swings into the saddle the Long Rider's eyes have been opened. He realizes he faces a choice between collaboration and resistance. Should he listen to those who urge him to seek safety within an urban existence? Does he follow the herd and direct all his energies toward obtaining the comforts of life?

Not being satisfied with what appears to be his predetermined destiny, Long Riders have to resolve to change it. They respond to an ancient message implanted deep within their DNA that urged them to undertake a migration away from predictability. They instinctively knew that even on a planet where every place had supposedly already been explored, the last great unresolved mystery was to be found hidden within their own souls.

Such freedom is worth a little hardship. Long Riders are the modern mounted pilgrims of the sunrise. They have set themselves a goal which seems far beyond their reach. They are often scared before setting off because they are literally riding into unknown country on many levels. But they have determined to pay the price to find their soul's desire.

**Challenges.** Many dream of making an equestrian journey. Few ever summon the courage to set off on the difficult path towards self-reliance. When they do, it doesn't take long for the romance to be stripped away remorselessly. Awaiting those who depart is the bare and barren truth. A host of physical and emotional challenges will force them to confront the limits of their strength. They learn to endure hardships and heartaches. Adversity teaches them perseverance. Overcoming illness bestows confidence. Ignoring hunger develops an iron resolution. Facing the unknown gives them courage.

Long Riders aren't imbued with magical powers. They aren't born with special talents that qualify them to undertake such difficult trips. When confronted with ordeals they have to resist and find a way forward. They must overcome uncertainty and summon the will to continue. As the miles fall behind them, a mixture of courage and curiosity grows stronger as the outline of who they once were grows dimmer. The deeper they dig within themselves, the stronger becomes the desire to complete the journey no matter what. A growing sense of individual identity fuels their desire to accomplish something special in their lives.

**Changes.** Lao Tzu, the Chinese philosopher credited with founding the concept of Taoism, warned, "The farther one travels the less one knows." Wisdom is not automatically gained by self-sacrifice. Discomfort is no guarantee of knowledge. Many a fool has ridden 10,000 hard miles and returned home just as ignorant as the day he left. Thus, a journey may be arduous but not be counted a success on another level. What is surprising is that no matter where their diverse journeys have taken them, Long Riders who return often share a surprising number of discoveries in common.

Roger Pocock spoke for many when he said that an equestrian journey gave him an increased sense of energy, strength, well-being and alertness. Many have reported learning how few material possessions one needs to be happy. The stark reality of life in the saddle has demonstrated the value of simplicity. While food, shelter and friends remain high priorities, "things" have greatly diminished in importance. They have learned the truth of the saying, "The more you know, the less you need." After having won through so many hardships, such travellers have learned to be grateful for yesterday, to live for today and remain hopeful for tomorrow. They accept good fortune, or bad, with equal equanimity. One part of their apprenticeship has been the need to survive in all weathers. Constant exposure to the elements has taught them to respect and reconnect with the natural cycles of the seasons. Unlike a competitive event, the horse had not separated the traveller from those he met. It revealed to the Long Rider the essential unity of mankind, as the horse's soothing presence enriched countless lives along the way.

**Lessons.** I have spent time with many of the greatest Long Riders. I always met them alone at our first encounter. That is because they radiate intensity. They have the dignified bearing of those who stand apart. There is always a distance in their eyes. When they speak, you hush and listen. They were sleepless souls awaiting another dawn departure. And every meeting still echoes in my memory. The path they chose to follow was complex and often hidden. They had elected to push beyond the boundaries of their previously-known lives. The further they rode the more narrow notions they left behind. Competitive riders are about control, the search for robotic equine perfection, the glorification of ego, the worship of money. The vast majority of so-called 'explorers' are publicity-hungry adventurers seeking thrills and recognition. Long Riders belong in neither of those camps. They crossed rivers and rode over mountains to find personal secrets.

American Long Rider Andi Mills made momentous personal discoveries riding across that country in 2007. She wrote, "The first one thousand miles drove home the realization that the destination is not nearly as important as the journey to reach it. I learned the cavernous difference between 'needs' and 'wants.' I learned, not only to endure and overcome difficulties, but to truly embrace them for the valuable lessons they teach me. I learned to be content in my circumstances, no matter what they might be at the moment and most importantly, I learned that true contentment is a choice. By the time my journey came to an end, I no longer held any illusions about myself. I knew exactly who I was and exactly who I was not. How many people live and die, not knowing that simple truth?"

**Perspective.** In the beginning of most journeys, the overwhelming emotion is apprehension. Anyone who rides a great distance and survives an assortment of perils will certainly return with many a tale to tell, as travel has represented a period of discontinuity from previous activities and beliefs. What is unique is when the traveller recognizes that they have undergone an internal alteration as well, that there has been a realignment of their emotional compass. "It is a rare fish that knows it swims in water," an ancient proverb states.

Yet many Long Riders have recognized the power of this period and understood that it has influenced their reflective consciousness. They realised they had returned enriched with more principles and were more receptive. They understood that they had not escaped from their previous problems. Only now they were more able to put them into perspective. Bit by bit the effect of the journey sinks into the deep parts of your soul and leaves an impression ever afterwards which renders everything else feeling tame by comparison. It has taught you things about yourself that you could not have learned in any other way.

One vital lesson learned by many is the need to balance the reality of daily action against inner tranquillity. Millions of tourists set off on holidays every year. Few come back wiser from the experience. Their goal was to get a tan, not take their destiny into their own hands. They were not required to travel in such a way that every faculty had been extended. They had not returned with a new vision of their lives and the world won through hardship.

The journey changes many of us. The older we get, the stronger and more obvious become the marks as they draw nearer to the surface.

**The Brevity of Life.** We are here but a moment. Where we came from, and where we ultimately return to, remains a mystery which defies the attempts of priests and atheists to solve. All we know is that for a twinkling of the universe's eye, we are here, cognizant, awake, alive – and capable of doing great things with our lives. Most are content with being defined as someone's offspring, sibling, spouse, aunt, uncle or friend. People rush to be associated with a sports team because it identifies them as members of a local or national herd. They seek friends on Facebook because it provides them with a collective identity. They use others to define themselves because they lack the courage to stand alone. The mystery of their existence is as visible to them as it is to anyone else, but they prefer to delay contemplation of the inevitable. It is always summer. Time is everlasting. They live their lives as if they are exceptions to the doom that awaits us all.

When you put your life into perspective, and factor in horses, you should ask yourself if what you do reflects who you are and what you symbolize. Does winning a blue ribbon, because your horse could make a certain movement or jump over painted sticks, constitute your legacy? Journeys have always symbolized more than mere geography. They are the migration of our soul searching for answers. From Ulysses to Tschiffely, a brave few have set off in search of more than a mere destination. What they have been seeking is a meaning to mysteries. What we do reflects who we are. Undertaking the journey is about far more than reaching the shore of a physical ocean. The water may have halted your physical progress, but in an indefinable way, you can never be stopped again – because you are no longer the person you once were.

**Peace.** In a purely physical sense many Long Riders conclude the journey after having defied perils, ridden through black nights and felt the blood running hot through their veins. The journey proves they were not among the complacent. Having faced challenges and overcome them, the Long Rider realises he doesn't have to prove anything to anyone. He has stood up to the test. As a result the traveller has returned not only safe but strengthened with a formidable power of the spirit. He has ridden the miles, yes. But in addition his soul has been replenished, a longing fulfilled, a thirst satisfied. Having ridden through the Terra Incognita of his own life, the traveller has found solace, quiet, freedom and clarity. Like the legendary Aimé Tschiffely, many a Long Rider set off as an underdog. Along the way the traveller found self-esteem, courage, patience and resilience. He learned not to care what may befall him tomorrow because of what he survived yesterday.

For many a sense of restlessness has been driven out, replaced by a feeling of serenity. Long Rider Samuel Butler explored New Zealand in 1862. He articulated this sense of serenity when he wrote, "There came upon me a delicious sense of peace, a fullness of contentment which I do not believe can be felt by any but those who have spent days consecutively on horseback."

Others realised how a long0held desire for something missing had been replaced by a sense of arrival. Ella Maillart, recalling how she rode from Peking to Srinagar with Peter Fleming in 1935 said, "It was a journey where nothing happened, but this nothing will satisfy me for the rest of my life."

Some achieve a serenity of the spirit when they comprehend that an essential inner need has been found; they have found themselves and become their own friend. In all these cases, and many more, an illumination has transformed the traveller. A simple journey has brought them into contact with higher truths. Along the way they have met a mysterious creature; themselves.

# Chapter 86 - Between Two Worlds

**The Dream.** Life isn't like the movies. No one rides happily into the sunset. Trouble occurs when dreams crash into necessity. Few Long Riders realize that returning from their journey will subject them to a painful emotional challenge; that the longer one has spent time in the saddle the harder it will be to adjust to the demands of domestic routine; that the transition process is often extremely difficult.

To understand what has been lost, one must appreciate what was discovered. The Long Rider has been floating along in a world that has little to do with the constraints of time. In such a world there are no nasty intrusions as can be seen in any daily newspaper. Harping critics fade away. The path of the sun takes on a new importance. The demands that obsess the majority of people, such as jobs and bills, no longer control the destiny of the Long Rider. As the journey progresses the feeling of freedom becomes overpowering. You long to prolong the sense of personal liberty.

**The Mirage called "Home".** There comes a time, especially amongst first-time travellers, when an invisible influence eventually exerts a silent message. Though they were initially anxious to depart, a longing to return home begins to seep into the Long Rider's psyche. Equestrian travel is filled with physical hardships and emotional challenges. Sitting alone by the fire, many a Long Rider has had time to wonder what fun his friends were having back home or if his family was worried about his welfare. At first it's easy to refuse to listen to these whisperings. But as the miles grow, and the troubles continue, a longing often develops to be re-united with loved ones, to re-visit favourite haunts with pals, to enjoy a delicious meal, to sleep in comfort, to give up wandering. If allowed to grow, these thoughts eventually tip the scales. The Long Rider is overcome with loneliness and longs to return home.

**The 3 Ds.** The journeyer passes through three stages; discouragement, danger, and finally disorientation. The first section of this book explains how nearly every would-be Long Rider has to overcome the resistance of those who oppose his plan to set off on an equestrian journey. This opposition has been documented through the ages. Pedestrians always have a long list of reasons why it is inadvisable for a seeker to depart from the safety of the village. Marco Polo was undoubtedly told he would never live to see distant Cathay. Finding the courage to ignore this discouragement is the first big D. The extensive fourth section of the book is devoted to a study of all the various types of dangers Long Riders may face; i.e. bandits, bears, bugs, bureaucrats, deserts, mountains, rivers, swamps, etc. The list is the most comprehensive ever compiled. What it does is to provide an in-depth look at what may await the traveller. Overcoming all these various types of dangers is the second big D. If you travel far enough you eventually find yourself standing at a lonely spot. The last big D is the one you confront when you return home. It is this sense of disorientation which is the final act of a true journey.

**The Initial Excitement.** At first you are too preoccupied becoming reacquainted with the luxuries of modern life to take any notice of forthcoming problems. After spending months or years in the saddle, riding from dawn to dusk, experiencing various degrees of discomfort, you can truly appreciate the comforts of life. Ah, that first night back. Real food, cheery faces, the joy brought on by not worrying over the welfare of the horses. But it's not all champagne bubbles and laughter. At first you can't believe the hot bath, the delicious meal and the soft bed. Then the disillusionment begins to creep in. It isn't just the displeasure of society giving you the cold shoulder that Long Riders find distressing. Many have grown so accustomed to a hard life, and to sleeping on the ground, that beds feel uncomfortably alien.

**Horses.** What you notice immediately is what's obviously missing; your horses. Modern life is composed of fragile relationships involving family, love, marriage, work and social friendships. Yet any of these alliances can disintegrate with little warning. The horse is the heart of the journey. His emotional continuity makes him a compelling and reliable friend. No matter how wrong things may have gone, he has always been there for you. It is extremely difficult to cope with the loss of your constant companion. You and the horse have formed a relationship that has been torn apart. This helps explain why many Long Riders report dreaming about their horses, thinking they can hear them grazing nearby. Others have said how much they miss waking up to the sounds of the horses snuffling at dawn. From a life full of equine sounds and smells, the returning traveller finds himself surrounded by an uncomfortable silence. One Long Rider reported that it took her two months to readjust, during which time she was prone to burst into tears and cry uncontrollably at the thought of the horse she had adored and been forced to leave behind in a faraway country.

**Living with Less.** One of the first things you notice when you unpack your few possessions and put away the saddlebags is how many objects surround you. Having lived on so little for so long, the re-entry into a world of obscene excess has a shocking effect. When asked what they missed most, many Long Riders report that they had been happy with what little they had.

**Reverse Culture Shock.** After having survived what one Long Rider called "the turbulence of re-entry," many travellers undergo what is known as reverse culture shock. Long Riders report various negative emotions when they return home. After living outside, houses feel too hot, dry, stuffy and oppressive. After enjoying long periods of silence, they are surrounded by noise. After being grateful for a simple meal, they are confronted with mountains of food that does not live up to their expectations. Massive emotional readjustment is often required because the onset of reverse culture shock may manifest itself in feelings of personal guilt, deep disappointment or resentment at the privileges and excesses which are a part of the modern consumer-oriented society. Many travellers eventually question the validity of their former lifestyle, values and beliefs.

**A Lack of Understanding.** It is not unusual for a Long Riders to feel they have achieved something significant. Without being boastful, they are entitled to a sense of pride. Many express the belief that they have discovered their true identity. While this may be cause for personal celebration, it often invokes an odd sense of isolation.

One of the tough emotional lessons returning Long Riders learn is not to expect to find either sympathy or understanding back home. Though they bear the same external name, after having survived so many challenges Long Riders often return so emotionally altered that their family and friends hardly recognize them. Before long the traveller realizes that he is no longer a part of his previous world. He has turned his life upside down by riding thousands of miles but life back home has been proceeding as if the journey had never occurred.

Upon your return it is not unusual to discover that your friends have never moved, either emotionally or physically, from the day you left. You'll discover the same people; sitting on the same bar stools, talking about the same old things, following the same predictable routines. It doesn't take long for a Long Rider to learn that conversation with such old friends is often disappointing and boring.

Though strangers often expressed an embarrassing amount of interest in your journey as you rode through their country, people at home display a shocking lack of curiosity about your adventures. A lot of people will pay polite attention to your tale, for about a minute, and then you had better be prepared for a long list of standard reactions to your trip. First they generally ask if you had a nice horse holiday. Then they will enquire if you are going to get a job and/or grow up.

One Long Rider reported, "People are generally not interested in hearing about your experiences. They cannot relate. And most are too busy to ask questions because it doesn't have anything to do with them. And you really do not want to go there because you know they will not understand anyway. The only people who understand are people who have done long rides or people who genuinely want to do a long ride.

**Resentment.** Upon his return, the traveller often involuntarily invokes a strong sense of unease and discomfort. When this occurs, those who step across the invisible line and break the taboos of society are punished in a variety of ways.

Many people sacrifice their dreams in exchange for financial security. Some betray their hopes because they are crippled with fear. Others become compromised and trapped by accident. Regardless of what hindered their escape, they harbour a sense of heartache and pain when they look back upon what their life might have been. When they hear the stories of a returning Long Rider, they know their dreams have fallen apart and that they have lived a life-lie. Remorse overcomes them when they realize they have wasted their chance. What was it they wanted to buy that was worth all their dreams? The majority of people are afraid to fly from the nest. Theirs is a life half lived, enclosed within walls, divorced from Nature, terrified of hazards; their allegiance is given to maintaining the settled order of things. They often display deep suspicion of a returning traveller and subject him to social stigma.

Never underestimate the emotional toll which may come into play with your immediate family, who are often angry. Many will not even acknowledge what the Long Rider did or grant it any significance. The traveller is often accused of shirking his duty and of not living up to expectations. Awkward conversations ensue. Family gatherings become painful. These unexpected displays of negative feelings fade with time but leave a shadow on your soul.

**Inarticulate.** You paid more than money for what you learned during the journey. You sacrificed comfort. You endured isolation. You had to fight to reach your goal. Upon your return you feel free; but at what cost? Many Long Riders report that after an initial dose of enthusiasm, they grow increasingly silent. One returning Long Rider wrote, "I don't know what to say. Words fail me. Things have changed on the inside, but I can't describe how."

**The Body's Reaction.** One reason Long Riders experience emotional trauma is because their bodies are undergoing a chemical change. Travelling across the countryside on horseback invokes a sense of spaciousness. Living in the open air is energy enhancing. Being physically involved with horses is invigorating. Witnessing the passage of the seasons stimulates the emotions. American specialists who x-rayed the brains of travellers found that this combination of heightened stimulus contributed to a sense of well-being. There is also evidence to suggest that the human body receives a chemical rush from travelling, as the journey into the unknown constantly produces adrenalin. Long Riders often experience an emotional slump after having spent long periods of time in the saddle. When the daily dose of constant vibrancy is withdrawn, their energy levels drop. Instead of elated feelings of happiness, they report a lack of motivation.

**Stress.** Even though Long Riders experience a tremendous emotional high when they conclude their journey, the physical and emotional changes which they then undergo often produce increasing levels of stress, anxiety and depression. Having survived the dangers of the journey, they must now overcome the challenges of the homecoming. Like soldiers returning from a war zone, Long Riders and various types of explorers report experiencing depression, anxiety and nightmares. Several astronauts, for example, have suffered mental anguish after completing their missions and then turned to alcohol to relieve their depression. Equestrian explorers aren't immune from such invisible interior wounds.

**Grief.** Few Long Riders realize that they are likely to undergo a grieving process when the journey is concluded. They have been deeply involved in an immersive experience which required them to be concerned with deeper and subtler things. Suddenly they return to a world full of striving and scheming and sorrow. They may find themselves surrounded by love but not by comprehension. The painful process of reintegration requires them to resume their well-ordered place in life. Feeling orphaned and lost, many experience a vast and secret misery.

**Long Rider Realignment.** A Long Rider needs to give thought to his return. You need to allow time to readjust to what feels like an artificial world. Most Long Riders say that the first two months are the hardest. It helps if you have a quiet place where you can retreat, re-think and restore your sense of emotional balance. Reward yourself by enjoying all of the luxuries you missed. Take pleasure soaking in a hot bath. Eat everything you ever day-dreamed about while you were starving in the saddle. Read a good book. Sleep late for two or three days running. See a movie. Visit old friends. Place all these well-earned moments deep within your memory banks. Don't become isolated. Be willing to discuss your journey but do so carefully. Because the journey just ended, it seems impossible that the details will ever fade. But every traveller forgets events, names, places, dates and details. As soon as you conclude your journey summon up the discipline to organize your journal, arrange your photographs, edit your film, work on your book and thank all the people who assisted you.

**Benefits and Discoveries.** Returning is not all bad. Many Long Riders come back with a sense of gratitude for what they have learned and experienced during the journey. On an obvious level the completion of a difficult and dangerous equestrian trip permits the traveller to put aside all questions of physical courage. But other discoveries are more subtle. Though they may not undertake another journey, many Long Riders have become aware that, in addition to having made history in their own life, they glimpsed the eternal along the way. In this way the aftermath of your journey helps keep you emotionally preoccupied, and extends your trip in a new manner, while you have time to readjust to your new circumstances and surroundings.

**Choices and Changes.** It also helps explain why many Long Riders undergo various types of major life transformations shortly after returning, including a change in job, career, marital status and housing. They are looking for new answers to life's complexities.

**The Courage to Continue.** The journey has caused you to no longer take life for granted. The homecoming requires you to remain loyal to what you have learned and who you have become.

# Chapter 87 - Honour

If honour is to be effective it cannot be imposed from the outside.

**A Mounted Brotherhood.** The strength of the equestrian brotherhood symbolized today by the Long Riders' Guild. Three of the most extraordinary Long Riders of the 19th century were part of a chain of events that resulted in the Baron reaching Tokyo. The American Long Rider Januarius MacGahan rode from Fort Perovsky, Russia, across the Kyzil-Kum Desert to Adam-Kurulgan ("Fatal to Men"), Kyrgyzstan in 1873. Two years later MacGahan advised British Long Rider Frederick Burnaby on how to reach Khiva. It was Burnaby's famous book, *A Ride to Khiva* that inspired Fukushima seventeen years later. Prior to his departure, Fukushima met Sven Hedin in Berlin. Sweden's greatest explorer and Long Rider gave the novice traveller valuable advice concerning his upcoming trip. Three heroes from three countries helped their Japanese comrade.

**Fly to your Brother's Aid.** The concept of receiving wisdom from a wise elder reaches back to the days of the Trojan War. Prior to leaving his home, Odysseus entrusted the welfare and education of his son to his friend, Mentor. It is his name which has come down through the ages to represent a trusted teacher and guide. Though the idea may be old, the practice remains alive today. What began with five Long Riders from three countries has now spread to more than 40 nations. In every case, one equestrian traveller inspires, encourages, warns or educates another. One helps you. After your ride, you in turn share your hard-won wisdom with those who follow in your hoofprints. The Guild has always been about aiding our fellows, not winning at their expense. In an unprecedented show of international equestrian brotherhood, Long Riders from five countries helped Filipe Leite prepare for his 10,000 mile journey from Canada to Brazil. This outpouring of generosity and support prompted Filipe to explain his feelings about being a Long Rider. "There is no competition. The horse unites us," he wrote.

**Inspiration.** As these examples demonstrate, Sir Isaac Newton wrote, "If I have seen further than others, it is by standing upon the shoulders of giants." Luckily Long Rider history is filled with examples of travellers who drew inspiration or were helped by their peers.

**The Last Enemy – Yourself.** These are inspiring stories. But life isn't always filled with noble deeds or honourable people. When he wrote his great classic on exploration in 1852, Francis Galton cautioned travellers to remember failure in travel could happen for a number of reasons. "An exploring expedition is daily exposed to a succession of accidents, any one of which might be fatal to its further progress. While Galton was primarily concerned with avoiding prowling lions, he did not consider the ethical accidents that might befall the unwary traveller. Few realize there is an invisible crevasse that lies across everyone's path. After having survived every sort of physical disaster, they are tempted to violate their conscience. Some compromise their honour day to day. Some fall prey to self-deceit. Some sell their souls.

**The Final Trap.** Every returning Long Rider can justly take pride in his accomplishments. But there is a thorn hidden under the rose. Long ago a Sufi mystic wrote, "If you wish to find the hidden treasure destroy the castle of egotism." That wise man understood that the lure of egotism attracts man like honey draws a bear. Self-centeredness is the weak point of man. It diverts a person away from that which is spiritual and leads him toward darkness and arrogance. In an age when people use Twitter and Facebook to reveal their every secret, in an age when people will go on television and do anything to gain fame, Baron Fukushima serves as a beacon of modesty, strength, resolve, iron will, courage and dignity.

**Fame.** Is the journey about serving self or helping others? There is no subject on which people are more apt to deceive themselves than the lust for fame. Dr Johnson defined honour as "nobility of soul." That nobility is endangered when the desire for celebrity becomes the primary motivation.

The very notion of a hero has been distorted in today's modern world. Increasingly people are tempted to define their self-worth solely by their public visibility. Yearning to be noticed and admired, they lose touch with their morality by becoming uncontrollable narcissists.

There is a difference between explorers and exploiters. Sir Ernest Shackleton warned, "I think nothing of the world and the public. They cheer you one minute and howl you down the next. It is what's in oneself and what one makes of one's life that matters."

The media can't be trusted to decide what is right or wrong; only your own conscience can make that decision!

**Addicted to Adoration.** In an earlier chapter I discussed the ethics of equestrian travel. That study focused mainly on the human's obligation to protect his horses. I have also written about how a traveller should not deceive the press or cheat the public. But sadly there have been occasions when equestrian travellers have become so enamoured with fame that they have ignored, erased or censored information about other Long Riders. These acts of deception were made in an effort to make the traveller appear bigger, bolder and braver to the press and public. Instead of using the ride as a portal to inner discovery it became a search for celebrity. Making a name took precedence over principle. They had not heeded the advice of the noted explorer, Colonel John Blashford-Snell who stated, "He who believes his own publicity is heading for a fall."

We have a responsibility to others. But not all honour it. Some practise self-delusion and deceit. Fame can be a blessing and a curse. Once some people get a taste of it, they become addicted. Because fame fills some starving corner of their psyche, they are unwilling to share a crumb of recognition with another Long Rider.

**Brotherhood or Commerce.** Sir Richard Burton wrote, "Man should seek honour, not honours."

Acknowledging the contribution of others is one of the keys to being a successful Long Rider. Yet the concept of comradeship is the last thing on some people's minds. They are the ones who are anxious to impress the public and the press with the false impression that they were the first, the fastest, the bravest, etc.

Aimé Tschiffely warned against what he called "headline grabbers." He cautioned the public to be wary of "vain men who have written so-called confessions to be sold to gullible readers."

Much of equestrian travel involves ritualistic behaviour. Some acts, like feeding and brushing, reach back to the dawn of man's relation to the horse. That is why even though every modern Long Rider journeys in the present, he is always aware of the past. And you would not think that anyone would pretend to the press and the public that "no one else would dare do this." But you would be wrong. It was Sir Richard Burton, again, who wisely wrote, "He knew it all by heart, but his heart knew none of it."

**Ethical Exploration.** There are other types of individuals who occasionally infest the equestrian travel world in an effort to aggrandize their ego or enlarge their bank account. The first clue is that their stories are chiefly concerned with the incredible dangers they supposedly survived. For some, the desire to undertake an equestrian journey is a false display of rugged-ness. Those are the ones who stress the hardships. They prove that the accumulation of miles is no guarantee of success. The horse can never deliver them because the true goal of the journey will forever elude them. They will never arrive. Their journey is endless because, being blind, they never truly set out. A real Long Rider comes back not with tales of suffering but with an address book filled with the names of new friends. In his book *As a Man Thinketh*, James Allen wrote, "Circumstance does not make the man; it reveals him to himself."

**Chivalry in a New Age.** The concept of a mounted brotherhood is nothing new. Throughout history, mounted men have attempted to recognize the finer qualities in their lives. Has honour waned since the era of horses passed? Is nobility a birth right or is it defined by one's actions? Events throw light on the character of Long Riders, past and present, which demonstrate that they are striving for perfection, not pretence. Long Riders are Comrades not Competitors and that at the end of the day what matters is personal validation. It's not enough to strive for mere miles. Mastery of technique is an empty vessel. We don't want to beat the Baron and Aimé. The true goal is to strive to be like them.

# Section Seven – The Equestionary

The Equestionary was conceived by Swiss Long Rider Basha O'Reilly, a noted linguist. Equestrian explorers quickly learn that being able to communicate in the native language increases their chances of success. Yet knowing how to greet people, count in the local currency or ask for simple directions is not enough. Long Riders have special linguistic needs. Vitally important words that are required on a daily basis, such as hay, stable, farrier, saddle, etc., are not to be found in standard phrase-books. That is why the Long Rider Equestionary provides fifty images of those objects and situations most likely to be of use or concern to equestrian explorers. Armed with the Equestionary, even if you cannot say horse or saddle, you can point at the appropriate picture and establish basic communication.

## Points of the Horse

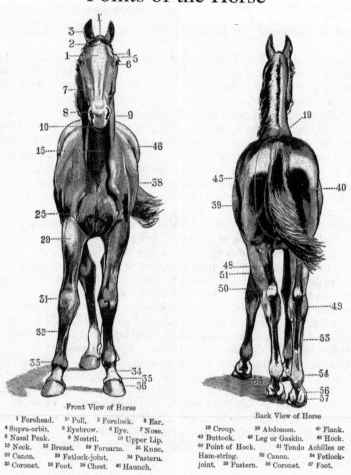

Front View of Horse

Back View of Horse

[1] Forehead.  [1'] Poll.  [2] Forelock.  [3] Ear.
[4] Supra-orbit.  [5] Eyebrow.  [6] Eye.  [7] Nose.
[8] Nasal Peak.  [9] Nostril.  [10] Upper Lip.
[15] Neck.  [25] Breast.  [29] Forearm.  [31] Knee.
[32] Canon.  [33] Fetlock-joint.  [34] Pastern.
[35] Coronet.  [36] Foot.  [38] Chest.  [46] Haunch.

[19] Croup.  [39] Abdomen.  [40] Flank.
[43] Buttock.  [48] Leg or Gaskin.  [49] Hock.
[50] Point of Hock.  [51] Tendo Achilles or Ham-string.  [52] Canon.  [54] Fetlock-joint.  [55] Pastern.  [56] Coronet.  [57] Foot.

254

# Equine Digestion

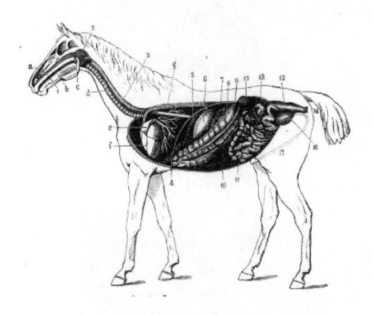

# Equine Skeleton

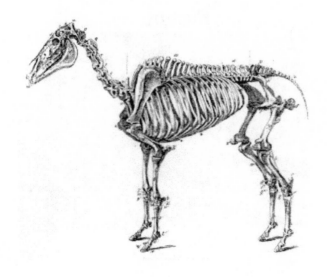

# Barn

# Stalls

# Pasture

# Hay

# Grain

# Water

# Camping

# Yurt/Ger

# Western Saddle

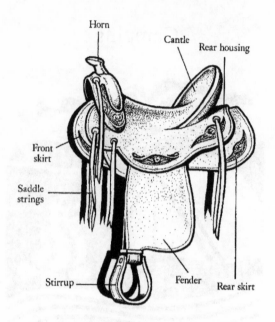

Horn

Cantle

Rear housing

Front skirt

Saddle strings

Stirrup

Fender

Rear skirt

# English Saddle

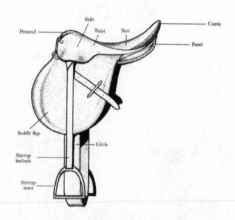

Skirt

Pommel

Waist

Seat

Cantle

Panel

Saddle flap

Girth

Stirrup leathers

Stirrup irons

# Bridle

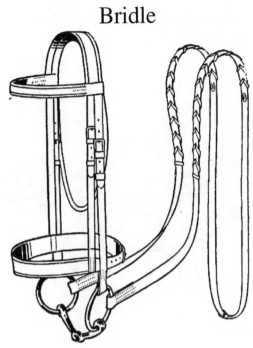

## Parts of a Halter

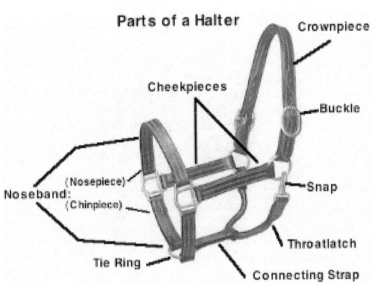

Crownpiece

Cheekpieces

Buckle

(Nosepiece)

Noseband:

(Chinpiece)

Snap

Throatlatch

Tie Ring

Connecting Strap

# Adjustable Pack Saddle

# Pannier

# Horseshoe

# Farrier

# Hoof

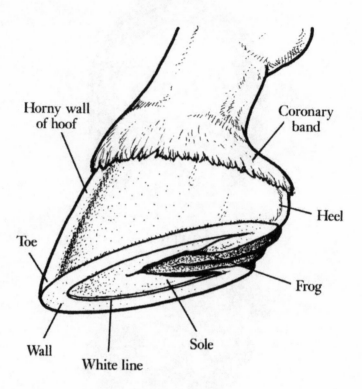

Horny wall of hoof

Coronary band

Toe

Heel

Frog

Wall

White line

Sole

# Hoof Boot

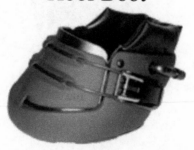

# Accident

# Doctor

# Danger

# Wolf

# Bear

# Lion

# Mountain Lion

# Jaguar

# Crocodile

# Rattlesnake

# Vampire Bat

# Scorpion

# Mosquito

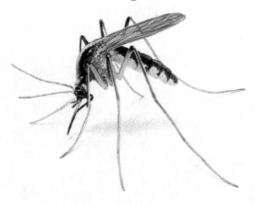

# Wasp

# Border

# Traffic

# River

# Bridge

# Ferry

# Tunnel

# Cattle Guard

# Mountains

# Mountain Trail

# Jungle

# Quicksand

# Desert

# Snow

# Thermostat

# Section Eight – Long Rider Knots

The following knots are those most often used by Long Riders around the world.

## Central Asian Nomad Fast Release Knot to tie your horse

# Securing the lead rope

R. Wauters.

# Securing the Reins

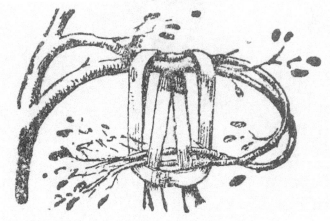

# Western Saddle Cinch Knot

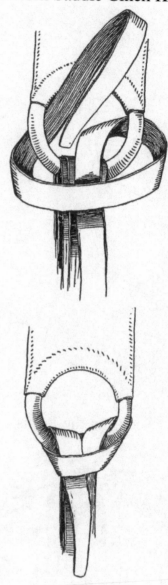

# Other Important Knots

## Clove hitch

## Bowline

CPSIA information can be obtained
at www.ICGtesting.com
Printed in the USA
LVHW092137290419
616043LV00009B/454/P